The Complete Book of

———

WILLS, ESTATES & TRUSTS

ALEXANDER A. BOVE, JR., ESQ.

The Complete Book of

WILLS, ESTATES & TRUSTS

· THIRD EDITION ·

A HOLT PAPERBACK

HENRY HOLT AND COMPANY | NEW YORK

Holt Paperbacks
Henry Holt and Company, LLC
Publishers since 1866
175 Fifth Avenue
New York, New York 10010
www.henryholt.com

Distributed in Canada by H. B. Fenn and Company Ltd.

Library of Congress Cataloging-in-Publication Data

Bove, Alexander A., date.
  The complete book of wills, estates & trusts / Alexander A. Bove, Jr.—3rd ed.
    p. cm.
  Includes index.
  ISBN-13: 978-0-8050-7888-6
  ISBN-10: 0-8050-7888-6
    1. Wills—United States—Popular works.   2. Executors and administrators—
United States—Popular works.   3. Estate planning—United States—Popular
works.   4. Probate law and practice—United States—Popular works.
5. Trusts and trustees—United States—Popular works.   I. Title.
KF755.Z9B68 2005
346.7305—dc22   2005045707

Henry Holt books are available for special promotions
and premiums. For details contact: Director, Special Markets.

First Edition 1991
Second Edition 2000
Third Edition 2005

Designed by Victoria Hartman

Printed in the United States of America

7 9 10 8 6

To the memory of Clement A. O'Brien, Esq.,
with profound gratitude for the inspiration,
encouragement, and love he so freely gave me,
and
To my wife, Cathy, whose love, tolerance,
and understanding have contributed
as much to my books as I have

Contents

Introduction to the Third Edition

Is the federal estate tax law really going to be repealed? If it is, can we forget about estate planning altogether? Does a child of a sperm donor have a right to inherit from the "father's" estate? Even though the child may be born years after the father's death? What are the legal implications for an estate when a person's body is deep frozen after death for possible "revival" in the future? And what if that person is "revived"?

The answers to those questions, as well as a number of other interesting and important new developments and updates, are the reason for this revised and expanded edition of *The Complete Book of Wills, Estates & Trusts*.

As some of you may know, our estate, gift, and generation-skipping tax laws have changed substantially, allowing larger exemptions in some cases, smaller in others. New and unique concepts and issues relating to inheritance have been brought about by scientific and medical advancements, including the donation and storage of sperm to be used in the future to produce children. This edition explores the attendant questions, including whether there is a way to protect the estate of a sperm donor from claims of future "children" conceived against his will or without his knowledge or even after his death. I also explore issues surrounding the heretofore science-fictional issue of deep-freezing the body after death to wait for future development of a cure for the cause of death. And what if a frozen deceased actually did return? Can she get her property back? My discussion of the interesting case of the famous baseball player, Ted Williams, whose body was frozen after death, sheds some light on this, as well as how to avoid disputes if you do decide to go into biostasis (the deep freeze) after death.

Another important area that warranted expansion is that of asset protection planning. As the number of lawsuits and the size of judgments grow, so does the field of asset protection trusts. This edition fine-tunes some of the steps to be taken to protect your assets and includes reports of real cases showing how asset protection trusts can work.

Also in the trust area, a whole new section has been added on the subject of purpose trusts. This is a new (for the United States) type of trust that can have many unique uses, including asset protection and closely held business succession planning. It is also a subject you are most unlikely to see discussed in any other book of this type in the United States.

In some circumstances, one of the most important documents in an estate plan can be a durable power of attorney. This is often the case where a person who becomes incapacitated has no trust but should have one, or has a trust but it is unfunded. In either case a properly drafted durable power of attorney can "save the day" (as well as saving thousands in legal fees). For this reason and in light of numerous legal developments on the subject since the last edition, I have not only expanded my discussion on the durable power but added a sample form as well.

Lastly, hundreds of smaller changes and updates have been added to almost every chapter reflecting changes in the law and clarification of subject matter, all to the benefit of my readers, whom I thank for making this book a success.

Boston, Massachusetts

The Complete Book of

———————

WILLS, ESTATES & TRUSTS

The World of Wills

I have nothing, I owe a great deal; the rest I give to the poor.

—the will of Rabelais, the fifteenth-century satirist

Was Rabelais serious or was this just another example of his wonderful satire? Did this single sentence make a valid will?

Whether it did or not, it certainly helped immortalize Rabelais, since it is hard to find a discussion of wills that does not make mention of his. Rabelais, no doubt, would have been immortalized regardless of his will, since he left the world so much more in the form of his literary works. But for those of us who leave little more than some money and a few greedy relatives, the fact is that a colorful or unusual will may offer some prospect of immortality that we would not have otherwise. Although the world of wills can be colorful, however, it can also be grim. A will can be a source of security to a family or it can bankrupt them, as we will see.

Your Own Nobel Prize

Most people know, or at least think they know, what a will is, and they generally treat a will with a certain degree of respect. After all, wills are almost universally regarded as a sort of permanent memorial, a person's final statement to the world, offering, in many cases, a touch of immortality. A perfect illustration of this is the will of Alfred Nobel, who truly immortalized himself through the provisions of his will.

Just a year before his death in 1896, Nobel wrote out his will, which, despite its humble and relatively simple language, gave birth to one of the most widely known and respected memorials in the world—the Nobel Prize. This is what he wrote that formed the foundation for the prizes:

> The whole of my remaining realizable estate shall be dealt with in the following way: the capital, invested in safe securities by my executors, shall constitute a fund, the interest on which shall be annually distributed in the form of prizes to those who, during the preceding year, shall have conferred the greatest benefit on mankind. The said interest shall be divided into five equal parts, which shall be apportioned as follows: one part to the person who shall have made the most important discovery or invention within the field of physics; one part to the person who shall have made the most important chemical discovery or improvement; one part to the person who shall have made the most important discovery within the domain of physiology or medicine; one part to the person who shall have produced in the field of literature the most outstanding work of an idealistic tendency; and one part to the person who shall have done the most or the best work for fraternity between nations, for the abolition or reduction of standing armies and for the holding and promotion of peace congresses. The prizes for physics and chemistry shall be awarded by the Swedish Academy of Sciences; that for physiological or medical works by the Karolinska Institute in Stockholm; that for literature by the Academy in Stockholm, and that for champions of peace by a committee of five persons to be elected by the Norwegian Storting. It is my express wish that in awarding the prizes no consideration whatever shall be given to the nationality of the candidates, but that the most worthy shall receive the prize, whether he be a Scandinavian or not.
>
> Paris, November 27, 1895
Alfred Bernhard Nobel

Through this "simple" will, carefully handwritten by Nobel himself in the Swedish language, Nobel thought, no doubt, that he had included all the necessary provisions to carry out his now-famous plan.

Actually, Nobel's will was very poorly drafted (he disliked lawyers and, therefore, decided to write it himself) and resulted in protracted legal battles, requiring the court to clarify and interpret important issues relating to, among other things, the selection of candidates and awarding of the prizes. Nevertheless, after years of court proceedings in several different countries and about a half-million dollars (a respectable fortune in those days) in fees, legacies, and expenses, the remainder went to establish permanent immortality for Nobel.

Then there are other types of immortality—one that results when the deceased was a popular figure *before* his death, so there is a great deal of continuing public interest in how he left his estate, and another where there is a bitter and very public dispute over the provisions of a will, or both, such as in the case of the late Howard Hughes.

Hughes, the eccentric Nevada billionaire, died in 1976, a bitter, emaciated, ninety-two-pound remainder of a man, and almost instantly the fights began over his estate. Over forty wills surfaced after his death, each claiming to be the billionaire's last will. The most famous of these was the "Mormon will," purportedly found on the desk of an official of the Mormon church. The Mormon will, which appeared to be in Hughes's own handwriting, left one-sixteenth of his $4 billion estate to Melvin Dummar, a gas station operator who, as the story goes, picked up a poor old man on a deserted road and gave him a lift to Las Vegas and a quarter to make a phone call. The poor old man turned out to be Howard Hughes, who, in a gesture of generosity totally foreign to his reported character, left Dummar a princely chunk of his estate.

The fairy tale would have been complete had the Mormon will been declared valid, but after a trial that took the better part of a year and several million dollars in legal fees, Dummar and the Mormons lost the case. Despite the appearance of forty wills, the courts finally decided that Hughes died without a will. To this day, however, the estate has not been completely settled, and it most likely will continue for many more years to provide a comfortable annuity to the battalions of attorneys who represent the estate and its labyrinthine interests in oil wells, real estate, airlines, television stations, hotels, and casinos.

The estate of Hughes and Nobel were admittedly extremes. Still, some of us may achieve a touch of immortality by creating our own little "Nobel" prize in the form of a small scholarship fund or a research grant, while others may unwittingly achieve the same result as Hughes by leaving no will, a defective will, or several wills, or even a valid will that becomes the subject of a bitter dispute. Or perhaps we will express some wish or bequest so unique that it finds its way into newspaper articles and law books, such as that of Sandra West, late of California, whose will directed that she be buried "in my lace nightgown . . . in my Ferrari, with the seat slanted comfortably." Whatever the case, the fact remains that our wills will be governed by the same principles and rules of law as those of Howard Hughes, Alfred Nobel, and Sandra West.

In the cases of Nobel and Hughes, it is interesting (and essential) to note, for instance, that both of these famous estates consisted almost entirely of *probate property,* and this is why their wills were so important. A person's will deals only with property or assets that are part of his *probate estate,* and the probate estate is governed by the probate process. In this chapter, we will look at the power as well as the vulnerabilities of probate, and the complexities as well as the absurdities of the process.

Technically, the probate process involves a "proving" of the deceased's last will (i.e., that it was a properly signed, valid will and that it was the last one the decedent made). But as a practical matter, the probate courts also deal with disputes relating to the transfer of the property of a deceased person and claims against his estate. Therefore, if the deceased left a will, it is the job of the probate court (some states call it the surrogate's court, orphan's court, or chancery court) to decide whether the will was valid according to the laws of the applicable state, and if it is declared valid, the probate estate will be disposed of according to the will. If the will was not valid, or if the deceased left no will, then the probate court will order the deceased's property disposed of through the probate court according to state law.

If, in the meantime, there are any disputes relating to the estate or claims against the estate made by the decedent's creditors, employers, family members, or anyone else, or if there are bills to pay or anything else that could possibly interfere with the final settlement of the probate estate and payment of bequests to the beneficiaries, the probate court will deal with it all, as part of the probate process. Here's how it all happens and why, step by step.

The Probate Process—Step by Step

In a civilized society, a legal mechanism for dealing with a deceased person's property is essential. Think of the chaos that would result if, when someone died, the law allowed anyone free access to take all or any part of the deceased person's property on a "first come" basis. Instead, we have developed a system that protects and sometimes directs the distribution of property on a person's death. Our laws recognize that some order must be maintained in the situation, and so they provide, among other things, for what is called the right of "freedom of testation" and a legal process to deal with those estates that have exercised that right, as well as those that have not.

Freedom of testation simply means the right to leave your property on your death in almost any manner you choose. Few people realize that this is not a "natural" right. It would be quite possible, for example (though it would certainly meet with resistance), for the government to rule that on a person's death, all of his property would belong to the government. Such an approach, however, would, among other things, discourage the acquisition of property and would soon undermine our capitalistic system. Therefore, we are "allowed" to freely acquire property during our lifetime, to keep it or dispose of it as we wish, and, on our death, we are "allowed" to decide, subject to certain obligations to keep our spouse and children in mind, who will get what is left. These decisions, if you want them to be carried out, must be reflected in a valid will or some other legal disposition, as more thoroughly discussed in chapter 11; otherwise, the laws of the state will decide how your property will be divided. Whether or not you decide to exercise your "freedom of testation" and make a will, the dividing and transfer of the property that is part of your "probate estate" can only be done by the probate court.

When we talk of your "probate estate" (or "probate property") in this sense, we mean any type of property that stands in your name *alone* at the time of your death or that would require action on the part of your executor or administrator to transfer. It would not include, for instance, jointly held property or assets that are payable to a named beneficiary at death. It includes only property over which you *alone* would have control. From a "legal" perspective, therefore, if on death we wish to transfer any of our "probate" or "estate" property to someone who survives us, or if our estate is to be given to the spouse and children equally because we left no will, just how would this be accomplished? They could not simply "take" the property because they would not have legal ownership of it. And on what legal grounds could they support their ownership if they did take it? This is why we must have some orderly legal process if we are to recognize any rights to transfer property at death, and this is where the probate process comes in.

Therefore, whether you decide to write your own will or to have no will at all, whether you are a beneficiary of an estate or a creditor, and whether you think there will be no disputes or you can't wait to start one, it is very important for you to understand how the probate process works. This is because probate is the system that determines and governs the distribution of the probate estate to the heirs and beneficiaries, the payment of estate debts after death, the resolution of disputes and claims against the estate, and contests against the will.

STEP 1: FINDING THE WILL

When a person dies, the first thing that must be done concerning distribution of his property is to determine whether he left a will. In most cases, family members will know or have an idea that there was or was not a will. If not, a search of the deceased's papers and safe-deposit box may offer some leads. If the deceased had a lawyer or saw one before his death, the lawyer should be asked if he has any knowledge of a will.

In many states, it is a crime to conceal a will, and most states have laws requiring anyone in possession of a will to submit it to the probate court within a certain period (often thirty days) after a person's death, with penalties for failure to do so.

Rather than conceal a will, however, if someone in possession of a will does not want it probated, he is more likely to simply destroy it. This is also a crime, but it is almost impossible to prove that a person has concealed or destroyed a will unless someone actually saw him do it. There are, unfortunately, a number of cases where there was a strong "common sense" inference that a will had been destroyed but no way of proving it, and no copies or other evidence existed to show what it said. In one case, a man we'll call Irving notified his girlfriend, Rosie, who was his close companion for twelve years, that he had made out a will leaving everything to her. Before he met Rosie, Irving had a will in which he simply left his estate to his brother and sister, his only two relatives. On Irving's death, the will he told Rosie he made out could not be found. Several months later, Irving's brother "discovered" the old will among Irving's papers and submitted it for probate. Although she felt certain that Irving's brother had simply torn up the new will, Rosie had no standing to object to the old will and no proof, other than Irving's statement to her, that he had made a new one. There was nothing she could do to prevent the old will from being allowed.

STEP 2: STARTING THE PROBATE OF THE ESTATE

Once the will is located, it (the original) is sent to the probate court in the appropriate district of the state where the person was domiciled (had his permanent residence) at the time of his death. If the original is lost or destroyed, a verifiable copy may be submitted to the probate court, but the parties seeking to have the copy allowed must be prepared to satisfy the court that there was no funny business. Submitting the will to the probate court, by itself, does nothing other than to place the will on record with the court. In order for any action to be taken on the will, someone, usually the executor named under the will, must ask ("petition") the probate court to approve the will as the last will of the deceased. If for some reason the executor does not offer the will for probate, any interested party, even a creditor of the deceased, may do so.

Petitions for the probate of a will are relatively simple forms available at the probate court for the district or county of the decedent's domicile. This is not to say that there are no complexities, but the request (petition) for probate itself is the easy part. In substance, it simply asks the court to allow the will that has been submitted to the court as the decedent's last will.

If there was no will, then the petition takes a different form. It suggests to the court that the decedent left no will and asks that a person (named in the petition) be appointed as administrator to represent the deceased's estate. If there is no will, the deceased's probate property is distributed according to the laws of the state (as more particularly discussed in chapter 2). Whether or not there was a will, most states require that the petition include the names and addresses of all of the "heirs at law" (generally meaning those persons who the law says will inherit if there is no will). Usually this would be the spouse and children, or the parents and siblings.

STEP 3: NOTICE TO HEIRS AND INTERESTED PARTIES — TIME TO CONTEST

In most states, after the petition for probate is filed, the probate court will order that notice of the petition be given to the heirs and other "interested" parties (those who may not be heirs but who may be named in the will) and, in some cases, that "publication" must be made. Publication is the placing of legal notice in the local newspaper to the effect that John Jinx, a resident of Boston, Massachusetts, has died and a petition has been submitted to the court asking that Jane Jinx be appointed as the executrix (or administratrix if there was no will) of his estate. The publication will also suggest that if you wish to object to the allowance of this petition, you or your attorney should file an appearance on or before a certain date. In those states that require notice, this designated date (sometimes called the "return date") is very important because if no objections to the petition are received by that date, the court will allow the petition. This does not mean if you miss the date or later discover that you should have objected that you cannot, but an objection filed after the date designated by the court as the "deadline" will be accepted by the court only if there was a good reason for the failure to file the objection within the allowed time. If adequate notice is not given as required by the state's laws, no probate may be allowed.

About a third of our states take the reverse approach and immediately allow the petition for probate and appointment of executor as soon as the will is filed, *without* notice to the beneficiaries. This does not mean, however, that no one can object. In fact, in those states that allow the will without notice, a person who wishes to contest the will or the appointment of an executor often has a much longer period within which to do so—usually until the estate is settled and the executor is discharged by the court.

In those states where notice and/or publication is required, the information in the newspaper publication will also be sent directly to you if you are an heir or an interested party in the estate. Obviously it must be sent to you sufficiently before the return date to give you adequate time to object to the allowance of the petition if you wish to do so.

The filing of an objection to either the allowance of the will or the appointment of the executor (or administrator) is surprisingly straightforward. All you (or your attorney) need to do to begin the contest is notify the court that you object. That's it. A brief letter to the appropriate court will suffice, saying something such as, "I object to the allowance of the petition of Jane Jinx requesting that a certain document be allowed as John Jinx's will and that Jane Jinx be appointed as executrix," (signed) Jesse Jinx. Naturally, you will at some point (from only a few days to sixty days in some states, much longer in others) be required to *specify* just what it is you object to and why, and the laws at this stage begin to be somewhat more complex, so it would be foolhardy to attempt to go much beyond this point without an experienced lawyer. Judges are generally not sympathetic to people who try to represent themselves in will contests.

STEP 4: APPOINTMENT OF THE EXECUTOR/ADMINISTRATOR

If no one objects to the petition for the allowance of the will or (if there is no will) to the petition for administration of the estate without a will, then the court will usually appoint the executor named in the will (or the administrator named in the petition) to be the legal representative of the deceased's estate. Once formally appointed by the court, the executor or administrator will take legal title to all of the deceased's probate assets, so that estate property may be "dealt with" in the process of settling the estate. In other words, all of the deceased's bank accounts, securities, and other assets (real estate is subject to special rules in many states) that are a part of his probate estate will be titled, "Jane Jinx, Executrix, Estate of John Jinx."

The executor, or the administrator if there was no will, is the person responsible for all aspects of settling the estate, including paying debts and taxes, dealing with claims against the estate, and ultimately distributing the estate property to the beneficiaries. After receiving his appointment, however, one of the first things he must do is prepare and file an estate inventory.

STEP 5. FILING THE ESTATE INVENTORY

Within one to three months (depending on the particular state) after the executor has been appointed, he is required by law to file a "complete" inventory of the estate's assets. (This would include only the *probate* assets as described below.) The inventory is submitted to the court and, like all other papers submitted to the court, becomes a matter of "public record" (available to anyone who wants to look at it).

Briefly, there are two reasons for the filing of the inventory. First, the inventory indicates to the court the items of property for which the executor will later "account" (tell the court in detail what he did with all these items when the estate is settled). Second, it lets the beneficiaries, creditors, and all other interested parties know the contents of the deceased's probate estate. If the executor delays or refuses to file an inventory, any interested party may ask the court to order him to file one, although if there are no disputes or contests, executors often file their inventories late.

The probate inventory will include *any* type of property (stocks, bonds, real estate, furnishings, jewelry, copyrights, claims against others, etc.) that *belonged to the deceased* at the time of his death. Normally, this only includes property that stood in the deceased's name alone, but could very well also include property that was being held by someone else, including joint property, for example, that the executor believed should be a part of the deceased's probate estate. Otherwise, nonprobate property, such as jointly held property, life insurance or retirement plan benefits payable to a named beneficiary, or assets in a living trust, will not be included in the probate inventory.

STEP 6: PAYMENT OF CLAIMS

In order to facilitate an orderly settlement of the estate within a "reasonable" period of time, every state provides for specified time periods within which claims against the estate *must* be made; otherwise, they will not be collectible, no matter how valid. The period usually begins at a specified time (say three months) *after* the executor has been appointed or has given notice to creditors, and ends from six to twelve months after that. Unless the court for some reason allows an extension, it is only within this period that a creditor may make a formal claim against the estate, and state courts are fairly strict on this point. The executor, however, has an obligation to notify all known creditors and to make a reasonable effort to identify creditors, so that they will have the opportunity to file a claim within the special period. Since this period is specified as being "open" to creditors' claims against the estate, the executor must be careful not to prejudice creditors by distributing all or too much of the estate property to beneficiaries before the end of the specified period. If that happened, then the executor would be held *personally liable* for valid creditors' claims, and for this reason, executors will not, as a rule, distribute estate property before the end of the special claims period.

This is not to say that claims may not be paid by the executor before or after this special time period, since the executor can pay valid, undisputed claims almost any time he wants. It is usually the disputed and particularly the unknown claims that worry the executor and apply to this special period. Once the period expires, the executor need worry only about known claims that he intends to pay, other valid expenses, taxes, and, finally, distribution to the beneficiaries.

STEP 7: PAYMENT OF DEBTS, FEES, EXPENSES, AND TAXES

Simultaneous with his assessment of what claims may be made against the estate, the executor will begin to determine the remaining debts, fees, and expenses that he is aware of (such as doctors' bills, utility bills, outstanding charge account balances, and of course legal fees and executors' fees), since all of these items will have a bearing upon the estate taxes that may be due in the estate. In fact, part of the executor's job is to file the estate tax return and see that the taxes are paid when due (taxes are usually due within nine months after the date of death, unless an extension is granted). Claims and expenses for which there is no dispute are usually paid by the executor within this nine-month period.

STEP 8: FILING THE ESTATE TAX RETURNS

Putting all this information together, the executor will prepare (or have a professional prepare) the deceased's estate tax returns showing all the property included in the estate, reduced by allowable claims and deductions, to arrive at the tax due, if any. Filing of the estate tax returns does not mean the estate is settled. In fact, the federal and/or state governments may take several months to a year after filing to "accept" the returns or to respond by asking for more information or, in some cases, in deciding that the estate will be audited. Until the returns are accepted and the final tax liability (if any) is agreed upon and paid, the executor should not distribute all the assets of the estate. If he does and if there is not enough money left in the estate to pay the balance of the tax due, he will be *personally liable* for payment of the remaining tax on the probate estate.

Note that if the estate is "small" enough in size, it may not be necessary to file a federal estate tax return at all. That is, if the value of all the property included on the deceased's federal estate tax return does not exceed the allowable "tax free" amount ($1.5 million in the year 2005), then no federal return is due. (See chapter 14 for a discussion of estate taxes.) This does not mean that the state in which the deceased lived or owned property would not require its own estate tax return or a separate estate tax, since state laws vary on this. In many states, even though no estate tax may be due, it may be necessary to file a return just to "prove" that no taxes are due so the beneficiaries can inherit the property without fear of a tax or a state lien on real property being discovered later. If estate tax returns are filed and finally accepted, the federal and state governments will normally give the executor a "closing letter" stating that no further taxes are due in the deceased's estate. In most cases, receipt of the closing letter(s) is quickly followed by distributions to the beneficiaries and the closing of the estate itself.

STEP 9: GIVING THE BENEFICIARIES THEIR MONEY (FINALLY)

After all tax matters for the estate are settled and all bills and expenses paid or amounts set aside, the executor may then prepare to distribute what is left to the beneficiaries according to the terms of the deceased's will, or according to the laws of the state if the deceased left no will. If there was a contest and a negotiated settlement, the executor would prepare to make the full distributions required under the settlement. (If there are lawsuits still outstanding against the estate, it is unlikely that final distributions will be made until these are settled.)

Before the executor will actually make payment or transfer property to beneficiaries, however, he will prepare a release for each beneficiary to sign, indicating that the beneficiary accepts the proposed distribution in full settlement of any claims or legacies he has in the estate and releases the executor from any further claims or personal liability. Together with the release, the beneficiaries may also receive a copy of the "final account" that the executor proposes to file with the probate court. This is a detailed financial report of all the assets of the probate estate, the income and expenses, disbursements, and other transactions made by the executor on behalf of the estate during estate administration, and the proposed final distribution of the remainder to the beneficiaries, leaving a balance of zero. The beneficiaries are usually asked to review and assent to the executor's account, but if they object, they may notify the executor or the court.

If you are a beneficiary of an estate, you should *not* sign a release until you have seen and are satisfied with the executor's account. It will be difficult, after you have signed the release, to object to excess executor's fees, or legal fees, or some other estate expense or distribution. (For more on this, see chapter 8.)

Once the beneficiaries sign the release and assent to the executor's final account, they can then expect to receive their inheritance from the estate (although, in many cases, if there is enough money in the estate, they may have already received an advance on their inheritance).

STEP 10: CLOSING THE ESTATE

When the executor has paid or settled all debts, fees, and taxes and has prepared his final account, and assuming he has already obtained the assents and releases of the beneficiaries, he will submit his final account to the probate court asking that his account be "allowed." Allowance of the account means that the beneficiaries and the court have accepted this report as a complete and accurate record of the settlement of the estate. When this happens, the estate may be closed and the executor discharged of all duties and liabilities.

If this is all there is to it, then, why are estate settlements so confusing, time-consuming, and expensive? Usually because things seldom go according to plan. If there are minors who may inherit, the court will usually take extra pains (and delays) to see that they are protected. If the deceased left property in more than one state, then you can be sure of substantial delays and extra legal costs. There may also be a dispute over claims, or over what belonged to the deceased and what didn't, or there may be difficulty in locating the beneficiaries and getting their assent, as in the case of the New York man who left specific bequests of $3,000 each to several cousins in Poland. By the time they were located and the necessary communications authenticated and certified by the proper authorities, more than two years had passed and a sum equal to the bequests had been expended. (Keep this in mind if you plan to leave something to people in other countries.)

As to the reason it takes so long to settle an estate, even *without* complications, a quick review of the ten steps above will help you see that each of these steps is vulnerable to interference by heirs, spouses, creditors, and the vagaries of the system. Furthermore, each step may be taken only in its due time. If, for example, bequests are paid before debts are settled or claims made, the executor could be personally liable for any shortfall, so he will be sure to wait the necessary time before payment. Similarly, taxes are almost never paid before the due date of nine months after death, since to do so would be depriving the estate of the use and interest on that money. And after the taxes *are* paid, the executor must then wait until he is told by the government that no further taxes are due, before he can make complete distribution of what is left. For all these reasons, you should, in most cases, have a lawyer to help you—but not just any lawyer.

Do You Really Need a Lawyer?

Something that Howard Hughes and Alfred Nobel had in common was that they both disliked lawyers, and each, therefore, wrote his own will. But had Hughes or Nobel anticipated the hundreds of thousands of dollars in legal fees (*millions* in Hughes's case) that would be generated by their stubbornness, they might have bitten the bullet and paid a lawyer to plan their estates properly.

As suggested above, in all but the smallest and simplest estates, it is a good idea to consult an attorney—but not just any attorney. Although the issues of hiring, paying, and firing (if necessary) an estate attorney are more thoroughly discussed in chapter 14, suffice it to say here that for preparing your will, you should find an attorney who is experienced in preparing wills (and other estate documents, such as trusts). For help in settling an estate, you should find an attorney who is experienced in settling estates and who will charge you on an *hourly* basis for his work, rather than a percentage of the estate. In some estate cases a premium over the hourly rate may be appropriate, but in most situations it is not called for.

You should also keep in mind that in settling an estate, your lawyer does not have to "take over" the entire estate. He can simply guide you in assembling the necessary information, obtaining appraisals, filing forms that he has completed, etc., so that you can, if you wish, do a good deal of the groundwork while he supplies the professional advice, thereby keeping the legal fees to a minimum. In fact, if he is a busy attorney, he will appreciate this arrangement as it takes some of the time pressures and less productive tasks away from him. From your perspective, however, you have a professional to guide you through the complications of estate settlement, and if a mistake is made, he is responsible. By writing your own will or settling someone's estate on your own, *you* are assuming all of the responsibility for matters in which you are not trained or familiar. If you try to do it yourself and mess it up, in addition to whatever penalties and personal liability you or your beneficiaries may face, you'll probably accomplish just what Hughes and Nobel accomplished—generating thousands of dollars in legal fees that could have been avoided.

2

Do You Really Need a Will?

To my dear friend Mrs. George Hale, I give and bequeath the sat-
isfaction of being remembered in my will; and I leave my lawyer,
Huber Lewis, the task of explaining to my relatives why they
didn't get a million dollars apiece.

—from the will of Edwin O. Swain, who died penniless

Since Swain didn't have a dime, did he really need a will? Even
if you do leave money or property, can't you just place everything into joint
names or into a trust and forget about your will?

Actually, everyone has a will, whether he likes it or not. That is, every
state provides laws that dispose of a person's estate if he did not make
arrangements to dispose of it himself. Technically, of course, these laws do
not constitute a "will," but they do accomplish the very thing that a will is
designed to do—dispose of your property at death. They are called the laws
of "intestacy" or the laws of "descent and distribution," and they attempt to
divide the estate in a manner that follows the usual tendency of people to
provide for their families. For instance, in most states, if a person dies
"intestate" (without a will), his property will pass one half to his surviving
spouse and one half to his children. This does not mean, however, that if
such a division is satisfactory to a person he need not bother to make out a
will. The laws of intestacy do not distinguish between adults and minors, for
instance, so if the deceased died without a will and left minor children, the
court would have to appoint a guardian (even though there was a parent surviving), who would administer the funds for the minor until the age of
majority (eighteen in most states). And if the child suffered from a disability, the guardianship could continue indefinitely. Most of us would rather

determine for ourselves the terms and conditions for providing for our families, depending upon the individual family's circumstances, and the way to do that is by making out a will. In addition to these concerns, there are many other important factors, as we will see in this chapter, including an overview of the shares your relatives will take if you die without a will, what property they will divide and what property is beyond the reach of these laws, and the options offered to you through your will.

Heirs and Shares

Most of our laws of succession are derived from the early English laws, but fortunately they have been modernized. In old England, real estate was considered to be the most important and valuable family asset (as it often is today), and the law provided that a wife could *not* inherit real estate from her husband except for the right to live there if she survived him. Under the English law of primogeniture, ultimately all of the husband's real estate would pass first to the eldest son, or to that son's children, if any, otherwise to the next eldest son, etc., the males always being given preference. Fortunately, as I said, we now follow the modernized version of this law, which basically treats males and females equally and does not discriminate against wives.

Briefly, the order of inheritance where there is *no* will follows the general pattern outlined below, but be sure to keep in mind that specific state laws may differ, and the laws in the community-property states (Arizona, California, Idaho, Louisiana, Nevada, New Mexico, Texas, Washington, and, for some purposes, Wisconsin) may differ substantially with respect to the share of a surviving spouse. You should also note that, when a person dies without a will, there is no way to change any of these state-ordered distributions, no matter how unfair or unintended they may be.

It is not unusual, for instance, for a "divorced" spouse to inherit a surviving spouse's full share because death of the other spouse occurred before the divorce became legally final, or before the proceedings were completed. In other cases, the spouses may simply be estranged for years, never having formally obtained a divorce, and the law allows such a surviving spouse to take a full share, since in the eyes of the law she is still a surviving spouse.

With all this in mind, here is a brief outline of the usual distribution of a person's *probate* estate, when there is *no* will, keeping in mind in each case that it applies to what is left *after* payment of estate debts, expenses, fees, and taxes, and that state laws may differ:

a. If the deceased left a spouse and children, the estate will pass one-half to the surviving spouse and one-half to the children. If a child is also deceased and left children of his own, those children (i.e., grandchildren of the person who died without a will) will divide the share of their parent. (In a number of states, instead of fifty-fifty, the shares are one-third to the surviving spouse and two-thirds to the children, or child, if only one. Furthermore, some states differentiate the shares of real estate and other types of property.)

b. If the deceased left a spouse and no children or grandchildren, the estate will pass one-half to the surviving spouse and one-half to the "next of kin" (basically meaning blood relatives of the deceased). Many states provide that where there are no children or grandchildren, the surviving spouse will take the whole estate up to a certain amount, and the rest will be divided as stated above. (For example, the spouse may take the whole estate up to $200,000, but if it exceeds $200,000, then she will take $200,000 plus half the rest.)

c. If the deceased left children or grandchildren but no spouse, the whole estate would be divided equally among the children. (As explained above, if a child died before the deceased, leaving children of his own, those children would divide the share of their parent. For instance, if Jane died leaving two children, A and B, plus four grandchildren whose father was C, a deceased child of Jane, then the four grandchildren will divide C's one-third share of Jane's estate.)

d. If the deceased left no spouse and no children or grandchildren, the whole estate would pass to the deceased's *next of kin*.

Next of kin generally means surviving blood relatives if there are no lineal descendants (i.e., no children, grandchildren, great-grandchildren, etc.) of the deceased, and with respect to next of kin, there are "orders of preference" as to rights of inheritance. In most states, for example, if the deceased left parents and brothers or sisters, the deceased's parents will first inherit the estate. Next would come brothers and sisters equally (if the parents did not survive the deceased), then children of deceased brothers or sisters, then more distant relatives.

For example, say that Brewster dies without a will, survived by his ninety-two-year-old mother, a brother, and two nieces who are children of Brewster's deceased sister. In this case, Brewster's mother will inherit his entire estate. If she died before Brewster, then Brewster's estate would pass one-half to his brother and the other half to his two nieces equally. (The two nieces would take the share their mother—Brewster's sister—would have taken.)

The *spouses* of these persons in any of these categories, including spouses of children and grandchildren of the deceased, would almost never inherit under the laws of intestacy. For instance, say that Webster died without a will, survived by two of his three children. One child died before him, leaving a spouse, but no children of his own. Webster's estate will pass only to his two children. The spouse of Webster's deceased child will not inherit.

Similarly, *stepchildren* of the deceased, and nephews and nieces of the deceased's spouse, are never considered next of kin. If these persons are the *only* surviving "relatives" of the deceased, then the deceased's property will pass to the state. To illustrate, say that Stanley, a widower, dies without a will, leaving a stepson, and two nephews from his wife's side of the family. There are no other relatives. Stanley's estate will pass to the state where he had his principal residence at the time of his death.

A child of the deceased born after the deceased's death will inherit just as if he were born during the deceased's lifetime. Adopted children are treated the same as natural children for inheritance purposes. Up until recently, illegitimate children in most states could inherit only from their mother, unless the father acknowledged the child as his during the father's lifetime. (A 1986 U.S. Supreme Court decision changed this, however, since it held that state laws could not discriminate against such children.)

Now that you have all this technical data under your belt, you must remember two critical points:

1. These rules apply *only* to inheritance where the deceased left *no will;* and
2. These rules apply *only* to property that passes through the deceased's *probate* estate.

Therefore, if the deceased left a will (and if the will is allowed by the probate court), *none* of these rules will apply, except for the rule relating to adopted children. Adopted children are treated as natural children unless the will specifies otherwise. If, on the other hand, the deceased had a will, but it was later lost or destroyed and is considered revoked, then these rules *will* apply, no matter how unfair their application may be. Similarly, if the deceased left no will but left all of his property in joint names with others (or in some other form of ownership that avoided probate), there will be no property to which the rules can apply! Let's look at a couple of cases that illustrate these points.

Jack Dawson remarried a few years after he lost his first wife, Sally. His relationship with his second wife, Flora, seemed excellent, so he made out a new will leaving almost his entire estate to her and only small gifts to his three children. Subsequently, however, the relationship between Jack and Flora began to deteriorate. They argued constantly and Flora was making Jack's life miserable. Jack became more and more upset until one day, while sitting in front of the fireplace in their living room, Jack decided to confront Flora with his anger. He waved his will in front of her face and told her he had decided to revoke it, whereupon he threw the will into the burning fire and stormed out of the room. Flora rushed to the fireplace and retrieved the will, which was singed but intact. A few months later Jack died.

When Flora offered the will for probate asking that the entire estate pass to her, Jack's children objected, as he had told them of the incident, thinking that his will had burned in the fire. He did not make out another one.

Under such circumstances, the court held that Jack's will was revoked. Since he did not make another, he died without a will, and his estate was divided half to Flora and half to his children, even though Jack wanted Flora to get nothing.

When Mary Trindle was widowed at age sixty-two, she moved in with her daughter, Angela. As Angela's family grew, their home became too small, so Mary bought a new home, in her own name and Angela's name as joint tenants. Although Mary's other three children visited her regularly and remained on good terms with her, Angela was the one who took care of Mary. Because of this, Mary gradually placed all of her other assets in joint names with Angela, including bank accounts, securities, and even her government savings bonds, so that Angela could "get at" the money if anything happened to Mary. On Mary's death, the other children looked for their share of Mary's estate, since Mary died without a will and the state laws provided that the children would share Mary's estate equally in that case. Unfortunately, these laws only apply to "estate" (*probate*) property, and Mary's jointly held property passed automatically to Angela, *outside* Mary's probate estate. The other three children split nothing equally.

Probate Property vs. Nonprobate Property

The executor or administrator of the deceased's estate has a duty to collect all of the estate assets. Estate assets—more often called *probate assets,* or assets comprising the *probate estate*—include all of the property which the executor or administrator is entitled to administer for the benefit of all parties "interested in the estate." Such parties include not only beneficiaries and heirs but also the deceased's creditors. It is very important, therefore, to distinguish probate property from nonprobate property, to separate just what is available to beneficiaries, heirs, and creditors from what is not. As explained earlier (and as I will repeat many more times throughout this book), the heirs, beneficiaries, and creditors of the estate are normally entitled only to the *probate* property, and property that avoids probate is likely to avoid the reach of these parties.

One way to approach the question is to ask exactly what property *belonged* to the deceased at his death. For the most part, this would include items that were held in the deceased's name *alone,* or if held with others, held in a manner that did not permit the other owners to take the deceased's share on his death. For instance, if the deceased had real estate under a tenancy in common with his brother, then the deceased's share would be a part of his probate estate and would not automatically pass to his brother. Note the difference between a tenancy in common and a joint tenancy: Under a joint tenancy (discussed in more detail in chapter 11), the survivor takes all of the property without probate, whereas under a tenancy in common, the share of each tenant passes through his probate estate. The difference is normally revealed in how the title reads (although evidence to the contrary could change the result): "A and B" (without any additional words) and "A and B as tenants-in-common" generally indicate a *tenancy in common,* while "A *or* B" or "A and B *as joints tenants*" or "A and B *jointly,*" or "A and B, *jointly with right of survivorship,*" would all indicate a *joint tenancy.*

In addition to the more common types of assets such as real estate, securities, bank accounts, business interests, works of art, etc., that are regarded as probate property if they are in the deceased's name alone, here are other types of property interests that may be considered probate property:

1. *Partnership share.* If the deceased was a partner of a partnership, the remaining partners are required to account to his estate for the deceased's interests in the partnership (although it is not impossible to hold a partnership share in joint names or in a trust, to avoid probate).

A share in a limited liability company is generally treated the same as a partnership share.

2. *Lawsuits.* If the deceased had started a lawsuit against someone before his death and it is the type of action that survives his death (such as a contract action or other type of suit to recover property damages), then his executor or administrator may continue the action and any recovery will be a part of the probate estate. If the deceased's death was caused by someone's negligence, then most state laws provide that the executor or administrator of the estate may bring a "wrongful death" action, part of which may be subject to probate.

3. *Life insurance policies.* If the deceased was the insured under a policy and if the policy proceeds were payable to the deceased's "estate" (usually a bad idea), then the proceeds will be probate property. If the deceased was the *owner* of a policy on someone else's life, then the policy *itself* (not the proceeds, since the insured person would still be alive) would be a part of the deceased's probate estate.

4. *Gifts made just before death.* If the deceased made "death bed" gifts and if, because of this, there is not enough money in his probate estate to pay his creditors, the gifts may be ordered back to the estate, to become probate property.

Once again, it is only the *probate* property that is disposed of by the will. Nonprobate property passes outside the probate estate and is not disposed of through the will. So if you have a nonprobate estate (where all the assets pass to others without the need of the will), why do you need a will?

Options Your Will Offers You

For one, you could make a statement similar to that of Edwin Swain at the outset of this chapter, simply "mentioning" people in your will but not leaving them anything, thereby enabling you to honestly say, "I want you to know I have mentioned you in my will." On the other hand, you could actually "leave" them bequests of the thousands of dollars you don't have, as Cora Johnson did.

Cora gave a great deal of thought as to how she wanted to leave her "fortune." She finally went to her lawyer in Boston and had him draw a will, enumerating several bequests and legacies to favorite friends and charities that amounted to about $700,000. The only problem was that Cora's entire estate was less than $100. It seemed that Cora had been informed that she was about to inherit a fortune from the estate of a close friend of hers from New York. (According to Cora, after her friend made out her will, she subsequently became very ill and mentally incompetent, so Cora was confident that her friend's will could not later be changed.) Unfortunately, Cora never revealed the identity of her friend to anyone, and, according to the probate records, Cora's estate never received the funds. (In fact, Cora's will has mysteriously disappeared from the probate court records in Boston!)

In addition to disposing of property that you don't yet have and, of course, property that you *do* have, here are other options that a will offers, some of which can be exercised *only* through your will.

NAMING A GUARDIAN FOR YOUR MINOR CHILDREN

Even if your spouse survives you, it may be necessary to name a guardian for your minor child or children. Although the parent is the natural guardian of the child's *person*, she or he is not the natural guardian of the child's *property*. If the minor child receives any property through the estate, such property must be held by a guardian (or, in some cases, a custodian, as noted below). If no one is nominated (the will merely *nominates*, the court *appoints*—but the court is normally bound to honor the wishes of the deceased, unless inappropriate), then the court will make its own nomination and appointment. Furthermore, in your will, you can provide for a *successor* guardian. That is, you can say, "If my husband cannot serve as guardian of my minor children, then I nominate my brother and his wife, John and Jean Johnson, to be guardians."

GIVING DIRECTION TO GUARDIANS

Few people (including attorneys) think of this. If is quite permissible to add in your will instructions to your guardians regarding the care, education, or domicile of your minor children in the event both parents are deceased. For instance, you might say, "In the event my wife and I are both deceased leaving minor children, I direct that my guardians see that they are provided with counseling to help them deal with the loss of their parents. I further direct my guardians to use their best efforts to place my minor children in schools (or private schools) of a caliber and reputation similar to those of the Newton public school system (or the Tom Brown private school, etc.), and if possible, I would like them to continue to live in the general area of Maintown, California."

Not all of these instructions may be carried out to the letter, but it would certainly be clear that the guardians would be authorized to make any reasonable expenditures to carry out your wishes, and you have made it clear to your guardians just what your wishes are. For example, despite its importance to the mental well-being of the child, it is quite rare for the guardian to provide a child with counseling on the loss of his or her parents.

NAMING A CUSTODIAN

If you make bequests of money or property to a minor child, a guardian must normally be appointed, since a minor child cannot take title to property. Unless other provisions are made, the guardians, once appointed, must submit an annual account to the probate court and must ultimately make the property available to the child when the child reaches the age of majority (eighteen in most states). If instead you name a *custodian* to hold the property (generally, this is allowed for amounts up to $10,000), you will be dispensing with the need for a guardian (for *this* property only), and the custodian, in most states, is not required to file an annual account to the probate court. Furthermore, most states allow the custodian the option of holding the property until the child reaches age twenty-one, even though eighteen may be the age of majority.

UNBORN BENEFICIARIES

If a will provides that shares of the estate may be taken by a person born *after* a person's death (this is often done unintentionally), then there may be what are called "unborn" or "unascertained" beneficiaries. For instance, say that Bill leaves his estate three-fourths to his children, equally, and one-fourth to his grandchildren, equally. On Bill's death, one of his daughters is pregnant. The child-to-be is considered an unborn beneficiary on Bill's death, since he or she, as Bill's grandchild, will take a share of Bill's estate. In order to see that such beneficiaries are not shortchanged by the executor or the other beneficiaries, the probate court will often appoint a special guardian (usually a lawyer known to the court) to look over the actions of the executor and others on behalf of the unborn beneficiary. This special guardian is sometimes called a "guardian ad litem," and he is entitled to charge a fee for his services, which are often superfluous. Many states allow a testator to *dispense* with the appointment of a guardian ad litem by including instructions in the will to that effect, and doing so can save the estate considerable time and expense.

INSERTING A NONCONTEST CLAUSE

If you are making bequests under your will and have more than a nominal probate estate, you may want to consider a "noncontest" or "anticontest" provision. This is designed to discourage disgruntled beneficiaries and basically provides that if they contest the will, they will lose their share. (Noncontest provisions are discussed in much greater detail in chapter 10.)

CHOOSING OF EXECUTOR

Without a will, you cannot choose the person who will handle the settlement of your estate. In your will you may not only name one or more executors, but, as with guardianship, you may name successors if these individuals cannot serve. This can be extremely important, since an orderly and expeditious settlement of the estate can be enhanced by a properly selected executor. (This is discussed in much greater detail in chapter 9.)

SURVIVAL AND SIMULTANEOUS DEATH PROVISIONS

Although it does not happen often, family members do die in common disasters or within a few days or weeks of one another. The first situation relates to "simultaneous" death, where it is impossible to tell who died first. Under the laws of all states, you have a right to declare in your will who is considered to survive in this case. This can be important, especially in the case of jointly owned property, for instance, where, if you do not specify who is the survivor, then "each is considered to have survived the other." The *expensive* effect of this (without a declaration in your will) is to split the joint property and require one-half to pass through each estate.

There are also tax reasons for using a simultaneous death election. The spouse with the larger estate should normally declare that, in a common disaster, the other spouse is considered to have survived. In the typical estate plan, this has the effect of "equalizing" the estates and bringing both into a lower estate tax bracket.

The other "survival" provision deals with those cases where a beneficiary survives you by a few hours or a few days or weeks. This is quite different from a common disaster. In this case, it is clear who died first.

The problem is that you normally want a beneficiary to inherit and use the property for the rest of his life—not for a few days or weeks. The other problem in this situation is that the bequest would go from your probate estate to the *beneficiary's* probate estate (since he or she died just after you), causing *double* probate costs, delays, and legal fees. For these reasons, many lawyers add a standard provision that says, "In order for a person to be considered to have survived me under this will, she or he must have survived me by sixty days." (Sixty days is somewhat arbitrary but considered reasonable.) You should not make the "waiting period" more than several months, however, since the provision itself would then operate to hold up the probate process, as the executor is forced to wait to see who survives the prescribed period.

BUSINESS INTERESTS
If the probate estate includes business interests that are "personal" to the deceased, such as a sole proprietorship or a partnership interest, it is very important that the will contain *specific* provisions authorizing the executor to carry on the business. If there are no such provisions and the executor continues the business without authority, he will be *personally liable* to the persons he deals with (in the business) and he will also be *personally liable* for any losses incurred by the business while he acts without authority. (If the provisions are not in the will, the executor would normally ask the probate court for the authority, but this would be an added expense.) See appendix II for a sample provision.

**FUNERAL ARRANGEMENTS, LAST COMMENTS,
AND BODY "DISPOSAL"**
Your wishes regarding funeral arrangements or other special instructions will normally be carried out unless they are frivolous and wasteful. As to body disposal, you may be surprised to hear that after your death, you have no property rights to your body, and wishes that you express in this regard *may* be carried out, out of respect, but are not legally enforceable against your family or beneficiaries. Organ donations fall somewhere in between, as they are allowed by law in most states, but if, in fact, your family objects to your body being cut up and the parts sent to various institutions, the institutions will not contest it.

In your will you can also, of course, express personal wishes, make statements of observation or appreciation, or even express opinions about people, but most lawyers discourage this, as it often leads to trouble. If, for example, you want to finally tell someone what you really thought of him over the years, it could get your estate in trouble, or at least lead to additional expenses. There are a number of cases, for instance, where testators disinherited lineal descendants (children and grandchildren), stating that it was because they were illegitimate, and many of these cases resulted in lawsuits against the estate.

The more common cases of vituperous testators, however, simply express not so pleasant feelings about a spouse or a child, or, of course, an in-law, as in the case of the father whose will left his son-in-law "fifty cents to buy a good stout rope with which to hang himself and thereby ridding mankind of a most infamous scoundrel." Rumor has it that upon hearing of this special bequest, the son-in-law responded, "Too bad my poor father-in-law did not live to enjoy the bequest for himself."

CONDITIONAL BEQUESTS

Conditional bequests, designed to "force" people to comply with otherwise unenforceable or nonbinding requests (such as marrying within a certain religion or carrying out special funeral arrangements), are also possible, but they must, of course, be within the law. For instance, you cannot make a bequest conditional upon the beneficiary committing a crime or doing something that is against public policy. Other than that, however, you do have a great deal of leeway, since no matter how eccentric the condition, the beneficiary does have the right not to carry it out and refuse the bequest, as in the case of the California man who left his nephew $5,000 on the condition that the nephew, who was a professional gambler, "pledge himself to religion and become a man of the cloth." The nephew, to whom $5,000 was little more than a week's wages, graciously refused the bequest, finding the "paper" more attractive than the "cloth."

In short, there are many things you can do, some things you may do, and a few that you must do—and can only do—in your will. And since you simply cannot know what your family and property circumstances will be at your death, what will be in your probate estate, or what will be the cause of your death, you'll always need a will.

3

What Is a Will?

Dear Edward,
This letter leaves me in bed with high fever. I do not know whether I
should live to see morning. You have from childhood always shown
yourself to be a friend, now I am sick and have one more favor to
ask—in case I die see that old Buffington has nothing of mine, not
even a lock of my hair. Eliza did what she could for me and I want her
to have our home in Yazoo City. Buffington has not given me a cop-
per. I could say more but am too sick.

Truly yours, Mamie Buffington

Mamie wrote this letter on Christmas day in 1898 and died a few short months later. Subsequently, Mamie's letter was offered for probate as her will. "Old Buffington" was Mamie's husband, who, for obvious reasons, objected to its allowance, claiming the letter was not a valid will. Was it? Doesn't a will have to be witnessed? Or notarized?

In most states, a will, to be valid, must follow very strict requirements of signing and witnessing, and in some cases, notarizing as well. In others, however, a simple statement entirely in the handwriting of the deceased, and signed (and dated) by him or her, can be considered a valid, enforceable will, if it is made with the intent that it be a will. Such wills are called "holographic" wills, meaning entirely handwritten by the person who signed it.

The case of Mamie Buffington took place in Mississippi, a state that recognizes holographic wills, and Mamie's letter was held to qualify as a valid will. (A holographic will need not be witnessed—it need only be completely handwritten, signed, and dated by the testator.) "Old Buffington," therefore, didn't get a "copper," or even a lock of Mamie's hair. Though the Buffington case is not a recent one, the law is still the same in those states that recognize the validity of a holographic will. And the disputes are still the same, as well. In fact, many authorities feel that the continued allowance of the holographic wills actually introduces disputes, since it encourages a person to attempt to make his own will simply by writing it out, even if it is just a "simple" letter! There are many special and important provisions that should be in a will that are practically never in a holographic will. But even in those states that recognize the handwritten "holographic" will, all *wills,* whether handwritten or not, must meet certain requirements, and wills that are not handwritten must be signed with certain formalities to make them valid. In this chapter, we'll see just what is needed to make your will valid, whether handwritten or not.

Formalities of a Will

1. The will must be in writing. Except for special cases, such as holographic wills (and, in the case of certain life-and-death situations, oral, also called "non-cupative," wills), ordinary wills *must be in writing, must be signed by the testator* (the person making the will), and *must be witnessed by two witnesses* (some states still require three witnesses).

Unless a will meets *all* the necessary requirements, it will not be valid, *no matter how close it comes.* But if it does meet the necessary requirements, it *will* be valid (unless disallowed on some other grounds, such as incompetence of the testator), even though some of its features are unusual.

For instance, the "writing" need not be in English. A will may be written in any language, even in a language the testator did not understand, so long as he understood the contents and *intended* that the document be his will. Of course, if it is in a foreign language, the will must be translated into the language of the court in which it is probated.

As to what material the will is written on, this has been the topic of many unusual court cases and interesting articles. The only requirements are that it be written or inscribed on a substance that results in a readable and reasonably permanent record. (A will written on a block of ice or scratched in the sand, therefore, would probably not be valid.) Records show that a number of wills were written on the backs of envelopes and train tickets, and one was scratched on the fender of a tractor by a dying man. But perhaps one of the more unusual is the famous "petticoat will" case of California. There, the testator, George Hazeltine of Los Angeles, was in a hospital, dying. He sought to make out his last will, but a piece of paper was nowhere to be found. Obligingly, one of Hazeltine's nurses lifted her dress and tore off a piece of her petticoat, on which Hazeltine wrote out his will. It was witnessed by two nurses and later actually offered for probate in the Los Angeles probate court. Because of the novel circumstances, the petticoat will enjoyed national attention. It was disallowed, but *not* because it was written on a petticoat.

Photographs or tape recordings are not valid as wills as they are not considered "writings," nor are videotape recordings, convincing as they may be. Therefore, unless you want to go down in wills history as the person who chiseled his will on the outside of the fifty-second floor of a skyscraper or engraved it on the head of a pin, you'll probably be far better if you just have it typed on paper, like the rest of us. After all, it's not what the will is written *on*, but what it *says* that matters.

2. *The will must be signed by the testator.* With the exception of a "non-cupative" will (one that is made orally in a life-and-death situation, such as a soldier in battle), this is a basic and very strict requirement for *every* type of will in *every* state. What constitutes a signature, however, may surprise you. For openers, it need not be legible. (When you think about it, however, this rule may be perfectly reasonable, since with the exception of English teachers, few people have legible signatures.) A misspelled signature is also valid, probably for the same reason illegibility is not fatal, the essential ingredient being that the testator *intended* the mark to authenticate the document as his will. In fact, any "mark" intended to act as authentication if sufficient, such as a line, a dot, an "X," or even a fingerprint could be sufficient. And a testator who is physically unable to sign is permitted to have *someone else* sign for him, as long as the testator understands the contents of the will and the other person signs the testator's name *in his presence* and *at his direction.* Without this provision, illiterate testators would not be able to make a will, nor would people who were paralyzed or simply too ill to sign. A good illustration of this is the will of Christopher Reeves, the actor who played Superman and who later became paralyzed from the neck down as the result of a horseback-riding accident. Reeves's will was actually signed by his wife, Dana, in his presence and at his direction. The will as signed by Dana (of course, she signed Christopher's name to the will) was duly admitted to probate in the Westchester County Surrogate's Court.

Those who *can* sign, however, need not necessarily sign their legal name— although it is silly not to, as this just increases the chance of litigation, as in the case of "Nannie" Rodgers. Mrs. Rodgers's will contained bequests of real estate and money and was very poorly written. To make matters worse, she signed it, *"Aunt Nannie."* Of course, the heirs contesting the will claimed, among other things, that her signature was not valid. In upholding the will, the Kentucky court said, in effect, that the testatrix may sign her full name, or an abbreviated name, or even an assumed name, so long as there was no intent to deceive, and so long as it was her intent that the instrument operate as her will. Aunt Nannie's signature was valid but the probate of her will was delayed by the contest.

On the other hand, if the testator does not *finish* signing, the signature will *not* be valid. For instance, say that a testator intends to write out his full name, such as "Grover Lambeck," but after writing only "Grov" or "Grover La" (or any part of the full name without completing the signature or the mark he *intended* to make), he suddenly drops dead or has a stroke or simply stops writing, then the partial mark or partially written name is *not* considered a signature. Of course, if what he wrote was all he *intended* to write, as in the case of Aunt Nannie above, then the partial signature would be valid.

Generally, the signature is only required once, and customarily it is placed *at the end* of the will. In many states the signature may be placed anywhere on the will, so long as the will was complete when the testator signed it, he knew of its contents, and he intended the signature to authenticate the entire will. It is foolish, however, to sign anywhere but at the end. If a bequest is written in *below* the testator's signature, for example, immediate and obvious questions arise as to its validity.

To ensure that no changes or additions are made after the will is signed, most attorneys will have the testator initial or sign each page of the will. While this is good practice, it is not a legal requirement to the validity of the will.

3. *The will must be witnessed.* Most states require that there be at least two witnesses to the testator's signature. Note, however, that *the witnesses do not need to know the contents of the will.* The witnesses must be competent (legally able to testify that they witnessed the will), but in most states they need not necessarily be adults. The fact that they may later become incompetent, or die before the testator, has no effect on the validity of the testator's will.

A witness should not be a person who is named as a beneficiary under the will, nor should he or she be the spouse of such a beneficiary. If this happens, the beneficiary may not be allowed to take his bequest under the will, although for all other purposes the will may still be valid. And it is only the witness or the spouse of a witness to which this rule applies. It does not affect a bequest to some other relative of a witness. For instance, Robert is a witness to the will of his brother Morris, and Morris's will leaves a $10,000 bequest to his nephew (Robert's son), George. The fact that Robert witnessed his brother Morris's will will not cause George's bequest to be disallowed.

Furthermore, qualification of the witness is important only *at the time the witness signs.* A subsequent "disqualification" will not matter. For example, Joe makes out his will leaving half of his estate to his niece, Priscilla. One of the witnesses to Joe's will later marries Priscilla. Priscilla will still be eligible to receive her bequest, since she was not the spouse of a witness at the time of the signing.

If a will has *more* than the required number of witnesses, it will still be valid, but if it has *fewer* than the prescribed number, it will not.

If a witness also happens to be named executor or trustee under the will, this has no effect on the will or on the appointment of the witness as executor or trustee, since neither of the appointments is considered to be a bequest or benefit under the will.

As to the actual signatures, the same rules as discussed above for the signature of the testator apply to those of the witnesses. That is, though it is preferable that they sign their full name, any mark or abbreviation will be sufficient so long as they intend it to operate as a witnessing to the testator's signature.

4. The testator must sign "in the presence of" the witnesses and the witnesses must sign "in the presence of" the testator and "in the presence of" each other. The testator must sign his will "in the presence of" the witnesses, but most states also allow the testator to *acknowledge* his signature in the presence of the witnesses. In other words, he could simply say to the witnesses, "This is my will; I signed it yesterday, and today I would like you to witness my signature." (This is considered the same as signing it again in their presence.) Their subsequent signatures as witnesses in his presence would then be valid.

If the testator is actually in the presence of the witnesses when he signs, that is also sufficient, even though the witnesses do not actually watch him sign. Similarly, the witnesses must sign in the presence of the testator, and he must be in a position to be able to see them sign, even though he does not actually watch them do so, or could not, as in the case of a blind testator. For these reasons, lawyers will usually gather the testators and all the witnesses in a room for the signing, allowing no one to leave until the signing and witnessing is completed. If, for example, the testator signed, then one witness signed and was called out of the room before the other witnesses signed, the validity of the will could easily be questioned in most states.

Signing Your Own Will at Home

If you haven't already noticed, the formalities of executing a will are quite rigid—"almost" is no good. That is, if you are one witness short, or if no one saw the testator sign, or if a witness was called out of the room before the signing was completed, the entire will could be held invalid. Therefore, if it is necessary for you to have your own will signed "at home," or somewhere other than your lawyer's office, here are some helpful hints.

1. The testator should read the will over to be sure it leaves his property as he wishes. Handwritten wills should be avoided wherever possible, except perhaps in cases of extreme emergency, even in those states that recognize "holographic" (handwritten) wills. If there are errors in the will, the will, or at least the corrected pages, should be retyped in full. Erasures, crossing out lines, and writing new provisions in the margins should be avoided whenever possible, as they raise obvious questions. If such changes must be made on the face of the will, the testator should sign his name in the margin beside *each* such change, and the witnesses should then sign or initial below the testator's mark to show that the changes were made to the will *prior* to its signing.

2. The will should be "integral." That is, each page should logically follow the one before it, and preferably, each page should be signed or initialed by the testator. (Some attorneys also have the witnesses initial the pages as well.) Finally, the pages should be fastened together. These steps are *not* required by law but are an excellent idea to prevent a later questioning as to whether the document presented for probate was the *exact* document that the testator signed as his will.

3. Be sure that the witnesses are competent and that none of them is mentioned as a beneficiary in the will or is the spouse of such a beneficiary.

4. At the time of the actual signing, the testator and the required number of witnesses should be brought together in a room. If the testator is not known to the witnesses, they should be briefly introduced. The testator should then announce to the witnesses something such as: "This is my will. I have carefully read it and I understand and approve of the contents. Now I would like you to witness my signature." The testator should proceed to initial each page, and then sign his name in full at the end of the will, in front of the witnesses. The witnesses should then sign, in front of the testator, and none of the witnesses should leave the room until everyone has signed. The witnesses should

also write their addresses beside or below their respective names. If a witness's signature is not legible, his name should be printed below it. The date of the signing and witnessing should be included.

Many states also allow the addition of a "self-proving affidavit" to the will. This is a statement that is later offered as proof that the will was properly signed and, if no one objects, the affidavit will avoid the necessity of bringing one or more of the witnesses before the court (after the testator's death) to testify as to the signing. If your will has a self-proving affidavit, then a notary public would also have to be present, since the affidavit must be notarized.

5. When signing is completed, the will is usually handed to the testator, and he decides where to keep it. Of course, it should be kept in a safe place. Some testators leave it with the attorney, and some states allow for depositing the will in the probate court for the district where the testator resides. This is for safekeeping only, and does not constitute legal action of any kind. (Later in this chapter more details are given on where to keep your will.) Wherever it is stored, a copy of the signed will should be left with the testator's attorney for his files. If the original is lost, the availability of such a copy may prove extremely valuable. Note that only *one* will is signed. The only times a "second" will is signed are to amend the first will, to make a new one, or in cases where the testator has property in a different *country*.

Who May Make a Will?

Anyone having "testamentary capacity" may legally make a will. Do you remember hearing the phrase "of legal age and sound mind"? Basically, this is testamentary capacity.

Legal age is not necessarily the age of majority. Every state allows a person age eighteen or over to make a will, though in many of those states the age of majority is twenty-one or twenty or nineteen. Once "legal age" is reached, however, a person has the right to make a will, so long as he is of "sound mind," often a much more difficult question than that of legal age.

A person is of "sound mind," according to the law, when he or she can understand in a general way:

- the nature and extent of his property,
- the people to whom he would "normally" leave such property, and
- the manner in which he is leaving such property under his will.

This does not mean that only an intelligent person or one who is generally regarded as "normal" can make a will. The standard of capacity necessary for making a will is actually not very high, and a person meeting the requirements outlined above may at the same time be regarded as weird or eccentric by his peers. Such persons, as well as those who are not weird but merely "slow" or "dull," and even some who are under a guardianship or conservatorship for mental incapacity, could make a perfectly valid will if they are capable of the basic understanding stated above. It is the level of such understanding that is the test, rather than the reasonableness of the will itself.

A person, therefore, need not be in "perfect" mental health or be totally aware of every facet of his financial and business situation to make a will. Rather, an essential issue is whether the testator knew to whom he wanted to leave his property and understood that his will would accomplish this. In this regard, it is not necessary that the testator be able to understand the meaning of the technical terms in his will, nor must he be able to comprehend the legal steps necessary to carry out his plan. Similarly, it is not necessary that the testator understand the intricacies or even the exact amount of the property or estate he presently owns.

All that is necessary is that the testator is *capable* of understanding them when he makes out his will. In other words, if the testator *thought* he had only two parcels of real estate but in fact had *five* parcels, a bequest of "all my real estate to B" would cause all five parcels to go to B, so long as the testator had the *capacity* to understand the nature and extent of his estate. *The fact that he did not realize what he had is not relevant.* This point is further illustrated in the case of the will of Nancy Shaw, who thought she was leaving only $500 to Campbell College, but in fact left the school nearly $20,000!

After a number of communications with her attorney, Nancy had him make out a will that contained about forty specific bequests, which, she believed, practically exhausted all of her estate. Thinking that the balance would only amount to about $500, she wrote her attorney, "If there is any money left in my estate it may go to Cambell College," and this was incorporated into her will.

During the trial, evidence was offered that Nancy Shaw was somewhat eccentric, that on occasion she broke down without apparent reason, and that she thought her relatives were plotting to take her estate. There was also evidence showing that Nancy Shaw had never been to Campbell College (or to any other college for that matter), or that she even knew anything of the college, except that there had been a picture of the college hanging in the church she attended. Finally, there was evidence to show that if Nancy had known how much Campbell College would receive, she would have left it to her other heirs.

This belief, however, was not important to the validity of Nancy Shaw's will, the Kansas Supreme Court said. The essential issue was whether Nancy was capable of understanding the extent of her property. The evidence of the specific bequests and the bequest of "any money left" was itself enough to convince the court that she did have the capacity to understand, and Campbell College was allowed to receive the bequest.

It is interesting that although evidence of Nancy Shaw's eccentricities was brought in this case, it was not regarded as having a bearing on her capacity to make a will. Although extreme eccentricities, especially if evidenced by the provisions of the will itself, can at least *suggest* a certain lack of capacity (or, to put it another way, they would elicit the reaction that only a crazy person would include such a provision in his will), courts are reluctant to treat this, by itself, as conclusive of the testator's lack of capacity.

Take for example the case of James Kidd, a gold prospector who was declared dead by an Arizona court in 1963 after having mysteriously disappeared several years earlier. Kidd's will left the bulk of his estate "to go in a research or some scientific proof of a soul of the human body which leaves at death I think in time their [*sic*] can be a Photograph of [the] soul leaving the human at death, James Kidd."

Although Kidd's bequest could certainly be considered eccentric, it was not, by itself, an indication that he was mentally incompetent or did not have the capacity to make a will. In fact, in the Kidd case, after some "soul-searching" on the part of the probate court judge, Kidd's money was actually given to the American Society for Psychical Research in New York City, to establish a fund to carry out, as near as possible, the search for evidence of the "soul" as provided in James Kidd's will.

Rather than pure eccentricities, therefore, there must be an actual lack of mental capacity to render the will invalid. The more common cases are those where the person is clearly mentally deficient, usually from a medical standpoint. The obvious persons in this group would include those who are mentally retarded or mentally disabled, who are unable to form and understand a testamentary plan. Another form of incapacity, however, is often more difficult to distinguish—that is, where a person is considered to be "mentally deranged."

A mentally deranged person may appear to be quite normal and able to understand very well the "natural objects of his bounty" and the extent of his estate, but because of his derangement, he is considered unable to make a rational testamentary plan. A person suffering from extreme paranoia, for example, thinking that his wife and children are plotting to kill him, may make a will leaving his estate to a casual friend whom he trusted. Such a person is said to be mentally deranged and suffering from, in the words of the law, an "insane delusion."

An insane delusion is a false belief that results from a diseased or deranged mind, a belief that operates against all facts and reason. A false belief by itself, however, is *not* delusion. The fact, for instance, that a person disinherited a child because he falsely believed the child was not his is not an insane delusion and would *not* warrant a finding by a court that the testator did not have the necessary mental capacity on the basis that he was suffering from an insane delusion.

To suffer from an insane delusion, a person must believe in a state of facts that does not exist and that no rational person would believe to exist. This is, in part, why eccentricities are not considered to be insane delusions. They may constitute strange or queer behavior, but they often have no bearing on the testator's capacity or belief in making his will. And even where there is an insane delusion, as a general rule the insane delusion will only invalidate a will if it operates to cause the testator to make a disposition of his property that is clearly a *result* of the delusion and *contrary* to what he might otherwise have done. Accordingly, if the delusion, no matter how insane, did *not* affect the disposition of property, the will may be held valid, as illustrated in the case of Oren Eveleth Emery of Iowa. Oren believed his son was trying to kill him. Nevertheless, he made out a will leaving all his property to that son, even though he had other children. The other children contested Oren's will, arguing, among other things, that Oren was suffering from an insane delusion (that his son Emery was trying to kill him) and, therefore, the will should be set aside. The court observed that if this delusion had affected Oren in any way, it would have been to omit his son rather than leave the property to him, so although it was in fact an insane delusion, it did not invalidate the will.

In the case of Louisa Strittmocher, the court did overturn her will because of insane delusion, although some might disagree with the court's conclusion. Evidence in that case showed that Louisa Strittmocher, who never married, had such an insane hatred of men that it affected her capacity to make a will.

Louisa Strittmocher apparently had a normal childhood and was quite devoted to her parents, yet she later wrote: "My father was a corrupt, vicious and unintelligent savage. Blast his wormstinking carcass and his whole damn breed." Additional evidence showed that she had a morbid aversion to men and that she "looked forward to the day when women would bear children without the aid of men and all male children would be put to death at birth." She became a member of the National Women's Party and began talking of leaving her estate to the party. Sure enough, she made out her will to that effect, and just a month later, she died.

Strittmocher's heirs contested the will, offering testimony from Strittmocher's physician, who stated that, in her opinion, Louisa Strittmocher suffered from severe paranoia. The New Jersey court agreed, holding that Strittmocher was suffering from an insane delusion and lacked the capacity to make a will. Accordingly, the will was held invalid and the money went to Strittmocher's heirs.

In summary, there are many factors that influence our ability to make a will, but anyone who has the "capacity" to make a will may make one. Capacity generally means the ability to understand what it means to own property, to understand in a general way what it is you own, to understand that there are people to whom you would "normally" leave your property (even though you decide not to leave it to them), and to understand that you can dispose of your property by making out a will.

You do not have to be in "perfect" health, either mentally or physically. You simply have to have the capacity. Persons under guardianships for mental weakness, for instance, can still make a will if they have the required understanding, even if only for the brief period in which they made the will. Likewise, persons who are extremely ill or very old, or suffering from a severe handicap such as blindness or deafness, can make a will. Even persons who are otherwise healthy, however, may "lose" their capacity to make a will because of an insane delusion.

Wills Made in Another State

Regardless of where your will was made out, the laws require it to be probated in the place where you had your principal domicile (residence) at the time of your death, assuming it needs to be probated at all. (As discussed previously, if a person's estate consists entirely of nonprobate property and if there is no other requirement or request that probate be initiated, then the will need not be probated.)

But what happens if you made out your will when you resided in Boston,

Massachusetts, then moved to Charlestown, South Carolina. Is your Massa-chusetts will still "good"? Must you rush to make out a new will? Does the Massachusetts will now cover *all* of your property, including that in Massa-chusetts, South Carolina, and in other states?

The general rule is that if your will was properly executed according to the laws of the state in which you executed it, then it will be valid in another state if you subsequently move, even though the laws of the new state are different. For instance, say that you reside in Massachusetts and you make out a will, under which only two witnesses are required. You later move to South Carolina, which requires three witnesses to a will. If you should die in South Carolina without having made a new will, your Massachusetts will will most likely be valid in South Carolina, as it was properly executed under Massachusetts law when you resided there. The question is, however, whether this "foreign" will has the necessary validity to dispose of your property in South Carolina, Massachusetts, and elsewhere. When a person dies leaving property in another state (in his own name), it becomes neces-sary to take out probate not only in the state in which he was domiciled (resided) at the time of his death but also in those other states where he left such property. This procedure is called "ancillary administration," which is a fancy term for additional probate, additional legal fees, and additional delays. (This is covered further in chapter 11.) Fortunately, the ancillary administration does not require the will to be proved all over again, but it does require proper certification of its proof in the domiciliary state (South Carolina, in our example above), so that the foreign state or states can see that it was held to be a valid will according to the probate court in the state of your residence. After certification of this proof is submitted to the satis-faction of the court in the "foreign" state, then ancillary probate will be allowed in the state where the property is situated.

If you do have property in other states, you should consider making arrangements that will preclude the need for ancillary administration on your death (or disability). The two principal ways of accomplishing this are through joint ownership and through a living trust; in my opinion, a trust is by far the more preferable method.

If property in a foreign state is held by the deceased and another as "joint tenants with rights of survivorship," then on the death of the deceased, the other joint tenant will own the foreign property without the need for pro-bate or ancillary administration. The problem is that this will not apply to the need for probate due to mental incompetence (or guardianship, for instance) of one of the joint owners, nor does it provide for the contingency that the other joint owner might die first. For these reasons, a simple, living trust (as discussed in detail in chapter 12) is preferable, as it can provide for both of these contingencies, avoiding ancillary administration in each case.

Despite all this, it is very important to understand that each state has the absolute right to impose its own laws on all property situated within its boundaries, regardless of what a will provides and regardless of whether the property is held in a trust or under a joint tenancy. It is this principle that in part makes the issue of foreign wills unsettled. The state laws are not consistent, for example, as to the rights of a surviving spouse at death. Say that state X allows a spouse to take a "forced share" (the share she can take regardless of the provisions of the deceased spouse's will; see chapter 7) of one-third the estate and state Y allows her to take one-fourth the estate. And say that the deceased died a domiciliary of state X, also leaving property in state Y. His surviving spouse, if she elected to take her forced share, would take one-third the property in state X and one-fourth the property in state Y. In the same context, states can decide whether the spouse's share should include property held in joint names with another or held in a living trust. This does *not* mean, however, that a foreign state can extend a spouse's rights to property outside that state.

As a general rule, therefore, it is a good idea to have your will reviewed by a local estate attorney if you change domicile to another state. If you have property in states other than that in which you live (that is, in which you have your principal residence), you should definitely take steps to avoid the necessity of ancillary administration in the "foreign" states. And if you think your surviving spouse will attempt to disregard your will and take her forced share, plan ahead.

What Property Will Pass under Your Will?

As briefly noted in chapter 2, the provisions of a will apply only to property held in the deceased's name alone or property that is held or payable in a way that it must pass through the deceased's *probate* estate. Ignorance of this essential fact has caused fights, bitterness, and disappointment in many a family.

Quite often, for example, a family is shocked to find that even though Dad's will left the home to his two children, they will not get it because it was held in joint names with his second wife. Since it was held jointly, the home did not pass through Dad's probate estate and, therefore, did not pass under the terms of his will. For this reason, anyone making a will *must also* review the titles and status of each asset and item of property that he or she has, to ensure that the specific property will pass under the terms of the will or bypass the will altogether. This is not to say that I recommend that all of your property pass through your will. *I do not.* I do recommend, however, that if you are to have a will and if your will contains bequests of property, that you take the necessary steps to see that your wishes are carried out. To do this, you should review your assets to see just what will pass under your will (through your probate estate) and what will not.

Property or assets in *your name alone,* such as a home or a bank account or a stock certificate, must pass through your probate estate and, therefore, under the terms of your will. But as you will see in the discussion that follows, there can be many instances when the title to property is deceiving, or where there may be no "title" problem but an improper beneficiary designation, or where property you did not know you would have at your death comes into your probate estate.

Tenant-in-common. In cases where you are a tenant-in-common, the disposition of your share on your death is not so readily apparent. For instance, if you are a co-owner of property with someone else, the property or other asset is not in your name "alone," but your share may nevertheless be a part of your probate estate. The main difference between a tenancy in common and a joint tenancy is that the share of a deceased *joint* owner will pass to the surviving joint owner, thereby avoiding probate, while the share of a deceased tenant-in-common will pass to the deceased tenant's *probate* estate. Since it becomes part of your probate estate, it will pass under the terms of your will.

Unfortunately, it is not always easy to tell whether the property was owned under a tenancy in common or a joint tenancy, as people often confuse the two, assuming that if there are two (or more) names on the title, it is a joint tenancy. *This is not so.* Title standing in the names of "A and B," for example, without any other words or designation, is a tenancy in common, and if A dies, his share (presumably one-half) will pass to his probate estate. Of course, if the title reads "A and B, as tenants in common," then it is even clearer.

Life insurance or other arrangements with named beneficiaries. In most cases, life insurance proceeds (or any other financial or benefit plan that allows funds to be paid to a beneficiary named by you) are payable directly to the named beneficiary (to a spouse, or to children, or to a trust, for example) on your death, without further legal action. Because of this, the funds will avoid probate and will not pass under the terms of your will. In certain cases, however, they can *become* probate assets because of a slipup in planning.

For example, say that you are the owner of an insurance policy on your life, payable to your spouse as beneficiary. Your spouse dies *before* you and you never added another ("secondary" or "contingent") beneficiary. In this case, the proceeds would be payable to your *probate estate* and, therefore, would pass under the terms of your will.

Some advisers (*not* this one) actually recommend that your life insurance proceeds be payable to your estate. In other words, the beneficiary description would read, "The estate of the insured," or words to that effect. Unless there is some clearly compelling reason to do this, I would strongly recommend against this designation for the following reasons:

1. It will increase legal and administrative fees for settlement of the estate;

2. It will expose the insurance proceeds or other benefits to creditors of your estate;

3. It will expose the funds to an estate tax (which may have otherwise been avoided); and

4. It will ensure a substantial delay before your beneficiaries can enjoy the money.

Otherwise, it's a great idea!

Trusts. Creation of a "living" trust (which is discussed in more detail in chapters 11 and 12), naming yourself and/or your spouse as trustee, and placing your assets into the trust during your lifetime, has become a very popular method of avoiding probate. Some attorneys, however, draft such trusts to provide that on the death of the grantor (the person who created the trust), the assets remaining in the trust will be distributed "to the grantor's estate." This is sort of like building a lifeboat and then poking a large hole in it. I strongly advise against such trust arrangements; they carry the same hassles and headaches as life insurance policies designating the estate as beneficiary.

Lawsuits and inheritances. There may also be assets that must be probated and pass under the terms of your will whether you like it or not. These are usually assets that become "yours" *after* your death, or *on account of* your death, such as damages recovered as a result of lawsuits brought for personal injuries that lead to your death, or inheritances from a person who died shortly before you, leaving you a share of her estate.

The first situation could arise, for example, where a person was injured in an auto accident and, after a period of suffering, died. The executor of that person's estate would sue the negligent party for personal injuries (on behalf of the deceased) as well as for causing the deceased's death. The portion of the recovery received by the executor that is attributable to the personal injuries will become part of the deceased's probate estate and will pass under the terms of the deceased's will. The other portion usually passes according to special state laws relating to the distribution of "wrongful death proceeds," in most cases going to the deceased's spouse and children.

The second situation would usually arise, for example, where Uncle Bill died and left $25,000 to his nephew Bob. Before Uncle Bill's estate was settled, however, nephew Bob died. The $25,000 bequest from Uncle Bill would have to be paid to nephew Bob's estate (i.e., to his executor) and would then be distributed under the terms of nephew Bob's will.

Probate of nonprobate property. It is sometimes possible for your executor to question transfers or arrangements you may have made during your lifetime to avoid probate on your death. If he is successful, this has the effect of turning nonprobate property (that would pass outside your will) into probate property (that will pass under the terms of your will). For the most part, this exposure normally lies with jointly held property. For instance, say that you opened a joint bank account with your daughter and placed half your savings into it. Meanwhile, your will leaves "everything" to your three children equally. Noting this inconsistency, your executor could easily argue that the joint bank account you had with your daughter should be part of your probate estate, that you added daughter's name merely as a convenience, and that you never intended that she should get more than the others. If the executor were successful (which is quite possible if there were sufficient evidence to show your intentions), the bank account would pass to your *probate* estate and the funds, therefore, would pass according to your will. (If you have such joint bank accounts and do not wish them probated, you should write out a statement to that effect, in your own words, indicating your wish and intention that the other joint tenant should own the balance in the account on your death, and send your written statement to the other joint tenant.)

In short, do *not* assume that your will will take care of all of the property you own at the time of your death. If you are like millions of others, you have some property that will pass under your will and some property that will not. The best estate plan considers and coordinates the best disposition of *all* of your property, probate and nonprobate, according to your wishes.

Joint Wills

A joint will is a *single* document signed by two testators, properly witnessed, and designed to act as a will for both of them. It is generally agreed by lawyers and other estate advisers that having a joint will is a bad idea and little better, if not worse, than having no will at all. The most perplexing issue is why anyone (or rather any two) would have a joint will in the first place.

In the typical joint will, husband and wife leave all of their property to each other, and on the death of the survivor, all of the property to their children. Since this is all in *one* will, complicated legal questions arise. For instance, can the survivor change her mind and make a *new* will? Some cases have held that she cannot, since the joint will could be considered irrevocable—after all, the first spouse died thinking that the surviving spouse would honor their agreement to leave their one will intact. But what if the surviving spouse decides that one of the children should be left out for some justifiable reason? Could the newly omitted child contest the new will on the basis that the joint will was irrevocable? Or could he sue the estate of the surviving spouse for breach of contract? A few cases have considered this possibility.

Then there is an estate tax problem with joint wills. If one spouse leaves property to another pursuant to a *contract* rather than voluntarily, then the amount left to the surviving spouse will *not* qualify for the tax-free marital deduction applicable to bequests to spouses (see chapters 12 and 13). If the joint will, therefore, is held to be a contract between the spouses, which it usually is, then the estate, depending on its size, could end up paying needless additional estate taxes, just because of the joint will.

In short, there is *no* reason to have a joint will. If you want to lock in a bequest to certain beneficiaries after the death of the surviving spouse, you can do this through an irrevocable trust, and still enjoy the tax-free marital deduction. If you intended to use the joint will as some gesture of your love for each other, make separate wills and stick to roses and holding hands.

Where to Keep Your Will

Once your will is prepared and properly signed and witnessed, you should be careful to keep the original in a safe place. Most law firms have safety vaults for storage of original documents, such as wills and trusts, and this is one possibility. If you prefer more formal storage, the probate courts in most states will accept the will for safekeeping for a small fee. If you store it with the probate court, it is not released to anyone but you or your personal representative (guardian or conservator) until your death. A third alternative would be to place the will in your safe-deposit box. This introduces other questions, such as who else has access to the box and will there be a delay in getting into the box at your death. The laws of most states allow a search of the safe-deposit box, after death, to determine if it contains your original will. Finally, you could keep the will in your desk drawer or glove compartment, but these locations are clearly not advisable. Of the three "safe" locations—i.e., your lawyer, the probate court, or your safe-deposit box—I suggest either of the first two, to eliminate positively any chance of monkey business with the instrument.

4

How to Cancel or Change Your Will

*"The reason I asked you to come here and bring my will with you,"
Graham said to his daughter, "is that I want to revoke it. I intend
to make a new will and reduce your share, as well as that of your
brother." Graham was blind. He asked his daughter to hand him
the sealed envelope that contained his will and she did so. After
feeling the envelope with the seal he had previously placed on it
and satisfying himself that it was the one that contained his will,
he handed it back to his daughter and told her to throw it into the
fire. Pretending to do so, she actually threw another piece of
paper into the fire, calling her father's attention to the odor and
the crackling of the burning paper, whereupon Graham was satisfied that his will was destroyed. Before he could make out
another will, however, Graham died.*

Was this an effective revocation of Graham's will? Should the
daughter be prohibited from offering the will for probate since she interfered with her father's wishes that it be destroyed? What if the will was, in
fact, destroyed? Could the children then offer a copy of the will for probate?

Or how about this scenario: Graham asks his daughter to open the envelope and hand him the will. After she does so, Graham asks her to identify
the particular page that leaves a share of his estate to his son and daughter.
She reads through the will and instead identifies the page *following* that
bequest, whereupon Graham takes his pencil and draws lines through the
entire page, adding at the bottom of the page the words: "I hereby reduce
my son's and my daughter's shares to one-fourth my estate instead of one-
half my estate." He then initials the page, which in fact contained some

small monetary bequests to friends and charities, and hands the will back to his daughter, satisfied that his wishes will be carried out. Will they?

Was this a valid amendment to Graham's will? Would it have been a valid amendment if he had written on the correct page? Are the bequests to friends and charities revoked since he crossed them out and initialed the page? We will find out in this chapter.

The Formalities Required for Changing a Will

As explained in chapter 3, wills are serious business. They must be in writing and signed and, except for holographic (handwritten) wills, which are allowed in a number of states, they must be witnessed with very strict formalities according to the laws of the state governing the validity of the will. This is because the law takes very seriously the disposition of a person's property after his death and wants to be absolutely sure that the person understands the terms of his will and that there is no (or little) room for doubt about his intentions. In view of this, changing or revoking a will is of no less importance, since both similarly affect the disposition of a person's property after death. Therefore, they must also conform to the law; otherwise, they will not be honored.

Changing the terms of a will is normally done (and best done) through a "codicil." A codicil is an amendment or change to a will, signed with the *same formalities* as a will (that is, with two or more witnesses, etc.), and has the added effect of "republishing" the original will that it amended (except insofar as it is changed by the codicil). Republishing is the same as restating the previous will (even though all of the provisions of the previous will are not actually repeated in the codicil). This means that a properly signed codicil can actually correct a deficiency in the signing of the original will.

For instance, say that in his will, Charles left half his property to his sister, Charlotte, and the rest to charity. Charlotte's husband was a witness to Charles's will, the effect of which would be to negate the bequest to Charles's sister, as explained in chapter 3. Later, Charles executes a codicil to his will, adding a $2,000 bequest to his favorite pub, and the codicil is witnessed by two new, independent witnesses. The effect of the codicil is not only to amend Charles's will to add the $2,000 bequest but *also* to republish (restate) his *entire* will (except as it is affected by the change) and "correct" the previous error in execution, so that his sister's share will then be valid.

Even the wording used in a typical codicil suggests the importance of the formality in language and execution. One might read, for instance:

I, Graham Cracker, of Boston, Mass., having made my last will dated January 29, 1989, hereby make this codicil, amending said will as follows: I hereby delete Article III and substitute the following Article III in its place: . . .

In all other respects (or, "Except as modified by this codicil"), I hereby ratify and confirm my said will in its entirety, signed (Graham Cracker), witnessed in his presence and in the presence of each other, (*Witness A*) and (*Witness B*).

Unfortunately, in changing their wills, many people would rather not pay an attorney to do it properly. They prefer to do it themselves by marking up their original wills, writing in their own changes, crossing out bequests, and generally handling it in a fashion they think is proper, without regard to what the law requires—after all, it is *their* will.

As a general rule, this is about the riskiest way to do it. Although some states recognize "partial revocation," which is what happens when you simply cross something out of your will, to do so positively invites a will contest and litigation. Furthermore, if after crossing provisions out, you add some new provisions, such as a new beneficiary or a different bequest, then this constitutes a *change* (as opposed to a revocation) that can *only* be valid if it is made with the *same formalities* as the original will itself.

For instance, say that your will, in part, leaves $5,000 each to A, B, and C. You want to omit C, so you cross out his name on the will and initial the change. In *some* states, this could be treated as a partial revocation and operate to omit C's bequest. However, if you omit C and add D, or reduce C's bequest from $5,000 to $500, simply by writing it in the margin of the will without following the necessary guidelines for executing a will, your proposed changes will be *useless,* having no effect at all. Furthermore, even in those states that might acknowledge your right to cross out C, the question arises as to what happens to the $5,000 that you originally left to C before you crossed him out. Since C does not now get the $5,000 (assuming your change is honored), then it must go to someone else, and this now has the possible effect of changing some other part of your will, which can only be done with the *same formalities* as executing the will itself.

Therefore, in our example above where Graham made his changes on the wrong page of the will, he neither reduced his children's shares nor changed the specific bequests to his friends and charities. All of these were *totally unaffected* by his markings on the will because the changes were not made with the same formalities required in making and signing the original will. For the same reason, it did not matter that he had made the attempted changes on the wrong page. It would have had no legal effect in this case (other than to stimulate a will contest).

In short, you should *never* try to amend your own will by crossing out pages or paragraphs and substituting the new provisions on your own. (Initialing or signing your name in the margin beside your change only confirms that you don't know what you're doing.) If you want to make a change that will have the intended legal effect, do it through a properly executed codicil and avoid the probability of a long and expensive will contest.

Changing Your Will (Intentionally or Unintentionally) by Disposing of Your Property

It is quite common for a will to be affected unintentionally by the testator selling, giving away, or otherwise disposing of an item of property that he has mentioned in his will. For instance, in his will, Rob leaves his collection of books to his son Jeremy. Later, Rob decides to donate his book collection to the New York Public Library, which he does. On Rob's death, his will still leaves the book collection to Jeremy, but there is no book collection for Jeremy to take. Must Rob's executor purchase a similar book collection to give to Jeremy? Can Jeremy sue the estate for an amount equal to the value of the book collection? Can the executor substitute some other item of equal value? Since Rob allowed the specific bequest to remain in his will, isn't this an indication that he wanted it to stand? If the books were stolen or destroyed before Rob's death rather than given away by Rob, would this change the result?

The answers to all of these questions would at first glance seem to hinge upon the issue of Rob's intention. That is, did he intend that his son, Jeremy, receive a book collection on his death, no matter what? Originally, the courts did look to the intention of the testator, but the law later evolved into the "simple" and sole question of whether the item of property is in the testator's estate at the time of his death. If it is not, the bequest is said to be *"adeemed,"* and the beneficiary gets nothing, regardless of the circumstances leading to the ademption (disposal) of the property. This principal is clearly illustrated in the unsuccessful lawsuit brought by Maude Welch to force her husband's estate to give her the car her husband owned.

In his will, Maude's husband, M. C. Welch, left the following bequest: "I hereby give and bequeath to my wife, Maude Trickle Welch, twenty-five thousand dollars cash, my Packard automobile, and all my household goods, furniture, and jewelry." The rest of the estate was left to M.C.'s brother and sister. Just before his death, however, M.C. traded in the Packard automobile for a Lincoln, which he still owned when he died. Maude, of course, claimed the Lincoln should be hers, since M.C. clearly wanted her to have a car for her use. The fact that he didn't change his will was simply an oversight, Maude claimed. The estate countered with the argument that M.C. did not leave Maude a Lincoln, but a Packard, specifically. Since he did not own a Packard, Maude should get nothing in this regard, as the bequest was "adeemed."

The court agreed with the estate. The will, they said, was plain and unambiguous. It read, "my Packard automobile," and to hold that this language should mean any other automobile that M.C. owned would be to change the law of wills. The court said:

> The rule is universal that, in order to make a specific legacy effective, the property bequeathed must be in existence and owned by the testator at the time of his death, and the nonexistence of property at the time of the death of a testator which has been specifically bequeathed by will is the familiar and almost typical form of ademption. This may result from a variety of causes, such as a gift during the lifetime of the testator of the particular article which was the subject-matter of the legacy, or its consumption, loss, or sale, and in each of such instances the courts have held that the legacy is adeemed. Where the testator substantially alters the form of the subject-matter of his bequest as by making wool into cloth, or a piece of cloth into a garment, the legacy is adeemed, because the subject-matter cannot be restored to its former state.

But supposing that, after buying the Lincoln, M.C. had purchased another Packard (not the one he first owned). Would the second Packard go to Maude under his will? It would, since the will operates as of the time of the testator's death, and it would be presumed that he wanted *this* Packard (i.e., the one he owned at the time of his death) to go to Maude. He would, in effect, have *restored* the "adeemed" property so the bequest could be carried out. A similar result would occur, for instance, in the case where Woody leaves his "beach house on Cape Cod" to his daughter, Wackie. Later, Woody sells the beach house, and still later he buys another beach house on Cape Cod. Wackie would get the second beach house, since it adequately satisfies the description in the will. If the second beach house were located somewhere else, however, a different result would occur.

This rule of ademption only applies to *specific* bequests or legacies (other than money). That is, those bequests addressing and identifying a specific item or items of property, even though in some cases the specificity itself may be general. For instance, "all my automobiles," or "my entire collection of books," or "all my household effects," or "the silver tea service that belonged to my grandmother." All of these are specific bequests of property, subject to ademption, to the extent that the described article or articles are not a part of the testator's estate. Where a group of items is involved, the bequest could be adeemed in whole or in part, such as where only half the original book collection was left at the testator's death, or where only three pieces remained of grandmother's five-piece tea service, in which case, the beneficiary would receive the portion that remained. On occasion, however, the question of what remains can be confusing, as in the case of Mary De Garmendia.

Mary had two valuable strings of pearls and in her will she left one to her friend Natalie and the other to Mrs. R., another friend. Just before Mary's death, however, she had the two sets of pearls combined to make a single string. Obviously, this presented a problem and Mary's executor took the position that Natalie's bequest had been adeemed, since there was now only one string of pearls.

In its opinion, the court noted that ademption could result not only through loss or destruction of the object but also from changes that cause a loss of its identity. For example, if the stones in a diamond bracelet were removed and placed in several other pieces of jewelry, a bequest of the diamond bracelet would be adeemed. In this case, however, neither of these (i.e., neither a disposition nor a loss of identity) had really occurred. The executor had one collection of pearls bequeathed to two persons and this was no different than if the two beneficiaries were left a stack of books or a herd of cattle. The property could easily be divided by the owners, as it had not lost its identity nor was it destroyed.

Of course, if the article or articles were destroyed, then the case of ademption (and therefore, loss of the bequest) would be clear, right? The answer is an unequivocal maybe. Among other things, it depends upon *when* the articles were destroyed. An interesting case that illustrates this point is that of Anne Shymer, who died when the *Lusitania* sank. In her will, Anne left her clothing, jewelry, laces, and other personal articles to her mother. Most of these articles, however, went down with Anne and the *Lusitania*. As a result of insurance claims made for the lost articles, Anne's husband, as executor of her estate, received about $9,000 as reimbursement for the articles, and Anne's mother contended the funds should be paid to her, since they were a direct reimbursement for the articles that were left to her in Anne's will. Anne's husband, however, argued that the bequest was *adeemed,* since the articles were clearly lost, so the money should pass with the rest of the estate.

The court, on the other hand, noted that an ademption, to have the same effect of eliminating the bequest, must take place *during the lifetime of the deceased.* Here, there was no evidence that such was the case, and the reimbursement rightfully belonged to Anne's mother as reimbursement for articles otherwise bequeathed to her and lost *after* Anne's death.

In sum, when the specifically bequeathed item of property is lost, destroyed, stolen, or otherwise disposed of *during the deceased's lifetime,* the beneficiary loses out and generally has no recourse. But does the same rule apply to money?

Involuntary Changes in Your Will— When There Isn't Enough Money to Go Around

In his will Sal left $50,000 to his wife, Sally, and the rest of his estate went to his four children equally. As it turned out, Sal's entire estate after expenses amounted to about $50,000, just enough for the bequest to Sally. Does this mean his children will get nothing?

In another will, Sebastian left the following bequests: $10,000 to each of his two children; $30,000 to establish a scholarship fund in his name; the home he lived in (worth about $200,000) to his wife (for total bequests of $250,000); and the rest of the estate to his mother and sister equally.

After expenses, Sebastian's estate was about $400,000, more than enough to cover all of these bequests, but shortly after his death, a claim was made against his estate by a former business partner he had cheated years earlier. The partner sued Sebastian's estate and the court awarded him $275,000. When the estate pays this amount (which takes priority over the bequests), what happens to the rest? Will the children get their shares? Will there be a scholarship? Will the wife get the home? Will the swallows come back to Capistrano?

These cases reflect the principal of "abatement" of bequests in a will. *Abatement* is the forced reduction of bequests or shares when the testator's estate does not contain sufficient assets to pay debts, expenses, and all the prescribed bequests in full. When this happens, the bequests are "abated" (reduced) according to certain rules, unless the will specifies otherwise.

As a general rule, the first bequest to suffer is the "residuary" bequest.

This is the one that usually says, "I leave all the rest, remainder and residue of my estate to." The residuary bequest is the "pot" from which all expenses and shortfalls are generally funded, before any reduction for specific bequests (i.e., bequests of specific sums of money or items of property). (Remember, the will can provide otherwise.)

Therefore, in Sal's case, Sally would receive her specific bequest and the children would receive nothing. And if there were not enough to provide for Sally's full $50,000 bequest, she would simply take whatever money there was, to apply toward it. Of course, if there is not enough in such cases, the beneficiaries have no recourse, since there is no obligation (nor ability) on the part of the testator to leave more than he has.

In the case of Sebastian's estate, the same rules apply, but the situation is a bit more complicated, since there are specific bequests of both money and real estate, and the estate, even though valued in excess of the $275,000 judgment, does not have adequate cash to pay the judgment. The next question is: Is all the cash used up first and then the remaining items sold to raise the necessary additional cash? Or does everyone pay a proportionate share of the cost?

Unfortunately, the rules are not consistent from state to state. Many states follow the common-law rule, which favors the use of "personalty" (anything other than real estate) to pay the costs before ordering the sale of real estate, while others treat both realty and personalty alike for purposes of abatement. Once this preference or nonpreference is established, then the bequests will be abated proportionately.

That is, say that in Sebastian's estate the abatement of realty and personalty were treated alike. The total estate was $400,000, less a judgment of $275,000. Specific bequests totaled $250,000, leaving a "residuary estate" of $150,000. As noted above, the residuary estate would be applied first, so that the $150,000 would be applied in full toward the $275,000 judgment, leaving a balance of $125,000 due on the judgment. There is $250,000 left in the estate ($400,000 less $150,000), of which $125,000 must be applied to pay the balance of the judgment. In other words, each of the specific legatees must pay a proportionate share of the $125,000 (by *reducing* the amount they get), but just how is it divided?

The rule of abatement provides for a proportional reduction based on the relationship a given share bears to all the shares. That is, if two equal beneficiaries had to abate their shares they would each be reduced by the same amount. Similarly, if A was to get $10,000 and B was to get $20,000, A would abate his share by one-third the shortfall, and B would bear two-thirds the shortfall.

In Sebastian's estate, then, where the specific bequests totaled $250,000 and the shortfall was $125,000, and assuming that bequests of real estate and personal property are treated alike for abatement purposes, then each beneficiary would bear the following share of the $125,000 shortfall:

			(Shortfall)		*(Reduction of Share)*
2 children	$20,000	x	$125,000	=	$10,000
($10,000 each)	$250,000				($5,000 each child)
Scholarship	$30,000	x	$125,000	=	$15,000
($30,000)	$250,000				
Wife	$200,000	x	$125,000	=	$100,000
($200,000)	$250,000				

That is, instead of receiving $10,000 each, the children would receive only $5,000 each, and instead of $30,000, the scholarship would only be funded with $15,000.

Unfortunately, the wife's share is in the form of real estate and in order for the abatement of her share to be carried out, the real estate would have to be sold. If she did not want this to happen, she would have to borrow against it and pay the $100,000 herself.

Abatements can produce harsh results, but fortunately they are not a common occurrence. If there is a question about there being enough funds to pay all debts, expenses, and all specific bequests, you should try to deal with it ahead of time, but as we saw in Sebastian's case, it is not always foreseeable.

How to Revoke Your Will

In a sense, complete revocation of your will is much simpler than changing it because the revocation, when effective, is absolute and complete, and the ways a will can be revoked are fairly well defined in the law. For instance, if you tear up your will into small pieces with the intention of revoking it, it is clear that you have legally revoked it. Despite the clarity of the legal requirements for revocation, however, people will still find ways of complicating and confusing the issues.

As a general rule, you can successfully revoke your will by:

1. Physical acts done to the will (i.e., tearing it up or burning it);
2. A subsequent writing (such as a new will) formally revoking the previous will; or
3. Getting married after the will is made, unless the will was made in anticipation of the marriage.

1. REVOCATION BY PHYSICAL ACTS DONE TO THE WILL

Just about every state has specific laws providing that a will can be revoked by acts such as "burning, canceling, tearing, obliterating, destroying, mutilating, and cutting" the will, or one or more words to that effect.

As clear as such acts may appear at first glance, however, they are the subject of a great deal of litigation. There are many cases, for instance, very similar to that of Graham, described at the very beginning of this chapter. Graham, who was blind, asked his daughter to throw his will into the fire. She pretended to do so, and Graham was left to believe his will was revoked. Of course, it was not. Though he asked that it be destroyed, the will remained in good condition and was presented for probate at Graham's death. The fact that the daughter deceived Graham was a separate matter and did not cause the revocation of his will.

In a somewhat similar case, which illustrates the same principle but with a different result, Samuel decided to revoke his will, so he carefully took the large envelope that contained the will and tore it in half. Because the folded will was so much smaller than the envelope, however, only a corner of the will was torn, and none of the "writing" was damaged. Was Samuel's will revoked?

It is not necessary that the tearing, burning, mutilating, etc., be a complete physical destruction of the will beyond recognition. In fact, even the slightest charring or tearing is sufficient, so long as it is done with the *intent* of revoking the will. If the testator directs someone else to destroy the will, as in Graham's case, it *must* be done in his presence. If he is not present, the revocation is not effective even though he may have directed it.

Presence and *intent* of the testator, therefore, are essential ingredients in these cases, *along with the physical act itself.* For instance, say that Erin Gobrah has two wills and wants to revoke one of them. By mistake she tears up the wrong one. Is either will revoked? No. Neither will was revoked by the act of tearing, since there was *no intent* to revoke the one that was torn by mistake, and the one intended to be revoked was not torn.

In short, there must be some form of physical destruction done to the will either by the testator or by someone else in his presence and at his direction, done with the intent to revoke. The destruction need not be complete, but need only reflect the testator's wish to destroy or cancel the will. Although the testator himself can change his mind and recover the will before the destruction is complete, interference by *someone else* without the testator's authorization will *not* prevent a revocation if the other elements are present.

Therefore, in Graham's case, no revocation occurred, since even though he had the *intent* to revoke, nothing was done to the will. And in Samuel's case, there *was* a revocation, even though his wife retrieved the will, since he had the intention to revoke the will and the physical act of destruction, though not complete, was done to the will.

2. REVOCATION BY A SUBSEQUENT WRITING

If you are the nonviolent type, and burning, tearing, and obliterating things do not appeal to you, you may prefer to revoke your will by a safe, simple writing.

You may have noticed, for instance, that most wills begin with language such as, "I, Mildred Smith, make this my will *hereby revoking all wills and codicils previously made by me.*" If properly signed and witnessed or otherwise meeting the state's requirements for a valid will), this "writing" would operate to revoke all previous wills and codicils. The writing revoking a previous will need not itself be contained in a will, but it would be more than a little foolish to have nothing more than such a writing, unless you do not want a new will, or unless the new will accidentally omitted the standard revocation clause. If for some reason, such as those just mentioned, a bare writing solely to revoke the previous will becomes necessary, the writing itself must meet the *same formalities* as the will, that is, intent, competence, and all the required signatures.

Confusion occasionally arises as to whether a writing that revokes a codicil to a will or a direct destruction (revocation) of the codicil itself revokes the underlying will. The general rule of law in this case is that revocation of a codicil does *not* revoke the underlying will, but only the codicil.

3. REVOCATION BY GETTING MARRIED AFTER THE WILL IS MADE

If a person marries after he makes his will, the general rule is that the marriage will automatically *revoke* a will that he made prior to the marriage, unless the will was made "in anticipation of" the marriage. That is, a will made in such a case will actually state something such as: "Having in mind my forthcoming marriage to Ruth Roth, I hereby make my will."

The requirement of anticipating or contemplating the marriage in no way means that the new wife or husband must be a beneficiary under the will. She will have her rights in any event if you leave her out, as explained in chapter 7.

While marriage will revoke a will that does not anticipate the marriage, a divorce generally does not. At one time, a divorce had no effect at all on a previously made will, but now most states provide that a divorce will revoke the particular *bequests* made in the will to the ex-spouse, and often will similarly revoke the appointment of the ex-spouse as executrix of the will. In other respects, the will would remain valid after a divorce.

Reviving a Previously Revoked Will

Occasionally a testator will revoke his will because of a belief in a point of fact or law, which after his death is discovered to be mistaken. Is there anything the beneficiaries of the previous will can do?

For instance, take the case of Domenica Lunedi, a widow, who made a will leaving her entire estate to her only child, Domenic. While skiing with friends in the Alps, Domenic became lost, and after a number of intensive searches, he was given up for dead. Two years later, convinced that Domenic was gone, Domenica revoked her will by making a new will, expressing her love for Domenic and leaving her estate to various hospitals and universities in Domenic's memory. Shortly thereafter, Domenica died. As it happened, Domenic was lost and seriously injured, but not dead. By the time he made his way back home, however, his mother was dead, and he found himself left without a dime.

While a revocation, if properly executed, absolutely revokes the previous will, some revocations, such as Domenica's, could be viewed as *conditional* revocations that are dependent on the condition being true. In other words, if Domenica had known that Domenic was not deceased, she would clearly not have revoked her previous will. And her belief that he was in fact deceased was apparent by the gifts to the charities in "memory" of Domenic. In such cases, courts have held that the revocation was dependent on the condition and if it could be shown on the *face* of the revocation that there was a material mistake on which the revocation was based (here it was clear in the revocation that Domenica believed Domenic to be dead), then the revocation will not be effective and the previous will will stand.

The same rule can apply to individual bequests that are revoked by a subsequent codicil or by a new will. In one case, for example, where a man made a codicil that revoked some bequests to certain relatives stating, "they being all dead," the bequests were allowed to stand when it was discovered that the relatives were, in fact, alive.

But don't rush to the courts just because your uncle left you out of his will on the basis that he thought you were unemployed but, in fact, you had a job. If the court believes that your uncle would have left you out in any event and the mistaken belief was not the motivating and principal factor behind the change, the disinheritance will stand.

5

Common Will Provisions

A word is not a crystal, transparent and unchanged; it is the skin of a living thought and may vary greatly in color and content according to the circumstances and the time in which it is used.

—Justice Oliver Wendell Holmes

Few attorneys would disagree. Most of the millions of will contests over the past two thousand years have turned solely upon the meaning of a word or phrase. After all, a will is no more than a collection of words. It is the meaning of those words, however, that truly challenges the mind and the purse. But, as Justice Holmes tells us, meanings are not always clear. So where does that leave us?

Personally, and with the greatest respect for Mr. Justice Holmes, I think Humpty Dumpty put it considerably more succinctly, when he said to Alice: "When I use a word, it means just what I choose it to mean, neither more nor less."

Just what words *should* go into your will? Aren't there parts of every will that are just about the same? So what's the big deal about "words"?

A Question of Words, and the Use of Boilerplate Language

Use of the "right" words can make or break a will. Many people feel, however, that lawyers who draft wills never think about the words they use; they simply pull a standard form off a shelf and—bingo!—they have a will. Such standard forms and provisions are called "boilerplate," because, like the interchangeable metal plates of cylindrical boilers, the very same language is to a certain extent interchangeable from one will to another, word for word. Use of such "boilerplate" forms and provisions causes many to believe that an attorney might not even be needed if one can get one's hands on the right forms.

Part of this is true. The fact is that we *do* have hundreds of different forms and standard provisions relating to wills, which can in fact be readily used, word for word, from one will to another. But it is *only* the competent and knowledgeable use of such forms and individual provisions that enables an attorney to produce a "good" will at a fair price.

It is *not* true that lawyers do not think about the words they use. (Of course, as with any business, trade, or profession, there are varying levels of competence, and some may be able to show exceptions to the previous statement.) But a competent attorney will never use a document that he has not read and does not understand. If your attorney cannot explain to you the reason for and meaning of each provision in the will (or trust) he has drafted for you, you should change attorneys.

What many fail to realize is that the use of standardized forms and provisions by an attorney is actually quite advantageous to the client. These forms usually represent suggestions by legal scholars and specialists as the result of many years of study of court decisions, changes in the law, and just plain, practical experience, and, if the right form is chosen, *you* are getting the benefit of all that. It would be nearly impossible and financially prohibitive for your attorney to spend the same amount of time researching and developing these provisions just for you on an individual basis. You wouldn't expect your doctor to personally mix the drugs and chemicals of every prescription he gave you. Somewhat similar to the physician with the medicine, the critical role of your attorney in this respect is to have the knowledge of the standardized forms and provisions that will best protect your interests and satisfy your objectives under the law.

Although many standard provisions are necessary and helpful, some are superfluous or useless, and still others can actually be harmful. Unfortunately, attorneys who do not pay attention to the "words" they are using, or the unsuspecting testator who decides to save a few dollars by making his own will from a "form" book, frequently perpetuate such useless and potentially harmful provisions.

For instance, for many years (perhaps a hundred or more!), attorneys and many form books have continued to use the standard will provision regarding debts. (In fact, I wouldn't be at all surprised if your own will has one.) It is usually somewhere near the beginning of the will and says something like this: "I direct my Executor to pay all my just debts and expenses as soon as practical after my death, etc." This is a totally useless provision that in some cases could lead to the payment of claims that otherwise might not have been paid. *Of course* your executor has to pay your "just debts and expenses"! So why do you have to direct him to do so? You don't. Just because the provision is "standard" does not mean it should be used in every case.

This is not to say there is no individualization in a will. There are always special provisions or insertions that must be drafted for each particular family. But in most wills, the majority of the provisions are boilerplate. Following is a list of those boilerplate provisions that you'll find in most wills, and *why* you should find them there.

Some Common but Necessary Will Provisions

1. Exordium clause. This is the opening phrase of your will stating that it is, in fact, your will. The usual language is something such as: "I, Grover Lambeck, of Brooklyn, New York, declare this to be my last will, revoking all prior wills and codicils made by me."

This is all the exordium needs to say. It is *not* necessary to begin "In the name of God, amen," or "Being of sound mind and mindful of the vicissitudes of life," or, as in the case of a chorus girl's will stating, "Being of sound mind and fantastic body," and so on. (If you have to *tell* everyone you are of sound mind, maybe you have a problem.)

As to recital of domicile, it is not absolutely necessary, nor is it legally conclusive that you are in fact domiciled where you say you are, but it is a *good idea* to have it, because at least it offers evidence that this is where *you* declared your domicile to be at the time you signed the will.

2. Survival clause. For every bequest you make under your will, including the residuary bequest, you should consider whether you want the named beneficiary to receive the bequest *only if she or he survives you.* If this is the case, then you *must* add the words, "if she (or he) survives me," after each such bequest. If you do not, then the bequest will automatically pass to the beneficiary's probate estate if she does not survive you.

Furthermore, as explained in chapter 2, you can actually specify (within reason) just how long a beneficiary must live after you in order to be considered as having survived you for purposes of your will. This provision can be very important when, for example, a beneficiary dies a few hours or a few days after you. In such a case, you probably would *not* want the bequest to take effect.

For instance, your will can state that "a beneficiary shall not be considered to have survived me or another, for purposes of this will, unless such beneficiary shall have survived me or such other for a period of thirty (30) days." Thirty days is arbitrary and is not the required number for any legal purpose. It could just as well be ten days or sixty days, but most experts agree it should not be more than six months, as this can create estate settlement delays and uncertainties and, in the case of a surviving spouse, cause a loss of certain estate tax savings.

If the beneficiary does not survive you, then the share he would have received will pass to your residuary estate and be distributed along with that. (The residuary estate is what is left over after payment of all bequests and all expenses, taxes, and claims.)

To illustrate how the survival clause might work, say that Quincy's will provides, "I leave the sum of $50,000 to my brother, Randolph, if he survives me." The will also contains a sixty-day survivorship clause, requiring a beneficiary to survive Quincy by at least sixty days if he or she is to take the bequest. While traveling together, Quincy and Randolph are in an accident and Quincy is killed. Randolph hangs on for a few days, then dies. Under Quincy's will, Randolph (or his estate) will inherit nothing, as he did not survive for the sixty-day period required under Quincy's will. Without that provision, Randolph's estate would have been entitled to the $50,000 bequest since Randolph survived Quincy, even though only for a few days. Thus, *after* Quincy's estate was settled, the $50,000 bequest would have to be paid to Randolph's estate (adding costs and delays) and would then be distributed according to Randolph's will, if he had one, and, if not, according to the laws of the state where Randolph resided.

3. *Simultaneous death (common disaster) clause.* Related to the survivorship clause just discussed, the simultaneous death clause is, in fact, somewhat different. All states have adopted what is called the Uniform Simultaneous Death Act, which provides that if the testator and a beneficiary die under circumstances where it is impossible to determine the order of death, then the *testator* is considered to have survived the beneficiary, unless the testator's will provides otherwise. It is not harmful to have both a simultaneous death clause *and* a survivorship clause in a will, especially where a spouse is involved. In such a case, the will frequently provides that the spouse is excepted from the survivorship clause, and in the event of a

simultaneous death, the will declares that the spouse with the smaller estate will be considered to have survived, for the purpose of reducing the federal estate taxes. (See chapters 12 and 13 for a fuller discussion of this.)

4. *Tangible personal property.* Although the concept and handling of tangible personal property is discussed in greater detail later in this chapter, it is mentioned here only to point out that it should be separated, as a *specific bequest,* from the residue of the estate. For instance, "I leave all my tangible personal property to my wife, if she survives me. If not, I leave such tangible property to my three children equally, or all to the survivor(s) of them."

Tangible personal property normally consists of household furnishing, jewelry, clothing, automobiles, and other "moveable" personal effects, and frequently it is simply taken by the surviving spouse and children without any formalities. Because of the federal income tax laws dealing with the treatment of distributions from an estate, however, this innocent taking of such tangible personal items in some cases can actually be taxable as *income* to·the recipients. An exception to such tax treatment applies to specific bequests under the will and, therefore, it should be separately bequeathed as suggested above.

5. *Powers of executor.* Generally, lawyers make much more of executor's powers than is frequently necessary, especially in smaller estates, since an executor has certain inherent powers necessary to carry out his duties to settle the estate, whether or not stated in the will. But it does not hurt to provide more extensive powers so as to eliminate any question on the part of third parties dealing with the estate, and in larger estates where the extent of the executor's duties is occasionally unknown, greater powers are quite appropriate. Furthermore, there are certain powers that *must* be specifically stated, including the authority to continue the deceased's business and the power to deal with or sell the deceased's real estate, if necessary. Therefore, if you have a business or real estate, your will should contain the necessary powers to allow the executor to deal with these items. (These issues are discussed in greater detail in chapter 9.) Most states have "statutory" executor's powers, which may be incorporated in the will simply by referring to the applicable law of the state.

If a *trust* is created under the will, it is essential that the trustee's powers also be detailed. They may be similar to the executor's powers but are frequently more extensive because such trusts are generally designed to continue for many years.

6. *Guardian appointment.* If you have minor children, you want to be

sure your will deals with appointment of a guardian for them, as well as a successor guardian if the initially named guardian can't serve. And remember, this is actually a nomination rather than an official appointment. (This is covered in greater detail in chapter 2.)

7. *Executor appointment.* As with the guardian and other "appointments" under your will, this is a *nomination* rather than an official appointment. The official appointment of an executor comes from the court if no one objects to your nomination. As with the guardians for minor children, you should nominate a successor executor, in case the first one named cannot serve. (Executors are discussed in detail in chapter 9.)

8. *Bond.* With only a *few* exceptions, every "fiduciary" (i.e., executor, administrator, trustee, and guardian) must give a bond to secure the faithful performance of his duties, although in a few states the bond can be avoided. A bond is basically the person's promise to make good if he causes a loss to the estate as a result of his negligence or wrongdoing in carrying out his duties. The bond can be a personal bond "without sureties," meaning that it is backed only by the executor's personal assets, or it can be *with* sureties (outside guarantees). The sureties can either be *personal* sureties (friends of the executor who agree to pay if he runs off with the estate's money) or *corporate* sureties (an insurance company that guarantees payment). This provision usually states, "I name Bob Blank as executor and direct that he be allowed to serve without bond, or if a bond is required by law, then he should serve without sureties on his bond."

It is argued that a bond with corporate sureties adds to the expense of administering the estate and this can be true, but, in fact, the costs are usually very small in proportion to the amount of money that is covered. If the executor and the primary beneficiary are the same, however, there may hardly be a need for a bond, for if he takes the estate's money, he is taking it only from himself. But if they are not the same, you may want to consider at least a personal bond.

9. *Tax apportionment clause.* This important provision typically states that all inheritance and estate taxes are to be paid from the *residue* of the estate. The usual purpose of the provision is to leave specific bequests intact, on the assumption, for instance, that if Sam leaves $1,000 to each of his four sisters, he wants each of them to receive the full $1,000, and not $1,000 minus taxes and minus legal and executor's fees. The typical apportionment clause allows them to get the full amount, and the estate taxes on their shares will be paid from the residue.

Most states have apportionment statutes providing that *unless* the will states otherwise (which is what the standard tax apportionment clause does), each beneficiary will bear his pro rata share of the taxes based on the amount he receives and taking into account tax exemptions and other allowances. In practical effect, therefore, the typical apportionment clause anticipates that the specific legatees (i.e., beneficiaries who receive specified sums or specified items of property), if any, will receive only nominal amounts and that the residuary legatees (those who receive the residue of the estate) will receive the bulk of the estate. In this case, it is acceptable that they should also pay the taxes.

Problems can arise, however, when the specific legatees, as well as beneficiaries who receive property *outside* the will (through joint ownership, for example), receive a disproportionately large part of the estate. If, in this case, the will has a "standard" tax apportionment clause providing that the residuary estate pays the tax, there will almost certainly be trouble, not to mention an unfair distribution of the estate.

For instance, say that Merriweather's will has the usual tax apportionment clause, and his total estate is $200,000. He leaves $50,000 to each of his three daughters and the rest to his son. State inheritance taxes amount to $16,000, and expenses and legal fees (which are normally paid out of the residue regardless of the apportionment clause) come to an additional $6,000. The son, who receives the residue, will therefore receive $50,000 less $16,000 in taxes and less an additional $6,000 in fees, or a net of $28,000, while the daughters will each receive the *full* $50,000! If the apportionment clause were omitted from Merriweather's will, it would have caused each of the daughters to pay her fair share of the tax (although his son would still have paid the expenses).

Therefore, before you approve of the "standard" tax apportionment clause, take a careful look at the specific bequests you have made, as well as the items of property that pass outside your will, and see if the burden of tax payment is where you want it.

10. Avoid "extra" guardians. Whenever there are minor children who may stand to inherit from the estate, or even the possibility that a child, *yet unborn,* could inherit under certain circumstances, many states, in an effort to "protect" the interests of such minor children, will require that a guardian ad litem (GAL) be appointed on behalf of the minor child. This will be done *even though* one of the spouses is already appointed as guardian under the will, on the basis that since the spouse herself is also a beneficiary, she cannot be totally disinterested when it comes to the child. Therefore, the court will appoint a GAL (who is usually an attorney known to the judge or to the clerk of court) to review the estate matters on behalf of the minor child.

Despite this, it is possible in most states to *dispense* with the necessity of such an appointment, provided you feel comfortable that the persons you have appointed will do an honest job. The dispensation clause usually says something like this:

> If any occasion shall arise during the administration of my estate, or in connection with any matter or procedure connected with my estate, calling for the appointment of a person to represent the interests of persons unborn or unascertained or the interests of any other person, I direct that such appointment shall be dispensed with, if permitted under the law of the applicable jurisdiction.

Note that these are by no means all the provisions that should or will be in your will. No doubt there will be numerous others to carry out your special wishes and objectives. For instance, there may be a noncontest clause (discussed in chapter 10), or several conditional clauses (discussed in chapter 6), or you may even come up with some new ones on your own!

Understanding the Difference between Real and Personal Property

What is "property"? The term *property* is often interpreted by the lay public to mean real estate. In fact, property, in the basic legal sense, means anything that is capable of ownership. In this regard, it could include everything from a theater ticket to a yacht, from a share of stock to a movie contract with MGM, from an apartment lease to ownership of the Empire State Building. All involve a property right of some sort, and all property rights are divided into two basic categories: real and personal.

Real property is any property interest in *real estate*—(that is, land. A property interest in real estate could include a lease or a mortgage, as well as a deed to the real estate itself. (When buildings are constructed on the land, they generally become a part of the underlying real estate.)

Personal property is any property interest in anything *other than* in real estate, and could include shares of stock, a promissory note, a piano, an automobile, or a copyright.

Personal property is divided, in turn, into two categories: *tangible* personal property and *intangible* personal property. Basically, *tangible* personal property includes things you can move and touch and that have some "inherent" value, such as furniture, jewelry, clothing, paintings, collectible coins, rugs, etc.

Intangible personal property includes things that in themselves have *no* value, but which represent the *right* to something else. For instance, a share of stock, which represents the right to dividends and a share of assets if the company is liquidated; a copyright, which represents the right of ownership in a book, a song, or a work of art; a royalty interest, which represents the right to a share of profits in some resource; or a promissory note, which represents the right to collect money from someone.

Most wills separate only *tangible* personal property from the rest of the estate, and, therefore, the rest of the estate normally includes *intangible* personal property plus all real estate. Quite often there are more problems associated with tangible items of nominal value (i.e., mother's engagement ring) than there are with other estate property of much more substantial value, as illustrated below.

Dealing with the Oriental Rugs, the Coin Collection, and Mother's Jewelry

These items, as you now know from the above discussion, are all considered tangible personal property. In most estates, the blanket provision leaving all tangible personal property to a spouse or children is usually *intended* to include only the normal household furniture, clothing, and other articles of nominal value. You should be aware, however, that this same blanket provision will automatically include *all* of your tangible property, whether valuable or not. If you have items that are of sufficient value that you feel should be separated, then do so; otherwise you could invite questions and possibly trouble, as did the famous artist Mark Rothko.

Rothko left his wife his New York town house and all the tangible personal property in the town house. As it was, the town house contained a few million dollars' worth of Rothko's paintings. Rothko's executors sued his wife, contending that the paintings should not be included under the tangible property clause. The court held that the will was clear and that the widow was entitled to the paintings.

Similar problems arise when beneficiaries are given the choice of "an item" of tangible personal property. Just what is "an item"? Of course, one item might be a piano or a clock, but what about a sixty-piece service of silverware? Is that one item or sixty? Or how about a stamp collection? Is that one item or one thousand? The question is illustrated (and answered) in the case stemming from the estate of Blanche Marston.

Mrs. Marston was a wealthy woman from an affluent suburb of Boston. In her will she provided for numerous friends and relatives, and the bulk of her estate, including the proceeds from the sale of tangible items not left to individuals, went to the Marstons' charitable foundation. The bequest in question was to one Michael Lonigro, who was given the choice of "any three items of tangible personal property." Lonigro chose, as *one* of the three items, Mrs. Marston's extensive stamp collection, worth about $11,000. Marston's executors objected, of course, on the basis that this should not be considered as one item. The Massachusetts court held for Lonigro. It would be quite foolish, the court said, to treat this single collection as twenty thousand or thirty thousand individual items of personal property. Mrs. Marston, in other parts of her will, had already indicated that she regarded her silver collection as having a "unitary character," and the collection of stamps should be treated no differently.

This treatment of collections as a single item of personal property is generally accepted, but within reason. A "collection" of jewelry, for instance, is not consistent with this view unless it is truly in the nature of a collection that was accumulated more as a unit than simply as a series of pieces that have the same character. In any event, to avoid the problem you should be specific and state how *you* want any such valuable "items" to be distributed.

LEAVING A "MEMORANDUM"

A statement as to the disposition of your tangible personal property is safest in the will itself, but many people are reluctant to do this because it makes public the items you owned (a will is placed on file at the probate court for any interested party to view). An alternative used by some is a "memorandum" given to your executor, containing a list of items and the respective beneficiaries to receive those items. Such a "private" memorandum is perfectly legal and binding *if* it meets certain requirements. First, it must be in writing and in existence at the time the will is signed; second, it must be identifiable as the paper referred to in the will; and third, the will must state that the memorandum is in existence. In other words, you must have it written and preferably signed and dated at or prior to the time the will is signed. If you do all this, the executor is bound to follow your instructions on the memorandum. But if you do meet these requirements, then the memorandum could become "public."

Instead, most people regard such a memorandum as some sort of a tangible flexible will (as to their tangible property), allowing them to modify the memorandum from time to time as they see fit. Although it is permissible to do so, your executor is *not* legally bound to follow it. As a result, if you leave your tangible property to your executor to be distributed "according to a memorandum" you will leave with him, and if the memo does not meet the above requirements, the executor may be able to do whatever he wants with those items, or, more likely, there will be a fight over them.

Of course, if the executor can be "trusted" to carry out your memorandum, then things should go as you wish. In fact, where children are involved, many attorneys (this one included) recommend that you write a "letter" to your children—which really amounts to a memorandum in a sense—asking that they honor the wishes you express in the letter relating to distribution of your tangible personal property. Although it is *not* legally binding, it usually places considerable moral pressure on your children to carry it out.

Another caveat: If a child is named executor of your estate and the executor is given authority to divide your tangible personal property among all the children in "substantially equal shares," this could also lead to problems in some cases. If you think there could be such a problem, simply name an independent person, a "special executor or administrator" if necessary, solely for the purpose of making decisions on the equitable division of your tangible personal property. Another option we often use to help avoid disputes is to provide that each child will be able to select an "item" of property in turn, by seniority or by drawing straws, stating in the will that sets or collections are to be kept intact where practical. If you do have one or two items that are disproportionate in value to the rest (such as a stamp or coin collection, or a single valuable painting), you should deal with these *separately* and should *not* lump them in with other items of your tangible personal property.

Finally, if there are large items of tangible property or items that require special handling that are bequeathed to individuals, you may want to consider (though it is not necessary) having those individuals pay for freight, insurance, storage, or other special costs attributable to the distribution of those items; otherwise the estate will have to pay those costs.

Leaving Something to Charity

Believe it or not, not everyone wants to make his children rich. There are many who believe that their money will be put to much better use by leaving some or all of it to charity. As explained at the outset of this book, however, there is no inherent right to bequeath your property to anyone or any organization; it is only the good grace of the state that allows you to do so. There are, therefore, a number of limitations and "safeguards" imposed on us by these laws. One of them is the limitation on charitable bequests.

In early England, so much property was being acquired by churches and monasteries that the Crown became fearful of the tremendous power that the Church could wield; in addition, it was regarded as contrary to the nation's economic growth. To counter this trend a law was enacted that made it illegal to leave property to a charity. Although we have no such law in the United States, these concerns, together with the strong tendency to protect the family, have led to laws in a number of states that either limit the amount you can leave to a charity or require that the will containing the charitable bequest be executed within a specified time before your death, or both.

The time limitation is intended to prevent a person who is facing death from being unduly influenced by a charity or by the idea that he might buy a way into heaven. The time limitation usually provides that the charitable bequest will be invalid unless the will is signed at least a specified number of days or months prior to the testator's death. For those states that have them, the time limitations run from thirty days to six months before death. If a codicil to the will is made within the prescribed period, whether it violates the provisions depends on the terms of the codicil. Generally, if it reduces the charitable bequest or leaves it unchanged, it will not violate the time-period requirement. If it increases the bequest, however, it may be invalid as to the increase, if not the entire amount, depending upon the state's law.

Limitations on the amounts that can pass to charity vary from state to state. In the few remaining states (e.g., Florida, Georgia, Idaho, Mississippi) that still impose such limitations, however, the limitations usually apply only if the deceased left a spouse and/or children or grandchildren. If there were no such heirs, the limitations generally will *not* apply, and the testator can, if he wishes, leave his entire estate to charity. You can be fairly certain, however, that if there is a limitation and there is an heir to contest it, it will be contested.

For example, in one New York case (under a now-repealed New York statute limiting charitable bequests), an eccentric spinster left almost all of her $40 million estate to charity. Before you could say "the root of all evil," over two thousand claims were filed contesting the charitable bequest and asking for a share of the $40 million. Relatives came out of the woodwork and, of course, most had their own attorneys. There were so many contestants and attorneys that special arrangements had to be made for hearings because they could not all fit into the courtroom. One creative "relative," however, stood out above the rest. He testified that he was the son of the spinster's deceased brother (which would make him her only nephew) and, if true, this would also entitle him to the entire estate. As evidence, he offered a Bible in which was recorded the marriage certificate of his mother and the spinster's brother. Because of the massive size of the estate and the vigorous contest, the whole matter was widely publicized and this new "heir" quickly made the headlines. Unfortunately, a simple inspection of the Bible by the court disclosed that it was published twenty years *after* the date of the marriage certificate it contained, and the "nephew" was dismissed as a fraud and subsequently sent to jail.

As to the rest of the two thousand–plus relatives, only nine were recognized by the court and they shared the estate with the charity (and the lawyers, of course).

Even in those states that do not impose restrictions on charitable bequests, if the testator gave what the heirs feel was "too much" to a charity, you can be pretty sure there will be trouble, especially if the circumstances surrounding the charitable gift appear suspicious. A recent case illustrating what would appear to be "suspicious" circumstances is that of the famous and colorful pianist, Liberace.

Only two weeks before his death, Liberace, in the terminal stages of his decease, signed a new will leaving the bulk of his multimillion-dollar estate to a charitable foundation. The lawyer who drafted the will was named executor of the will and was also named as director of the foundation. As soon as Liberace's heirs and previous beneficiaries learned of this, they filed proceedings to contest his will, the outcome of which we probably will never know, since after a few years of private battle, the matter was apparently settled out of court.

Some Final Words about Words

Although there is certainly no question that a will is no more than a collection of words, there is the very serious question of *whose words are they?* You go to your lawyer and tell her, "I want to leave this to Jack, that to Jill, and the rest to Mrs. Hill," which you feel should take no more than two or three sentences. Later she sends you a "draft" of a ten-page document, containing thousands of words, considerably more than a simple disposition of "this, that, and the rest."

Later, after you have signed a document you never really understood, you meet an untimely death (death is almost always untimely), and a will contest arises over whether you meant "this" when you said "that," and what is included in "the rest." The lawyers each build a convincing argument over why *you* wrote the will the way *you* did, witnesses are brought to testify as to *your* intentions and whether or not these intentions were reflected in *your* will, and then the court launches into its basic rules in interpretation and construction of wills to decide, once and for all, what *you* meant in the words of *your* will, which, in fact, was drafted by your lawyer.

"Words are given their plain meaning," begins the judge, "and the answers must be found within the four corners of the will." "But the words were not really those of the testator," one lawyer responds. "His *lawyer* chose the words. And since it was a person skilled in the use of words, why should we give them their 'plain' meaning? They should be literally and technically construed, since we cannot now ask the testator what he meant!" "All right," the judge says, "to determine the intent of the testator, perhaps we should consider outside evidence." "But if we open the door to outside evidence," says another lawyer, "doesn't this destroy the sanctity and security of the will, which was so carefully executed before witnesses and all, just for that purpose? If there was a mistake," she says, "it was the *lawyer's* mistake. She didn't say it right."

"But how do we determine that?" replies the judge. "What about the accepted legal doctrine that there is a presumption of a just and reasonable meaning to the will, that the will speaks for itself as of the moment of death, and that the latter of two inconsistent provisions should prevail?" And so it will go, on and on and on, usually until the parties settle.

Actually, all of the arguments and principles mentioned above are valid and have been the basis of many court decisions in will contests. As to the question of whose words they are—they really should be a combination of yours and the lawyer's. Given the complexities of the law and the many provisions that belong in a will, which would be nearly impossible for a layperson to draft and understand, it is a fact of life that you should engage a competent attorney to draft your will and that many, if not most, of the words will be the lawyer's and not yours. This does *not* mean, however, that you need not or should not read it over carefully and ask questions about any provisions that you do not understand.

Only by asking, for example, would you know what a tax apportionment clause is and then be able to see whether your estate is being divided as you have instructed. Actually, the dispositive provisions (those that dispose of your property) should at least be able to confirm that "this part, that part, and the rest" of your estate will be divided as you directed and that, although the very words may not be yours, the thoughts are yours.

6

Uncommon Will Provisions— Controlling from the Grave

I leave to my banker, Mr. Hubert Pingrey, the sum of £1,000, provided that, within six months of my death, he walk the length of Bond Street, at midday and not on a Saturday or a Sunday, dressed in women's clothing, which should give him an inkling of the feelings to which he subjected me before advancing me a loan.

—from the will of J. Pemberton Casey

This is what is known as a *conditional bequest*. In this particular case, the banker, Mr. Pingrey, declined to meet the condition, which is always an option of the beneficiary. Conditional bequests, as one would imagine, take all manner of shapes and forms, and they seem to offer a testator some guarantee (if the condition is valid and accepted by the beneficiary) that his wishes will be carried out after his death, or in some cases, as we will see, a guarantee that if his wishes are not carried out *before* his death, the beneficiary will not inherit.

The condition attached to the banker's bequest above may seem somewhat silly or eccentric to some, quite poignant to others. A study of the history of wills reveals that such bequests are limited only by the imagination of the testator, provided they meet the requirements of the law. As the U.S. Supreme Court said in one case of a conditional bequest, "The right of a testator to attach to a gift in his will any lawful terms he sees fit, no matter how whimsical or capricious, is widely, if not universally, recognized." And we will see just how whimsical and capricious a testator can be.

The Requirements of a Conditional Bequest

1. THERE MUST BE A CONDITION

This requirement may sound obvious, but it is a fact of law that the courts will not impose a condition where there was none, or where it was not made *clear* that a condition existed. In interpreting the language of wills, there is a presumption in favor of *vesting*. That means there is a presumption that the bequest should go to the person named, with no strings attached, unless the will *clearly* states otherwise.

For example, language such as, "I would like it if Gerard were to use this bequest for such and such," is *not* a conditional bequest. Similarly, language like, "I leave my son, Alexander, $50,000, knowing that he will be generous to his sister, Andrea," does impose upon Alexander the condition that he must provide for Andrea if he wants to keep the $50,000.

If a condition is to be imposed on a bequest, therefore, it must be clearly stated as a condition, as in the case of the bequest to Mr. Pingrey at the outset of this chapter, where it was clear what Pingrey had to do before he could receive his £1,000.

2. THE CONDITION MUST BE LEGAL AND NOT AGAINST PUBLIC POLICY

If Mike leaves an annual income to his brother Mack, "so long as he continues to deal in drugs," or "provided he beats his wife once a month," or "provided he uses the funds in a movement to overthrow the U.S. government," such conditions are clearly illegal and would be totally ignored by the court.

In such cases, where the condition is clearly illegal, or where the condition is unclear, or where it fails to meet any of the other legal requirements, the condition is void and the bequest generally passes directly to the beneficiary *free* of any condition.

If a condition is not illegal when it takes effect (at the time of death) but later becomes illegal, then once again it becomes void. For instance, Mr. Fields owns a liquor store on a popular street in Philadelphia. The store was in the family for generations, and Fields would like it to continue as such. In his will, therefore, Fields states, "I leave to my son, W.C., an annual income of $20,000 provided that he continues to operate our family liquor store on Thirteenth Street, Philadelphia," and W.C. does so. A few years later, however, the city zoning board makes it illegal to operate a liquor store on Thirteenth

Street. In this case, since the condition *became* illegal, it also became void, and W.C. could continue to get the income, even if he had to close the store.

Conditions that are against public policy are not as easy to determine. The rules of public policy are not written down anywhere and are always a matter of objective and reasonable judgment at any given time. What was against public policy fifty years ago may be perfectly well accepted today, and what is considered against public policy in one court may be considered acceptable in another, although the underlying principles on which it is based remain the same. On this point, one court said that a condition is against public policy if it "contravenes any established interest of society, or conflicts with the morals of the time, tends to injustice or oppression, restraint of liberty or legal rights."

This reference comes from a case where the testator, a Mr. Schmitz, left a sum of money in trust for four (of six) brothers and sisters, on the express condition that "no one [of the four] of them shall at any time after my death have any communication with [the other two] verbally or in writing, nor live under the same roof with them, for twenty years."

Of course, there is nothing at all illegal in this condition, but is it against public policy? "The family is the origin of all society and all government, and this condition is damaging to and encourages dissension in the family relationship," said the court, citing numerous other cases containing conditional bequests prohibiting children and grandchildren from speaking to the testator's ex-spouse, requiring children to attend schools that would separate them from their parents, and prohibiting an aunt from visiting or communicating with certain nieces and nephews. Clearly, they said, Schmitz's condition forbidding brothers and sisters to speak to one another is against public policy and was held void. (Conditions prohibiting marriage or having children, or encouraging divorce are similarly against public policy, as discussed in greater detail later.)

If there is more than one condition, and one is illegal (or against public policy) while the other is valid, the court will ignore the invalid condition altogether but will enforce the valid condition. For instance, Jacob Hawke left his property in trust for ten years. If at the end of that time his son had "reformed his intemperate habits" *and* divorced himself from his wife, the son would receive the property. The court held that the condition to obtain a divorce was not enforceable, but the condition to reform was, and the son would have to satisfactorily perform under the second condition, within the prescribed period, before he could inherit the property.

3. THE CONDITION MUST BE POSSIBLE TO PERFORM

If the condition stated in the will is or becomes impossible for the beneficiary to perform, through no fault of the beneficiary, then the condition becomes void. For instance, Bradford leaves his estate to his son Brad on the condition that he take care of and support Bradford's wife for ten years after Bradford's death. Three years after Bradford's death, his wife dies. Brad is, of course, excused from the condition since it is now impossible to perform. Similarly, Atkinson leaves a parcel of land to Educatum University on the condition that the university construct a dormitory on the land within three years of his death. The town rules absolutely that such a building may not be constructed on the land. The university will receive the land free of the condition.

4. THE TIME FOR PERFORMANCE SHOULD BE CLEAR

Conditional bequests generally fall into two categories—condition *precedent* and condition *subsequent*. The bequest to our banker friend, Pingrey, at the outset of this chapter, was a condition precedent, meaning that *before* Pingrey could get his bequest, he must perform the condition of walking down Bond Street in women's clothes. Mr. Schmitz's bequest, in which he placed funds in trust for his brothers and sisters on the condition that *thereafter* (for twenty years) they should not speak to another brother and sister, illustrates a condition subsequent. If they did so within the twenty-year period, the benefits they were receiving under Schmidt's will would stop. Under a condition *subsequent*, therefore, the bequest would be given to the beneficiary subject to the carrying out of the condition. If he did not carry it out, he would have to give the funds back; under a condition *precedent*, the bequest is not given until the condition is performed.

In both cases, the time for performance is critical to the condition. In the banker's case, he had six months; in the brothers and sisters' case, twenty years. The condition would not fail, however, just because *no* time is specified for performance. In such cases, the court would give the beneficiary a "reasonable" time to do whatever it is you have requested he do.

If no specific time is stated and the condition appears to last forever (such as "$1,000 to Shirley, provided she never changes her name"), other practical problems are introduced, since the condition would require either the funds to be held until it was clear the beneficiary had performed (which would be a little ridiculous, since it may take a lifetime) or the beneficiary to give back the funds if she violated the condition. Because both of these alternatives are impractical, it is likely that the court would order the conditional bequest be held in trust, and the *use* of the funds offered to the beneficiary for the indefinite time period, subject to a loss of the use if the condition was breached. If the amount of the bequest was small enough so as not to warrant being held in trust (as in the case of $1,000 bequest), the court could order the bequest paid outright to the beneficiary, since keeping it in trust would only result in additional, unnecessary costs to the estate.

5. THE CONDITION MUST BE CAPABLE OF BEING CARRIED OUT

To be enforceable, the condition must be *capable* of performance and *certain* as to the determination of performance. In one case, a wealthy banker left a large chunk of his estate to a nephew on the express condition "that he shall never, on any occasion, read a newspaper, his favorite occupation." What's wrong with this condition? It is certainly not illegal and probably not against public policy—but it is impossible to determine performance. How would anyone be able to tell whether the nephew continued to read newspapers, especially if he washed his hands regularly?

Referring again to the case of Mr. Schmitz, public policy was not the only issue. Even if it was held not to be against public policy for Schmitz to forbid his brothers and sisters to speak, how could it be monitored and enforced? Interestingly, Schmitz *did* contemplate this problem and authorized his trust to spend up to one-half the estate income to enforce these rules, including the authority to "pay any person" $100 for furnishing conclusive evidence that the brothers and sisters had spoken, and he also provided that the trustee would be the sole judge of the validity of such evidence. Nevertheless, the court felt that the condition was void on account of its *uncertainty* of performance. Trust funds would have to be used, probably without effectiveness, to "spy" on the brothers and sisters, and it would be a continuing waste of the court's time to decide, upon someone's appeal, whether, in fact, they spoke and thus breached the condition.

There are many, perhaps hundreds, of other cases restricting modes of dress, prohibiting drinking, or requiring the living of a "clean life," all of which lead to the same problems of monitoring performance. Some clever testators seem to anticipate this and couch their conditions in different, more identifiable terms of performance, such as that of a wealthy Englishman named Sargeant, whose will provided his nephews with a substantial annual income, but only under certain conditions: "As my nephews are fond of indulging themselves in bed in the morning, I wish them to prove to the satisfaction of my executors that they have got out of bed in the morning, and either employed themselves in business or taken exercise in the open air, from five to eight o'clock every morning from the fifth of April to the tenth of October, being three hours each day, and from seven to nine o'clock in the evening from the tenth of October to the fifth of April, being two hours every evening; this is to be done for some years, during the first seven years to the satisfaction of my executors, who may excuse them in case of illness, but the task must be made up when they are well, and if they will not do this, they shall not receive any share of my property. Temperance makes the faculties clear, and exercise makes them vigorous."

6. THERE MUST BE A PLAN FOR UNMET CONDITIONS

A critical element to a conditional bequest is called a "gift-over," meaning that you must provide what will happen to the bequest in question if the beneficiary does not meet the condition. If you do not, the condition may be ignored. In other words, you might say, "I leave one third of my estate to my son, Hotschott, on the condition that within one year of my death, he writes a five-thousand-word essay on why he thinks I was a great father. If he fails to do so to the satisfaction of my executor, then the said one-third of my estate shall pass to my English teacher, Geraldine Scripter, of Quincy, Massachusetts, or to her heirs if she does not survive."

Taking this strategy one step further, you might consider including a provision to the effect that if for some reason a court holds that the conditions you placed on the bequest were invalid and unenforceable, then in that event, the property would pass to your backup beneficiaries. This would be an extremely important provision to include if there is a question that your conditions may be considered against public policy.

Having in mind all of these requirements, you can now conjure up your most creative conditional bequests. But to get you started, here are some of the more typical ones.

Some Varieties of Conditional Bequests

1. PROHIBITIONS AGAINST MARRIAGE

Perhaps one of the most common conditions you will find is the attempt to restrain or prohibit the future marriage of a beneficiary. Closely aligned with this is the condition that a beneficiary must obtain a divorce to be eligible to receive a bequest. The condition encouraging divorce has been repeatedly struck down by the courts as being clearly against public policy. Conditions prohibiting or discouraging marriage or remarriage, however, are not as absolute. Generally (although there is at least one exception explained below), *total* restraints against marriage are considered against public policy and therefore void. *Partial* restraints, however, are another matter.

A total restraint against marriage would be where, for instance, Cabot leaves half his estate to his granddaughter, Buffy, provided she never marries. Such a condition would be void, and, barring certain other provisions in the will, the bequest would go to Buffy without conditions. Restraints against a remarriage, however, are often upheld (perhaps on the basis that this helps the beneficiary avoid making the same mistake twice?), and if the condition prohibits the remarriage of a spouse, it is almost always upheld if it is "fair and reasonable" under the circumstances. In other words, it is perfectly okay to provide, "I leave my estate in trust and the income is to be paid to my husband, Lothario, for his life, provided that if he remarries, then his income is to cease and all remaining funds are then to be given to St. Concetta's Convent."

Partial restraints on marriage are more difficult to pin down as being either legal or illegal. A partial restraint does not prohibit marriage altogether, but merely prohibits marriage under certain conditions. For example, "I leave $50,000 to my daughter, Candy, provided she does not marry before the age of twenty-two," or "provided she does not marry someone of Italian extraction," or "provided she obtains the consent of her aunt and uncle, if they are not deceased, prior to becoming married." Generally, a partial restraint will be held valid unless it is "unreasonable." But what is unreasonable? Presumably, a partial restraint would be unreasonable if because of its terms it virtually prohibited marriage under most circumstances, or under reasonably foreseeable circumstances, such as when a man was prohibited from marrying any woman under six feet four inches, or when a person was prohibited from marrying before she reached the age of fifty. These conditions virtually prohibit marriage under reasonable circumstances, and therefore would be void.

Note that the question of reasonableness here does *not* mean logical, objective, unbiased, or unbigoted. There are many conditions upheld by the courts that are clearly "bigoted" in the common usage of the word. For instance, it is not unusual for a testator to leave funds to a child or grandchild provided she or he does not marry a person outside the Jewish faith, or the Catholic faith, or some other religious affiliation. Generally these restrictions are upheld.

In one case, with a much more narrow restriction, funds were left to children on the condition that, "If either one of my children should marry [a person from] T. W. Phillips' family, then I only give him or her the sum of three dollars, to be all that he or she is to receive under my will." As one might expect, the daughter married into the Phillips family. She contested the provision on the grounds that it was an unreasonable restraint against marriage. But clearly it was not, the court said. Given the broad range of "permissible" restraints under the law, restraints against marriage into a single family was not unreasonable. She got three dollars.

2. PROHIBITIONS AGAINST RELIGIOUS AFFILIATIONS

Although the courts are not totally consistent on this point, bequests that are subject to the condition that the beneficiary adhere to a particular religion, renounce it, or study it, or marry, or refrain from marrying someone in a particular religion, all have been held to be valid and enforceable. In one case, funds were left to a priest on the condition that he withdraw from the priesthood and from any other order or society associated with the Roman Catholic Church. The condition was held to be valid. In another case where the condition was upheld, funds were left to a child on the condition that the child be educated in or brought up in the Catholic faith. And still another upheld condition left the funds on the condition that the child only marry a person of the "Hebrew faith."

Contentions that such conditions are against public policy on the basis that they are unconstitutional as a restraint against religious freedom have generally been overcome on the argument that individual actions or transactions (i.e., a bequest under a will) are not bound by state guarantees of constitutional rights and that the right of the testator to use his funds to encourage or discourage the following or promotion of a particular religious belief is no less a right to religious freedom on *his* part. Unless the conditions were illegal or would injure someone or operate against public policy, they will be upheld, "no matter how specious, how intolerant, how narrow and prejudiced or dogmatic they may appear to others."

3. CONDITIONS PROHIBITING THE USE OF ALCOHOL, TOBACCO, GROWING MUSTACHES, ETC.

These conditions, sometimes called reformation or character-improvement conditions, are almost as common as the conditions frequently placed on marrying. The usual problem with the character-improvement conditions, however, is monitoring them. Aside from that, and aside from the possible embarrassment of the beneficiary when the world learns that he is "immoral" (according to the testator) because he is addicted to drink, smoking, or whatever, they are perfectly legal, and if they meet the necessary requirements of conditional bequests, they are generally upheld.

But to be upheld, the terms of the condition must be clear and definite. Conditions for character improvement may often appear clear, but they are usually very indefinite. It is easy to understand that "if Bart stops gambling for five years, he can have one-half my estate." But how would we know what Bart does unless we assign a private detective to follow Bart around day and night for the next five years? And what do we mean by "gambling"?

Or how about a condition that dictates how a person should dress? Such as the condition in the will of a minister who left his daughter a substantial bequest under the following terms:

> Seeing that my daughter Anna has not availed herself of my advice touching the objectionable practice of going about with her arms bare up to the elbows, my will is that, should she continue after my death in this violation of the modesty of her sex, all the goods, chattels, moneys, land, and other that I have devised to her for the maintenance of her future life shall pass to the oldest of the sons of my sister Caroline.
>
> Should anyone take exception to this my wish as being too severe, I answer that license in dress in a woman is a mark of a depraved mind.

The minister's condition by itself is valid but, once again, there are problems with its definitiveness and practicality. Must we follow Anna around for the rest of her life hoping that at some unsuspecting moment on a hot day she will roll up her sleeves? Another, perhaps more serious, problem with this bequest (and most others like it) is *who is holding the money?*

The "legal" approach to such a bequest would be to give Anna the funds "subject to divestment" (taking them away) if she breached the condition. Meanwhile, she could presumably do with the funds as she pleased. If I were Caroline's oldest son (the bequest provides that he will take the money if Anna dresses "immodestly"), I would ask the court to have the money held in trust so that Anna could not give it all away and then roll up her sleeves in defiance of the condition! But for how long? This is another common problem with such bequests. The will says, "should she continue after my death"— again, for how long? Since there is no specified limitation, the answer would be, for the rest of Anna's life! Such a vague and indefinite condition would definitely fail.

In addition to the monitoring aspect, however, remember that the condition must be clear. Many conditional bequests have failed because of confusion and uncertainty, such as the case where the testator left his estate to his two grandchildren "provided that they did that which was right." Well, you may know what he meant and I may know what he meant, but who is to judge—and (again) the question of for how long arises. Must they do "what is right" for just a while after Grandpa's death, or for the rest of their lives? Should they file some sort of reports on what they did, when, and with whom? In this particular case, the condition was disregarded and the grandchildren received the funds outright.

So, if you want to improve a person's character by encouraging him or her to stop drinking, smoking, gambling, or fraternizing with lawyers, you should think out carefully just what it is you do want, consider the steps reasonably necessary to monitor the character improvement, and *spell them out* clearly, in terms, definite enough that it can be determined (by someone other than yourself) whether your conditions were met. Then you should appoint someone to decide or provide a method of determining whether the condition has been carried out. If the condition is otherwise clear and determinable but no one has been designated to judge whether or not your condition has been met, *the court* will appoint someone to do so.

4. OTHER "INTERESTING" CONDITIONS

A valid condition bequest can be a great persuader, since the beneficiary stands to lose the bequest if he ignores the condition. As a result, testators have used conditional bequests to cause (or at least attempt to cause) beneficiaries to dress a certain way, follow a particular profession, adhere to or reject a particular religious belief, keep a particular family name, refrain from talking to certain other family members, not to marry into a certain family, etc. Here is a reasonably typical example of one of these conditions, perhaps a bit out of the ordinary but nonetheless worthy of reporting (the names were changed just a little to protect the "innocent").

Ansel Emmernecker had a substantial estate that included an elegant farm and more than enough funds to support it. His wife had died some years before, and he was left with an only son, Gifford, who himself had two children. Emmernecker's will left his entire estate in trust for his son, Gifford, provided that if Gifford refused to comply with the terms of his will, the estate would be sold, Gifford would get nothing, and the funds would be held in trust for Gifford's children under the same condition, which was this: Emmernecker's will required that Gifford and his children shall keep the family name of Emmernecker, and "whenever necessary in the course of his life to write or spell the name of Emmernecker, he shall spell it exactly as it was spelled in this instrument and was spelled by my ancestors."

For some reason, Gifford had thoughts of changing his name. Attorneys he consulted told him he could change it to something like Higgens Emmernecker, or Gunther Emmernecker, but if Gifford wanted to keep his father's bequest, he had to keep the surname, Emmernecker, and he even had to *spell* it that way. According to the records, however, Gifford had in mind something more American and less conspicuous, perhaps something like Engelbert Humperdink. So Gifford asked his attorneys to take legal action to see if there was a way they could "break" the condition.

The attorneys then argued that the court should ignore the condition as it was unduly harsh and might even interfere with Gifford's acting career. In the event that, without thinking, Gifford made some innocent mistake, like signing an autograph as "The Giff" or "M.N. Ecker" or "The Necker," he could lose the entire bequest. Furthermore, it was not clear how the trustees could monitor use of the name, and Gifford's attorneys argued that if a condition is vague and uncertain, the law should not require it to be carried out.

The court was not sympathetic. The opinion, eloquently written by the well-known justice Arbus Plasikowski, stated that "the testator's purpose was to perpetuate the ancestral spelling of the surname he proudly bore and in furtherance of that end he required his beneficiaries carry on the use and spelling of that name if they wished to receive the annual income from the trust." Emmernecker's condition was held to be valid and enforceable, and the Giff kept his name.

5. BEQUESTS TO CATS, DOGS, AND CHICKENS

At first glance, it would appear that discussion of a bequest to a cat, a dog, or some other animal does not belong in the category of a "conditional" bequest. Upon further examination, however, you will see that, in fact, that is the only way to carry out such a gift.

As noted very early on in this book, the right to leave property on your death is not a natural or inherent right, but rather it is only a privilege permitted by law, and therefore compliance with the law in this regard is essential if you want your property to pass according to your wishes. One facet of the law regarding the right of passing property on death deals with the identity of the beneficiary. Generally speaking, a beneficiary must be a person or a legal entity capable of appearing in court and accepting the bequest. That is, you cannot leave your money to a bridge or a flagpole (though it may be possible to leave money in trust for the *maintenance* of a bridge or a flagpole—see "Special Purpose Trusts" in chapter 12).

In this context, you can readily see that a cat, a dog, or a bird falls into the same category. And the more you think about it, the more you can see this rule makes sense. After all, you couldn't very well expect a dog to have a bank account or a credit card or own real estate, or an old chicken to be placed in a nursing home or make a will leaving its property to the rooster down the road. Unfortunately, this does not stop people from leaving their estates to a favorite pet. When this happens, however, the bequest is usually disregarded, and the estate passes to the next person designated or, if there is none, to the deceased's "residuary" estate (as explained in chapter 5).

For instance, say that Old Mrs. Osborne leaves $50,000 to her two favorite chickens, Pick and Peck. All the rest of her estate is left to her nephew, Sylvester. In this case, Sylvester will get the entire estate, and Pick and Peck won't get so much as a grain of wheat.

More and more such testators, being aware of this problem and perhaps having the common sense to seek advice, are beginning to realize that there *is* a way to provide for their pets without leaving them any funds directly, that is, through a conditional bequest. Old Mrs. Osborne could have provided for Pick and Peck by stating in her will, "I leave $50,000 to my farm hand, Perdue, on the condition that he takes care of my chickens, Pick and Peck, for the remainder of their lives."

Of course, Mrs. Osborne should include some simple means of having Perdue show that he is complying with the provisions, such as an annual chicken checkup by a vet, with a report to the court or to the executor. Otherwise, there is always the temptation that Perdue would put the chickens on the wrong side of the gravy, with no one the wiser and Perdue $50,000 richer. Even with all the reporting, however, it may be that, depending upon how the court decided to treat the conditional bequest, Perdue would be given the funds, subject to his carrying out the condition. If this happened, he would be more or less free to use the money as he wished, subject to an order to return what was left if he mistreated the chickens. To be certain, it would be best if Mrs. Osborne had the funds placed in a trust for a period of years; otherwise Perdue could conceivably spend the money and then disregard the conditions of the bequest.

If a testator contemplated leaving a large sum for the benefit of an animal, perhaps the best way would be to leave the sum to a charity whose function it was to provide for such animals, on the condition that the charity assume the care of the testator's animals after his death. You could even take this one step further and provide for the *creation* of such a charity on your death, if you have enough money. A case in point is that of Jonathan Jackson of Columbus, Ohio, whose will left a sum to be used for the construction and maintenance of an elaborate home for cats (his own cats included). Jackson's will contained detailed plans of a cat house that would include dormitories, conversation areas, exercise grounds, an auditorium where the cats could listen to "accordion music," and, of course, "rat holes" for their daily sport. He left out a cocktail lounge. (For more on trusts for pets, see "Special Purpose Trusts" in chapter 12.)

Conditions on Burials, Funerals, and Memorials

Generally, these conditions, or more accurately *instructions,* are governed by the same rules discussed above for conditional bequests. Primarily, they must be legal and must not be against public policy. Where special burial or memorial instructions are involved, however, it seems that the public policy issue is the one that must be dealt with more often than the "legal" questions. There is nothing inherently wrong, for instance, with being buried just about anywhere you choose, but it would certainly be against public policy to allow someone to be buried in the center of a busy highway or entombed in the wall of a shopping mall. Similarly, you can have your ashes scattered anywhere you want, but to ask that they be scattered over all the Caesar salads served in a popular restaurant might be met with objection.

In short, it is not always easy to tell what is or may be against public policy and what is not. In one case, for example, a midwestern woman's will directed that she be buried with all her jewelry. The executor of her estate, however, refused to do so on the basis that it would be wasteful and therefore against public policy. The probate court judge agreed and disallowed the provision, ordering that the jewelry be sold and the proceeds distributed according to other provisions of the will. "If the practice is developed in our state," the judge said, "to foster the burying of valuables with the deceased, our cemeteries, like the tombs of the pharaohs, will be ravaged and violated."

On the other hand, the burial instructions under the will of Sandra West, which in principal were similar to the above case, were carried out without question. As mentioned earlier in the book, Mrs. West's will directed that she be buried "next to my husband, in my lace nightgown . . . in my Ferrari, with the seat slanted comfortably." The Ferrari in this case was worth much more than the jewelry in the other case, but apparently no one objected to carrying out the bequest and the court would not take it upon itself to object, so the instructions were carried out. The Ferrari, with Mrs. West at the wheel, dressed in her baby-blue lace nightgown, was buried inside a large wooden crate, encased in cement to reinforce the necessarily large grave and to discourage grave robbing.

Just because someone leaves such instructions, however, is no guarantee that the instructions will be carried out. The public policy and reasonableness arguments can always be raised by those objecting to the use of the funds in a capricious or wasteful manner. Sandra West's estate exceeded $3 million, so no doubt her brother-in-law, the sole heir of her fortune, was pleased to accommodate good old Sandra by burying her in her Ferrari automobile, especially since her will provided he wouldn't get a cent if he didn't comply with her burial instructions. If, on the other hand, the Ferrari was the principal asset in Sandra's estate, perhaps he would have felt differently—and perhaps a court would have felt differently as well. Furthermore, if she left survivors who were dependent on her and who would have need for such assets, it is unlikely her wishes would have been so smoothly carried out.

Occasionally, testators will attempt to get creative with parts of their bodies, and such instructions are approached very cautiously by the courts, as it is generally considered highly disrespectful and against public policy to use parts of the body for purposes other than those relating to science or medicine. The courts are reluctant to honor such requests as that of John Reed, who purportedly directed that his head be separated from his body and used as a stage prop to represent the skull of Yorick in Shakespeare's *Hamlet*.

On the other hand, if you are famous, the courts may feel that the world may, upon your request, have the opportunity to view what is left of your body, as in the case of a well-known English judge named Jeremy Brentham. Judge Brentham directed that his body be bisected and his skeletal remains be dressed in black coat, white shirt, and "drab" accessories, and properly displayed. If it is not still there, Judge Brentham's clothed but beheaded skeleton was viewable for many years in the Anatomical Museum of University College in London, with his head carefully placed between his feet.

If a body is to be kept intact, about the only creativity available is through special burial instructions, and the process of cremation offers additional "opportunities." While it is perfectly acceptable to order cremation, some testators become quite imaginative as to the disposal of their ashes, keeping in mind that the same public policy and practicality aspects govern the disposal of ashes. But even where the request seems quite reasonable, there could be factors that prohibit accomplishment. For instance, think about the practicality of the poetic instructions to "scatter my ashes over the seven seas."

To do this, one would have to engage a person to travel to each of the appropriate parts of the world and employ a ship or a plane, from which the ashes would be scattered over the seas. I actually had a client who wanted his ashes shot off into outer space. When I explained the cost of renting space on a rocket ship and the regulations regarding the placing of objects into orbit, he discovered it was likely to cost more than the amount of his entire estate. He quickly reconsidered and settled for scattering them over the tomato plants in his backyard.

THE DEEP FREEZE—COMING BACK FROM THE DEAD

In more recent history, there has developed a special situation that raises all kinds of complicated legal questions and issues relating to wills and disposition of the body. Under the unproven theory that if a body is properly prepared and frozen (far beyond ice-cube level) shortly after death, it may be revived at some time in the future when, hopefully, a cure is found for the cause of the death. A good deal of public attention was focused on this concept when the famous Red Sox baseball slugger Ted Williams purportedly directed in a contract signed prior to his death that he be deep frozen, despite the fact that his will directed the cremation of his body (talk about extremes!). Assuming the contract was valid (one of the central questions in the estate dispute), Ted Williams apparently believed that it might be possible in the future to reverse the freezing process and restore life functions to his body or even just to his head. According to information from ALCOR Life Extension Foundation, a company that will freeze and store your body after death, either the whole body could remain frozen, or they have a special, reduced price for just the head (what they euphemistically refer to as "neuro-suspension," something we authors frequently experience).

John Henry and Claudia, two of Williams's children (and thus some of his "next of kin"), believed that their father did want his body to be frozen, purportedly so that he might be reunited with them in the future. At the same time, however, Bobby Jo (another of Ted's next of kin but one left out in a different kind of cold) believed the will clearly reflected Williams's last wishes, directing that his body be cremated and the ashes sprinkled at sea, and, she argued, those wishes should be honored. Which of those wishes and legal documents to honor became the subject of a bitter legal dispute among Ted's children.

While Williams's body remained frozen in a stainless steel tank at ALCOR, the fight (and the legal fees, of course) continued. In the meanwhile, Ted's son, John Henry, who led the fight to disregard the will, died, and reportedly was also headed for the deep freeze himself in the hopes of being reunited with his father one day in the future. Not all remained tranquil or perfect in purgatory, however. It was reported in a *Sports Illustrated* article that Ted's body had been decapitated and the skull cracked. Furthermore, the $120,000 cost of the freezing and storage process was not fully paid, and Ted, or what was left of him, might have to be evicted. As of this writing, the fight to have Ted's body returned remains unresolved, but a report in the May 4, 2004, edition of *Florida Today* indicated that attorneys for Ted's daughter, Bobby Jo Ferrell, had found a case precedent exactly on point, which they feel should convince the court to order Ted's body returned to Florida for cremation as he instructed in his will.

As noted, numerous legal issues arise when a person leaves such instructions, particularly including the question of whether Ted had the "right" to dispose of his body after death.

In general, whether it is your body or your ashes, reasonable requests you make that are not against public policy will be carried out, *provided* your spouse and/or children do not object. Believe it or not, as a general legal principal you do *not* have an absolute property right in your body (or ashes) after your death. Although your wishes will be given the first preference, they can be thwarted, and, as clearly demonstrated in the Ted Williams case, can lead to serious family disputes and huge expenses. One way to help avoid this is to make your bequests *conditional* upon those wishes or instructions being carried out (assuming, once again, that they are not unreasonable, impractical, or against public policy). Although this is no guarantee, it will certainly make the beneficiary think twice before deciding to disregard your instructions.

Furthermore, in the case of a deep-frozen body, what if the "deceased" was in fact revived in the future? What rights would he have? Could he get his property back? (No court, at this time at least, would ever agree to suspend the disposition of property at death for such a reason.) Thus, anyone thinking of being deep frozen may also want to think about setting up some sort of really long-term trust just in case.

MEMORIALS

Memorials (including memorial ceremonies that are to be repeated on a periodic basis after death in memory of the deceased) are really a separate category, as they do not, generally, need to be conditional, and they are designed to live on far beyond the death of the testator and, in many cases, his relatives. The two most common memorials, for instance, are the grave-yard type—which include monuments and mausoleum—and those that are charitable in nature, such as scholarships, for instance, or medical or scientific research grants, or artistic endeavors. Graveyard monuments, etc., are fairly straightforward and usually involve a onetime expense shortly after death to erect the monument. If the expense is not outrageous in proportion to the estate, the instructions will usually be carried out. Charitable memorials are relatively easy to set up under a will and most can go on "forever" in the name of the testator. For example, say that Friswold leaves $100,000 to Boston University to establish a scholarship in her name. Usually, the terms are that the school will use only the *income* from the $100,000, meaning that the $100,000 will remain intact virtually forever, each year producing a scholarship grant in the Friswold name.

Then there are memorials that are *not* charitable, and the law provides that these cannot go on forever, although they can nevertheless continue for many years after the testator's death. Briefly, in most states, a noncharitable bequest that does not pass outright to a particular person or organization cannot continue any longer than twenty-one years after the death of some designated person (or persons) who was alive at the time of the testator's death. For instance, Snodgrass leaves two children and three grandchildren surviving him at his death. His will provides that the annual income from one-eighth of his estate is to be used for the rental of a billboard that can be seen from the perpetually packed Southeast Expressway in Boston, Massachusetts. The billboard sign is to display a large picture of Snodgrass, smiling, with the caption, in large letters:

> Sherman Snodgrass, smiling at you from that big expressway in the sky.
> He'll never be stuck in traffic again.

Snodgrass could provide that his noncharitable memorial would continue each year (after his death) until twenty-one years after the death of the *last* survivor of his two children and three grandchildren. It wouldn't matter which one of them survived, but twenty-one years after the death of the last one, Snodgrass's billboard display would have to cease (assuming no one torched it before that). In the states (fourteen as of 2005) that have abolished this rule, noncharitable trusts can last forever.

"DRINKS ON THE HOUSE IN MEMORY OF WHATSISNAME"

One of the more imaginative and festive memorials is that of one Ernest J. Milani of Norwell, Massachusetts. Ernie provided that a portion of his estate be set aside in a "Memorial Trust," where each year, on Ernie's birthday, the income from the trust is to be used to provide free drinks to all of the patrons who happen to be in his favorite tavern on that evening, to raise at least one toast "in memory of Ernie Milani." Unless the money is used up earlier, this liquid memorial could continue for about one hundred years after Ernie's death, by which time they will probably have long forgotten who he was but will no doubt toast him with fervency anyway.

If you're thinking of a special memorial such as this, you must be careful to cover every contingency; otherwise you will simply add to the cost of it, or perhaps risk losing it completely, on the basis that it is indefinite or uncertain and cannot be carried out. In the Milani memorial, for instance, provisions had to be made in the event the named tavern ever closed down or moved, or in the event his birthday fell on a Sunday or a holiday when the tavern would be closed, or in the event of a storm or other minor catastrophe, and, of course, he provided for "reasonable" tips for the bartender and other servers. Here's looking at you, Ernie!

It should be noted here that Ernie's memorial trust may or may not be regarded as "charitable" by a court. Whether the annual providing of free drinks for the public falls into that category would remain to be seen. In Ernie's case, the trust was funded with a nominal amount, so it is likely that it would not be a big issue. If a large amount of funding is involved, however, it would be wise in such a case to consider a "special purpose" trust, which can be established for a noncharitable purpose (see chapter 12).

Defaming from the Grave—Having the Last Bad Word

For some testators, a will offers the opportunity to say things they were reluctant or afraid to say during their lives. Sometimes they were afraid to say it because they were afraid of the results it would bring, so they chose the coward's way out—hiding behind the will, where the victim could not reach. But is this so? Isn't it possible for the victim to sue the estate for libel?

Research into the question of defaming from the grave discloses a great number of angry, sarcastic, and slanderous statements left by testators who wanted to have the last bad word, most of them toward wives, husbands, or children (or those who, in the eyes of the testator, "pretended" to be children), and of course, toward in-laws. Here are just a few:

For my tyrannical wife, who did not give me any peace during the last twenty-four years since I am married to her I leave one dollar for which to buy a rope and hang herself. There was not a married man yet more miserable yet.

—from the will of Daniel Ross

And the Marquis d'Aligre said:

to my son I leave the pleasure of earning a living. For twenty years he thought the pleasure was mine.

But perhaps one of the most vituperative epitaphs of all was that of a harried husband, who left

to my wife, ANNA WALTERS PRESTON, one-third of my estate. It is my earnest desire and everlasting wish that the above-named adulteress and fiend in human form, to whose wiles I fell a victim while temporarily separated from my first wife, this harlot whose insidious lies, poured into my ear daily, caused me to take the step which made a reconciliation with my first wife impossible, this she-devil who, in an effort to ruin my good name, has for the last three years circulated the most damnable lies about me ever uttered by human tongue, this unnameable beast, who has made life for me a living hell for the last three years or more, and by whom I stand in daily fear of being murdered while asleep I repeat, it is my everlasting wish that this woman, whom I am compelled by law to call my wife, shall not receive one cent more of my very modest estate than she is entitled to under the laws of the State of Pennsylvania.

—Harry Preston

One gets the distinct impression that Harry and Anna didn't get along too well. Or at least that was the way Harry viewed it—so he really let her have it in his will. There is no evidence, however, that Harry ever spoke that way to Anna until his death. We'll never know.

What we do know, however, is that in certain cases such language can give rise to a lawsuit against the estate for libel. Even though the bulk of such suits are unsuccessful, it can cost the estate thousands of dollars just to defend against such a suit, without considering the cost of any settlement. Furthermore, chances are you won't even get the satisfaction of having your nasty words become public, since the modern trend is to simply *delete* the slanderous expressions from the will, so that the "public" would see the will without the damaging language. For example, if your will says, "I leave to my no-good, worthless failure of a daughter, Fluzie, the sum of $1,000, provided she stops sleeping with every bum she meets," the court is likely to delete what is called the "nondispositive" parts, so that as far as the public is concerned, your "will" reads, "I leave to my daughter, Fluzie, the sum of $1,000."

If for some reason you feel absolutely compelled to have a few nasty last words, then, instead of putting them in your will, you might consider writing a personal letter to the one you so dislike. It will probably have a much more lasting effect.

7

Spouses' and Children's
Rights to an Estate

I leave to my husband, Dom Witte, the sum of Five Dollars, to be given to him at the rate of ten cents a month, because he was so good to me.

—from the will of Barbara Witte

$\mathbf{M}$ust Dom settle for this? As a surviving spouse, doesn't he have "special" rights, or can he be disinherited and left with "ten cents a month"? And what about children? Aren't we legally obliged to leave them something?

As to spouses, most testators do want to provide for them and do so in their wills. But then there are those like Harry Preston, mentioned in the previous chapter, who thoughtfully referred to his wife as a "she-devil" and a "fiend in human form." Interestingly enough, however, Harry had the presence of mind (or perhaps heeded professional advice) not to attempt to completely disinherit her, but rather he left her "not one cent more than she is entitled to under the laws of the state of Pennsylvania." In doing this, Harry acknowledged, as any testator in this situation must, that most states give a surviving spouse the right to a certain share of the estate regardless of the provisions of the will.

Children are an entirely different matter. Even though a parent has a natural as well as a legal obligation to provide for minor children, there is generally no legal requirement that a parent leave a part of his estate to a child, whether a minor or not. This is not to say that children never have rights to contest a will or take a share of a parent's estate, but, as we will see, these rights are far less direct than those of a surviving spouse.

Disinheriting a Spouse—With and Without a Will

When the deceased spouse leaves a will disinheriting a spouse, most states allow the surviving spouse to *ignore* (or "waive") the will and take what is called a forced share. The laws of those states that allow a surviving spouse to take a forced share are very specific in the amount that the spouse may take, but this does not mean that questions do not arise. For instance, if state X says that a spouse can disregard the provisions of the deceased spouse's will and take one-third of the "estate," does this mean one-third of the estate that passes under the will? Or does it also include one-third of the life insurance, as well as one-third of the property in trust and one-third of the joint property?

It used to be that the surviving spouse's right to waive the will and take forced share applied only to the deceased's *probate* estate, and in many states that is still the case. The modern trend, however, extends this right to what is called the "augmented" estate, which includes *nonprobate* property, such as property the deceased spouse placed in trust (depending upon the extent of control and enjoyment the deceased spouse retained in the trust), certain jointly held property between the deceased and others, and, in some cases, gifts made by the deceased spouse within two or three years of his or her death.

In those states where the surviving spouse's rights only extend to the deceased's *probate* estate, it would be a very simple matter for a spouse to disinherit the other spouse merely by creating a nonprobate estate, and, in fact, this is what the modern-day Harry Prestons are usually advised to do if they wish to disinherit their spouses.

For instance, if Harry placed all of his property in a living trust, Anna Preston's rights to waive the will would not extend to the trust and she would have received nothing. This could still be the case in states where the spouse's rights extend only in the *probate* estate, but beware the modern trend in state laws to go beyond this.

Generally, the spouse's election to waive the will and take a forced share *must* be exercised within a certain period after the will is submitted to the probate court and the executor is appointed. Unless the will itself can be attacked on some other grounds, little can be done before that. Normally, this involves waiting until the will is submitted for probate and allowed (by the court) as the deceased's last will. When this happens, the executor is appointed to administer the estate. Thereafter, the spouse must, within the prescribed time, file her written election to take the share allowed by law despite what is provided in the will. This time requirement is usually very strict and must be carefully followed. For instance, if state Z allows the spouse to waive the will provided he or she files a waiver with the probate court within six months of the appointment of the executor, the spouse's election *must* be made within that period. If it is made a week or even a day late, it is likely to be lost, despite the fact that he or she may have an excellent excuse for being late.

Many states require that the election can be made only if the surviving spouse lives long enough to make it, while others allow the election so long as the spouse survived the deceased at all. In the first case, if the election must be filed no later than six months after the death of the first spouse, then a surviving spouse who died within six months of her husband could not make the election. In the latter case, even though the surviving spouse died shortly after the first, the *executor* of the surviving spouse's estate could still make the election, on her behalf, to take a share of the first spouse's estate. That share, once received by the executor, would then pass to the surviving spouse's estate.

If the waiver is made effectively, the surviving spouse's share, according to the laws of the estate, will generally be given priority over other shares under the will, but *not* over the debts, expenses, and taxes of the estate. After those are accounted for, then the "net" estate is arrived at, which is the amount on which the spouse's forced share is based. Once the forced share is paid, the rest of the estate can be distributed according to the will (or other arrangements, if the forced share involved nonprobate property).

In some cases, taking a forced share can upset the bequests under the will that was waived (although this is not usually a consideration of the surviving spouse who waives the will). For instance, say that Osgood has a will leaving $60,000 to each of his two daughters and the rest of his estate to his secretary. Osgood has intentionally omitted his wife, Prettygood, from his will, since he has a strong hunch she has been seeing another man, but he can't prove it. Osgood's will was prepared by his lawyer and signed by Osgood in the lawyer's office with the proper formalities, after the lawyer carefully reviewed the will with Osgood, who was satisfied with the contents. A few months after signing the will, however, Osgood decided to change it. He made an appointment with his lawyer and while on his way to the lawyer's office, Osgood suffered a fatal heart attack brought about by the shock of finding a parking spot in downtown Boston.

Osgood's "estate" consisted of the home, which he owned jointly with his wife, Prettygood, and two bank accounts, in Osgood's name, worth about $150,000. Shortly after Osgood's death, his will was offered for probate and when Prettygood saw that she had been left out, she rushed to her lawyer, N. Tangle, to see what she could do about it. Tangle tells her she does not have a good case to attack the validity of the will itself, since it appeared to have been properly signed and there was no indication that Osgood was not competent when he made the will or did not understand the contents of the will. Osgood's will, therefore, was probably valid, and Prettygood's only recourse, Tangle advised, would be to allow the will to be probated and then, within the prescribed time, waive the will and take her forced share as Osgood's surviving spouse. She followed Tangle's advise and did so.

Osgood's executrix (the secretary) was then required to give Prettygood her forced share, after payment of the debts and expenses of Osgood's estate. In Massachusetts, where Osgood resided, the surviving spouse was entitled to one-third of the first $75,000 of Osgood's probate estate and a life estate in one-third the rest of the estate. (A *life estate* is the right to use the funds or property during a person's life. In a case like this, it usually, but not always, means that the spouse would receive the *income* from one-third the remainder of the estate.) No adjustment is made for property or assets that passed directly to the surviving spouse outside the probate estate. In other words, Prettygood would be allowed to keep the home, which was held in joint names with Osgood, and, in addition, she could take her forced share as described above. (Some states require that amounts received by the surviving spouse outside the probate estate, such as through joint ownership, be taken into account when computing the "forced share" of a surviving spouse.)

Prettygood's forced share, then, would amount to $25,000 outright (one-third of the first $75,000) and a "life estate" in $25,000 (one-third the balance). Briefly, the life estate would consist of the *income* from the $25,000 and, in certain instances, parts of the principal, depending upon Prettygood's future circumstances. In effect, since this is a "life" estate, it requires the court to set aside the second $25,000 for the rest of Prettygood's life. After Prettygood's forced share is dealt with, the rest of Osgood's will can be carried out, but obviously the taking of the forced share will upset the rest of Osgood's will.

For purposes of the forced share, Osgood's estate, after expenses, consisted primarily of $150,000 in bank accounts (the jointly held home passed directly to Prettygood). The forced share reduced the bank accounts by $25,000, plus another $25,000 to set aside for Prettygood's life estate, leaving only $100,000 to distribute to the named beneficiaries. Osgood's will, however, left $60,000 to each of his two daughters and the rest to his secretary. Clearly, there is not even enough to satisfy the specific bequests to his daughters, let alone the secretary. So what happens?

Although it depends to some extent upon the law of the particular state, the general rule is that unless the testator expresses a contrary intent in his will, the *residuary* estate will bear the cost of the forced share. Of course, if the residuary estate is insufficient to cover the forced share, it has to come from somewhere, so then the specific bequests would be ratably reduced to make up the difference. And this is exactly what happened in the above example of Osgood's estate. The residuary estate (which was left to the secretary) was not enough to provide the $25,000 share plus the $25,000 life estate, so the excess would be taken from the daughters' shares. Instead of getting $60,000 each, therefore, the daughters would receive $50,000 each, and the secretary would get nothing—at least not until the death of Prettygood.

On Prettygood's death, her "life estate" in the $25,000 would be over and, assuming the full $25,000 remained, the two daughters would each receive $10,000 (the balance of their $60,000 bequest) and the secretary would receive the "residue" of $5,000. As a practical matter, Osgood's executor (or his daughters) would probably have tried to reach a settlement with Prettygood to avoid having to tie up estate funds for the rest of Prettygood's life, but settlement is totally at the option of the estate. The surviving spouse cannot force the estate to pay any sooner or any more than is allowed under the law.

If the state in question required all beneficiaries, including the residuary beneficiary, to proportionally bear the cost of the spouse's forced share, then in Osgood's case the daughters would have borne the bulk of Prettygood's share, since they received the bulk of the estate. That is, since the total estate, after expenses, was $150,000, and each was to receive $60,000, they would each "pay" 60/150 times the forced share and the secretary would "pay" 20/150 times the forced share. But, as noted above, this is not the general rule.

Not every state has such a complicated forced share. In fact, most states simply give the surviving spouse the right to take one-third or, in some cases, one-half the estate outright, but short of that there is very little consistency among the states. Some restrict the spouse's rights to real estate that the deceased spouse owned at his or her death; others include all of the deceased's property but limit the election to "probate" property. Still others, and this is becoming a trend, as discussed earlier in this chapter, allow a spouse to take a share of the "augmented" estate, which goes far beyond the probate estate and includes jointly held property, certain gifts made by the deceased before his death, and certain trusts created by the deceased during his lifetime.

Usually, if a state's forced share allows the surviving spouse to go beyond the probate estate, it also requires the spouse to "account" for nonprobate property that he or she received on account of the death of his or her spouse. That is, the spouse would be required to take into consideration the value of *all* of the property she receives on account of the death of the other spouse, including property they held jointly, in trust, and other nonprobate assets that passed to the survivor.

As I said, however, there is little consistency, except for the fact that every state has some provision that prevents, or is designed to prevent, disinheritance of a surviving spouse. In community property states, the spouse's protection is not in the form of a right to elect against the will. There is no need for such statutes because the community property laws themselves give the spouse a right to one-half of *all* the property acquired by the spouses during the marriage. Since one-half the marital property already belongs to the surviving spouse, there is no way that the deceased spouse could leave it to someone else in his or her will.

It is also important to note that the surviving spouse's forced share does *not* qualify for the estate tax marital deduction (see chapter 12). Therefore, amounts that a spouse takes as his or her forced share will be fully subject to federal estate tax, whereas amounts voluntarily given him or her by the deceased spouse will not because of the marital deduction.

It is very common to confuse the spouse's right to a forced share of the estate with the share a surviving spouse would take if the other died *without* a will (intestate). Although in some states the two may bear a resemblance, *they are not the same.* In fact, except for those few states where the forced share is by law *equal* to the intestate share (Arkansas and Minnesota, for instance), the forced share is usually *less* than the share a spouse would take if the other died without a will.

As described in chapter 2, when a person dies without a will, his surviving spouse can take from one-third to all of his estate, depending upon the particular state's laws, whether there are children, and, most important, the extent of the *probate* estate. Does this mean, then, that if I want to disinherit my wife, I simply place all my property in joint names with, say, my daughter and tear up my will? In some states, yes, but in others, no.

As noted earlier, the trend in many states is to make it harder rather than

easier to circumvent the rights of a surviving spouse. It is finally being realized that the intention behind such laws is to protect and honor the marital
relationship and to respect, even after death, the rights acquired by marriage. If a spouse is to be given rights to the "estate" of a deceased spouse,
therefore, such rights should encompass *all* of the property that he or she
owned and enjoyed at the time of his death. It is ludicrous to strictly limit
such rights to the *probate* estate of the deceased spouse, when in fact the
bulk of his or her estate often avoids the probate process entirely, and it is
even more ludicrous to allow such rights to hinge upon the existence of a
will. Based on this reasoning, a number of states are allowing a spouse to
take a forced share of the "augmented" estate (which, as explained, includes
nonprobate property) regardless of the fact that the deceased spouse left no
will. And for those states that do not yet recognize this trend, I suggest it is
only a matter of time.

Well, then, exactly what do I do if I am the Harry Preston type, intent
upon leaving my spouse the absolute minimum and preferably nothing?

Short of giving the property away, not very much, if the trend continues.
In the meantime, however, in those states that have not yet adopted the augmented estate concept (there are about twenty-five of them), you can create
a living trust (discussed in greater detail in chapter 11), name yourself as
trustee, and transfer all of your property to this trust. It can allow you to
enjoy the property so long as you are alive and well, and on your death the
trust can direct that all of the remaining trust assets be paid over to, say, your
children, or anyone else you designate as a beneficiary in the trust. Since
this arrangement would avoid probate, it would also, in those states that
base the forced share on the probate estate, avoid the reach of your surviving spouse. Unfortunately, it is not something you can absolutely count on,
since the state laws are changing rapidly. Your next best bet would be to give
your spouse the minimum amount that the law requires on the *condition*
that if she makes any attempt to get a penny more, she will lose the share
you have given her. This does not necessarily guarantee that she won't get
more than you have given her, but it does mean that in order to get it she has
to risk losing the share you left her.

There are also occasions where a "spouse" who is not a spouse may have
rights on the death of a partner—the "common law" marriage. In a number
of states, if a couple lives together as husband and wife for a specified number of years (usually seven), then in the eyes of the law of that state they can
be considered married. In such cases, the surviving common-law spouse has

the same rights as a "legally married" spouse, including the right to waive the will and take a forced share, as discussed above.

Since it is not uncommon today for couples to live together for extended periods of time without being married, the rights of common-law marriage are becoming a more common concern. Those who do not necessarily want to share their respective estates with each other may find that the death of one after having cohabited for the required period of time might very well produce rights to the surviving partner that were never anticipated. For instance, in New Hampshire, if a couple lives together *"as husband and wife"* for three years before the death of either, the other has rights to the estate of the deceased partner similar to those of a surviving spouse.

To avoid this problem as well as other complications, such as the disruption of the estate by the surviving spouse of a "legal" marriage, couples should consider entering into an agreement that fixes their respective rights on death, as discussed later in this chapter.

Rights of Divorced or Separated Spouses under a Will

Generally, once a divorce becomes final, the divorced spouse has no legal claim to the estate of his or her ex-spouse, unless, of course, the terms of the divorce decree call for some sort of payment on death. (It is not uncommon, for example, for a decree to provide for a lump-sum payment to the surviving ex-spouse in lieu of alimony.) Other than in such cases, no liabilities or responsibilities exist for ex-spouses. However, problems frequently arise during that period of time during which the spouses are "ex" in each other's eyes but not in the eyes of the law.

Just about every state allows for or requires a "cooling off" period after the initial divorce decree during which the spouses are still legally married. It usually takes anywhere from one month to a year after this decree before the divorce actually becomes legally final and the couple is no longer husband and wife. If a spouse dies within this period, the surviving "spouse" has all the rights of the surviving spouse, just as if divorce proceedings had never been initiated, and even if the deceased spouse was efficient enough to have changed his or her will, the surviving spouse is entitled to take his or her forced share of the estate. If the spouse did not get around to changing his or her will (and the will happened to provide for his or her "spouse"), the survivor would then have the chance of either accepting the bequest under the will or taking a forced share, whichever gave her more.

This potential problem is even more exaggerated when the spouses are legally separated but not divorced, or when they are simply "estranged." In either case they are still considered husband and wife, with all the attendant rights on the death of a spouse.

In all of the above cases (a nonfinal divorce, a legal separation, and even an estrangement), it is advisable for the spouse with the larger estate to have the other spouse enter into an agreement (even if a price has to be paid for it) providing that in the event of the death of a spouse, the other agrees to waive (not to exercise) any rights she or he may have to the other's estate. If the agreement is properly drafted and consideration (payment) is given, such agreements (discussed below in greater detail) can be legally binding and can avoid the problems mentioned above.

EFFECT OF DIVORCE ON A WILL

While in most states marriage automatically *revokes* a will made before the marriage (unless the will was made in anticipation of the marriage), the opposite rule applies to divorce. That is, as a general rule, a divorce does *not* revoke an existing will. Because of ignorance of this rule, the families of many deceased ex-spouses found themselves sharing the estate with the surviving ex-spouse who was named as a beneficiary of the will, which the deceased forgot to change, or didn't bother to change because he thought the divorce somehow changed it. As a result of the clear inequity of such situations, almost all the states have enacted laws that provide that although a divorce does not revoke an existing will, it *does* revoke the provisions of such a will that favor the divorced spouse.

For instance, say that Tristan has a will leaving three-fourths of his estate to his loving wife, Isolde, and the remaining one-fourth to his son, Wagner. The will also provides that if Isolde does not survive Tristan, the entire estate will pass to Wagner. After many years of a harmonious marriage, however, the music stops and the couple obtains a divorce. After the divorce, Tristan immerses himself in his work of setting the Dead Sea Scrolls to music and so forgets to change his will. Suddenly one day, while writing an aria for the lead camel, Tristan aspirates on his penpoint and dies. When the will is later offered for probate, Isolde arrives to claim her share. She is informed, however, that in Alaska, where they resided, the law provides that a divorce revokes any provisions in favor of a former spouse, and since Isolde was only a former spouse, the bequest to her in Tristan's will was revoked. In such a case, the will is treated or interpreted as if Isolde (the divorced spouse) *predeceased* Tristan (even though in fact she did not), and so the estate would pass to his son, Wagner.

Despite state laws revoking will provisions for a divorced spouse or, in a few states, revoking the will altogether on divorce, it is important to note that such measures have *no effect* on beneficiary designations that the deceased spouse may have made on life insurance policies, retirement plans, and the like. Many court battles have been fought, and *lost*, in an attempt to recover insurance or other proceeds paid to the ex-spouse as beneficiary because the deceased simply forgot to remove her name.

The laws of some states go one step further with this concept of revoking will provisions for a former spouse, and, in the event of divorce, *also* revoke the appointment of a former spouse as *executor* of the deceased spouse's estate. Obviously, it can be embarrassing if the divorced spouse is appointed executrix to administer the estate for the benefit of the deceased's new bride! To avoid creating such a difficult situation, it is a lot easier, less traumatic, and cheaper to simply make out a codicil after the divorce, stating your wishes for the disposition and administration of your estate.

Premarital (and Postmarital) Agreements—and Wills

It is interesting that first marriages are almost never accompanied by a premarital agreement, whereas second (and further) marriages are almost never without one. Whatever the reason, if either party of a marriage, first or otherwise, is at all concerned with limiting the rights of a spouse on divorce, separation, or death, an agreement should certainly be considered. Here, we will concern ourselves with the use of such agreements to prevent lengthy estate contests and to avoid the disruption of the forced share otherwise available to a surviving spouse.

For many years, the law effectively prohibited a married couple from entering into legal contracts with each other on the theory that to allow one spouse to sue the other would undermine the family unit, which is viewed as the cornerstone of our society. Eventually, as lawsuits for divorce and related property disputes became more common, it was successfully argued that each member of the couple was a legal individual and should be able to contract with anyone, including the other spouse. It is, of course, now widely accepted that for most purposes a couple can enter into a legally binding agreement with each other and, as a result, couples began to discover that such agreements could even include, to a point, their financial responsibility to each other under a variety of circumstances. It should be noted here that a contract to do something that is against a particular law or against public policy will not be enforceable in any event, so that a husband could not avoid by contract, for example, his legal responsibility to support his wife and children.

Marital agreements fixing a spouse's rights at death are becoming quite common, especially where there are children from previous marriages. Such agreements are available in every state, including the community property states. Since the law is different in each state, it is difficult to outline the precise form of such an agreement in every case, but briefly, the agreement would state the share of the respective estates that each agrees to give the other on death. In return for such a share, the surviving spouse agrees to waive all other rights he or she may have to take anything further, such as (and specifically including) his or her right to waive the will and take a forced share of the estate. Furthermore, the agreement should also contain some provision regarding any jointly held assets that the couple may acquire. If it is desired that the jointly held assets should pass to the survivor on the death of one, the agreement should clearly say so. And if it is desired that the jointly held assets should go to the surviving spouse *in addition* to any other share stated in the agreement, it should state that as well.

Perhaps the most important element to ensure the enforceability of marital agreements is *independent representation.* Do *not* allow the same attorney to represent both parties. It is absolutely essential that each party have independent counsel advising him or her of his or her rights, and many attorneys make it a practice to have the attorneys sign the agreements as well, stating that they have explained the agreement to the client and they are satisfied that the client understands the contents and the rights and liabilities involved.

Although most marital agreements are premarital (made *before* the marriage), it is quite possible in most states to enter into *post*marital agreements. If, for example, a couple is married for twenty years and decides to fix their respective rights at death (it usually happens after a dispute, but not always), they can at that point enter into a postmarital agreement. Generally, all of the same principles apply here as apply to premarital agreements, subject, of course, to the laws of a given state; it can be every bit as binding on the surviving spouse and, like the premarital agreement, it can avoid a will contest.

Children's Rights under a Will

Most people are under the impression that they *must* leave their children something in their estates, since if they don't, an omitted child has the right to contest the will and take a share of the estate. Perhaps the most common offshoot of this misconception is the practice of leaving one dollar to a child you wish to disinherit.

In fact, in every state, with the very limited exception of Louisiana, a parent has the power to disinherit a child simply by leaving his estate to someone else (other than the child). And whether the child is left one dollar or nothing at all, she may contest the will.

What gave rise to this practice of leaving one dollar to a disinherited child are certain laws based on the presumption that parents normally do not wish to disinherit their children. The laws that reflect this presumption provide that if a child is omitted from a parent's will, he is nevertheless entitled to a certain share of the estate (these are called "pretermitted" child statutes).

In general, these laws protecting omitted children are of two types—one is the Missouri type, which provides that if a child is not mentioned in the will, he or she will automatically take a share of the estate, regardless of the reason for the omission, and the second is the Massachusetts type, which provides that if a child is not provided for in the will, he or she will take a share of the estate, *unless* the omission was intentional on the part of the parent.

In order to show that the omission was intentional, lawyers would have their clients (who wanted to disinherit a child) leave the child one dollar, or perhaps have them include a statement declaring their intent, such as, "I intentionally make no provision for my son, Randolph." When advised of the need to make such a statement, a number of testators have felt compelled to go a step further, embellishing the intentional omission with more colorful comments, such as the New Yorker who left his son "the generous sum of one dollar, which is twice what he is worth."

This is not to say that such language prevents a child from contesting a will. As explained in detail in chapter 10, anyone who has standing and who has a reason can contest a will, and children who are disinherited are often likely contestants. The point is that there is *no* legal obligation on the part of a parent to leave something to a child, even though the child may be a minor whom the parent was legally obliged to support while he (the parent) was alive, although this rule (where a minor child survives a parent) has changed in a few states, and there may well be a trend developing across the country not to allow a parent otherwise responsible for providing for a dependent child to avoid the responsibility on death.

Sometimes a child is omitted unintentionally because she was born or adopted *after* the parent made out his will. Because of the presumption in favor of children, most states provide that a child born or adopted after the parent made out the will is entitled to a share equal to the share she would receive if the parent died without a will. As noted above, however, some states will not allow the child to take a share if it appears that the omission of the after-born or adopted child was intentional. Unfortunately, the question of intent of the deceased parent in either case is, in most instances, strictly interpreted, so that an intentional omission of a child on the mistaken belief that the child was dead is still an intentional omission. This has led to some very sad results. There have been a number of cases, for instance, when a parent who has not heard from a child for ten or twenty or more years omits him from the will, thinking he is dead. In such cases, the omission was intentional and therefore enforceable, even though it was based on a misunderstanding on the parent's part. (Note that the language of the will in such cases is important. If the mistaken belief is actually stated in the will as the basis for the omission, then even though the omission was intentional, thereby precluding the child from taking a share under the omitted-child law, the child may be able to void that portion of the will on the grounds of *mistake*. An example would be: "Because my son John is dead, I omit him from this will.")

Assumed death and actual disappearance are not the only causes for omission based on a mistake that can leave a child without a share. There have also been a number of cases where a father omitted a child because he thought the child was not his own, as in the case of Owen Schlock of New York.

Owen and his wife, Sarah, were caretakers on a parcel of property in upstate New York. According to the records, Owen's "only fault" was that he drank too much. Several months after his marriage to Sarah, he heard some rumors around town that Sarah was not "true to him." About a year and a half after the marriage their son, Homer, was born. It was not until eight years later, however, on a night Owen came home intoxicated, that he accused Sarah of having had "connection with someone other than himself," claiming that Homer was not his son. For the next thirty years Owen continued to make similar comments, but only while intoxicated and never in the presence of anyone but Sarah. Finally, he made out a will leaving nothing to his son, Homer, who was, in fact, his son.

Under these circumstances, since Owen was of sound mind (he was sober when he made out his will), and since he deliberately omitted his son, Homer, from his will, Homer was effectively (though unjustifiably) disinherited, and there was nothing he could do.

As discussed above, there are a number of states, such as New Hampshire, Missouri, and Alabama, that do not require proof that the omission was intentional. In those states, a child not provided for or mentioned in the will will automatically take a share of the estate, regardless of the reason for the omission.

Interestingly, when a child is improperly omitted from a parent's will, the rights of that child can pass down to the child's children if the child is already deceased at the parent's death. For instance, say that Mallard asks his lawyer to prepare a will leaving all of Mallard's estate to his three children, Huey, Dewey, and Frank. When she comes to Frank's name, however, the lawyer's three-fingered typist misses a few keys and the will leaves the estate only to Huey and Dewey. The will is signed by Mallard without realizing that Frank has been inadvertently omitted. As it happened, shortly after the will was signed, Frank was killed in an auto accident, survived by his wife and two young children. And shortly after that, Mallard died of a heart attack at the sight of his lawyer's bill.

Because Frank was not intentionally omitted from Mallard's will, he should be entitled to a share. But Huey and Dewey come forth and say, "Personally, we liked Frank, and had he survived, we probably would have shared the estate with him, but it's a shame he didn't. Frank's children were never entitled to a share." In fact, those states that have laws protecting omitted children provide that the rights of an omitted child can be exercised through that child's *lineal descendants* if the child is deceased, and case law supports the fact that the omitted child need not have survived the parent for this to be so.

In my example, therefore, Frank's two children would have the right to share one-third of their grandfather's estate because of the fact that their father, Frank, was an improperly omitted child.

Remember that *any* mention of the child in the will is adequate to show that she or he was not accidentally omitted, so that even if the child is merely referred to in some context other than a bequest, such as naming him executor, it is probably sufficient evidence of an intentional omission.

An even more difficult question arises where an after-born child is the result of the artificial insemination of the deceased's sperm after his death. Here it is difficult to argue that the child was omitted intentionally since the child was not even considered to be in existence at the time of the testator's death, let alone the time he made his will. This issue of whether such children qualify as "omitted" children has yet to be resolved by the courts, but, as noted in the discussion below, it has been considered in a few states in regard to whether such a child would qualify for Social Security benefits.

Surprisingly, an omitted child does not get his share by contesting the will since, presumably, the will was properly executed. Rather, before distribution is made to the other beneficiaries, the child must ask the court to order that a distribution be made to him as an omitted child, under the appropriate law of the particular state.

A parent who wishes to disinherit a child must also be careful that the remainder of his estate is properly disposed of under his will; otherwise the intentional omission statement may be useless, and the undisposed-of property will be treated as "intestate" property (as if the parent died without a will) and, of course, under the law the child will take a share of that. Therefore, be sure your will has a "residuary" bequest (it would be unusual if it didn't, but it *has* happened, especially with home-drawn wills), leaving "all the rest, residue and remainder" to so and so.

Adopted children. For purposes of inheritance, adopted children are treated the same as natural-born children. They will inherit from their adoptive parents and *not* from their natural parents. When they are adopted, they *lose* the right to inherit from their natural parents' estates. This does not prohibit, however, both sets of parents from providing for the child voluntarily.

Illegitimate children. Until very recently, the general rule was that an illegitimate child could only inherit from his or her mother and not from the father, unless the father acknowledged the child to be his (although the father could, of course, voluntarily provide for the child). A 1986 U.S. Supreme Court decision changed all that, holding that such laws were unconstitutional and that a state may not prohibit an illegitimate child from inheriting. The effect of this decision gives an illegitimate child the same inheritance rights as a legitimate child, including the right to a forced share if he is improperly omitted from the will. The effect of this, in turn, could be to force fathers of illegitimate children to "acknowledge" involuntarily the illegitimate child by intentionally omitting the child from his will. For instance, one might envision a will stating, "I intentionally omit that bastard son of mine" (which raises the question: Could this be introduced as evidence in a paternity suit?).

Children of sperm donors. Modern science is creating complicated legal problems, many of which were totally unanticipated in developing the technological advances. A number of these surprise issues surface in the area of inheritance law. For instance, say that Jack and Jill are married, but Jack is terminally ill at a relatively young age. Both of them are desirous of having more children, so Jack preserves and stores his sperm for this purpose. After Jack's death, Jill is impregnated with Jack's sperm as they planned, resulting in another of "their" children, but this one is born nearly four years after Jack's death. Does the child have rights to Jack's estate long after it is settled? And what if Jill dies before Jack, Jack later remarries, and dies sometime later. After Jack's death, his second wife learns of the stored sperm, is impregnated with Jack's sperm, and bears Jack's child. Does this child have any rights to Jack's estate even though Jack never consented to the arrangement?

One Massachusetts case, decided in 2002, dealt in part with the former issue (where the deceased consented), but the legal question that arose was whether the child born after the one parent's death would increase the surviving spouse's rights to Social Security benefits. The case involved a young couple married three and a half years with no children. It was discovered that the husband had leukemia and would likely be unable to father children once the disease progressed. The couple arranged to store the husband's semen and preserved it for possible future use by the wife. In October 1993 the husband died, and in October 1995 the wife gave birth to twin girls after being artificially inseminated with her husband's sperm. The wife then applied for mother's benefits and child's benefits under Social Security. Her claim was denied by Social Security on the basis that she did not establish that the twins were her deceased husband's "children." Subsequently, a U.S. administrative law judge held that the children did not qualify for benefits because they were not entitled to inherit from the father's estate under Massachusetts law. Then Massachusetts's highest court, the Supreme Judicial Court, reviewed the case. The court held that the children did qualify as children of the deceased husband and the surviving spouse's benefits should be measured accordingly. The court went on to note, however, that such an opportunity should not be allowed to take place at just any length of time after the father's death and that a reasonable time period, perhaps two years, should be established as a limit beyond which such rights would be cut off. Otherwise, it would not be equitable or reasonable to require other heirs or legatees to wait indefinitely for their rights to the estate to be settled. (The court also held that paternity must be clearly established and that the deceased father must have affirmatively consented to posthumous conception and to the support of any resulting children.)

In another case on the same issue as to whether an after-born child who was not "in utero" on the testator's death would qualify for child's Social

Security benefits, a lower court decision against the child was appealed to the federal circuit court of appeals. That court (in the Ninth Circuit) held in 2004 that the child did qualify as a "child of the testator" and should receive benefits. It was also noted, however, that the issue continues to be unsettled and unpredictable.

Perhaps an even more potentially troublesome issue arises with "anonymous" donors, typically resulting where healthy men are paid for donating their sperm to sperm banks, to be purchased and used by infertile couples or even single women to produce children. Depending on the arrangements made with the sperm bank, it may be possible for the sperm's purchaser or the child to discover the identity of the donor. Does the child in such a case have any rights to the natural father's estate? Typically, two situations apply. In many instances a couple unable to otherwise bear children will utilize the stored sperm. Since the resulting child is not of the husband, the husband might legally adopt the child, and the rights of the child to the estate of the natural father are then cut off. Where this does not happen, however, it may be that the child does have rights to the natural father's estate, but it is not always clear. In one case in Washington state, for instance, the court held that the previously anonymous donor had no (lifetime) responsibility for the support of minor children produced by his sperm. To (help) avoid the question of right and liabilities in such cases, it is typical for the anonymous donor to sign a legal waiver of financial and parental responsibilities on making the donation and for the recipient/purchaser of the sperm to also sign a release, waiver, and confidentiality agreement on receipt. But in the eyes of the law, who can sign for the child? In such cases, it is not at all clear that a parent, here the mother, can waive the legal rights of the child.

All this adds up to a potentially risky situation for the donor, unless, as noted, the child is later legally adopted. As to the legitimate father who stores his sperm for use after his death, he would be well advised to simultaneously establish some form of trust for the child or children who may result from the use of the sperm, since it could be that, depending on how long after his death they are born, the law might not provide them with any rights. (Note that such a trust would present some very interesting drafting challenges and should only be undertaken by an attorney expert in the field of trust law.)

Special Family Allowances

Every state has laws that offer some protection for the welfare of a surviving spouse and, to a lesser extent, minor children of the deceased in cases where the deceased did not provide for them in his or her will or where the family requires financial assistance while the estate is being settled. For the most part, these provisions favor the surviving spouse, and amounts allowed for the care of minor children, surprising as it may seem, are usually quite limited. In Massachusetts, for instance, while a widow's allowance is only limited by need and by the proportion the allowance bears to the total estate, allowances for minor children may not exceed $100 per child. As noted previously, however, a minor child has the right to sue the estate of a Massachusetts parent for support, since the parent had the legal obligation to support the child while the parent was alive. Most states, however, do provide shelter, at least, for the minor child for a period after the parent's death.

Such "shelter" provisions, frequently called "Homestead" rights, usually allow the surviving spouse and the deceased's minor children to continue to live in the home (even though it may have been left to someone else under the will), at least until the children reach the age of majority, and, in many cases, the surviving spouse may continue to reside there for the rest of his or her life, whether there were children or not.

WIDOW'S ALLOWANCES

Actually, *widowers* are now generally permitted to receive allowances from the estate, too, but for hundreds of years such allowances were given only to widows because of the husband's legal obligation to support and provide for his wife. These widow's allowances stood in addition to any Homestead allowance.

The purpose of the allowance, which is paid out of the deceased spouse's *probate* estate, is to provide for the care and support of the surviving spouse *during the period of administration* of the deceased spouse's estate. Knowing how long it can take to settle an estate, and considering the fact that distributions are not normally made to beneficiaries for many months at best, the probate courts are empowered under the laws of every state to order that payments be made from the estate to the surviving spouse from the estate for his or her maintenance and support.

The widow's allowance ordered by the court takes priority over all other debts of the estate and may be paid to the spouse even though the estate is insolvent, or being sued or contested. It may be given to the spouse whether or not she is named as a beneficiary under the will, and even where there was no will. Furthermore, the allowance is available to the spouse *in addition* to any forced share she may take or other benefits she receives from the estate. Since it takes first priority, the allowance could, if large enough in proportion to the rest of the estate, disrupt or even reduce other bequests. In fact, if the estate were small enough, it could be used *entirely* for the widow's allowance and there would be no "estate" to administer, despite the fact that the deceased spouse left a will that contained bequests to others.

The amount of the allowance is always up to the court, which takes into consideration the size of the estate and the circumstances of the widow, such as age, health, general needs, and manner of living. It is this last consideration that often gives rise to the greatest discrepancies between what the widow thinks she should get, what the estate thinks she should get, and what the court gives her.

In one case in Georgia, the widow, Marylou, applied to the court for a year's allowance from her husband's estate, which was valued at over $300,000. In Georgia the procedure was to appoint an appraiser to determine approximately how much money Marylou would need for the twelve-month period. The appraisers came up with a figure of $75,000. After the executor (a bank) of her husband's estate recovered from the shock, they appealed to the court on the basis that the amount was excessive. The court agreed and reduced the allowance to $50,000. The executors, still unhappy with the amount, appealed to a higher court, arguing that while Marylou's husband was alive, he never spent more than $1,800 a year for support of the both of them! Since when did her manner of living warrant an expense of $50,000 for twelve months? The higher court agreed that the lower court was too generous and suggested that the amount of $3,500 would be more appropriate.

That was in 1950.

Only a year later, another case on widow's allowance illustrated even more dramatically how the accustomed manner of living has a great deal to do with the allowance. In this case, Millicent Hearst asked the court for a mere $10,000 a month to tide her over while the estate of her husband, William Randolph Hearst, was being settled. In view of Mrs. Hearst's accustomed style of living (and, of course, the size of Hearst's multimillion-dollar estate), the court granted her request.

Although the court has wide discretion in deciding the amount of the allowance and, in most cases, the length of time it will be paid, it has no discretion as to the persons who are entitled to be paid. For instance, even though a spouse may have been legally separated from her husband for years before his death, she may still be entitled to a widow's allowance on his death. And no matter how needy a widow may continue to be, if she remarries after her husband's death, any widow's allowance will immediately cease, as she is then no longer his widow.

The allowance is not automatic. It must be applied for by the surviving spouse within a reasonable time after the death of the other spouse and, as noted above, if the executor of the estate or the beneficiaries feel it is excessive, they can appeal the order. Few spouses would voluntarily waive the allowance after the other's death, but if the couple executed a prenuptial agreement waiving or limiting the spouse's allowance, this would obviously have a bearing on the court's order.

Since most estates take quite some time to settle, it is a good idea to consider applying for the widow's allowance soon after the death of a spouse to provide quick, liquid funds for the support of the survivor. However, if the surviving spouse already has adequate funds (from joint bank accounts, etc.) and is the beneficiary of the estate as well, she may forego the allowance, use her own funds for support, and simply wait for the estate to be settled. On the other hand, if she is not the only beneficiary, or if there is a substantial number of creditors who stand to take too large a bite out of the estate, then the surviving spouse should definitely apply for the widow's allowance.

8

Estate Management

One hundred dollars shall be expended by my executors for the purpose of buying booze and canapes for my friends. On second thought make it three hundred dollars because I don't want my friends to go away sober or serious.

—from the will of Wayne Morris

Clearly this is not a bequest but rather a direction to the executor of Morris's estate to spend a certain amount of money in connection with the funeral "ceremony." As such, is it a valid expense of the estate? If the expenditure were larger and therefore reduced the shares of the beneficiaries, would it still be honored? Is it paid before creditors of the estate are paid? Is it the executor's obligation to pay all such expenses out of estate funds? What if he uses his own funds? Can he later recover the money from the estate?

Who Pays the Debts and Expenses of the Estate—and When?

The administration of an estate operates on the same principle that applied when the testator was alive—a person must first attend to his own debts and expenses before he can give away what is left. With the exception of certain priority allowances given primarily to the surviving spouse as discussed in chapter 7, the beneficiaries of an estate can only take what is left after the appropriate debts and expenses of the estate have been paid. This, of course, leads to the questions of which expenses must be paid first and what is appropriate. In early English law (on which much of our law of wills is based), the deceased's funeral expenses and the costs of proving the will were given first priority over all other debts and expenses, and this is still generally the case. Using the general assets of the estate (that is, assets that are not already specifically encumbered by a mortgage or lien), the priority of payment is as follows:

1. Funeral expenses
2. Administration expenses
3. Taxes (federal and state)
4. Expenses of last illness
5. All other debts

Out of respect to the deceased and because of the obvious need to dispose of the body with dignity, funeral expenses are generally paid before any other debts or expenses of the estate. As explained below, however, there are certain limitations. For instance, funeral expenses must be reasonable in proportion to the entire estate, if possible, though in an estate of only a few thousand dollars this may not possible, for the entire estate may be consumed by the funeral expenses. On the other hand, the cost of a huge and extravagant monument may appear quite reasonable in a $10 million estate.

If the estate is insolvent (i.e., where the debts exceed the value of the estate), the funeral costs are still given priority but are often limited in amount. Furthermore, in such cases, the court would understandably not be so lenient in what it allowed as a funeral expense, although reason and respect for the deceased would still prevail. For instance, in one Pennsylvania case where the estate was insolvent, an unusually high sum had to be paid for a special oversized casket because of the huge size and weight of the deceased. The cost was questioned by the creditors as unreasonable (it wasn't clear what they suggested as an alternative), but the judge found it to be proper and allowable, since there was no other, less expensive way to inter the deceased with dignity.

In situations as the one above, the deceased's creditors have to act fast because the burial often takes place right after death and long before the will is probated or the executor is appointed. However, if the person is already buried (and the expense incurred) before the creditors have a chance to challenge the incurrence of the expenses, they can subsequently challenge the *payment* of those expenses, asking that their own claims be given equal priority. If the court feels that the burial expenses were excessive, it could limit the payment of such expenses and the gravedigger or funeral director might just have to take less than he bargained for. The typical estate, however, is *not* insolvent, and so in most cases the funeral and burial expenses are given their due priority, and, if reasonable, they are seldom questioned.

Funeral expenses have been held to include not only the direct costs of the funeral and burial but also the cost of burial plots, perpetual-care contracts, Masses, and, more commonly, tombstones and monuments, keeping in mind the ever-present requirement of reasonableness in proportion to estate. If in your will, for example, you direct that your executors engage a sculptor to carve a twenty-foot-tall marble statue of you holding a golf club, it is unlikely to happen unless you have a million-dollar estate and a place to put the statue. Furthermore, unless you tie the direction for such an elaborate memorial into a conditional bequest (as discussed in chapter 6), there is always the chance that your heirs will challenge the instructions. This is just what happened in the estate of Billy Rose, the famous showman and at one time the largest individual shareholder of AT&T.

Rose's will directed that a large and elaborate mausoleum be built for him (although Billy himself was an unusually small man). Unfortunately, his two sisters, who stood to inherit the $30 million estate, didn't agree and instigated a lengthy court fight to revise the will. Poor Billy had to lie in cold storage for two years before the case was finally resolved and he got his mausoleum.

Quite often, a surviving spouse will pay funeral expenses out of accessible funds in a joint bank account, even though there are other assets in the probate estate. If the estate is solvent and the surviving spouse is the sole beneficiary of the estate, this is not a problem. However, if the estate is insolvent or if the spouse is not the only beneficiary, she should seek reimbursement from the estate for the funeral expenses she paid; otherwise, she would just be increasing, at her own expense, the amount available to creditors and other beneficiaries.

Finally, the question of whether allowable funeral expenses would include the cost of refreshments, or "booze and canapes" as directed by Wayne Morris at the outset of this chapter, would depend upon whether the estate was solvent and upon whether the expenses were reasonable in proportion to the estate. This is just the type of expense that would be disallowed in an insolvent estate but unquestioned (if reasonable) in a solvent one. I suppose if there is a question, you could always give your executor the option of having a "cash" bar.

After funeral expenses come expenses of administration. Commonly, these would include executor's fees and attorney's fees in connection with proving the will, handling all matters for the executor in administering the estate, and defending an attack against the will or the estate. In addition, they would include all costs in discovering, collecting, and maintaining estate assets. As with all priority amounts, however, administrative expenses must be reasonable under the circumstances and anyone having an interest in the estate, such as creditors or beneficiaries, can ask the court to review and possibly disallow them if they are unreasonable.

Next in order of priority come taxes or other amounts due to federal and state governments. Of these, the federal taxes take first priority, then the state government. The type of taxes that fall into this level of priority normally include estate and inheritance taxes and income taxes owed by the deceased (and assessed by the government) *up to the time of death.* Taxes that accrue *after* that date are generally not given the same priority.

After taxes come the expenses of the deceased's last illness, but not in all states. In many states, these expenses are simply lumped in with all other expenses after the three enumerated above. In those states that give priority to expenses of the last illness, such expenses would normally include costs such as physicians' and hospital bills and medication relating to treatment of the illness that ended with the deceased's death.

After this category, the states vary considerably in giving preference to any other items of debt. Some, for example, recognize wages due to employees or rents due from the deceased as a tenant. However, as a general rule, the first three—*funeral expenses, administrative expenses,* and *taxes*—are given priority in all states.

The person responsible for the payment of all such charges is the executor of the estate (or the administrator, if there was no will). This responsibility is a very serious one, since if the executor fails to pay a debt that should have been paid or pays a debt that should not have been paid, he will be *personally* liable for those funds out of his own pocket unless he can show good cause for his error. As noted in earlier chapters, the executor normally will *not* pay any questionable debts until the creditor makes a claim against the estate for payment; every state provides a specified "open" period within which such claim must be made. If an unsecured creditor fails to make his claim within that period, he is likely to lose his right to recover unless he can show he never received notice of the person's death.

Many claims are not questionable, however, and the executor may, if he wishes, pay them at any time, assuming there are available funds to do so. If an executor in good faith uses his funds to pay a valid claim, he may later be reimbursed by the estate. In fact, if a third party advances funds to the executor for payment of a valid estate debt or if the third party pays the debt herself, she is similarly entitled to reimbursement from the estate, as illustrated above where a wife paid her deceased husband's funeral expenses out of her joint bank account. In either event, however, whether it is the executor or a third party, if the debt was overpaid or should not have been paid, there would only be partial or no reimbursement, accordingly. If the estate is insolvent, then a prudent executor will pay *no* debts at all until he has received approval of the probate court, since overpayment or improper payment will result in the executor being personally liable.

Even though an estate may be solvent and have plenty of assets to cover all costs, the next logical question is which of the estate assets are used to pay them. For instance, say that my uncle Mike left an estate consisting of $10,000 in cash and a home worth $80,000. His will leaves me a specific bequest of $10,000 and he leaves "all the rest" to my aunt Agnes (Uncle Mike's sister). As it turns out, there are debts and expenses of $13,000. Where does the money come from? Will I lose my $10,000 bequest?

The general rule is that unless the will provides otherwise, debts and expenses are first taken from the "residuary" estate, leaving the specific bequests, to the extent possible, intact. Therefore, in my example above, I would receive my $10,000 bequest because there is enough value in the residuary estate to cover the debts and expenses. Unfortunately for Aunt Agnes, however, there is only the home. In such a case Agnes would either have to come up with the $13,000 on her own, or sell (or mortgage) the home to pay the estate expenses. Relatively speaking, she would be much better off if she raised the money on her own, since a sale of the home under these circumstances would involve considerable additional estate expense, which *she* would indirectly have to bear.

If, on the other hand, there was enough cash or other liquid assets in the residuary estate, then the rule is that these assets are used first, and the real estate, if any, is *not* sold until the cash and other assets ("personal property") are used up. After the personal property in the residuary estate is used, then the real estate (in the residuary estate) may be sold and used to pay the expenses. When *all* of the residuary estate is used up, then and only then (*unless* the will states otherwise) are the specific bequests used to pay the debts, in the proportion they bear to each other. (This is called "abatement" and is discussed in detail in chapter 5.)

Investing Estate Assets

After paying all of the estate's debts and expenses, or perhaps while waiting until it is time to pay them, what do you do with all of the estate's money? Can you just deposit it in a simple bank account? If there are securities, must you hold them or should you sell them? In short, is the executor responsible for actively investing the estate's assets? Many people are under the mistaken impression that he is.

In fact, unless the will or the laws of the particular state specifically direct otherwise, the executor is under *no* duty to invest the estate funds. His primary responsibilities include discovering and collecting estate assets, paying all appropriate debts and expenses, and distributing the balance to the beneficiaries. This is not to say, however, that the executor need not pay attention to existing investments or that he can leave funds "idle." At the very least, any cash or liquid funds should be deposited into interest-bearing bank accounts. In this context, he is not necessarily bound to search for the highest income-producing investment; his first consideration must be protection of the principal, even if it means accepting a lower return.

If, on the other hand, the will instructs the executor to invest estate funds or state law imposes some duty to invest, then he must do so, and, when doing so, he must follow the "prudent man rule," which basically suggests that he invest in securities of well-established companies with long-term dividend records or, in the case of bonds, with ratings that are considered safe and suitable for this type of investment. Most states have what is called a "legal list" of investments that are considered suitable for funds held by fiduciaries, such as executors and trustees. Investments in securities included on the legal list or that are similar in all other respects, therefore, will usually be acceptable investments for an executor who is obliged to invest estate assets.

Occasionally, the executor "inherits" a questionable investment that the deceased was holding during his lifetime and is faced with the choice of making an unauthorized sale or watching the investment gradually sink in value. In such a case, he is not obliged to sell, but prudence should motivate him to ask the court and/or the beneficiaries for permission to do so. Obtaining the permission of either would normally take the executor off the hook for selling or failing to sell.

If the questionable investment consists of something the executor cannot sell, such as shares of stock in a small or privately held company, then he is under no obligation to take action other than to exercise the estate's right to vote as a stockholder of the company and to keep aware of the status of the stock and the company. An executor who is *not* obliged to invest would be well advised to avoid doing so and should simply place the funds in a safe bank, or, if there are large sums of money, perhaps in U.S. Treasury bills or notes. If an executor is not under a duty to invest but decides to do so anyway, he can be *personally* liable for any losses resulting from a bad investment, *even though* he acted in good faith, unless he can show that he made the particular investments at the beneficiary's *specific* request or at the court's direction.

The risk of personal loss for bad investments can be a serious one, especially where there are two or more executors and the investments are entrusted to one of them; this often happens when a family member and a professional person, such as an accountant, are named co-executors. Usually, the nonprofessional will let the professional do the investing, paying little or no attention to what he does with the funds, unaware that he could be personally liable for the professional's bad judgment. This is almost exactly what happen in the Shoddenfart estate.

Willi Shoddenfart's will named his brother, Otto, and his account, Morris, as co-executors of his estate. After Otto and Morris were appointed by the court, Otto, not being very familiar with the technicalities of the job, left everything up to Morris. Although Willi's will made no mention of investing, there was quite a bit of cash in the estate—around $250,000—and Morris felt it would be in everyone's best interests to invest it "wisely."

During the next year or so while the estate was being settled, Morris did some investment "research," consulted with certain experts, and finally placed the estate funds in a number of securities that he thought would surely appreciate, as well as some very high-yielding bonds. Since Otto was co-executor, he was asked to co-sign the checks Morris made out to pay for the investments as well as checks to pay estate bills, but Otto never even inquired what the checks were for. In fact, he was quite pleased that Morris was taking care of all estate matters, feeling that even if he asked, he probably wouldn't have understood anyway.

As it turned out, a few of the stocks didn't do as well as Morris had hoped (they dropped about $57,000 in value by the end of the year) and two (out of three) of the high-yielding bonds defaulted on their interest payments. In the meanwhile, Morris didn't forget to take his executor's fee of $7,200, and Otto was thrilled to receive a check for $3,000 as his "fee."

Willi's spouse and son, the beneficiaries of his estate, complained to the court, asking that Morris and Otto be held responsible for the stock losses and lost interest, and return their fees as well. Morris claimed that he acted in good faith and that he took the trouble to get expert advice, so he should not be liable. Otto argued that he had nothing to do with the whole matter, that he didn't know a bond from a doughnut, and that Morris never told him a thing about what he was doing, so how could he be responsible?

The court noted that Willi's will gave the executors no authority to invest the funds, and therefore, any investments made by the executors were made at their own risk. Furthermore, as co-executors, they had the duty to act jointly. When Otto was asked to sign checks he had at that time an opportunity *and an obligation* to inquire of Morris where the estate funds were going and why. He could not avoid that responsibility by ignoring it, and so he was held to be *equally* liable with Morris for the losses, and they were ordered to return the fees they received, as well.

Accounting to the Court and to the Beneficiaries

One of the primary duties of an executor or administrator is to provide an "accounting"—a detailed and accurate report of all estate assets and transactions relating to such assets. As explained in chapter 1, the executor is first required to determine the extent of all assets belonging to the estate, listing them on the inventory that is required to be filed with the probate court. The inventory is *not* an accounting but generally serves as the starting point of the executor's account, since those are the assets he has to administer and deal with in the settlement of the estate. As also noted, the *inventory*, and now the executor's *account*, deals with *probate* assets. Therefore, jointly held assets, insurance proceeds payable to a beneficiary other than the executor, and assets held in a trust will *not* be included in either the executor's inventory or the executor's account unless the executor takes the position that despite the ostensible title or arrangement to avoid probate, they are *probate* assets and he intends to take the necessary legal steps to bring them into the probate estate, as discussed in chapter 2.

After his appointment by the court, the executor is normally required to file an accounting at regular intervals, usually on an annual basis, although the probate court can order him to account at any time. If no account has been filed and the estate is ready to be settled, the executor will file his "first and final" account.

The first annual account will usually begin with the assets shown on the inventory; then it will show any additional assets that have come into the executor's possession. It will list all income and sources of that income, and it will show any losses realized, as well as all disbursements, including payment of estate debts, widow's allowances, expenses, and taxes. The balance of all this is what the executor has in his hands at the time of the account. This report will be filed each year until the estate is settled, showing the complete status of the estate (in probate) at the end of each accounting period. If the account is a final account, it will also show distribution of the balance of the estate to the beneficiaries, so that the balance shown on the account to the probate court is zero. When this happens and the court (and all other interested parties) approve of the account, the executor is discharged and the estate is closed.

If after the estate is closed the executor discovers additional estate assets, he must file a supplemental account and go through the approval process once again as to the new assets.

Where there are co-executors, only one account need be filed, but each executor must account to the court for all estate assets in his actual possession, and, as discussed above, each is fully responsible for administering the estate, even though only one does the work.

If someone other than the executor is in possession of estate property but won't give it up, that third party may be compelled to account to the court as to that property. Indeed, this very important legal mechanism is often used to recover estate property that has been taken by someone without authorization.

In one case, for instance, one of four daughters was taking care of her mother and decided, after her mother died, that she would help herself to the mother's jewelry. The mother's will named another daughter as executrix and left her jewelry to the four girls equally. The executrix filed a request in the probate court asking that her sister be ordered to give an "accounting" of the jewelry she had in her possession and to deliver it to the executrix for administration in accordance with the mother's will. The other daughter steadfastly refused, and the court finally ordered her arrested for contempt of court with the threat of jail if she didn't comply. She was then persuaded to turn over the jewelry.

Similar exposures to penalties such as personal liability and even jail time face the executor who fails to account when obliged to do so. Not only can the court compel an accounting from the executor or administrator, but *any* party who has an interest in the estate can ask the court to order him to account. Obviously, this includes all beneficiaries of the estate, but it also includes creditors of the estate. The creditors of *beneficiary* (as opposed to creditors of the *estate*), however, may not compel an accounting unless they have legally attached the beneficiary's interest in the estate. (In this case, the attachment would occur when a court, in recognition of the creditor's potential claim against the beneficiary, ordered the beneficiary's share of the estate to be held in abeyance pending the outcome of the creditor's claim.)

Each beneficiary and anyone else having a legal interest in the estate are entitled to notice of the executor's accounts; otherwise, the accounts cannot be approved by the court. Notice usually consists of sending the beneficiaries and other interested parties a copy of the proposed account. This is required in order to give the beneficiaries and other parties an opportunity to review the executor's financial administration and see that their interest and assets are being properly handled. It also gives the beneficiaries the opportunity to *object* to the executor's account if there are any entries or transactions that the beneficiary wishes to question. The beneficiaries' objections to entries or transactions should be sent to the court in writing with a copy to the executor, and should be very specific as to the items that are in question and why. A general objection to the account without specifics will usually be dismissed by the court.

Despite all of these serious requirements to account to the court and the beneficiaries, the executor's account can be waived in most states if all interested parties assent to the waiver. Of course, this assumes that all creditors have been paid and that no new creditors will surface within the allowable period. Dispensing with the account, where allowable, can help to keep the estate "private," since the account, like all other documents filed in the probate court, becomes *public* information once it is filed.

Waiver of accounts, and in many cases even inventories, is not uncommon in estates of the rich and famous in order to keep estate matters private, even though the will or the estate had to be probated. In the case of President John F. Kennedy's estate, for instance, the probate records at the Suffolk County Probate Court in Boston show that he left a will and that an executor was appointed, but that's it. There is no inventory, no accounting, and no other estate information in the public file. Since no interested party ever complained about it, nothing else was done, and technically, to this day, the estate was never closed!

However, if the executor's account is never filed and the estate is not closed, the executor is never discharged from responsibility. This means that at some future date a beneficiary could decide to challenge the executor's acts and, if the beneficiary was successful, the executor would be personally liable, long after the estate was "settled." For this reason, most professional executors (such as attorneys or banks) will always file their accounts, including a final account, and ask that the accounts be allowed (approved by the court). Once the final account is allowed, the executor is discharged.

Remember, only parties in interest can compel an accounting and, except in a very few states, such as New Hampshire, the court will seldom take it upon itself to compel one unless there is some apparent reason to do so, such as fraud or deceit or other improper conduct. If all the creditors are paid and all the beneficiaries are happy with the settlement, therefore, the estate could be settled quietly and privately, although there are risks of reopening for some reason at a later date.

When You Can Get Your Share

After all debts, expenses, and taxes are paid, and the final account has been approved, the beneficiaries can finally get their shares, although this does not usually happen as quickly as the beneficiaries would like. Because the executor, in most cases, must wait until the allowable period for creditors' claims has expired and until the tax authorities are satisfied, it may take a year or more, under the best of circumstances, before final distribution of the estate. Meanwhile, however, it is possible (and is often the case) for the executor to make *partial* distributions to the beneficiaries if such distributions clearly will not affect the ability to pay creditors and all other costs, including taxes.

Unfortunately, the executor has the right to withhold distributions if administration or circumstances of the estate call for it. For instance, distribution may be withheld pending resolution of a lawsuit against the estate, or where there is a contest over beneficiaries' rights under the will. Many states provide a certain period after which beneficiaries must be paid unless a court or the will permits otherwise. And even where a justifiable delay occurs, the beneficiaries would then be entitled to interest on their shares starting after the prescribed period by the laws of the state or under the terms of the deceased's will. For instance, in Massachusetts beneficiaries are entitled to begin receiving interest on their bequests if the bequests are not paid by nine months after the appointment of the executor. But if, for example, the deceased's will directs that the beneficiaries be paid six months after his death, interest on their bequests will begin at that time, not after nine months. Similarly, if the deceased provided that payments would not be made until two years after her death, interest on unpaid bequests would only begin to run after the two-year period provided in the will. A provision in the will to pay bequests early, by the way, does not give the executor the right to pay them out before debts, expenses, and taxes are paid; it merely determines the time when interest begins.

How you get paid. Unless the will provides that you should receive a specific item of property, your share may be paid out to you in any manner that gives you your fair share of the estate. For instance, if the will leaves you 100 shares of General Eclectic stock, then you will get 100 shares of this stock and not cash. If the estate does not have 100 shares of General Eclectic stock, and the bequest was not "adeemed," as explained in chapter 4, the executor must purchase the shares to fulfill the bequests.

With residuary shares, however, the beneficiaries often receive a combination of both cash and "in kind" distributions. A distribution "in kind" is one where you receive a share of the items that are left in the estate. For instance, say that after all debts, expenses, and taxes have been paid, there are three equal beneficiaries who are to divide $150,000, 300 shares of stock, and a car. Unless otherwise agreed, each will get $50,000 in cash, 100 shares of stock, and one-third the proceeds from the sale of the car (although, if they wished, they could own the car as tenants-in-common). Alternatively, if the car was worth about $12,000, two of the beneficiaries could receive 100 shares of stock plus $54,000 in cash, and the other beneficiary would get 100 shares of stock, $42,000 in cash, and the car. If the beneficiaries cannot agree on a split (such as where the item is not divisible and more than one wants it), then the executor can order the item sold and divide the proceeds, and if the item is auctioned off, then the beneficiaries can battle it out there.

If a beneficiary owes money to the estate (because he owed money to the deceased), his share of the estate may be reduced by the amount he owes and he will have little to say about it. This happens quite frequently, as where a child continually pressed the parent for "loans," which the parent advanced. If over a period of time the parent advanced a disproportionate amount to one child, she may decide to mention that fact in her will and provide that the child's share should be reduced by that amount. When this happens, the share *will* be reduced, regardless of whether the child even signed a "legal" note, and regardless of whether any such note was enforceable. About the only defense a child would have in such a case would be proof that he paid back the funds *after* the will was signed.

When the time comes to divide the spoils, the executor must make the necessary transfers to the beneficiaries. Shares of stock or other securities, for instance, can either be endorsed over to the beneficiaries or, as happens more often, be reregistered by the executor in the beneficiaries' names (or as they direct) and have them delivered to the beneficiaries. Cash or other liquid funds are, of course, paid by check, and personal property (such as furniture, jewelry, etc.) is often transferred by mere delivery of the item to the beneficiary, although occasionally it will be accompanied by a letter of "deed" stating that it is being transferred. If it is a valuable item of personal property, such as a work of art or a stamp or coin collection, you should ask for and keep some written verification that it came to you through the estate.

Real estate is handled differently. In most states, persons who inherit real estate (called the "devisees," where there was a will, or "heirs" where there was no will) *automatically* take title to the real estate on the death of the person from whom they are inheriting, subject, of course, to debts, expenses, and taxes of the estate. That is, there is *no* need for the executor to deed the property over to them nor for the court to order a transfer. The property becomes theirs on the deceased's death. This is occasionally the source of some confusion among beneficiaries, since they wonder how the property could be theirs if it is still "in the name of" a deceased parent and the beneficiaries have no deed with *their* names on it. The change in title is made "legal" by referring to the probate proceedings and the will at the registry of deeds where the property is recorded. The registry thus verifies the change of ownership and, therefore, there is usually no need for the executor to deed the real estate to the beneficiaries. If, however, the property is being *sold* from the estate to a third party, then the executor, after obtaining the court's permission to sell the property, will give a deed from the estate to the third-party buyer.

Even though the beneficiaries inherit the property as of the date of the deceased's death, it does not necessarily follow that they can sell it immediately. Because it may be subject to the payment of estate costs and taxes, a buyer would be reluctant to purchase it until he is satisfied that he can take the property free and clear of all such costs. The buyer will usually ask for some form of assurance (usually a release from the tax authorities and/or court approval of the sale) before the sale is finalized.

Real estate that is left to more than one beneficiary will pass to those beneficiaries as tenants-in-common (with no survivorship rights) unless the will provides otherwise. Thus, a bequest of the home "to my sons, Clark and Clive, in equal shares," leaves Clark and Clive as tenants-in-common. This makes sense, because under this form of ownership, if Clark dies, his half of the real estate will pass to his heirs, and vice versa.

Quick Settlement Procedures for Certain Estates

Many states have special, abbreviated probate procedures if the estate does not exceed a certain amount, if no one objects to the use of the "small estate" settlement procedure, and, of course, if the will does not direct otherwise. In Texas and Arkansas, for example, if the total *probate* estate does not exceed $50,000 in value, probate may be *avoided* simply by filing an affidavit (sworn statement) to the probate court explaining the status of the estate and disposition of the property (of course, estate debts and expenses must still be paid). Tennessee's "small estate" procedure is allowed if the probate estate does not exceed $10,000 and a similar affidavit is filed. Florida law permits you to avoid probate where the estate does not exceed $25,000; in Massachusetts the limit is $15,000 and in California, $100,000.

Some states, such as Arizona, Colorado, Indiana, and Hawaii, for example, allow an abbreviated probate procedure regardless of the size of the estate if the person requesting the abbreviated procedure files all the necessary information (including a copy of the will) and makes certain representations to the court, basically assuring the court that the abbreviated probate procedure is in the best interests of everyone involved and will not prejudice any interested parties, including creditors of the deceased.

The small-estate procedures only apply to *probate* property. Thus, if a Tennessee estate consisted of a half million dollars' worth of stocks and bonds the deceased held in *joint* names with his spouse (or in a living trust, which is preferable) and a $9,000 bank account in his own name, the estate could qualify for a *small*-estate administration, since the probate estate only consisted of $9,000, which is below the $10,000 limit for small estates in Tennessee.

Remember, however, that the use of the small-estate procedure is always subject to denial if anyone contests the disposition of property or if a valid creditor is prejudiced by it or if the testator's will instructs otherwise.

Whether the estate is large or small, however, the important thing is that it is properly settled and that the beneficiaries get their money as quickly as possible—at least that's how the beneficiaries see it. Occasionally, the deceased anticipates their eagerness to get at the money and provides for a waiting period of his own. A somewhat extreme example of this was the estate of Mr. Zalewsky, who must have had quite a sense of humor. Mr. Zalewsky left his will in an envelope bearing the instructions: "To be opened after my death." It was so opened, and inside there was another envelope with the words: "To be opened six weeks after my death." After the prescribed six weeks, that envelope was opened, only to find a third envelope, which directed: "To be opened one year after my death." Out of respect (there is no legal obligation to follow such instructions—in fact, if the location of the will is known, there is an obligation to produce it to the court within a very short time after the death), the heirs waited a year, opened the envelope, and, you guessed it, found a fourth envelope! Between envelopes, indecision, and ignorance, they ended up waiting *five years* until Zalewsky's will was finally uncovered and read, and when it was, it proved to be just as eccentric as the envelope game. Zalewsky provided that half of his estate was to be liquidated and the funds deposited in a bank account, to stay there with interest accumulating for one hundred years, at which time it would be divided among his descendants. Now *that's* a long time to wait.

9

Executors

I want it that mine brother Adolph be my executor and i want it that the judge should please make Adolph put up plenty bond and watch him like hell. Adolph is a good business man but only a dumpkoff would trust him with a busted pfenig.

—from the will of Herman Oberweiss

Although Herman may not have been very articulate, he seemed to have a pretty good understanding of the role of the executor. And even though he didn't trust his brother, he knew that the court could "watch him like hell" and that if Adolph messed up or ran off with some of Herman's money, Herman's beneficiaries would still be protected since they could collect on Adolph's "bond." So, was his brother a good choice? Should you generally name a family member as executor? Does it make a difference if the executor you name is also a beneficiary? Or should you name your lawyer? Or a bank? What if your executor resides out of state? Or what if you simply don't have anyone you can name—should you still make out a will?

The Russian term for executor is *dushe prikazchik,* which means "spokesman for the soul." And this is just what the executor is—one who speaks for the deceased in the settlement of his estate and the carrying out of the instructions in his will. If you make out a will, therefore, you certainly should name an executor. If there is simply no one you can name, it is possible, as you will see, to make out your will and leave the selection of executor to be done by someone or some institution you trust. In any case, the choice of executor should be well thought out, as it is an important job and the correct choice can make a tremendous difference in the smooth settlement of your estate.

Executor vs. trustee. The very first distinction you must make is the difference between "executor" and "trustee." Most people think they are one and the same, but their functions are *very* different. Your *executor* simply settles your estate and has no authority to decide who gets what portion of your estate. His job is finished when the estate is settled, which is usually a year or so after your death. Your *trustee* manages and distributes the money and/or property you left in trust, which often takes place after your estate is settled, and he may well have substantial discretion to pay or withhold benefits to or from your surviving spouse, children, or others. The trustee's job may last for many years after your death or after your children's deaths, and, in some cases, for years after the deaths of your grandchildren. Even when the executor and trustee are the same person or organization, the courts treat the positions as entirely separate.

Briefly, the executor's job is to collect and preserve all estate assets, pay all appropriate debts, expenses, and taxes, and distribute the remainder according to the terms of your will. (The executor is also responsible for burying the deceased testator in a manner suitable to his estate and his station in life.) If you have no will, an *administrator* is appointed by the court to do all of this, except that instead of distributing to people you choose, the administrator would distribute your property according to state laws of intestacy. You cannot name your own administrator.

The procedure for appointment of executor usually takes thirty to sixty days in most states. If there are pressing estate matters that must be taken care of immediately after death, those states allow for the quicker appointment of a "temporary" executor (or temporary administrator if there was no will). The temporary executor may be appointed very quickly (usually only a few days after application, if no one objects) and serves until the permanent executor is appointed.

Of course, if you have no estate to administer (that is, no *probate* estate), then it is not necessary for your executor to be appointed by the court, although, as discussed in detail in chapter 2, this does *not* mean you won't need a will.

If you do have a probate estate to administer, then on your death your will is submitted for probate and, unless there is some objection, the court will appoint the executor you chose in your will. No matter where you made out your will and no matter where your property is located, your will will be submitted for probate in the county of your *domicile* at the time of your death, even though you may have died in another county or another state. If you left property in your own name in another state, however, another set of probate proceedings will have to be taken out in that "foreign" state (called "ancillary administration"), but only after your will is first approved and your executor appointed in the state of your domicile. Your executor would then attend to the ancillary administration of the property in the foreign state. (This is usually a time-consuming and costly procedure and can be completely avoided with proper planning, as explained in chapter 11.)

The executor's bond. To secure the performance of his duties without damage or loss to the estate, the executor is required to file a "bond," which is simply the executor's personal promise to pay or make good any such damages or losses. This, of course, is only helpful if the executor is financially able to repay the loss, and it also assumes he is still around to do so! If you leave your millions to your children, and your executor runs off with your wife and your money, his personal bond won't do the children much good. For this reason, most states require the executor to have "sureties" on his bond. A surety is someone *else's* personal guarantee that if the executor causes losses to the estate and doesn't pay, then that person who provided the guarantee will pay. A surety can be personal (another individual) or corporate (an insurance company that insures against the executor's losses). Using individual sureties is less costly because you would normally use a friend or relative, and it is unlikely that he or she would charge you for this favor. Perhaps if friends and relatives realize the potential risk, however, they would charge you. In most instances, they sign as sureties without fully understanding what it means. Clearly, a corporate surety is best and, although it does involve a cost to the estate, it is usually very reasonable in light of the added safety it offers.

Unlike Herman Oberweiss, however, many testators have so much confidence in their executors that they include a provision in their wills that *dispenses* with the executor's bond, and many but not all states allow this. Most of the other states that do not allow the dispensation of a bond will instead allow the dispensation of sureties, so that the executor must give his personal bond but need not secure guarantees on it. Whenever a bond is required, the executor will not be appointed by the court until the bond is filed with the court. In general, most prudent professionals feel that a bond should always be required, whether you have a brother like Adolph or not.

Who Can or Should Be Your Executor?

You are free to choose just about anyone you want to act as executor of your estate, within certain limits, of course, and if your choice is within these limits, the court is obliged to follow your choice in most cases. Generally, you may not appoint a minor or incompetent person or, in many states, a convicted criminal. Otherwise, the appointment will not be rejected even though the person is extremely old, or suffers from a handicap, or has no business experience, or is a heavy drinker, or is a creditor of the estate, or a witness to the will, or a beneficiary, or is thought to be mentally or morally "impure." Having all this in mind, it is relatively safe to say that the law recognizes your right to select any competent person you choose and does not demand a high standard for the position. This is not to say that a court would approve an appointment that would lead to nothing but trouble, but, in general, it would give preference to your selection.

Don't forget that apart from court approval, one other approval is essential to your selection of executor—that of the executor himself. It's a good idea to discuss the matter with the person you choose to be sure he will accept the position. After all, it is not an easy job you are assigning him, and he can, if he wishes, decline the appointment after your death. If this happens, then the successor executor named in your will (if, in fact, you named one) steps up to the plate.

Since there is this right to decline, as well as the possibility of the executor you originally selected dying before you or becoming ill, or, in the case of a lawyer, a bank, or a trust company, going out of business, or, for any other reason being unable to accept the position, you should always name at least one successor executor. Although there is no limit to the number, it is rare to see more than two successors named. If you initially name two or three co-executors (that is, "I appoint my sons Andrew and Alexander as co-executors of my estate"), you must consider whether you want one or the other to serve alone if either can't serve.

You can also make the appointment conditional upon some other occurrence, such as the attainment of a certain age, completion of college, remaining single, being a resident of your state, etc.

Nonresidents, provided they otherwise qualify, are generally acceptable in most states, although appointing a nonresident may not be a good idea. First of all, there are practical problems a nonresident will face in dealing with property and creditors in another state, as well as in appearing in court, if necessary, and signing documents for the court, etc. Also, there may be added expenses because when a nonresident is appointed, he must appoint a resident "agent" in the local state for legal purposes. Furthermore, the estate will incur additional expenses in paying for the nonresident's travel to and from the local state to attend to the estate administration. If at all possible, therefore, try to keep your selection local.

And if for some reason you are simply at a loss to come up with any logical choice, then you can leave the choice up to someone else. That is, your will can say, "The executor of my will shall be chosen by the senior partner of the law firm of Nailem, Dodgem and Chargealot, but shall not be a member of that firm," or, "The executor of my estate shall be nominated and appointed by the then serving Rabbi of Temple Fitzpatrick in Boston, Massachusetts," etc. Very few testators use this substitute appointment approach, but if you decide to be one of the few, be sure the person or organization you choose to do the selecting is one that will make a sensible choice and remember that it is preferable to choose a position rather than an individual (i.e., "the senior partner of the law firm of Clark & Cluck," rather then "John Clark, Esq.").

Whomever you choose or whatever method you use, it must be *clear* and *definite.* If your will is considered to have failed to name an executor, the court will appoint one for you. This is illustrated in the case of Marshall Blackburn, who appointed "one of my sisters" as executrix of his will. When Blackburn made out the will all three of his sisters were alive, but when he died only *one* survived him. Therefore, it should have been pretty clear, you would think, that the one sister surviving would be the one to be appointed executrix. Not so, the court said. The appointment of "one of my sisters" was ambiguous and therefore an insufficient appointment. The "one" could easily have been either of the two who died, and, if so, the surviving sister would have no right to be named executrix. To hold otherwise, the court would be rewriting Blackburn's will and courts are always reluctant to do that. Blackburn could have easily avoided the problem by saying "my oldest surviving sister," which would have clearly selected a particular one, whether all three or only one survived.

Whether the original or the successor or one nominated by some other source, the executor is appointment only after notice is given to all interested parties that he was nominated by you and is about to be appointed by the court, if no one has a valid objection. Notice for the appointment of the executor usually accompanies and is integral to the notice for the probate of the will. Anyone objecting to the allowance of the will automatically objects to the appointment of the executor, since there can be no executor without a will. It is quite possible, however, to consent to the allowance of the will but object to the appointment of the executor, simply by wording your objection accordingly, but remember, you can't object simply because you don't like the person; you must have some valid grounds for objection.

As noted earlier, the standards for appointment of an executor are not very high, so grounds for objection are somewhat limited. That is to say, the person named by the testator in his will will normally be appointed by the court, despite lack of high intelligence or experience and despite the fact that the named person stood in a hostile or potentially hostile position with the heirs and beneficiaries. For example, I have seen a number of cases where the testator named his ex-wife as executrix to administer the estate for the benefit of his widow, and at least one case where a married man named his mistress as executrix. In all such situations, although the family and beneficiaries may fume with anger over the appointment, there is usually very little they can do, since that particular relationship does *not* disqualify the executrix from serving. In such cases, the court's response is: "We must appoint her; but if she subsequently fails to properly perform her duties as executrix, you are free to ask us to remove her."

Good choices/bad choices. Whether you made a good choice or a bad choice in naming your executor, that is, whether your executor will accomplish a smooth, tax-wise, and efficient settlement of your estate or whether he will instead milk the estate dry, prolong settlement, make questionable tax decisions, and continually fight with the beneficiaries, can only be determined after the fact. Other than the protection offered by the executor's bond, there is no guarantee that your lawyer will do a perfect job, or that a bank won't botch up the investments, or that your brother-in-law won't run off with the money. There are, however, some guidelines that may help reduce the possibility of a bad choice.

The first issue to consider is whether you should choose a professional, such as an attorney or a bank, or a nonprofessional, such as your spouse, your brother-in-law, or your barber. To a great extent, this depends upon the size and nature of your estate. If the estate is of moderate size (i.e., no complicated tax issues involved) and very liquid (i.e., savings, investments, and a home), and if you do not anticipate any family disputes, then I would say it would be acceptable to have a family member, such as a spouse and/or an adult, responsible child, as executor of your estate. If you do anticipate family disputes in the settlement of your estate (even though it may only be over who gets the grandfather clock or mother's engagement ring, which is often the start of a larger dispute), then you should consider having an independent executor, not necessarily a professional, but merely someone outside the immediate family.

If, on the other hand, your estate is somewhat more extensive, such as one that includes income-producing real estate or out-of-state property or a closely held business, or anything else that will require expertise in handling, or if the estate is simply a large one, then you should definitely consider a professional executor. If you do have a professional, remember that you can also name a family member to act as *co-executor* with the professional. This way a member of the family can keep closely involved with the process of settlement as well as all the necessary decisions and elections that must be made, and this in turn will remove some or all of the mystery that often accompanies a professional's handling of the estate that can make a family suspicious.

If you do make a bad choice (of course, *you* will never know it), your beneficiaries do have the right to ask the *court* to remove the executor, as discussed in detail later in this chapter. As you will see, you might consider giving them the right to remove the executor and appoint another. Although there is no certainty the *court* will honor your directions (I know of no case or law on the issue), it certainly can't hurt.

Executor's Powers

How many of you have heard the story about the newspaper advertisement that read, "Practically New Cadillac Sedan in Perfect Condition. Estate Must Sell—$50." Most readers dismissed the ad as a hoax, but one adventurous young man decided to check it out. Sure enough, he found a gorgeous, gleaming Cadillac, and the seller, the executrix of the deceased owner's estate and also his widow, confirmed that the young man could have the car for only $50! It seemed, so the story goes, that in his will, the widow's late husband specified that his Cadillac was to be sold and the proceeds paid to his mistress. Is this a true story? Did the widow/executrix have the power to do this?

One of the most common misconceptions about executors is the extent of their powers in administering an estate. It is often thought that the executor has the ability to change or withhold bequests or to otherwise exercise control over how estate assets will be sold or distributed, disregarding the provisions of the will. *This is simply not so.* As noted several times before, the executor's job is simply to settle the estate and distribute the remaining assets *according to the terms of the will* and in the best interests of the beneficiaries, whoever they may be.

The story of the Cadillac, the widow, and the mistress, therefore, is *not* true. If it were true up to the point of the sale for $50, then the story would go on to say that the mistress asked the court to order the widow to pay, out of her own pocket, the difference between the $50 and the fair value of the Cadillac. And the court would do it.

In fact, the executor's powers are derived from the will. That is, your will can contain extensive powers for the executor or none. If no powers are specifically granted, it is nevertheless presumed that the executor has the basic powers necessary to carry out the terms of your will, with the possible exception that if real estate must be sold, the executor must obtain formal permission from the court to do so (a "license to sell"). Although many simple form-book wills omit reference to the executor's powers, it is unwise to do so, since if there is a subsequent question of his authority, he must appeal to the probate court to decide the question, which adds unnecessary delays and expense to the settlement of the estate.

For this reason, attorneys drafting wills will usually grant the executor all "statutory" powers given by the particular state (most states have standard powers that may be granted simply by reference to the particular law), or they may enumerate specific powers. It is not unusual to make these powers very broad so there will be no question as to the executor's authority to enter into any necessary or advisable transactions in the settlement of the estate. For instance, an executor may be granted the powers to employ agents, attorneys, stockbrokers, etc., the power to exchange, mortgage, or lease property, to lend or borrow money on behalf of the estate, to compromise claims (reach a settlement with the claimant) for or against the estate, to retain existing investments or make new investments, and, if a business is involved, the power to continue the business.

Whether you want to or need to grant any or all of these powers to your executor depends upon the size and nature of your estate. The important thing to remember is that even though you may grant your executor broad powers, it does *not* mean that he can change your wishes as expressed in your will. For instance, the power to "mortgage, lease, or exchange property" does *not* mean that your executor can swap the Cape Cod summer home you left to your daughter for a winter home in Florida, nor does it mean he can place a big mortgage on it or lease it to someone else before he gives it to her. The only reason he would be authorized to do any of these things would be if it became necessary in the course of settling the estate for payment of debts, expenses, and taxes. And as discussed in chapter 8, specific bequests are generally the last items to be touched for payments of estate expenses.

Remember, it is the duty of the executor to act in the best interests of all parties of interest in the estate, and this clearly includes the beneficiaries, whether or not they all get along.

Executor's Fees

Under early English law, the executor of an estate was considered to be an honorary position, so his services were to be performed without compensation. In the United States that practice quickly changed. It is well established that executors (and administrators) are entitled to "reasonable compensation" for the services they render to the estate and the beneficiaries, and this is the case even though the executor may also be a beneficiary of the estate. Taking a fee is certainly not mandatory, however, and, in fact, it is not uncommon for a family member to serve without compensation. But when the executor is also a principal beneficiary, there are situations in which taking an executor's fee can actually save the estate some money, particularly in larger estates where a tax is due, even though the executor's fee is taxable income to the executor. For instance, if the estate is large enough to be in a 50 percent estate tax bracket and the executor has little other income and is in a 28 percent income tax bracket, taking a $50,000 fee will only produce a $14,000 income tax to the executor, but will save the estate $25,000, for a savings of $11,000.

To be properly payable, the executor's fee should be approved by the court *prior* to payment, and is then normally taken from the residual estate. If a beneficiary objects to the amount of the fee, she would usually do so at the time the executor files his account, or as soon as she learns of it, if the account is not yet filed. And *don't* confuse the executor's fee with the attorney's fee. They are separate and distinct roles and generate separate and distinct fees. The special situation where the attorney also acts as executor is discussed below. In both cases, by the way, the fees must always be "reasonable."

What is reasonable depends upon the particular circumstances of the case and is based on the amount of time, trouble, and responsibility involved in settling the estate and the manner in which the executor performs his duties. It is also based on the value and nature of the assets that come into the executor's possession and for which he is held accountable. The question here arises as to *when* the value is taken. Should it be at the date of death or at the date of settlement? Or some average value in between. If the estate is worth $100,000 at the date of death and because oil is discovered on estate land it is worth $5 million at the time of settlement, what value should be used? Since the size and extent of the estate's assets have a direct bearing on the executor's responsibilities, newly discovered assets or an increase in value of existing assets will usually entitle the executor to a larger fee. However, if the increase in value has no bearing on his duties or responsibilities, such as a jump in the stock market that pushes up estate investments, then the executor's fee would not normally be affected.

Using value as a strict basis of compensation can be arbitrary. For instance, the executor of a $200,000 estate consisting of rented real estate and involving battles with tenants, housing authorities, and disgruntled beneficiaries, versus the executor of a $2 million estate held entirely in bank accounts and publicly traded stocks, all payable to the executor (as the beneficiary of the estate): Is it fair that the second executor should receive a fee of four or five times that of the first, when the first may have put in much more time and trouble? In such a situation as that of the first executor, it is likely that the court will approve a fee higher than normal, in view of the circumstances. In the second situation, however, it is unlikely that a beneficiary (if it were someone other than the executor) would be successful in getting a court to *reduce* the fee because the estate was so simple to settle.

The actual amount of the allowable fee varies from state to state. Many states simply adopt the "reasonable compensation" approach with no fixed amount, while others publish a commission schedule, establishing what are considered reasonable fees based on a percentage of the estate. New York, for instance, has a permissible executor's fee schedule that ranges from 5 percent of the first $100,000 of estate assets up to (or down to) 2 percent of estate assets over $5 million. In a $2 million New York estate, then, the executor of the estate would receive a fee of almost $50,000! And if there were *two* executors on an estate of this size, *each* would receive the full $50,000 fee! (Many states require co-executors to share the fee, as discussed below.)

California's schedule may appear a little more "reasonable." Its rates range from 4 percent of the first $100,000 to 1 percent on $1 million and over. If we move the $2 million New York estate to California, the executor's fee would "only" be about $33,000. Texas, on the other hand, always likes to think big, and this includes its executors' fees. In this state, the fee can be as high as 5 percent of the value of the estate. If our $2 million New York estate were situated in Texas, the fee could be as much as $100,000 (almost as good as being a beneficiary under the will!). *Note* that these illustrations assume an "orderly" settlement of the estate without will contests, tax audits, or other disruptions.

For a few more comparisons of the fees on our $2 million probate estate:

- In Florida the fee would be $55,000 (and *double* that if there are two executors!);
- In Iowa the fee would be $40,000; and
- In Connecticut the fee (based on the *gross* estate, which includes *non-probate* assets!) could be $78,000.

In *all* states the standard fees may be increased, as noted above, if "extraordinary services" are rendered. Extraordinary services that can generate extra fees typically include the sale of real estate, defending a claim against the estate, a will contest, or handling an estate tax audit.

In any event, it is *always* a good idea for the executor to *keep very careful records* of the time he spends on all estate matters, including details of conferences or trips made on behalf of the estate and conversations and conferences with the estate attorney. This information can be very valuable in the event the executor's fees are questioned.

Occasionally, the question of executor's fees is addressed in the will. That is, some testators attempt to fix the compensation of their executor by providing a specified amount in the will. If a testator does so and the named executor subsequently accepts the position, then in most states he is bound to do the job for the stated fee, or resign (assuming the court allows him to do so). Some states, although not the majority, allow the executor in such a case to ignore or even remove the will provision limiting fees and take a "reasonable" fee instead. If the will provides for no executor's fee or a ridiculously low fee, it is likely that most states would nevertheless allow the executor to take a reasonable fee, as it would not be in the best interests of the beneficiaries to do otherwise.

Occasionally, a testator who is overly concerned about the executor's fees may discuss the matter with his proposed executor and reach an agreement for fees. If you are certain that this person will outlive you and you have a pretty good idea of when you will die and how large your estate will be at the time, this might be a good idea, since the executor would be bound by the agreement he signs with you, assuming he subsequently accepts the position. In general, however, such agreements are rare, since few people are in a position to foretell the future.

Where there are two or more co-executors, the question of fees can be a problem. Should they divide a single fee? Or should each take a full fee? Unfortunately, the states are not consistent on this point. Some require them all to share a single fee, others allow a full fee to each, while still others simply look at all of the services performed and attempt to arrive at a reasonable fee for everyone concerned, which would appear to be the fairest approach. In view of this, if you plan to name three or four co-executors, you should first check the law in your state (if you care about the fees).

Frequently, because the testator has so much confidence in his attorney, he will name the attorney as executor of his estate. This raises the obvious question of whether the attorney should be allowed a fee for acting as executor, as well as a fee for acting as attorney for the estate. One could argue various ways over the years, but today's view is that an executor who also performs services as the attorney for the estate is entitled to fees for all services rendered in both capacities, provided that such fees are reasonable under the circumstances. In any case, remember that any interested party has the right to object to both executor's fees and legal fees and that both the executor's fees and the legal fees must be approved by the court.

Removing an Executor

Removal of an executor is always an adverse proceeding, where the executor and the parties seeking removal each have their own counsel. There is a court hearing and a decision is made on the matter. This shouldn't be confused with the voluntary resignation by the executor when he simply does not want to or cannot continue his duties. (Even in that case, the executor's resignation is valid only when accepted by the court, and there must be a valid reason for it, although it is usually accepted, provided the resigning executor files his accounting up to the time of his resignation.) Forcible removal of the executor by angry beneficiaries is entirely another matter.

Once the executor is chosen by the testator and appointed by the court, the creditors and beneficiaries of the estate are usually stuck with him unless he dies or becomes incompetent, or unless they can prove serious misbehavior on his part. This is not to say that it is impossible to remove an executor, only that it is very difficult. In most cases, beneficiaries wish to remove the executor because he is moving too slowly, or he is rude and unfriendly toward them, or he acts like the estate "belongs" to him, or he repeatedly refuses to give the beneficiaries information, or he keeps the estate funds in a bank account instead of investing in something else. None of these reasons is grounds for removal.

The general rule is that a court will remove an executor only if it can be *shown* to the court that he is *incapable* of performing his duties, or that he is *unsuitable* for the position, or that he has become *disqualified* since he was appointed.

Disqualification would occur, for example, where the executor was convicted of a crime (unrelated to the estate) and sent to jail. Becoming incapable of serving would include, as mentioned before, any physical or mental handicap, whether permanent or temporary, that would prevent him from performing his duties. The last criterion, "unsuitable," is the one that requires constant interpretation.

Although the term *unsuitable* can encompass a variety of conditions that would cause a court to question a person's ability to impartially serve as executor, two that seem to arise more than any others are *conflict of interest* and *misconduct* by the executor. Conflict of interest might occur, for instance, when the executor is required to sell closely held stock from the estate to a company in which he himself is a stockholder. As executor he would want to sell at a high price, whereas as stockholder he would want to buy at a low price. By itself, this type of situation is *not* a reason to remove the executor. If the deceased knew that the situation would arise when he named the person executor, then it is highly unlikely that the court would second-guess the deceased. If the situation arose subsequently, there is still not cause for removal, unless it can be *shown* that the executor is about to conclude a sale of the stock at a price unfavorable to the estate. At that point, the court might remove him as executor, and, of course, he would be personally liable for the loss.

Perhaps the most common reason for removal or attempted removal of the executor is misconduct. As noted above, what constitutes the necessary level of misconduct to warrant removal is one thing in the eyes of the beneficiaries and quite another in the eyes of the court. Generally speaking, the misconduct has to be pretty serious, to the point where it is actually damaging or threatens to damage the estate. It can include everything from habitual drunkenness to stealing from the estate. In between, causes for removal would include failure to file an inventory or accounting (although filing late is not cause for removal), failure to obey a court order, failure to perform his duties as executor, and generally any waste or mismanagement of the estate. Some of these terms, such as *waste* and *mismanagement,* are as vague as the term *unsuitable* and about the only way to explain it is by referring to the U.S. Supreme Court's response when asked to define pornography: "We can't define it," the Court said, "but we know it when we see it."

A clear example of misconduct that constitutes grounds for removal was in a case involving an estate that included four pieces of income-producing real estate. Some of the real estate needed repairs and so the executor hired carpenters and painters to do the work. While they were at it, however, the executor thought he might as well have them do a little work on his own home, to the tune of about $11,000. The workmen obligingly billed the executor for work done on estate property, including the work on his home. The charge was only discovered when one of the beneficiaries checked the accounting and thought the bill for repairs was unusually high for the work done. An investigation quickly revealed what had happened and the executor was just as quickly removed, but only after he repaid the $11,000 plus interest to the estate.

Misconduct is not always so clear, however, and not always the type of misconduct that warrants removal. In another, slightly more colorful case, Arthur Friswald, a widower who left his entire estate to his three daughters, thought he was wise in choosing his accountant, John Hoopes, as his executor. In performing his duties as executor, Hoopes found it necessary to communicate regularly with the girls, and in doing so, he became somewhat quite friendly with them. In fact, he became more than friendly with two of them and began seeing each privately. Neither realized he was having an affair with the other, until one night when one decided to confide in the other and told her of the affair with Hoopes.

Not surprisingly, the two sisters became furious, and in addition to certain other actions and epithets irrelevant to this book, they immediately petitioned the court to remove Hoopes as being "unsuitable" for the position. In his own defense, Hoopes pointed out that he faithfully and meticulously performed his duties as executor of the estate, and his relationship with the sisters in no way interfered with this. He further pointed out that he did not charge the estate for any of the private "conferences" he had had with the girls. The court had to side with Hoopes. As contemptuous as his behavior may have been, it said, it was unrelated to and did not affect the proper performance of his duties as executor of the estate. The fact that Hoopes performed additional "duties" was not cause for his removal.

As angry as they were over the court's denial of their petition, the Friswald sisters reached a state of rage when they found that their father's estate would have to pay the legal fees for Hoopes's "defense" and that they would have to pay their own legal fees.

In fact, as a general rule, the question of who pays the costs for the removal proceedings depends upon the outcome. If the incumbent executor successfully resists the attempted removal, his legal fees will be paid out of the estate on the basis that there was found to be no wrongdoing and it is in the best interests of the estate to keep the executor on board. On the other hand, if he is found unsuitable and is removed, then the (former) executor will not only pay his own legal fees but may be ordered to make restitution to the estate for any damages, which may include the return of fees previously paid to him.

Similarly, if the parties seeking to remove the executor are successful (the action may be brought *only* by a party interested in the estate), then their legal fees may be paid from the estate, on the basis that their action resulted in a benefit to the estate, in the form of removal of an unsuitable person who interfered with the proper settlement of the estate. If unsuccessful, like the Friswald sisters, they pay their own way.

To possibly avoid situations like this, a testator might consider including a carefully drafted provision in his will allowing the *beneficiaries* to remove the executor, if in *their* opinion he is unsuitable or becomes unsuitable for the position. Although there is no law on the validity and effectiveness of such a provision, and although one could argue that since the executor is appointed by the court, his removal is solely within the power and discretion of the court, there would nevertheless be no harm in including such a provision. The most that could happen in such a case is that the provision would be ineffective and ignored, and the best (short of it helping to facilitate a removal) is that the executor, upon seeing such a provision, may simply be more careful about doing his job properly for fear of testing the removal provision in court.

10

Will Contests, Lost Wills, and Beneficiaries' Rights

I leave my cousin Irving the sum of one dollar and I wish absolutely that he not get a penny more under my will. He has been responsible for my death and God will punish him. If he fights this will in any way I shall always haunt him and do everything possible to scare him.

—from the will of Quincy Bigger

At some point, the threat of a possible will contest crosses the mind of just about everyone who makes a will. It is commonly thought that anyone who is related to you can somehow challenge or upset the settlement of your estate just by hiring a lawyer to contest the will, and it won't matter how *well* the will was drawn, unless you left the rascal one dollar.

Can *any* will be contested by *anyone* who wants to make trouble for the deceased's estate? At what point can the will be contested and who pays for it? Did Quincy Bigger have to leave his cousin one dollar to prevent a contest? If the threat of haunting the potential contestant, as Quincy said he would do, is not enough, is there anything else you can do?

Although the facts of a juicy will contest can have all the excitement of an Agatha Christie novel and therefore often make the headlines, only a very small percentage of wills are contested, and most of the contests are *unsuccessful*. Studies have shown that over 99 percent of all wills offered for probate are ultimately admitted to probate. Unfortunately, the potential threat from a practical standpoint is not whether the contest will be successful, but whether an attempt at contest will be made. This is because many disgruntled, would-be beneficiaries will hire an attorney to contest the will and "tie up" the estate, primarily in the hopes of forcing a settlement rather than on the basis of truly supportable grounds for a contest. Given the tremendous expense of litigation, questionable claims are all too often settled, although they lack merit. As we will see, however, the laws are gradually changing in this area, and contesting a will is no longer a matter of mere whim or angry reaction.

In any case, don't confuse a *contest* of the will with a *claim* against the estate. If the deceased owed you money for goods or services, or for a loan you made to him, or if he has property of yours that you intend to get back, the necessary procedure is to make a claim against the estate *after* the will is allowed by the probate court, which in most cases is a lot less expensive and time-consuming than contesting a will.

Who May Contest Your Will

Contrary to popular belief, not anyone can contest a will. The general rule is that only persons "interested" in the estate have standing and are allowed to contest the will. A person is "interested" in the estate if he stands to gain something if his will contest is successful. For instance, if you die without a will, your estate will pass to your spouse and children. Therefore, a child has standing to contest a will, since if he is successful in overturning the will, he will gain a share of the estate. As pointed out in chapter 7, however, this does not mean that you *must* leave something to your children. It is not that they have a *right* to a share of the estate, but only that they have *standing* to contest your will if they have grounds for a contest. If a person would receive more under the terms of your will than he would receive if you had no will or under a prior will, then he may not contest it, since he would not gain anything even if he were successful. A person who seems to have no connection with the deceased may nevertheless contest a will that excludes him if he were mentioned in a previous will (and can prove it).

In general, all "heirs" who would inherit if you left no will, but *not* heirs of the heirs, have standing to contest the will. For instance, say that your only living relatives are your mother and brother. The law provides that if you die without a will, your mother will inherit your entire estate. You make out a will leaving everything to your companion, Clarence, who is despised by your brother but accepted by your mother, since he has always been kind to her and never failed to remember her on Mother's Day. On your death, your brother desperately wants to contest your will, but your mother does not. In this case, only your mother has standing as an heir to contest the will and there is nothing your brother can do unless he was mentioned in a previous will. If, on the other hand, your mother died before you, or even after you but within the allowable period for filing a will contest, then your brother would have standing, as he would be your direct heir (if your mother predeceased you) or he would be able to contest the will as the beneficiary of your mother's estate.

Remember that a spouse's taking his or her "forced share" as explained in chapter 7 does not constitute a contest of the will. The forced share is a statutory right regardless of the provisions of the will.

Because of the "interested party" requirement, you need not, as a general rule, worry about stepchildren or divorced spouses, although these are often the source of the greatest concern to testators. A divorced spouse has no standing to contest, even though he or she was mentioned in earlier wills as a spouse. A stepchild has no right to inherit, but if a stepchild was mentioned in an earlier will, he or she would have the right to contest, as would any other beneficiary who had been omitted in a subsequent will. In some cases, the court's strict adherence to the interested-party rule where stepchildren are concerned can appear unfair and unjust, as in the case of Sally Everbrook. Sally's mother was divorced from her father, and when Sally was six years old, her mother married Sally's stepfather, Douglas Huber. Shortly after the marriage, Sally became known as Sally Huber. She was enrolled in school under the name Sally Huber, was baptized under that name, with the baptismal records showing Douglas as her father, and all school and hospital records showed her as Sally Huber and Douglas Huber as her father. And although Douglas had never legally adopted Sally, he continually referred to her and treated her in all respects as if she were his natural daughter. In 1978, Sally's mother died, and about a year later, her "father," Douglas, died. Douglas's will, which was made out just after his marriage to Sally's mother, left his estate to Sally's mother, if she survived, otherwise to his brothers and sisters.

Sally contested the will on the basis that considering all the facts and circumstances as well as the behavior and acknowledgments of Douglas, she should be considered his legal heir and be entitled to inherit at least a share of the estate. The court conceded that Douglas clearly treated Sally as his daughter, but this, unfortunately, did not change the fact that she wasn't his daughter. Douglas, for some reason, never legally adopted Sally and, therefore, she had no standing to contest the will or take a share of the estate.

In other will contest situations, there may be no family relationship at all, but merely a business connection between the deceased and the contestant. In one case, for instance, the testator made out a will leaving a substantial share of his estate to a business, the Mantis Corporation, to allow it to use the funds for business purposes, and left his stock in the corporation to other family members. Later, he made out another will, leaving nothing to the business and everything to his family. When the second will was offered for probate, a stockholder of the Mantis Corporation contested its allowance. The family asked the court to reject the contest on the basis that the stockholder had no standing to contest the will. Not so, the court said. Standing is not restricted to beneficiaries who are actually named in the previous will, but includes persons who may be affected by the carrying out of the terms of the will. As a stockholder of the Mantis Corporation, the contestant would have indirectly benefited by the previous will and, therefore, definitely was in a position to contest the subsequent will.

Creditors of the estate do not have the right to contest the will, nor do creditors of a beneficiary or heir in most cases. It is possible in many states, however, for a contestant to "assign" his rights to contest a will to someone else. In other words, an heir who has standing to contest could transfer his right to contest to another person either by sale, gift, or exchange, like any other property right.

When it comes to will contests, you can't eat your cake and have it, too. If you have accepted benefits from the estate, you cannot then turn around and contest the will, unless you can show you were somehow deceived into accepting such benefits just to prevent you from contesting the will. This might happen, for instance, where the executor offers out money or other property as a part of your "share" of the estate and has you consent to the will without seeing it. If this happens and you later wish to contest the will, you should attempt to return whatever was given to you to preserve your right to contest.

Grounds for a Contest

You *cannot* contest a will simply because you don't like the provisions, or because you received less than you felt you should have received, or because the provisions were, in your opinion, unfair. You must have *legal* grounds, which, if supported by the evidence, would cause the will to be rejected by the probate court. Briefly, legal grounds include:

1. *Lack of testamentary capacity*—the testator was insane or incompetent at the time the will was signed.
2. *Improper execution*—there were not enough witnesses, or for some other reason the will was not properly signed.
3. *Undue influence*—someone took advantage of the testator's susceptibility and caused him to make out a will different from what he would have made on his own.
4. *Fraud or mistake*—the testator was induced to sign the will as a result of fraud, deceit, or mistake.
5. *Revocation*—the will was cancelled or revoked by the testator.
6. *Bogus will*—the will offered for probate was not the will of the decedent. (This might include forgery, for instance.)

You needn't choose only one of these grounds to contest the will. If you have evidence that could lead to rejection of the will on more than one ground, you may contest accordingly. For instance, you may feel not only that there has been undue influence but also that when the will was signed, none of the required witnesses was present. The comments that follow on the several grounds are for your general understanding only and are not an exhaustive discussion of the issues; your attorney will be able to advise you in greater detail. Furthermore, in reading this section on grounds for will contests, remember that in most instances the detailed description of each of the grounds is contained in another chapter; for instance, the issues relating to an improper execution and testamentary capacity to make a will are discussed in chapters 3 and 4.

1. LACK OF TESTAMENTARY CAPACITY

As the question of testamentary capacity applies to wills and will contests, it is often very difficult to disprove. The court presumes that the testator was sane and competent, which means that if you feel the testator was incompetent at the time the will was signed, you have to prove it. This could be quite difficult if the will was signed several years earlier, for instance, since it would mean that you would have to produce witnesses and other evidence relating to the specific time the testator signed his will. And remember that eccentricities are not necessarily indicative of incompetence or lack of understanding, and that persons who are suspected of being incompetent can have moments of lucidity, so that even credible evidence of weird behavior and occasional incompetence may not be enough to support a will contest based on lack of testamentary capacity. And if the will was signed in a lawyer's office, you have an even slimmer chance of proving lack of capacity, because most attorneys are extremely careful in monitoring the signing of the will, which normally includes a brief discussion with the testator to satisfy the witnesses that he knows and understands what he is signing.

2. IMPROPER EXECUTION

Assuming there is some substance to the claim, improper execution may not be quite as difficult to prove as lack of testamentary capacity, since it goes to the actual facts and circumstances surrounding the signing, as opposed to an evaluation of the state of mind of the deceased from a distance. The requirements for proper execution of a will are discussed in detail in chapter 3 and, if it can be shown that *any* of the necessary requirements was missing, the will may be declared invalid and the contest successful. As noted above, however, if the will was signed in the lawyer's office, the chances of proving improper execution are slim. But many testators (to the delight of many lawyers who are paid to contest wills) write their own wills and also arrange for the signing and witnessing. Such cases are the ones most likely to sidestep an important legal requirement, as in the case of Claude Boxe.

Boxe was a well-to-do widower who lived alone in Buffalo, New York. He hated lawyers and so decided to write his own will. He had a brother, William, with whom he never spoke, and a sister, Virginia, who was a known prostitute. His will, therefore, left his entire estate to his only friend, Stanley Gillis, who lived nearby and was always ready to help Claude when he needed it. Aside from being poorly drafted and neglecting to name an executor, Claude's will made it clear that he wanted his brother and sister to receive nothing, and that any claims they made against the will or the estate were to be fought "at all costs, even if it means spending everything on those blasted lawyer's fees."

On the night the will was to be signed, Claude called in two of his neighbors to witness his will. When they arrived he signed the will and asked them to witness it. Just as the first neighbor stepped forward to sign, the doorbell rang and Claude left the room to answer it. It was his sister, Virginia, who had heard that Claude made out his will and she wanted to try to make amends with him. Refusing to listen, Claude slammed the door in her face and returned to the room where the neighbors, who had by then finished witnessing his will, were waiting. Claude apologized for the interruption and then dismissed them with his thanks. Later that night, he wrote a letter to Virginia, telling her never to come to his house again and that he "fixed it" so that she and "that no good brother of hers" would not get a dime from his estate.

About a year later, Claude died and his friend Stanley Gillis offered his will for probate. Virginia and William contested the allowance of the will, however, on the basis that it was improperly executed. When the facts came out, it became clear that there was an improper execution since the witnesses did not sign in Claude's presence, as required by law. But it was Virginia's fault, Stanley argued. She knew they were signing at that time and came to the house for the very purpose of disrupting it. Furthermore, Claude's intentions to omit Virginia and William were clear, not only in the will, but in the letter he wrote Virginia. That didn't matter, the court said. The letter had no legal affect and there was no indication of fraud on Virginia's part. Even if she had planned it, Claude was free to sign his will again (or to acknowledge his signature) in the presence of the witnesses. He did not; the will was not properly executed and was, therefore, invalid. And despite Claude's instructions to fight it to the end, there was plenty of money left to be split between Virginia and William (and their lawyer, of course).

3. UNDUE INFLUENCE

When someone influences a testator to make out his will and leave his property in a manner that he would not have done were it not for the influence, then the will is the result of "undue influence" and invalid. Almost every would-be beneficiary who is left out of a will thinks he has a case of undue influence against another beneficiary who is suddenly named to receive most or all of the estate. This seems to happen very often, for instance, where children are omitted in favor of a new spouse. Unfortunately, undue influence is extremely difficult to prove, as it is usually done subtly, over a period of time, and there is no specific act or incident that clearly reveals it. Therefore, it must almost always be shown by circumstantial evidence. (Here's an example of circumstantial evidence: You checked your mailbox and found some mail. Then you noticed prints in the snow of exactly the type of boot your mailman wears in the winter. Although you didn't actually *see* him deliver the mail, the *circumstances* strongly indicate that he delivered it.)

To *prove* that your stepmother mentally coerced your father to make out a new will that excludes you is no easy task. It is not enough to show that she nagged him constantly, or that she just pretended to love him, or that she threatened to leave him unless he would make out a will in her favor, or that it is not fair that she should get everything and you, the child, get nothing. You must be able to show that your father (or whoever the testator may be) was *susceptible* to the undue influence of another, that the culpable person (in this case, your stepmother) was in a *position* and had the *opportunity* to exert undue influence, that she did, in fact, exert it, and last but perhaps most important, that as a result of the undue influence, the testator (your father) *changed his will* in a manner reflecting the undue influence.

As you can see, none of these requirements can be quantified or stated as a specific, identifiable rule of law, the violation of which would make your case winnable. It is not at all similar to proving that the will was not witnessed by two people. With undue influence every case must be judged on its own particular circumstances, and the courts are required to *begin* their evaluation on the presumption that the will they see before them reflects the *uninfluenced* wishes of the testator. The burden of proving that the testator was unduly influenced rests with the contestant. This is not to say, however, that it is an impossible burden, but rather that because of the difficulty (and therefore, expense) in doing it, the estate must be fairly large before it becomes worthwhile. Here is one case where it was worthwhile.

Nathaniel Cooper was a brilliant businessman who, through a series of shrewd investments, made himself millions of dollars. He owned posh homes in Philadelphia, Manhattan, and Long Island and was attended to by a chauffeur and a battery of butlers and maids. He had one child, Robert, from his first marriage, and a second, Gerald, from his subsequent marriage to Roslyn Cooper. The relationship between Robert and Roslyn was strained.

In the late '50s, Nathaniel had a serious stroke that left him physically handicapped; although he could get around, he was not the same man. He became hypochondriacal and would regularly carry with him a suitcase full of medications, which helped lead to his becoming anxious and depressed. Throughout this period, his wife, Roslyn, attended to him and Nathaniel became quite dependent on her. The thought of losing her made him "utterly despondent."

Despite this, he had times, particularly in the mornings, when he could transact his business and attend to his investments. He continued to read voraciously and, in general, was in control of his financial affairs.

Nathaniel thought highly of his son Robert and loved him very much. He paid for his education and subsequently loaned him $3,000, but only after the loan was "approved" by Roslyn. He once said, "Someday he [Robert] will be a very wealthy man." Although she approved the first loan to Robert, Roslyn dissuaded Nathaniel from making a subsequent $10,000 loan to him because of their strained relationship, causing Nathaniel to say to his son, "If you could only get on good terms with Roslyn. I could do a lot more for you, but she knows every step I'm up to and she will make my life hell."

Nathaniel made a number of wills during his lifetime, and in every one but the last, Robert was one of the principal beneficiaries. In fact, on July 16, he made out a will, naming Robert as one of the principal beneficiaries, as he had done in the past, but then on July 19, just three days later, he made out another leaving virtually all of his property to Roslyn. It seems that during the three-day period, Nathaniel and Roslyn had a heated telephone conversation, after which Nathaniel went to his attorney and directed him to prepare a new will, leaving almost everything to Roslyn. Nathaniel died about eighteen months later, and Roslyn submitted his "last" will for probate. Not surprisingly, Robert contested it. What's your guess? Was there provable undue influence?

At the probate court level, Robert won. Then Roslyn appealed and she won. Then Robert appealed to the state's highest court, and he finally won. The whole business took almost *ten years* to litigate! And one can only guess at the legal fees involved.

Another interesting and illustrative point is this: The effect of the court's final decision was to throw out Nathaniel's "last" will and revert to the one he executed just before that, under which Robert was a principal beneficiary. But so was Roslyn and so was her son, Gerald! Although Robert "won" and Roslyn was found guilty of undue influence, this did not effect her share under the previous will.

The problem with illustrating the principles of undue influence through case studies is that no two people and, therefore, no two cases are the same. You may have a situation that appears to have an identical fact pattern to a particular case but could have a totally different outcome in the courts. That is, the same or nearly the same fact pattern may not constitute undue influence if it did not affect the way the testator made out his will. And remember that forcing the testator to *make out* a will is *not* undue influence. The test of undue influence is whether he made out his will exactly the way *he* wanted to, provided, of course, he had not been tricked into doing it.

It has been said that nothing is so intricate as a devious mind, and the challenge of influencing another to do one's bidding without realizing it is too tempting a challenge for the devious mind to pass by. If we start with the premise that we are not allowed to change a person's desire in making his own will, why not offer him facts that themselves will cause him to change his desire on his own? That way, the testator could not be said to have been unduly influenced, since he is doing exactly what *he* wanted to do. For instance, if a woman is convinced that her husband has been unfaithful to her, she may be inclined to change her will *voluntarily,* and leave everything (in excess of the husband's statutory share, as discussed in chapter 7) to her children. Then all we need to do is convince her of that (untrue) fact. Would this be undue influence?

In one case based on a similar approach, the children of an ailing testator placed a bottle of poison (complete with a label sporting a skull and cross-bones) next to their father's bed, together with a note saying "Mrs. B., give this to Mr. B. One-fourth of this bottle will kill the old devil; don't put it in his eggs as you did before; put it in his coffee. I'll be over Sunday. G.F." This, together with a few other carefully placed comments and bits of evidence, caused the father, Mr. B., to believe that his wife was trying to poison him, whereupon he made out a new will and gave the bulk of his property to his children. Shortly thereafter he died (*not* from poisoning) and his wife, upon learning that she had been bypassed, contested the disposition of his property. The children made the mistake of telling certain other parties of their plot, and the bottle of poison and the note were found not far from their home. They were ordered to give the property back to their mother. This type of plot overlaps between undue influence and fraud, and to contest the will successfully it is essential that the statements and facts presented to the testator were false and the testator must have relied upon them in making the will. If they were true, then the contestant has no case.

The person perpetrating the undue influence need not be a beneficiary under the new will, although in most undue influence cases, it is surely done for the money. It has happened, however, that the undue influence is applied merely to get revenge against a beneficiary or to benefit a person in whom the perpetrator is interested.

Occasionally, the "new" beneficiary will be so eager to get the testator to sign the will that the beneficiary himself will prepare it. Although by itself this approach is not illegal, such a will will definitely be subject to careful scrutiny by the court, and if there is a suggestion of undue influence, the beneficiary will probably have the burden of proving that undue influence did *not* take place. In general, it is *not* a good idea for the principal beneficiary of the will to prepare the will. If at all possible, an independent attorney should be consulted and she should confer with the testator, privately if possible, and explain the terms of the will. And so long as the attorney is not a beneficiary, your will will have a much better chance of surviving an attack. (The question of attorneys as beneficiaries is covered in chapter 14.)

4. FRAUD OR MISTAKE

As mentioned above, these categories, particularly fraud, can often be closely associated with undue influence, and in many will contests the contestant will allege *both* fraud and undue influence. Fraud will occur when the testator makes or signs a will as the result of having been willfully deceived as to the nature or the contents of his will or as to some facts that bear upon the disposition of his property. Mistake is the same, but *without* the willful deceit by a third person. The common element between the two is that the testator acted on false information. The sometimes unfortunate difference between the two is that a will is almost never invalidated because of mistake, whereas it is readily rejected where fraud can be shown.

Fraud can be either in tricking the testator into signing a will when he doesn't realize it is a will, or when the testator is given false information *with the intention of causing* him to make out his will based on the false information. An interesting example of the first variety occurred where one Randolph Brinkley decided that his elderly and ailing neighbor, Ms. Constance Hildreth, should finally repay him for all his "kindness." On a friendly visit to her home one day, Brinkley invited Ms. Hildreth to join an organization, of which he was a member in fine standing, devoted to the care and preservation of cats. Having three of her own, Ms. Hildreth was pleased to sign the "application form" that Brinkley had conveniently brought with him.

The form was actually Ms. Hildreth's will, neatly printed and leaving her entire estate to Brinkley. Realizing that the will had to be witnessed, Brinkley then visited two more of his neighbors and asked them if they would "sponsor" Ms. Hildreth as a member of this wonderful organization for cats, and they did.

Not long after, old Constance checked out of this life, and Brinkley brought the will in for probate. It quickly occurred to him, however, that he may have a problem when the witnesses were asked to testify that they saw Constance sign the "will." His only solution, he thought, was to get rid of the witnesses. So, on another of his neighborly visits, Brinkley brought them a gift of some delicious breakfast cake. Saving it for the next morning, the neighbors left it on their table. In the meantime, while the neighbors were out the landlord and his wife stopped by, and within minutes of helping themselves to a bite of the lovely cake, they both died of convulsions. Constance's will was declared invalid and Brinkley was hanged for murder.

The other type of fraud, referred to as fraud in the inducement, is more common than the type discussed above. Normally, it results from the proposal of the concealment of a material fact, which causes the testator to make out his will in a fashion that he would not have done were it not for the false information. An illustration of this not uncommon type of fraud is the Holmes case.

Samuel Holmes made out his will, leaving everything to his two nieces, Daisy and Florence. On Samuel's death, Daisy filed for probate of Samuel's will and listed herself and Florence as Samuel's only heirs (probate petitions normally require a statement showing all the known heirs of the deceased—relatives who would inherit if there were no will—whether or not they are mentioned in the will). The will was admitted to probate, but then another niece, Wilma Hober, surfaced to contest the will.

Wilma offered testimony from witnesses stating that Samuel thought his sister (Wilma's mother) was dead and that she had no children; otherwise he would have made the will in her favor. There was also evidence to show that Daisy knew that Samuel had another niece. In fact, Daisy had letters to Samuel from Wilma but destroyed them. And on Samuel's death, she took no steps to notify any heirs other than her sister. From all the evidence, the court concluded that Daisy fraudulently withheld information from Samuel that caused him to make out his will in her favor and differently than he would have otherwise. What is interesting, however, is that the court did not declare the will invalid, but merely the bequest to Daisy. The bequest to Florence was allowed to stand, as she had no part in the fraud, and Wilma got her fair share.

The problems that sometimes arise with the question of fraud are the cause and effect of the fraud. If the mistaken belief had nothing to do with the making of the will, the fraud may not overturn the will. For instance, say that Bartholomew seeks a CPA to head up the accounting department of his company. He hires Morris, who presented a phony résumé. In fact, Morris was not an accountant but had extensive experience as a bookmaker in New Jersey. He, however, does an extraordinary job and becomes so close to Bartholomew that Bartholomew, who has no close relatives, names Morris as beneficiary of his estate. Is Morris guilty of fraud? Well, he may be as to the securing of the position, and if he didn't get the position, then he never would have been mentioned in Bart's will, but does this fraud negate the will? Probably not, since it was Morris's good and faithful performance, as well as his close relationship, that led to the will, *not* his fraud in gaining employment.

Change the facts just a little, however, and we may have more of a problem. Say that Abbie and Kendall meet and fall in love. Kendall proposes, Abbie accepts, and they are married. The only problem is that Kendall is already married, but he decides not to tell Abbie, as he feels it would definitely put a crimp in her day. After they are married, they make out wills leaving everything to each other, as most couples do. Abbie dies first, and Kendall proceeds to take her estate under the will. Can Abbie's parents contest? Was Kendall guilty of fraud?

Or how about this—Abbie is seventy-six and Kendall thirty. Abbie has a few million and Kendall a few dollars. Does this change the picture? Would it matter if they were married for twenty years?

There is no hard-and-fast rule, except that if it can be shown that Kendall lied about his marital status *primarily* to gain access to Abbie's estate, then it is likely the will would be overturned for fraud. On the other hand, if it can be shown that Abbie would have provided for him even if she had known of the deceit (which might have been the case after twenty years but not after one year), then the bequest might be allowed to stand.

Mistake in making a will, as noted above, is virtually the same as fraud but *without* fraud. In the absence of fraud, a will is unlikely to be invalidated on the basis of mistake, except in the rarest of cases. That is, no matter how unfair the results seem to be, the courts will not reject a will simply because the testator mistakenly believed, for example, that his son was dead or that his daughter didn't need the money, or did not know that he left it all to his grandchildren, so long as the mistakes were innocent and no fraud was involved. An unfortunate illustration is the case discussed in chapter 7 where the testator disinherited his son because he mistakenly believed the son was illegitimate. Many other cases exist where the testator omitted one relative or another on the mistaken belief that the person was dead. In such cases, the will stands and the mistakenly omitted beneficiaries have no recourse. The *only* time that there may be relief for mistake is where the mistake is apparent on the face of the will *and* it is equally apparent on the face of the will that the testator would have provided for the omitted beneficiary had he known the true facts. For instance, in the case of the supposedly illegitimate child, the results would have been different if the father's will had said, "I leave my estate in equal shares to my lawful children, excluding my son, Irving, because I believe him to be the child of someone else."

Other types of mistakes, such as a misspelled or incorrect name, or mistake in the description of property, or leaving the same property to two beneficiaries, generally are resolved by offering evidence to the court as to what the testator meant or intended. They are seldom, if ever, a reason for voiding the will and, as a result, they do *not* involve a will contest, but merely a request of the court to interpret the terms of the will.

For instance, say that Donna leaves "my apartment number 3 in building 819 to my son, Alexander," but she does not own that one; rather she owns apartment number 9 in building 813. If it can be shown that Donna intended the bequest to be apartment 9, then the court will acknowledge the mistake and allow her son to take the corrected bequest. Similarly, if a bequest is made to "my daughter's son, Robert Jenkins" and the daughter's son is named Ronald Jenkins, the bequest will be honored.

In the above illustrations, the mistakes do not appear significant and the intention of the testator can be made clear or confirmed with admissible evidence. More serious issues arise where the mistake is that the testator thought he was signing his will but in fact signed something else. In the case of Constance Hildreth discussed above, the document she signed was not intended to be her will so it could have no effect as a will—testamentary intent is essential. But what about a case where I sign a document as my will, but which in fact is somebody else's will? Clearly, even though I had testamentary intent and the document was a will, it would nevertheless seem to be the type of mistake that would cause it to be invalid. Or would it?

Consider the odd case of Harvey and Rose Snide of New York. Pursuant to their instructions their lawyer prepared wills for each that simply gave the whole estate to the other, and if one did not survive, to their children. Each spouse was named executor of the other's estate. In other words, the wills were completely identical except for the names.

They met one evening at a friend's house, with the lawyer and witnesses, for the signing of the wills. Their attorney, Knot Toobrite (not his real name but an appropriate one for him), removed the wills from his briefcase and presented one to Harvey for signing and one to Rose, indicating to each that they were signing their will. The problem was that the lawyer gave each spouse the *other's* will, so that Harvey signed Rose's will and Rose, Harvey's. (Apparently, even after the wrong wills were signed Knot Toobrite didn't notice it!) Harvey died, and when his "will" was submitted for probate the guardian ad litem for Harvey's minor child contested its allowance on the basis of mistake and lack of testamentary intent, since it wasn't Harvey's will! In an unusual holding seemingly inconsistent with prior New York law, the court decided that the facts of this case were unique and that the wills would be reformed to the effect that Roses's name would be substituted for Harvey's where it appeared and Harvey's for Rose's, to conform to Harvey's intentions.

As a practical matter, it is *highly* unusual for an attorney to allow this to happen. After the signing of any documents, let alone a will, any competent attorney would examine each signed page for signature, date, notarization, etc., and the document as a whole would be reviewed for integrity (all pages present and in order, etc.).

5. REVOCATION

Revocation, as grounds for a will contest, would occur where a party offered a will for probate but the contesting party contends that the will has been revoked. This could happen, for example, where a subsequent will had been made, revoking the will offered for probate, or where the will offered for probate has been revoked but the instrument was not destroyed. For instance, a case discussed in chapter 4 describes the testator who threw his will into a fire and left the room. The beneficiary rushed to rescue the will, which was intact except for a slight charring. As pointed out earlier, the will was legally revoked by the testator, but if the beneficiary offers it for probate after his death, the testator will not be around to dispute it. It is easy and convenient to offer such examples in a book to illustrate legal principles, but as a practical matter, unless the contestants of the will can offer some testimony or other evidence that the testator thought he destroyed the will, the contest may be lost.

"Partial" revocation, however, is what gives beneficiaries the most trouble and perhaps generates the most in legal fees. Drawing lines through someone's name or bequest in a will and then initialing it generally spells trouble. (In fact, you might just as well write the word *trouble* across the page and leave it at that.) In most states this is not a revocation but rather an invalid attempt at changing the terms of the will, which can only be done through a properly executed codicil. So *don't do it.*

6. BOGUS WILLS

A bogus or inauthentic will generally involves fraud and, like certain other grounds for contest, overlaps with it. The story of Constance Hildreth's cats and Randolph Brinkley, discussed above in the section on fraud, is an illustration of a will that was rejected as not being the will of the deceased. The same would apply, for instance, where the will was originally that of the deceased but someone made an unauthorized change to it, then offered it for probate. This method can be quite difficult to detect, since, in most cases, the will was properly signed by the testator and witnessed according to law. But, as is often the case, those stealing from the dead are usually amateur thieves and don't cover their tracks very well, as illustrated in the case of the estate of Nora Winkle. About five years before her death, Nora had her lawyer make out her will, which was properly signed, witnessed, and notarized in the lawyer's office. The will left Nora's entire estate in trust for her husband for his lifetime, and on his death the remainder was to go to Nora's stepdaughter.

On Nora's death, the will was offered for probate. At first glance everything looked in order. The will was properly signed by Nora, the witnesses had signed, everyone's signature was notarized, and Nora herself had even placed her initials on every page. But something had changed. Instead of the remainder passing to the stepdaughter, the first page of the will stated that on the husband's death, the remainder should pass to Nora's brothers and sisters. Naturally, the stepdaughter stepped in to contest the will.

It seems that after Nora made out her will, one of her brothers went to Nora's lawyer and instructed him to make out a new will because Nora had changed her mind and decided to leave the remainder to her brothers and sisters. The brother specifically asked that the lawyer have the will typed on the *same* typewriter as that used on Nora's first will. The lawyer did so and waited to hear from Nora. Then one day while the lawyer was out, the new draft of Nora's will mysteriously disappeared from his office. In court, he later identified page one of the will in probate as the *second* will he had drafted and *not* the one signed earlier by Nora in his office. The brother (or someone) had placed Nora's initials on the *new* first page, substituted that page for the earlier one, and offered the "original" will for probate. Nice try, said the court, but no cigar. And no will either. The will offered for probate was not Nora's will and was therefore rejected.

How to Contest a Will

The exact procedure for contesting a will varies considerably from state to state, but certain basic steps and principles apply, nevertheless. With the important reminder that this is not a legal textbook and that the assistance of a competent attorney is *vital* to success, particularly in the case of will contests, the following are the basic principles.

States follow either of two methods of probate of a will—one is *with* notice to the heirs, the surviving spouse, and the beneficiaries under the will, and the other is *without* notice. In those states that allow a will to be probated without notice, such as Georgia, Virginia, and New Hampshire, the contest of the will is filed with the probate court *after* the will is probated. In these states, you usually have a much longer time within which to file your contest against the will. But the longer you wait, the greater the chance that estate assets will be used or expended. Once you file your action to contest the will, however, the probate process is usually suspended until the case can be heard or until interim administrators can be appointed to administer the estate while the contest is proceeding. It may be a period of years after the will is probated, but it is usually tied to the period of administration of the estate. That is, you should file your contest before or within a very short time after the estate is settled and the court issues a decree releasing the executor.

In those states that require notice *before* the will is allowed for probate, such as New York, Massachusetts, and Maryland, you must file your objections to the allowance of the will *before* the date set for the court's review of the will, which is often only a month or less after the petition is filed by the person who wants to probate the will. If you fail to file within that period, you may lose your right to contest the will. A few states that require notice allow you to contest on certain grounds before or after the will is allowed. It is *not* a good idea to wait, however, if you feel you have grounds to contest.

Whatever the state you file in, once your objections to the will are filed, the probate is effectively suspended and this, if nothing else, gives you a little leverage to gain a settlement, if a settlement is desired or possible. But as noted below, do *not* file groundless objections for the sole purpose of forcing a settlement, or you may find yourself with nothing but the requirement to pay legal fees—for *both* sides. If the estate requires management (and it almost always does) while the contest is pending, an administrator will be appointed by the court to continue the administration. Often co-administrators are appointed—one from each side (you should aim for this)—to keep matters honest. But if this is not agreeable to the parties or to the court, an independent administrator (usually an outside attorney) will be appointed by the court to serve until the contest is settled. Of course, the administrator(s) gets a fee for this.

If you do decide to contest, the very first thing you should do is consult with an attorney to determine whether you have grounds to contest and how soon you must file your objections. Remember, you should *not* delay in consulting an attorney; otherwise you may lose your right to contest. You should bring with you copies of any notices you have received in connection with the probate or proposed probate, copies of any correspondence to or from the deceased (or anyone else) relating to his intentions or his estate, copies of any previous wills or trusts that you may have, and, in general, any information that bears upon your involvement with the deceased or his estate.

If your attorney decides you have grounds to object, he will prepare the necessary pleadings to file a formal objection to the allowance of the will (or to revoke the allowance); at some point this pleading must specifically state, in detail, your objections, the *grounds* for your objections, and the *facts* on which your objections are based. While at one time it was relatively easy to tie up an estate on questionable grounds, the current trend in the courts is to *punish* frivolous and groundless objections by requiring the troublemaker to pay the costs and fees for *both* sides, so don't be surprised if your attorney discourages you from proceeding despite what might look to you like a good case.

If you get to the point where it is decided that you have a case worth pursuing and objections are to be filed, the next thing to do is to get out your wallet and get ready for a long, expensive, and unpleasant ride.

Costs and Delays of a Will Contest

After you get over the anger and hurt of being left out of your favorite aunt's will, or your father's will because he left his estate to his new young wife, you should think long and hard before you rush in to contest the will. As noted above, the first thing to do is establish whether you have grounds for a contest. If so, then you should think long and hard again because it can be a lengthy and expensive procedure with *no* guarantee of success. Even though you may have what appears to be a solid case, remember that you are bucking a strong presumption that the will is valid and that it actually reflects the last wishes of the testator. The statistics show that only a very tiny percentage of will contests is successful.

If, despite this, you decide to proceed, you should realize that *you* yourself are responsible for the fees and other costs of the contest, while the other side—the executor and other beneficiaries—is financially backed by the estate. Assuming that you would not challenge the will unless the estate was substantial in size, this means that they can afford to go the distance, while you may be mortgaging your home to do so. Most competent attorneys expert in the field will not take a will contest case on a contingent fee (you don't win, you don't pay) basis. There are, of course, exceptions to this, but in most cases your attorney will want a retainer and your promise to pay costs plus his ongoing fees (perhaps at a reduced hourly rate against a percentage of whatever you may win) to pursue the case actively. Costs would include stenographers' costs for depositions (there will probably be a lot of them), investigators' fees, and travel expenses if the depositions must be held in other states. It is not at all unusual for legal fees and expenses to run

$10,000 to $50,000 in an "average" will contest, and probably more if it goes to trial. Considering, again, that you may not be a winner, you must ask yourself if you can afford this kind of sport.

The good news is that, if you are successful, you will, at least indirectly, recover your fees and expenses from the estate, and the bad guys in most cases must now pay *their* costs out of their own pocket. It's sort of the winner-take-all concept, except that, in some cases, if the executor has acted in good faith, the courts have discretion to allow him legal fees, even though the will was ultimately rejected.

You must also consider the time involved. These fees are not expended over a month or two. They are more likely to represent a year or two, and much of your own time is often required. And then there is trial. Even after the preliminary pleadings and "discovery" period (depositions and other sources for information), there are potential delays in finally reaching the time for trial. And if you make it that far, then there is the possibility of appeal. And there may be more than one appeal. Just look at the Nathaniel Cooper case discussed earlier; it took *ten years* for that case to be finally resolved! Unless you have an "ironclad" case, therefore, you might be better off spending the money on a psychological counselor, to help you get over the hurt and realize that the money will not make you happier (unless, of course, it is a *really* big estate).

How to Prevent a Contest

Money can be a great rationalizer, particularly where estates are concerned. People who originally would not dream of suing their brothers, sisters, parents, or cousins suddenly feel quite justified in vigorously seeking their "rightful" share of an estate by contesting a will that left them out or did not leave them "enough." It is no secret that will contests are public, painful, and expensive, no matter who wins or loses, but is there a way to prevent or at least discourage a contest?

Basically, there are three ways to prevent a will contest: (1) include an anticontest provision in your will and give the beneficiary something to lose; (2) during your lifetime enter into a written agreement with the beneficiary where she agrees not to contest; and (3) put all of your property in a living trust.

ANTICONTEST PROVISION
Although I feel that a provision of this sort belongs in just about every will, for some reason it is very seldom used by the average law firm. While it is

impossible to take away a person's right to his "day in court," it is quite possible to discourage him from exercising that right by giving him something to lose if he makes that choice. Because of the lack of an anticontest provision in most wills, in the majority of will contests the contestant has nothing to lose except the expenses of waging the contest. And while such expenses may not be minor, they may pay off in the form of a settlement with the executor or the other heirs. What's more, the contestant may still be entitled to the bequest left to him under the will.

For instance, say that Dad has four children, Eena, Mina, Minnie, and Moe. In his will he left Eena, Mina, and Minnie $150,000 each, but only $20,000 to Moe. Moe contests the will and settles with the estate out of court for $30,000. Depending on the terms of the settlement, Moe might get not only this $30,000, but *also* the $20,000 left to him under the will. In effect, Moe has nothing to lose except the cost of the contest. (To make matters worse, the estate will have to pay its own legal fees, which in some cases could have the effect of reducing the other children's bequests under the will.)

An effective way to discourage people like Moe would have been to include an anticontest provision (also called a *noncontest* provision, a *forfeiture* clause, and an *in-terrorem* clause) in Dad's will. In simple terms, provisions of this type say that anyone who contests the will automatically forfeits any bequest made to him under the will; this provision is quite enforceable in most states.

Thus, if Dad's will in the example above provided that the $20,000 bequest to Moe was subject to the condition that he did not contest the will, it is likely that Moe would have thought twice before contesting the will and waving his $20,000 good-bye, not to mention the out-of-pocket legal fees he would incur. A noncontest clause will be useless, however, to prevent an omitted beneficiary from contesting the estate, unless he has something to lose, and this is the price you must pay to discourage the contest.

To make the clause work, the amount at risk must be a meaningful amount to the beneficiary, an amount that will make him think before he rushes to his lawyer's office and starts running up legal fees. The $1 bequests are certainly useless, as are those in the hundreds, I would say. And you can always get creative and offer payments over a period of years, say $2,000 (or more) per year for five years, depending on the size of your estate and how much you want to discourage a contest, but this would only prolong settlement of the estate.

Including a noncontest clause in your will does *not* mean that a contest is legally prohibited. It merely means a contestant will lose his share of your estate if he attempts to interfere with the probate of the will. If the contestant is willing to risk that loss and the contest is subsequently successful, the presence of the noncontest provision will be moot because the will itself would have been overturned.

For instance, say that you don't realize it, but you are the victim of undue influence. Your daughter has manipulated you into a position where you are totally dependent on her, and, thanks to her stories, you are becoming resentful of your other children. As a result, you make a will leaving your estate 50 percent to your daughter and 25 percent to each son, providing they do not contest the will. But your daughter is not satisfied with this. Before you sign the will, she changes the figures so that she receives 80 percent and the boys 10 percent each, again with the noncontest clause. The changes are imperceptible and you do not notice them when you initial each page and sign the will. After your death, the boys find out what their sister has done, but now they must decide whether to risk loss of their 10 percent (each) of your estate. What would *you* want to happen in this case?

To prevent such inequities and fraud from escaping judicial review, many experts object to the enforceability of noncontest clauses on the basis that they can discourage an otherwise valid contest and allow a "defective" or fraudulent will to prevail, as in my example above. In fact, a number of states, such as Iowa, Missouri, New Jersey, and California, provide that a noncontest clause will *not* be enforced against a beneficiary who is found to have *probable cause* for his contest. In as many other states, however, including Georgia, Pennsylvania, and New York, the courts have held that a noncontest clause can be effective, regardless of whether the beneficiary had probable cause to contest the will.

In other words, in the "probable cause" states, even though you had a noncontest provision the beneficiary could contest the will and still receive his bequest even though he *loses* the contest, *provided* he had good cause for filing the contest. What constitutes probable or good cause will depend upon the facts of each case. Obviously, a court can decide only if there was probable cause after a sufficient number of facts have been disclosed.

If you do decide to include a noncontest clause in your will, you must be sure to provide what will happen to the forfeited bequest if the beneficiary does contest. This is called a "gift over," and without it, the clause will be invalid. For instance, you might say (*not* in these exact words), "Any beneficiary who contests this will shall forfeit his bequest, and such forfeited bequest shall pass to the other named beneficiaries hereunder, in equal shares," or, "If my son George contests this will, his bequest shall pass instead to my son Charles."

The most frequent problem with this noncontest strategy of giving them something to lose is that if you really want to disinherit someone, you probably don't want to leave them anything like $10,000 or $20,000 (or more, depending on the size of your estate). This problem can be avoided almost altogether by leaving your property through a living trust, rather than through your will, as discussed later in this chapter.

AGREEMENT WITH THE BENEFICIARY

As infrequently as noncontest provisions are used, agreements with the beneficiary are even more scarce, with one exception—marital agreements. As discussed in chapter 7, premarital agreements or postmarital agreements or separation agreements usually contain a provision that neither spouse will contest the will of the other. Since fair consideration was given for this promise, it will be enforceable and can be used to prevent or stop a will contest in violation of its provisions.

Where beneficiaries other than a spouse are concerned, however, the occurrence is quite rare. If you are not on friendly terms with a beneficiary to begin with, it would seem highly unlikely, to say the least, that he would sign an agreement not to contest your will, even if you paid him. And as to beneficiaries with whom you have a good relationship, they will probably be taking a fair share of your estate anyway, so a noncontest provision in your will would do the trick and eliminate the embarrassment of asking them during your lifetime. Nevertheless, if somehow the unusual circumstances arise, it is possible to enter into an enforceable agreement with beneficiaries not to contest your will.

USE OF A LIVING TRUST

As I have noted several times throughout this book, your will relates only to property that is in your *probate* estate. It follows, therefore, that the contest of a will affects only the property in your probate estate, and that property passing *outside* your probate estate may not be affected by the will contest. Contesting the will, therefore, becomes worthwhile to the contestants *only if there is a substantial amount of probate property*. Without that, a will contest can be meaningless. For instance, say that Attilla, who is single, has an estate consisting of three tons of gold and six small countries, all in his own

name. He makes out a will leaving everything to his twelve sons, and nothing to his daughter, Honey. Since all of Attilla's property was in his own
name, it will pass according to the terms of his will, but *only* after the will is
allowed for probate. If Honey contests the will, therefore, all of the probate
property will be tied up and the sons will get nothing until the will contest is
disposed of.

Placing the property in joint names with his sons might avoid this exposure to a certain extent, but, as pointed out in chapter 2, jointly owned property can be attacked as probate property and in many instances can be
brought back into the probate estate. This is not, therefore, a reliable way to
avoid a will contest. So what should Attilla have done if he didn't want
Honey to inherit?

Attilla should have placed the gold and the real estate into a living trust
during his lifetime. He could, as discussed in chapter 11, keep control over
all the trust assets during his lifetime and provide (in the terms of the *trust*)
that, on his death, whatever remained would pass directly to his sons.
Although a trust is not impossible to attack, it is far more difficult to attack
than a will. A will does not take effect as a legal instrument until the death of
the testator and, even then, not until the probate court has allowed it. A trust,
on the other hand, becomes effective and operative as a legal instrument as
soon as the settlor (the person who creates the trust) places assets into it.
Since he does this during his lifetime, and since the trust is operating with his
full knowledge and, in most cases, control, it is difficult for a contestant of the
trust to argue that the settlor lacked the capacity to do it, that he was unduly
influenced, that it was improperly executed, or that someone fraudulently
induced the settlor to set up the trust. In fact, it is extremely *rare* to hear of
a case where a would-be beneficiary successfully attacked a living trust.

Another reason such attacks are far less frequent and far less successful
than will contests is that the contestant has no leverage. That is, through a
will contest the contest can tie up the assets of the estate for years, preventing everyone from getting the full benefit and use of the property. As a
result, the estate has an incentive to settle with contestants just to get rid of
them and begin enjoying property. When the assets are in a living trust,
however, the contestant, except in rare cases where trust assets are rapidly
disappearing, has no right to tie up the trust assets while he is attacking the
trust, and so the existing trust beneficiaries can go on enjoying the benefits
despite the contest. Because of all this, trust contestants usually find themselves wasting a good deal of time and money only to find that they have

little or no chance of breaking the trust. (For the details on how to have your own trust, see chapters 11 and 12.)

Finally, if you want to double your protection against a contest you can also consider including an anticontest provision in your *trust* as well as your will. All of the same rules and considerations relative to the inclusion of the anticontest provision in wills apply to its inclusion in trusts. And this includes the necessity of giving the contestant something to lose. That is, as with a will, if you want to discourage a beneficiary from contesting the trust, you should make a bequest to him, conditioned upon his agreement not to contest or attack the trust.

Despite all of this, I suppose that if there is enough money involved and someone feels shortchanged, it's a good bet that somebody will contest something for some reason, whether it be under a will or a trust, even though he or she may realize that the only guaranteed winners are the lawyers.

Probating a Lost Will

The mention of probating a lost will may cause you to ask two questions: If we are probating a will, even a lost one, what does this have to do with a will contest? And the second: How can you probate a will if it is lost?

As to the first question, it is not unusual for a person to make more than one will. It is also not unusual for someone to offer for probate a will that may not be the last will of the deceased, on the basis that if the last will cannot be found, it must be lost. If it is lost, it may give rise to the presumption in the law of many states that a will that was in the testator's possession but cannot now be found is presumed to have been cancelled or destroyed by him and, therefore, the will he made out *before* the lost will is offered for probate. But not everyone may agree that the lost will was destroyed by the testator, and so they would contest the allowance of the earlier will and, at the same time, offer to probate the lost will, in the manner to be reviewed shortly.

There is also the more devious situation in which the beneficiary of an earlier will who is omitted from the last will destroys the last will and offers the one before it for probate. If the other beneficiaries do not have a copy or any other evidence of the existence of the lost will, they could be out of luck. Furthermore, the same dastardly deed could be committed even if there was no prior will. This would happen, for example, where the wrong-doers stood to inherit more if the deceased died without a will, as happened in the case of LaVerne Ketcham.

LaVerne lived with her two sisters for many years. All three of them being single, they enjoyed a good relationship and each made out a will, leaving her estate to the other two. About two years before her death, however, LaVerne met young Adolfo, who swept her off her seventy-two-year-old feet. After a year of intense courting and romance, they became engaged to be married. And as a gesture of their faith and devotion to each other, LaVerne and Adolfo wrote out new wills leaving everything to each other, whether or not the marriage took place. Unfortunately, only a few months before the scheduled wedding, while LaVerne was boating with Adolfo, the boat capsized and LaVerne drowned.

Grief-stricken, Adolfo immediately asked LaVerne's sisters for the will so he could attend to LaVerne's last wishes. The sisters carefully searched through LaVerne's private papers, all of which were kept in their home, but could find no will. The sisters then petitioned for administration of LaVerne's estate on the basis that she left *no* will, in which case the two sisters, as LaVerne's only heirs, would inherit her entire estate. When Adolfo raised the question of the will LaVerne had recently signed, knowing that it was among LaVerne's papers, the sisters replied that they knew of no other will and that, even if there was one, the fact that it cannot be found raises the presumption that LaVerne herself destroyed it with the intention of revoking it. Adolfo continued to object, claiming there *was* a will, but that it must be lost, *not* revoked. He told the court about their pledge to each other, and even offered his own will as evidence to show proof that each provided for the other in a will. Therefore, he said, he should be entitled to LaVerne's estate. Was this enough? If the court believed Adolfo's story, could it allow LaVerne's estate to pass to him?

Generally, to probate a lost will, you must be able to prove, by satisfactory evidence, the contents of the will *and* its proper execution. If a copy of the lost will is available, this would certainly be acceptable evidence of its contents, and if the copy was taken after the will was signed and witnessed, then this would be convincing to help show that it was in fact signed and properly witnessed. It may not be enough, however, just as it would not be enough if it were the original. One or all of the witnesses must testify as to the execution of the will by themselves and by the testator. In other words, a lost will must be proved just like any other will, except that the original is not available. If there is no copy of the will, the will may nevertheless be proved and probated if evidence of its contents and execution can be proved. This may be difficult to prove, although it is not necessary to prove the exact words of the will, only the substance of the contents and intent. Nevertheless, it is still difficult, since witnesses do not usually read the will, and unless there is some corroborating evidence, such as testimony of the attorney who drafted it, proof is unlikely to be available. In Adolfo's case, he lost because he did not have a copy of LaVerne's will and had no idea who the witnesses were or who the lawyer was who made it out. Without this, the will could not be reconstructed.

Perhaps one of the most famous (although not terrible fascinating) attempts at probating a lost will was that in Howard Hughes's estate. After the much more interesting case of the "Mormon" will (discussed in chapter 1) was disposed of, it was then contended that Hughes had made out a valid will many years before, but it had been lost. The proponent of the lost will was the Howard Hughes Medical Institute, a charitable organization founded by Hughes during his lifetime. The opponents were Hughes's distant heirs, who stood to inherit what was left of the several billions after the estate debts and expenses were paid.

In its 1977 petition to probate the lost will, the institute attempted to show that Hughes had signed a will in 1925, leaving his entire estate to the institute. Although the institute presented a rough draft of the will, it was unable to show that it was ever signed, and could not produce witnesses or any other corroborating evidence of its execution. As a result, the court rejected it and in 1980 decided, once and possibly for all, that Hughes left no will. (Now, if you can just prove you were related to him . . .)

Occasionally, a will can be considered lost even though its whereabouts are known but no longer accessible. In a very bizarre case illustrating the point, justice won out. Young André Laysse was shocked at the sudden death of his wife, but even more shocked when he found that she had left him only the legal minimum from her small fortune. As soon as his wife's will was offered for probate, André and his mother went forthwith to the probate court and asked to examine the original will, since they felt his wife was insane at the time she made it out. When the court clerk removed the will from the file, André's mother snatched the will from the clerk's hands and, as he ran around his desk to recover it, she handed it to André, who, according to the *New York Times*'s account of the story, "quickly put it into his mouth, chewed it violently, and swallowed it without a pause, before the eyes of the astonished clerk."

Here was a truly lost will. Unfortunately for André, however, a carbon copy of the will was available, as well as the necessary testimony of the witnesses. Accordingly, the will was probated as written and, in addition to the small amount he was left under his wife's will, thanks to André's antics, he was also left with a case of indigestion.

11

Avoiding Probate and Wills Altogether

The key here, I think, is not to think of death as an end, but to think of it as a very effective way to cut down on your expenses.

—Woody Allen

Actually, death can *increase* the expenses for many estates, especially when there is a will contest, as we have seen. And even if there is no will contest, everyone knows that probating an estate can be time-consuming and expensive. Other than staying alive, then, is there any effective way to cut down on these expenses? Is it really worthwhile to avoid probate? What is the best way to do it? Should you just put everything in joint names?

Avoiding Probate through Joint Ownership and Other Do-It-Yourself Methods

There are four ways to transfer property at death. Only one is through probate. The other three are the result of some arrangement or disposition made by the deceased during his lifetime but designed to cause a transfer at his death. They include: (1) contractual arrangements, such as life insurance, where the promise of the other party to the contract involves a payment or transfer to named beneficiaries on the deceased's death; (2) joint ownership, where on the death of one of the joint owners the jointly held property is supposed to pass to the other; and (3) living trusts.

LIFE INSURANCE AND OTHER CONTRACTS
Contractual arrangements that can avoid probate include life insurance policies and company benefit plans, although these are often overlooked as

probate-avoidance schemes by the average person. When you pay insurance premiums, for instance, you are transferring funds to the life insurance company and the company agrees to pay the death proceeds to your named beneficiary. Meanwhile, assuming you retain ownership of the policy, you can have access to the cash value of the policy during your lifetime, and on your death the proceeds are paid directly to your beneficiary without the need for the probate process. There is, in effect, a legal contract between you and the insurance company, so no court or other outside party needs to be involved to authorize payment of the proceeds to the person named, *unless*, that is, you make the mistake of naming your "estate" as the beneficiary.

Briefly (and as also noted in chapter 2), there are four reasons you would name your estate as beneficiary of your life insurance policies: (1) to make the proceeds available to contestants of the will and creditors of your estate; (2) to increase the probate costs and attorney's fees; (3) to be sure that there will be a substantial delay before your beneficiaries receive the money; and (4) to be sure the proceeds will be subject to estate or inheritance taxes. In case you don't get my drift, if anyone advises you to make your insurance payable to your estate, get another adviser—fast!

Another illustration of a contractual arrangement that avoids probate would be certain company benefits that are paid after the employee's death, under an agreement or contract he had with his employer. For example, a contract might provide that on an employee's death his spouse will receive $25,000 per year for five years. These amounts are paid directly to the spouse (or other beneficiary) and do not pass through probate, since there was a contractual agreement to pay them to a specific person or persons (or to a trust, as described later) after death of the employee.

Finally, certain business agreements can provide that buyouts or interests in the business can be paid or transferred directly to a named person (or to a trust) on death. A partnership agreement, for instance, could provide that on the death of a partner, the partner's spouse will be paid his share, or that she can become a partner, thereby avoiding the probate of his share.

JOINT OWNERSHIP

Joint ownership of property is probably the most popular way of avoiding probate and transferring property at death, although this popularity may not be justified. The basic understanding of a joint tenancy between two owners is that on the death of one, the survivor automatically owns the whole of the jointly held property. It is thought of as a sort of inheritance.

From a legal standpoint, a valid joint tenancy is not a transfer at death at all, but rather the result of a *lifetime* transfer that "vests" or becomes the property of each succeeding survivor by "operation of law." In other words, the property really already belonged to the survivor, subject only to the claim of the other joint tenant. The property, therefore, is *not* inherited. When a joint tenant dies, his interest and any claim he might have held in the joint property disappears, so the property, which belonged to the survivor subject to the claim of the other, is now the survivor's free and clear of any claim. This transfer of ownership is said to take place automatically by "operation of law" and needs no outside action or verification by probate courts, lawyers, deeds, or the like. It can be quite a smooth transition from one tenant to another. That is, of course, if there are no objections. Unfortunately, where money and emotions are concerned, things don't always work the way they are supposed to.

Joint tenancies enjoy as many challenges inside the courts as they enjoy popularity outside because they are treated in such an arbitrary fashion by the creators of the joint tenancies. This, in turn, makes them quite vulnerable to attack.

Using joint tenancies to avoid probate can be extremely risky. It not only invites litigation when there is the slightest question of the deceased's intent, but (depending on the size of the estate) can produce extra taxes and even extra administrative (probate) fees—the very thing it was hoped the joint ownership would avoid! I have pointed out in chapter 2, for instance, the fact that a disgruntled heir or an aggressive executor can take the position that the jointly held property should be *probate* property because it was not a "true" joint tenancy.

Another risk of joint tenancy is the simultaneous death of the joint owners. Basically, this has the effect of converting the joint tenancy into a tenancy in common. This would result in one-half the property passing through the probate estate of each joint tenant, and would bring about extra fees, delays, and taxes, unless the will or trust of one of the joint tenants contains a provision dealing with simultaneous death.

And even if the joint property succeeds in passing to the survivor on the death of a joint tenant, there is still the problem of the property being probated in the estate of the survivor, who is then the sole owner. To hope that the survivor will create some new joint tenancies in the future is merely to defer to a later date the risk of the same tax and legal problems.

A possible and important exception might occur when the home—the principal residence—is held jointly (or under a tenancy by the entirety) by husband and wife. (Tenancy by the entirety is a special form of joint ownership for husband and wife.) Seldom are there objections or interferences with the surviving spouse taking this property on the death of the other. Therefore, unless some other type of ownership is recommended by advisers, married couples owning their home jointly or as tenants by the entirety need not rush out to change the title, unless they want to place it in a trust, which can offer all the advantages of joint ownership with none of the disadvantages. Similarly, a bank account or money market account of "nominal" size in joint names of husband and wife is helpful for quick access to funds on death or disability of the other. By nominal size, I mean an amount sufficient to meet emergency needs in the context of your particular family's lifestyle. For some families it may be $1,000, for others, $20,000. You must decide for yourself. (For a discussion of how joint property is taxed, see chapter 13.)

In short, it may happen that joint property will avoid probate, but the risks that it will not, and that even if it does it will produce other problems and concerns, far outweigh the possible benefits.

As indicated in the chart on page 173, an option that offers all of the advantages of joint ownership—including avoidance of probate, but with far less risk of interference—is the *living trust.*

LIVING TRUST

A living trust, simply stated, is a trust created during your lifetime that usually provides for the disposition of assets that are in the trust upon your death. In other words, you could provide that your living trust will pay out all income to you during your lifetime and, on your death, whatever is left would be given to your spouse. Since there has been a lifetime transfer of the property to the trust, and since the trust provides what is to be done with the property on your death, there would be no need for the probate court to be involved in the transfer of those assets on death. (Trusts are discussed in much greater detail in the section that follows.)

The *"trustee bank account"* is a special breed of living trust and deserves a few comments and caveats here because of its excessive popularity and the unnecessary risks involved. In the typical case, A will place his funds in a bank account entitled "A, trustee for B" or "A, in trust for B," each meaning the same thing, which is that A is to have complete control of the funds during his lifetime, and on A's death B takes what is left, without probate in A's estate. This is a flimsy, very risky, but sometimes workable trust arrangement, which, like the joint bank account, *may* avoid probate of the funds in the account in A's estate, provided no one objects. It is quite possible—and

Different Types of Co-tenancies
and Their Characteristics

Question	Joint property	Tenancy by the entirety	Tenancy in common
Survivorship rights?	Yes	Yes	No
Right to sell your share?	Yes	No	Yes
Right to divide (partition) the asset?	Yes	No	Yes
Can creditors reach share?	Yes	Maybe*	Yes
Included in estate?	Yes (unless w/spouse, then one-half)	Yes (one-half)	Only your share

Joint Property vs. Trust

	Joint property	Trust
Avoids probate?	Probably	Yes
Can save estate taxes?	No	Yes
Helps avoid creditor's attack?	No	Yes
Provides for the unexpected?	No	Yes
Affected by disability of owner?	Yes	No
Affected by simultaneous death?	Yes	No
Affected by divorce?	Yes	No
Easy to obstruct?	Yes	No
Can provide for spouse, children, and grandchildren?	No	Yes
Can protect from creditors of beneficiaries?	No	Yes
Can predict outcome?	No	Yes
Reduces overall costs and expenses?	No	Yes

* Depending on the state where the property is located. A number of states (e.g., New York, Massachusetts, Florida) prohibit creditors from reaching certain property held under a tenancy by the entirety.

there is a good deal of litigation on the question—for A's executor to attack the validity of the "trust" and attempt to bring the funds into A's probate estate. Then there is also the possibility that B will predecease A, and the funds will definitely be in A's probate estate. (Many people *mistakenly* think that if they place the beneficiary's Social Security number on the trustee bank account, he or she will be taxed on the interest. This is *not* so. Because the trustee has complete control of the funds and no completed gift has been made to the beneficiary, the *trustee* will be taxed on the income, regardless of whose number is on the account.) Furthermore, all of the funds in the trustee bank account will be subject to tax in A's estate.

Finally, assets in a retirement plan trust, such as a company pension or profit-sharing plan, an IRA or Keogh plan, or an IRA rollover account, will avoid probate provided they are payable to a named beneficiary and *not* payable to your estate. As noted, all of these arrangements are held through a trust, or something similar to a trust, even though you may not have realized it. For this reason, your named beneficiary will receive the funds or benefits without the need for probate.

Everything else you need to know about trusts is covered in chapters 12 and 13.

AVOIDING PROBATE IN MORE THAN ONE ESTATE

As mentioned above, any assets that are *in* your living trust at the time of your death will completely avoid the probate process, *provided* that you have named beneficiaries in your trust to receive the assets. For instance, in a typical case, a husband will create a trust to provide for himself and his spouse while he is alive, and on his death the trust will distribute what is left to his wife. (In larger estates, this is modified somewhat to save estate taxes—see chapter 13.) In this case, when the husband dies, the trust assets will be given to his wife, free of probate, and the assets will then be hers. But the problem is that on the wife's later death (or disability), all of *her* assets will then be fully probated. This can be avoided.

It is quite possible to design the trust in a way to avoid probate in *successive* estates. For instance, in the example above, say that the husband's trust provided that on his death, all of the assets would *remain* in trust for his wife's benefit, and she could withdraw whatever she needed, but what she did not use or withdraw would remain in the trust and on her death, whatever then remained in the trust would pass to their children. This would cause the assets to avoid probate in both the husband's estate *and* the wife's estate. It is possible to go even a step or two further and avoid probate in children's estates, etc., but there may be some complicated tax considerations to this and the details should be left to your tax lawyer.

Out-of-State Property—Double Your Probate, Double Your Legal Fees

Probate once is bad enough, but probate twice (or *more!*) can be double the trouble, expense, delays, etc. And this is just what happens when you die a resident of one state leaving property in another state. For instance, Jack has his home in Massachusetts, a second home in New Hampshire ski territory, and a third home in Florida. Each of the "out of state" properties is in Jack's name alone. On Jack's death, neither the New Hampshire nor the Florida property can pass to other members of his family according to his will until probate proceedings have been taken out in *each* of these states. The procedure is called "ancillary administration" (meaning probate in another state), and this cannot be done until Jack's will has been probated in Massachusetts. Even under the smoothest of circumstances, all of these procedures could take the better part of a year, not to mention the expense of hiring lawyers in all *three* states. And this is if nothing goes wrong. If Jack's will is contested in Massachusetts, the other properties are likely to just sit there until the dispute is resolved.

There are two simple ways to avoid *all* of this: the first is to place the out-of-state property in joint names. This way, on your death the property will avoid probate in the foreign state and the survivor will receive it straightaway. That's the good news. The bad news is that joint ownership can, as I have pointed out earlier in this chapter, lead to much more trouble than you ever bargained for. Just for openers, what if your joint owner dies before you? And if not, what happens on the death of the survivor? Answer: More probate, then more probate. By far, the better option is the second one, a simple living trust.

By using a living trust to hold the out-of-state property, you can avoid the exposure of double or triple probate, and you can easily provide for contingencies no matter who dies first, not to mention all the other advantages enumerated above. It may be that the particular state in which your property is located requires a special form of trust, but I can assure you, this is nothing compared to the time, trouble, and expense your estate will suffer if you leave the "foreign" property in your own name.

Avoiding Probate with a Durable Power of Attorney

Most people associate *probate* with *death*. Few, other than those who have had to deal with it, realize that probate may be necessary during a person's *lifetime*—specifically on the person's disability or incapacity. If a person becomes legally incompetent to handle his affairs, then his "affairs" cannot be dealt with unless he has a legal representative appointed to do so. Traditionally, such a representative is appointed by the probate court in the form of a guardian or a conservator for the person.

The procedure for appointment of a guardian or conservator is not unlike the procedure for appointment of an executor under a will, including notice to heirs and other interested parties, filing an inventory and annual accountings, and, of course, the opportunity of heirs and interested parties to object anywhere along the way. In other words, it is time-consuming, expensive, and very public. But, like probate at death, *it can be avoided.*

WHY A *DURABLE* POWER?

It is possible to appoint someone to act legally for you in the event of your disability or incapacity, and it is done through a durable power of attorney. The difference between a regular power of attorney and a *durable* power of attorney is crucial in this context. A regular power of attorney may give someone the authority to act legally for you, but that authority automatically *ceases* if you should become legally incompetent. If this happened, then it would become necessary to initiate probate proceedings to appoint a personal representative for you (i.e., a guardian or conservator), *despite* the existence of the regular power of attorney.

A *durable* power of attorney, on the other hand, survives your disability or legal incompetence and provides that the person or persons you named under the power will be able to act legally for you *even though you are incompetent.* Therefore, at least for purposes of financial dealings, it will normally *not* be necessary to have a guardian or conservator appointed for you if you have a valid durable power of attorney.

The durable power of attorney, which is recognized in all states, is a legal instrument, signed by you (it is a good idea to notarize it as well and some states require this), naming a person (it could be more than one) as your "attorney-in-fact," to act on your behalf and do almost everything you could do if you were available.

SCOPE OF THE POWER

The durable power can authorize your attorney-in-fact to sign checks, enter contracts, buy or sell real estate, deposit or withdraw funds, enter safe-deposit boxes, create trusts, run your business, make health care decisions on your behalf, make gifts and other transfers of property that you might have made, *including transfers to your living trust,* and just about anything else that you could have done, all *without* the need of seeking probate court permission to do so.

Note that the power could also be restricted to certain acts or for a certain period of time. While this type of power is not the one usually contemplated in an estate plan, it can be useful where, for instance, you are going to be away for a while and want to appoint someone to handle financial matters during that period. Or perhaps property is scheduled to be purchased or sold during your absence. You can appoint someone to negotiate and sign any documents, including a deed, to carry out the transaction in your absence. In any event, the power of attorney must be a *durable* one. Nowadays it is almost impossible to get any third party to deal with or honor a power of attorney that is not a durable one.

Obviously, giving someone all this power is a two-edged sword. While it ensures privacy and will save money and avoid publicity, the durable power of attorney at the same time can place tremendous powers into the hands of your attorney-in-fact. Actually, she could wipe you out with little trouble, and your only recourse would be to sue her (for breach of her duty to you), *if* you could find her. So be careful in whom you select as your attorney-in-fact. Some advisers feel that a fair safeguard to this potential problem is to name *two* attorneys-in-fact, who must act together on your behalf. I agree that this will at least reduce the risk, but it also necessitates two signatures on every transaction if you want the precaution to work.

THE SPRINGING POWER

When they hear of the extent of the powers that are customarily given to the attorney-in-fact, some people get a little nervous about it and ask if there is another way, especially if the chosen attorney-in-fact is someone other than a spouse. For this reason, some attorneys (*not* including this author) recommend the option of having a power of attorney that does not become effective *until* a doctor certifies that you are unable to care for yourself. This is called a "springing" power, and will at least defer the risk of being wiped out until you are incompetent and by then perhaps it won't matter to you.

Personally, I think springing powers only invite legal questions regarding the timing and continuance of the power.

For instance, a springing power must contain a number of additional, carefully drafted provisions (thereby adding potential problems in themselves) that define specifically what "springs" the power. Is it merely a doctor's letter or must it be something more formal? What must the letter say? (If the language in the letter is unclear, you can bet it will be near useless to spring the power.) Must the letter or certificate be recently dated? What if the doctor's letter is, say, a year old? Does the third party have a duty to ask for a new one? Or to contact the doctor to verify that the letter is still valid? As one can quickly see, the springing power is, in my experience and strong opinion, fraught with potential problems and is generally a bad idea, since there is a much better way to accomplish the same thing.

Instead, I recommend having the instrument confer the power *when it is signed,* but advise the attorney (i.e., the lawyer who drafted your documents) to *hold* the instrument until some later date or when the incompetence comes about. For instance, say that a client signs a durable power of attorney, naming a spouse or a child as attorney-in-fact. Without the original instrument or a copy of the *signed* instrument, the spouse or child has no authority to act under the power. In the meantime, the original is left with the client's attorney with written instructions to deliver it to the attorney-in-fact upon the attorney's receipt of a letter from a physician stating that the client is unable to handle his own affairs. Delivery of the instrument would then allow the attorney-in-fact to act under the power and take any necessary steps to complete the client's estate plan, including transfers of assets to the client's trust. In comparison to the springing power, it would also avoid third-party questions as to whether the client was, in fact, incompetent, since the durable power would not require that he be incompetent before it takes effect.

DURABLE POWERS AND JOINT OWNERSHIP

Many people are under the misconception that any assets they hold in joint names with a spouse or other person can easily be reached in case of an emergency or, for that matter, at any time. While this may be true for jointly held bank accounts, and while the *death* of either joint tenant will normally cause the survivor to have complete access to the asset, this is *not* true for jointly held securities or jointly held real estate while both (or all) joint tenants are alive. In those (and certain other) cases, and in cases where property is held under a tenancy by the entirety, if one of the joint tenants becomes incompetent, the only party that can deal with the incompetent joint tenant's share is the legal representative of the incompetent joint tenant. That would include a court-appointed guardian or conservator, or an attorney-in-fact under a durable power of attorney. Thus, even in the case of jointly held assets, a durable power of attorney can save time, legal fees, and court costs in dealing with assets.

SIGNING SEVERAL POWERS OF ATTORNEY

Where there are two or more family members (or others) that the principal would like to name, but he wants them to be able to act completely independently, there is the possibility of creating and signing separate powers for each. This will work if everyone is in concert and no dispute arises, but if the different attorneys in fact disagree, then the situation could become somewhat chaotic and expensive. There is no simple way to deal with this possibility in the document, so choose your attorney-in-fact carefully.

OUT-OF-STATE POWERS OF ATTORNEY

Most states will honor a durable power that was validly executed in the state of your domicile, and at least one state, California, specifically recognizes such a power under its law. This may work for bank accounts or tangible property in the "foreign" state, but it may not be any help where real estate is concerned. State laws regarding transfers of real estate are very precise, and a durable power that is valid in one state may not be sufficient to transfer real estate located in another state. Therefore, if you have real estate in more than one state, it would be a good idea to execute separate durable powers of attorney, each complying with the law of the foreign state with respect to durable powers *and* the laws regarding transfers of real estate.

COMPENSATING THE ATTORNEY-IN-FACT

Usually the attorney-in-fact is a spouse or other close relative, so compensation is not an issue. Nevertheless, as a "fiduciary," the attorney-in-fact is entitled to reasonable compensation for the services rendered. What is reasonable depends upon the circumstances and the nature of the services rendered, but factors to be considered include the time involved, the responsibility, and the urgency of the matter. It is acceptable, although not necessary, to include a provision such as "My attorney-in-fact shall be entitled to reasonable compensation for the services rendered in my behalf."

NAMING A SUCCESSOR ATTORNEY-IN-FACT

Your durable power should also provide for a *successor* attorney-in-fact if your named attorney-in-fact ceases to serve. And if appointment of a guardian becomes necessary despite the durable power (other relatives could insist on it), then in most states you can also name you own guardian in the instrument. Despite its flexibility and advantages, however, you should remember that a durable power of attorney *ceases at your death*. It is not a substitute for a living trust, and although it will help avoid probate during your lifetime, it will *not* do so on your death.

WHERE TO KEEP YOUR POWER OF ATTORNEY

While many people who do not leave their original documents with their attorney are inclined to keep them in a safe-deposit box, it is generally *not* a good idea to keep your durable power of attorney there. As noted repeatedly, the durable power is the key to dealing with assets and avoiding probate on a person's incompetence or incapacity. If the document is safely locked away in a safe-deposit box and the owner becomes incapacitated, the named attorney-in-fact (or the successor) may not have access to the box, and therefore the document will be useless. In general, it is a good idea to have your attorney store the durable power of attorney document (most law firms have facilities for the safekeeping of original documents) along with the instructions described above under "Springing Powers" to deliver the document to the attorney-in-fact at the appropriate time. This will avoid the unnecessary hassle, delay, and expense of dealing with the bank (or the court) to get access to the safe-deposit box.

Why You'll Still Need a Will

Even if you think you have transferred *all* of your property to a living trust or have it arranged in some other way to avoid probate, you'll *still* need a will.

This is because there is no way of knowing exactly what you will own and how it will be held at the time of your death. For instance, you may have all of your property in a trust, but then your great-aunt dies and leaves you one-fourth of her estate. Now you have another "asset" in your name, and unless you are efficient enough to transfer this to your living trust (a trust *can* hold *the right* to receive inheritances before they are received but not before the other person dies), your probate estate will include this inheritance.

Then there is property or rights that may arise just *after* or *as a result of* your death. With these types of assets, it is impossible to avoid probate. For instance, say that, for some reason, a death benefit from your employer is payable to your estate. If you have no will, this amount (as would *any* property that passes through your probate estate where there is no will) will pass to your heirs under the laws of intestacy.

The other type of "after death" asset that must pass through probate would be damages resulting from some accident that cause your death. If, for instance, you are struck by a car and die after suffering for a time, your *estate* would have the right to sue the driver of the car for "conscious pain and suffering" as well as for "wrongful death." Some or all of the proceeds recovered from the lawsuits, depending on the laws of the particular state, would pass under the terms of your will.

Finally, as noted in more detail in chapter 2, there are options you have that are only exercisable through your will, such as the naming of a guardian for your minor children and the naming of an executor of your choice to be responsible for settling your estate.

Therefore, even when it is virtually certain that there will be no probate, I still recommend the client have a will, exercising all of the available options in accordance with his wishes and having the bulk of his estate "pour over" into his living trust. This way, any loose ends that may arise are covered and coordinated with the client's estate plan. If it later turns out that, in fact, there is no probate estate and no need to use the will, then, although most states require that any person in possession of a deceased's original will must *file* the will with the appropriate probate court, the will is simply not actually submitted for probate.

12

Everything You Need
to Know about Trusts

Put not your trust in money but put your money in trust.

—from a Chinese fortune cookie

For many years now, trusts have been acquiring considerable allure and attention from large segments of the public. Few people clearly understand what trusts can do or just how they work, but nevertheless everyone seems to be pretty sure that trusts can do just about anything and can work wonders. It's almost true.

A trust can certainly provide for you and for your family; it can allow easy access to property, such as real estate, bank accounts, and securities while you're alive as well as during your illness or upon your death; and it can certainly cause your property to avoid probate.

But there are many different types of trusts, and the different trusts contain different provisions. Some may do the job you want, whereas others will not. You must be careful that your trust accomplishes your specific wishes, has all the necessary ingredients, and will do the job you chose it for. To help you understand whether or not it will, you'll need to know something about the basics of trusts and how they work.

The Basics of Trusts—A Working Overview

The fundamental trust arrangement involves a transfer of property to someone on his promise that he will hold it for another according to the transferor's instructions. It is a unique and useful relationship that clearly reflects its very name—a trust. However, like many legal principles and relationships, the modern-day trust has evolved to embody the latest legal and tax developments in many different areas. Nevertheless, no matter how complicated the trust instrument may be, the basics remain the same, and if you understand these, you will understand how a trust can help you.

According to some trust experts, the concept of the trust traces back nearly two thousand years to the reign of Emperor Augustus Caesar. At that time, a Roman citizen and his wife, who was not of the Roman Empire, wanted to leave their property to their children, but under Roman law the children were not allowed to inherit because their mother was not a Roman. To circumvent this law, the Roman left his property through his will to a friend, also a Roman, on his friend's promise that he would use the property to provide for the Roman's children after the Roman's death.

As it happened, the friend did not keep his promise. He betrayed the trust that the Roman had placed in him and used the property for himself. The Emperor Augustus, shocked at the betrayal, referred the matter to the Roman court for disposition. Prior to this, the use of such a bequest (in trust) had never been formally recognized by the court, but after the emperor's approval the trust arrangement became so popular that a special court had to be established to answer inquiries and determine the treatment of such cases.

This was one of the earliest recorded forms of a trust, but it contains all the basic ingredients of today's trusts. The Roman (called the *donor* or the *grantor* or the *settlor*) transferred property (sometimes called the *corpus*) to his friend (called the *trustee*), who promised to follow instructions to hold and use the property for the benefit of the children (the *beneficiaries*).

From its simplest form to the most complex, every trust is based upon the same principles and contains the same basic elements: a settlor, a trustee, some property, and one or more beneficiaries. A *living trust* is any trust that you create while you are alive. It is sometimes referred to as an "inter vivos" trust—meaning "among the living." A trust created upon the settlor's death is a *testamentary trust.*

The trust created by our Roman was a testamentary trust—that is, it was created at his death by instructions contained *in his will.* In order for the trust to take effect, then, the Roman's will had to be approved by a court through the probate process. If the Roman had created a living trust and had transferred his property to the trust *during his lifetime* with instructions for its disposition after his death, there would have been no need for the probate court to make the transfer. *The property already in the trust would have avoided the probate process.*

REVOCABLE VS. IRREVOCABLE TRUSTS

Under most living trusts, the creator or settlor will reserve the right to "alter, amend, or revoke" the trust. This simply means he can change the terms of the trust at any time; he can even cancel (revoke) the trust and take the trust property back. In short, the settlor can do whatever he pleases with the trust or with any property held in the trust. The retention of a right to change or revoke the trust—called a *revocable trust*—does *not* provide the donor with any immediate tax benefits but *does* allow the property in the trust to avoid the costs, delays, and publicity of probate, and *can* save estate taxes in future estates. Trust language should be *clear* about rights to amend or revoke and exactly what is required to do so. For instance, amendment or revocation is usually required in writing and delivered to the trustee. A change in the trustee's duties or responsibility may require the trustee's consent, but I prefer instead to give the trustee, in such a case, the right to resign rather than a veto power over such amendments.

The opposite of a revocable trust is an *irrevocable trust.* If a trust does not specifically contain the right to amend or revoke, most states' laws provide that it is automatically irrevocable, meaning that it generally cannot be changed "by the donor." Note, however, that certain powers to change (even revoke) the trust can be given to others, while the trust would still be irrevocable as to the donor. Although current tax savings can be realized through the use of an irrevocable trust, you should consider one only after proper advice and counsel. This is because you will be required to give up benefits, if not control, of the property, and since the document is relatively permanent, recovery of the property transferred to such a trust is unlikely. (The tax implications of trusts are covered in detail in chapter 13.)

HOW A TRUST WORKS

Whether your trust is living or testamentary, whether it is revocable or irrevocable, whether it is a simple trustee bank account (as discussed earlier) or a complicated family trust, once the trust takes effect it will work the same way. When property is transferred to the trustee, the trustee immediately begins to manage, maintain, or invest the trust property, whether it be cash, securities, real estate, or other property, according to the instructions given by the donor. For example, say that John gives $1,000 to Mary with instructions that she give him (John) all the interest it earns, and upon John's death, she should turn the balance over to his sister Adele. Mary's duties are quite clear. She will pay John all the interest up to the time of his death, then she will transfer the remaining funds over to Adele directly. Adele then owns the money outright, without probate; Mary's job as trustee is completed and the trust is terminated.

Of course, the instructions and/or the duties could be much more involved. John could have transferred real estate to Mary, or a large portfolio of securities, and Mary, as trustee, would be responsible for the proper management of the trust property. This might include renting the property, keeping it properly insured and in good repair, and so on. If she were holding securities, she would be responsible for keeping track of the progress of the various companies whose stock she was holding, or she might simply hire an investment adviser. But in any event, once the property is transferred to the trust, the trustee's responsibility is to care for it while carrying out the donor's instructions.

WHAT CAN A TRUST DO?

The trust instrument is one of the most flexible legal tools available today. Rather than enumerate all that it can do, the scope of its flexibility is better understood by stating what it cannot do: It cannot be created to do anything that is illegal or against public policy. Anything else is permissible. For example, a trust can:

- Run a business
- Provide for minors or elderly or disabled persons
- Pay medical or other bills
- Create a scholarship fund
- Provide for retirement, education, marriage, and even divorce
- Help carry out the terms of a premarital agreement
- Hold real estate, cash, securities, or any other type of property
- Provide protection for property against creditors of the donor and other beneficiaries
- Avoid probate and some administrative costs for property in the trust, not just on the first death but on one or more subsequent deaths
- Save taxes

Our Roman citizen established a trust to care for his children. Simple enough, and also one of the essential reasons for a trust. The Roman must have been a wise person. Even in the year AD 5 he knew that a youth and his money are soon parted, and that rather than give his children the money outright, it may be better to allow them only the use of the property until they reached an age of greater maturity, when they might better appreciate the value of money and the responsibility that goes with it.

Your reasons for creating a trust may be some, all, or none of the above. Or you may just want to avoid probate. Whatever the reasons, your trust can be specially tailored to accomplish your objectives, leaving little to chance. In light of this, it is foolhardy to rely upon the whimsical joint ownership form to dispose of your property when a simple trust can accomplish the same thing and more.

WHO SHOULD BE YOUR TRUSTEE?

If you *fund* your revocable trust (place your assets into it) while you are alive—and you are foolish not to—then you should usually be your own trustee. Many people—even some attorneys—raise eyebrows at this, since, for some reason, it is a little unconventional. I have had many clients and readers tell me that they have consulted an attorney on the matter and he or she said it couldn't be done. Regardless of what you are told, even by such poorly informed lawyers, it *can* be done and it is *highly advisable,* assuming you want to keep direct control and access to your funds and other assets. *Note* that this is rarely the case with an irrevocable trust.

Under trust law, it is quite permissible for you to be donor, trustee, *and* beneficiary of your trust all at the same time, so long as your trust provides for some other beneficiary (or beneficiaries) after your death—this is called "a gift over." Naming yourself as initial trustee allows you to maintain full control over your property as long as you wish and are able. In the event of your death or disability, your trust would provide for a "successor" trustee, who would take over that position for you and administer the trust property for your own and your family's benefit.

The successor trustee, who takes over if you are ill or deceased, is guided (and restricted) by the terms of your trust. He cannot use the funds for his own benefit (unless the trust allows it) or go against your instructions. If he does, he will be personally responsible for his breach of "fiduciary" duty— the duty of a trustee always to act in the best interests of the beneficiaries and in accordance with the terms of the trust.

Although naming yourself as a trustee is an easy choice, selecting a successor trustee is often not so easy. For larger estates, the successor trustee in many trusts, depending on the provisions, must often be an independent one for tax purposes. This would be the case, for instance, where you wanted the trustee to have maximum discretion to distribute trust income and/or principal to your spouse and children after your death. In this case, having a spouse or child as the trustee could cause a loss of tax benefits, although your spouse or child could serve as a co-trustee with the independent trustee, so long as the trust provides that she may not make unrestricted distributions to herself.

On the other hand, if you don't mind providing for a modest restriction on the trustee's discretion, you *can* name your spouse (and/or children) as successor trustee of the trust under which she is a beneficiary. Yes, you read that correctly. All that is necessary is to include what is called an "ascertainable standard" to guide the trustee in exercising discretion. The actual language would be something like, "The trustee may pay to my spouse such amounts of the income and principal of this trust as the trustee in her sole discretion determines is appropriate for my spouse's health, education, maintenance, and support." The words *health, education, maintenance, and support* are the magic words that comprise the ascertainable standard and will keep the trust assets (i.e., those in the "bypass" or "family" trust) out of the surviving spouse's estate, *even though* she is the trustee and the beneficiary.

Unfortunately, many attorneys like to get fancy and creative with the ascertainable standard and use words that the IRS and the tax regulations have not approved, for reasons I am at a loss to understand. If the IRS tells us *exactly* how to do it, why mess with it? The simple addition of the word *comfort*, for example, to the four approved magic words, has proved *fatal* in a great number of cases, causing the entire bypass trust to be taxed in the surviving spouse's estate. Note that this is not like a $50 fine. The cost of the wrong word can be the better part of a $1 million in 2006!

In many smaller estates (say, $1 million or less—I know that $1 million is not exactly "small," but in terms of modern-day estates and estate taxes, it is considered "small"), the donor is often named as the initial trustee of the trust that provides for his and his spouse's benefit during his lifetime. On the donor's death, his spouse becomes the successor trustee and the trust continues for her lifetime. On the spouse's death, a child becomes the successor trustee and at that point the child (as trustee) merely divides the remaining trust property (after payment of expenses and taxes) among the children. (More details on the options and tax implications of trustee selection are discussed later in this chapter.)

Our Roman citizen named his friend as trustee and it turned out to be a poor choice. His friend had no experience in such matters and proved to be untrustworthy. In those days, perhaps, there were few people who could have had much experience, but a more reliable person may have at least carried out the donor's wishes.

Being a trustee may be easy if you are the donor as well as the beneficiary. You can do with the property as you please and you have only yourself to answer to. If you become a trustee where *someone else* is the beneficiary, however, you're in a whole new ball game. Everything you do is subject to review and question by the beneficiaries. Investments, distributions, the timing of both, selling, buying, leasing, preparing and filing tax returns and trust accounts, all must be done with your fiduciary duty in mind; otherwise you could find yourself covering your mistakes with your own money! People who really understand the serious responsibility and duties involved usually do not wish to act as trustee for someone else unless they have considerable experience—and the time to do it. As a result, when it comes to choosing a successor trustee, more and more people are relying on those organizations that have the experience and the time to give the trust the necessary attention. They are called "corporate" trustees.

A corporate trustee is a bank or trust company chartered by the state to accept funds from members of the public under a trust agreement. Although there may be something to be said against corporate trustees, there are many more important points in their favor. Most corporate trustees have been in the trust business for years and know how to manage a trust. They have a reputation to uphold and so do not want bad press if they can avoid it. They have financial backing and stability, so the chances of their running off with your money are slim, if not nonexistent. Their fees are regulated by law or by the probate court and are usually disclosed to you before you name them as trustee.

On the other hand, corporate trustees have been accused of being cold and unresponsive to the members of the family, and have been known to be somewhat stiff and inflexible when it comes to interpretation of the trust provisions. In addition, for many years their investment performance had been questionable. More recently, however, their investment performance has improved substantially and generally is no longer regarded as a problem. In part, as a result of their "pirating" the best investment managers from the "private" sector, many banks now have investment records that rival those of the better mutual funds. All of these "other-handed" objections, however, can be dealt with by adding two provisions to your trust: First, have your spouse or another family member act as co-trustee with the bank. This will add the warmth and sensitivity that some feel is lacking in a bank trustee.

Second, give your spouse (or other responsible family member or members) the right to remove the corporate trustee and appoint a successor (corporate or disinterested) trustee. If your bank is performing poorly, this will facilitate a transfer to one that has a better record.

In some cases the power to remove and appoint a new trustee can have tax implications as noted in this and the next chapter. Furthermore, the power to remove can be abused, and in the wrong hands it can jeopardize the proper administration of the trust; but you'll just have to trust someone.

For "smaller" trusts, say $500,000 or less, corporate trustees are not economical, and in most cases they would not want such a small trust. In these situations, a trusted family member or professional (such as an attorney or accountant) may be your only choice, so choose carefully, and don't forget to consider including the power to remove the trustee in the terms of the trust.

Remember, this is a brief overview. There are many other legal and, more particularly, tax considerations in the selection of a trustee. These issues are discussed in more detail in chapter 13.

THE TERMS OF YOUR TRUST

If you are going to have a trust, be sure it has terms that the trustee can follow and that properly reflect your wishes. The lazy man's trust, the trustee bank account, for example, or the inadequate preprinted form, is little better than a joint account and, in many cases, offers more risks. The trustee bank account is a trust that, in effect, has no terms other than the trustee's absolute right to make deposits and withdrawals as he sees fit and the right of the beneficiary (subject to easy interference) to receive the funds on the trustee's death.

In order for the terms of a trust to be carried out, there have to be some terms. Where there is none or where the terms are incomplete or contradictory or confusing, there will be trouble.

The terms may be simple or they may be complicated, but they must be clear. They should cover lifetime distributions of income and/or principal, the conditions or guidelines for distributions, and the possibility that a beneficiary may die before the donor or before receiving his or her trust distributions in full. There should be provisions for successor trustees and for adequate trustee powers, as well as protection of the funds from claims of creditors (called a "spendthrift" provision), to name only a few. Attorneys experienced in drafting trusts are well versed in the numerous provisions that can and should be included, but the following is an explanation of the more important ones.

SPRAY PROVISIONS

A very common and valuable provision seen in most family trusts, and invariably in "dynasty" trusts, as discussed later, is the "spray" or "sprinkle" provision. Where there is more than one beneficiary, this provision allows the trustee to distribute (spray) the income and/or principal among the beneficiaries in varying proportions as the trustee feels appropriate, having in mind their individual needs and circumstances from time to time. In other words, the trustee need not make equal distributions among the beneficiaries, but instead can vary the distributions according to their particular needs, which undoubtedly is exactly what the parents would do were they alive.

STAGED DISTRIBUTIONS TO BENEFICIARIES

One of the considerable advantages of a trust over a will is the ability of the trustee to hold the beneficiary's share over an extended period of time, and during that time to provide for the changing needs of the beneficiary through trust distributions. But the question then arises: "At what point do we give Johnny his money?" If parents die before their children reach a "responsible" age (no one knows exactly what age that is), it is a routine matter to allow for the trust to continue as explained a moment ago, but for how long? Unless a beneficiary is disabled and will never be capable of receiving a lump sum, or unless there is a dynasty trust that by its terms is designed to last for several generations, we need to think about the best way to make a distribution of Johnny's share to Johnny.

In the typical family trust, after the death of the surviving spouse the trust will provide benefits for the children until they reach a certain age, at which time the trustee pays out the shares and terminates the trust. The "certain age" differs with most families, but even in the case of relatively "small" estates, since we are talking about the distribution of a couple hundred thousand or more per child, certain sensible safeguards must prevail. For instance, most would agree it is a little foolhardy to hand over $200,000 in cash to a twenty-one-year-old, or maybe even a twenty-five-year-old. And what about larger estates where the children are to receive upward of $500,000 each?

In such cases, estate planners will almost always recommend spreading the distribution over a period of years. This will give the beneficiary the opportunity to learn (hopefully) how to handle the money, or, if he spends it or manages it poorly, the experience is likely to cause him to be that much more careful with the next distribution.

In the typical case, distributions are slated for one-third at, say, age twenty-five or thirty, another third at thirty or thirty-five, and the balance at thirty-five or forty. Remember that while the child is waiting for these distributions, he remains a beneficiary of his share and can receive periodic distributions of income and principal according to his needs until the final distribution of his share is made. For instance, if a child gets married, or needs help in buying a home or starting a business, the trustee could make lump-sum distributions to the child, even though he has not yet reached the age specified in the trust. Many trusts contain language making it clear that the trustee can make such distributions. Furthermore, if a child dies before his share is distributed, the trust may provide that the remainder of the share will pass to or be held for the child's children, to be distributed to them at a certain age, or to the child's siblings, etc. This way, the remainder of the child's share avoids probate in the child's estate. Although it is typically subject to taxes in the child's estate, there are unlikely to be any taxes due to the child's estate tax exemption of $1.5 million or more, depending on the year of death.

TRUSTEE ACCOUNTING

Every trustee of every trust *must* account to the beneficiaries for his administration of the trust. Generally, a trustee's account is a detailed financial report of what the trustee received on behalf of the trust, what he did with the assets over the course of the accounting period (receipts, payments, expenses, etc.), and what assets are left at the end of the accounting period. Traditionally (and legally), the normal accounting period is annually, although most corporate (bank) trustees are set up to account to their beneficiaries on a quarterly basis.

Although there is a legal duty for the trustee to account to the beneficiaries whether the trust states it or not, it is nevertheless important to have a provision calling for an account so that the details can be spelled out as to when and to whom the accounts are to be given.

Where the settlor is also the trustee of the trust, it is not necessary that he account to himself. The accounting requirement is normally to protect beneficiaries who are not also trustees. In that event, it is not permissible for the trust to dispense with an accounting, and any trust provision that attempts to do so would be ignored by the courts as being against public policy.

Accountings must be given in writing to the beneficiaries in a form that is reasonable for them to understand. If a beneficiary questions any part of the account or the behavior of the trustee, he has the right to request an explanation from the trustee. Trustees who refuse or mismanage the trust are always subject to review and possible penalties by the probate court. If a trustee is found by a court to have acted improperly, the court will "surcharge" the trustee, meaning that the trustee will be ordered to pay the costs or expenses or damages *out of his own pocket.*

NONCONTEST TRUST PROVISIONS

In chapter 10 I explained how to contest a will and how to prevent a will contest. Briefly, a will contest is prevented by giving the troublesome beneficiary (or his children) a bequest that is *conditioned* upon his not contesting the will. In almost all states, this will work, although some states make an exception if the contesting beneficiary had reasonable cause to wage the contest. Trusts are no different in this respect, except that the provisions in the trust and the will can be coordinated, so that the bequest, whether it be in the trust *or* the will, can be conditioned upon the beneficiary not contesting either document.

To illustrate, say that Uncle Sam wants to leave all of his $1 million estate to his nephew, Bill, but fears that his other two nephews will make trouble. Uncle Sam could leave his other nephews, say, $25,000 each, under a bequest in his will, and establish a separate living *trust* solely for the benefit of his nephew, Bill. The will could contain a noncontest provision stating that if a nephew either contested the will *or* brought any action to set aside or attack the living trust, he would lose his bequest. Note that in this case, if the noncontest provision was in the trust and not in the will, it would be ineffective unless the $25,000 bequest was then placed in the trust. That is, the provision must be included in the document that gives the bequest, and the noncontest condition could then extend to cover the other document.

USING PREPRINTED FORMS — OR, THE BEST WAY
TO INCREASE LEGAL FEES AND EXPENSES

Everyone likes to save money, and saving money on legal fees is even better. As a result, there is a huge and extremely profitable market in preprinted legal forms of every type, from adoption papers to zoning applications, but by far the most popular have been the forms for living trusts. Being a member of the public as well as a lawyer, I can understand the feeling that if lawyers use preprinted forms, why shouldn't you, and forget the lawyer. But in my opinion, you ought to approach preprinted forms in the same way you would a cheap suit of clothes bought from a mail-order supply house. The price may be right, but you'd be a fool to think it will fit or be fit to wear. So it is with these forms.

In a popular but dangerous book on avoiding probate, there are several hundred pages of a variety of trust forms, with step-by-step "instructions" on their use. The instructions, however, fail to take into consideration all gift tax or other tax results (in fact, following the instructions will often result in additional taxes). In addition, they fail to consider the possible conflicts from one preprinted form to another when compared with your overall estate plan; they fail to consider adequately death or disability of your beneficiaries; they completely overlook coordination from one form to another; and, most dangerously, they encourage you to go merrily along arbitrarily filling in the blanks, without knowing the slightest thing about what you are doing. And for what? For a savings of legal fees, since the last thing you should do—such books tell us—is consult a *lawyer*. The fact that thousands, or maybe hundreds of thousands, of your dollars are involved doesn't seem to mean much to the forms salesman, but it's an awful risk for your family. The unguided use of such forms *might,* if you're lucky, result in avoidance of probate with some of your property, but it will more likely result in *added legal fees* for court interpretation of conflicting documents, *added taxes,* and *added costs* in the estates of the beneficiaries. You might as well have spent your money on a cheap suit.

When you think of the tens of thousands of dollars in savings that can definitely—not maybe, as with uncoordinated forms—be saved through the use of a professionally drafted and funded trust, properly coordinated with the rest of your estate plan, it is silly and reckless to try to do it yourself with the help of forms you know nothing about prepared by some would-be lawyer. The only one who benefits from these forms is the company who sells them to you.

Coordinating Your Plan—Putting Your Trust to Work

Some of you reading this may feel complacent because you already have a trust. If this is so, congratulations—maybe! Set aside your complacency for the moment to see if your trust has been "funded." (Most typical living trusts are *not!*) A trust is funded when property is transferred to it. Your trust will operate or have effect *only* as to that property that has been actually transferred to the trust.

Perhaps the most common estate-planning mistake is having a trust, then failing to fund it. By funding I do not mean a transfer of $10 or $100, or by naming the trust as beneficiary of your life insurance policy. I mean funding it with just about all of your property, as well as naming the trust as beneficiary of your life insurance policies (unless you have a separate life insurance trust, discussed later in this chapter) and, in some cases, provided your tax adviser approves, your retirement plans. Depending upon the state in which you live, you may need a different trust to hold your real estate, but this can easily be drafted to coordinate with the terms of any other trust (or trusts) you have.

The big mistake is going to the trouble of having a trust but continuing to hold most of your property in joint names, or in your own name alone. Your jointly held property will, unless someone objects, pass to the surviving joint tenant and *not* to your trust. As to this property, then, your trust becomes worthless. Property in your name will, of course, have to pass through probate. And then it may pass to your trust, but only if that is what your will provides and if no one successfully contests it. In either case, you have lost a very important feature that the living trust offers: avoidance of probate in your estate and possibly future estates. Furthermore, failing to coordinate your assets with your trust could foul up your *entire* estate plan.

For instance, I recently had a case in which a father had gone to a great deal of trouble to create a trust for his retarded daughter. With an attorney's help, he had set up an elaborate, well-drafted trust that provided for the daughter's care for the rest of her life since she was unable to care for herself. On the father's death, his widow came to me to determine the next step so that the trust could begin to provide for the child. An examination of the father's assets disclosed that everything he owned was in joint names with his wife. Nothing passed to the daughter's trust!

In the more common situation, the husband will have a marital and a family trust to accomplish his estate and tax planning, but most of his property, being jointly held, will pass outside the trust, rendering the trust useless and frustrating the estate plan.

Funding your trust, then, to the maximum practical extent possible will allow you to get the benefits intended by the trust, during life as well as after death. One of the important lifetime benefits is realized if you become disabled. If jointly held securities or real estate is involved, at least one-half the value of the joint property would be "frozen," and in any event a sale would not be allowed until the probate court appointed a guardian or conservator for you. If, instead, you had placed this property in a living trust, *no* court action would be required. The property would be immediately accessible by the trustee to provide for your care and treatment. This can be extremely important in the case of a widow or widower or other single person.

Once you have some familiarity with the trust concept, call your attorney and ask him how familiar he is with *funded, inter vivos* (living) trusts and whether he can develop an estate plan for you that is designed to *avoid probate.* Be frank and direct in your questions. If your attorney gets overly defensive or tells you that you cannot be your own trustee, he is probably not familiar enough with the area, and you should look around for another attorney.

Most bar associations have lawyer referral services, and they should be able to give you the names of two or three local attorneys who have indicated they have a familiarity with tax and estate planning, But, as discussed in chapter 14, don't assume that the lawyers referred to you are experts either. And don't be afraid to call these (or other) attorneys to request an initial conference—preferably a free one. Many attorneys are willing to give you fifteen minutes or a half hour (you shouldn't expect more than that) without charge to determine whether they can help you and to see if the "chemistry" is right.

Once you have selected and met with an attorney and he or she has developed a plan for you, stop where you are. At this point you should spend $500 or so and get a *second opinion* on the plan that has been presented to you. The second opinion may be that of another attorney, or your accountant (if he has the training to do so), or even your bank's trust department (an advantage here is that the bank and the bank's trust attorney will not usually charge you for their review). If the opinion is favorable, you may proceed with the plan. If not, the issues raised may be discussed and resolved with your attorney, and your final plan may then be implemented.

Part of your plan will undoubtedly involve funding or transferring property to your trust (if it doesn't, you probably don't have the right plan). This is the legal move that actually starts your trust. As previously discussed, once the trust is funded, it then takes effect. Funding, or placing property in the trust, is a lifetime disposition of the property, and from that point on the property will be administered and distributed according to the terms of your trust because it is *in* the trust, even though you may be the trustee. Following are basic instructions on how to fund your trust.

BANK ACCOUNTS

Once your attorney has prepared your living trust and you have made the decision to fund it, you should take a copy of the signed trust to your bank and have the bank either change the title on the existing accounts or simply open up a new account in the name of your trust, showing yourself as trustee. The bank will usually want to keep a copy of your trust on file; this is acceptable since its privacy is still respected.

If you are asked for a tax identification number, you should give the bank your Social Security number, since all interest on the account will be taxed to you. If, out of ignorance, the bank insists on a trust ID number (which is actually against the tax regulations!), this is still not a problem, as discussed in chapter 13.

Once you have opened a new account in the name of your trust, nothing else will change. You may make deposits and withdrawals, loans, open new accounts, pay bills, and anything else you would do on your own. The difference is that now the funds in the account are "managed and disposed" according to the detailed terms of your trust rather than according to chance.

STOCKS AND BONDS

Transferring securities to your trust can be a little more involved than transferring a bank account to the trust, but do not be discouraged. Whatever it takes, it's worth it, and there is a shortcut.

If the securities are registered in your name or in joint names, you must first determine whether or not you want to transfer them to your trust. Remember that for income tax purposes the dividends or interest on these securities will be taxed to each joint owner equally, and if this arrangement is saving you some income taxes, this might be a consideration. Furthermore, depending on the size of your estate, there may be estate tax implications to changing all of your securities from joint names to a trust, so, especially with larger estates, you should check with your tax attorney first.

A transfer of registered securities to your living trust is effected by signing or by having each joint tenant sign the back of the stock certificate (or a "stock power," which is a separate paper, available from your stockbroker) and by submitting these to the transfer agent whose name will appear on the certificate. Before sending these, you must have the signatures "guaranteed" by a stock-brokerage house or by a commercial bank, so the transfer agent can rely on their authenticity. (Certificates should always be sent by registered or certified mail.) The transfer agent will also want a copy of the trust. Fortunately, there is a shortcut.

I have found that a *much* easier way of transferring securities is through your stockbroker. If the securities are in street name (held by your broker) or are registered, you may simply open a *new* brokerage account in the name of your trust and have your broker place the securities into this new account. If you intend later to take delivery of the securities, you will ask him to reregister them in the name of the trust. Some houses charge a nominal "accommodation fee" to make the transfer for you, and whatever it is, pay it! Transfer agents are extremely difficult and unnecessarily picky when it comes to trusts, and the aggravation you are avoiding makes the accommodation fee well worth spending.

After the transfer, you, as trustee of your trust, may deal with the securities just as if you personally owned them. There will be no restrictions, except that if you want to trade on margin or deal with options, the brokerage house (for its own protection) will usually request special language in your trust. If you intend to make these transactions, instruct your attorney when the trust is being drafted. If you forgot or did not know, you may amend the trust to add the necessary language (the brokerage house will be glad to tell you the specific language they would like).

As with the bank account, you may "wheel and deal" with your stocks without interference, and if you are disabled, your successor trustee may take over, but his wheeling and dealing is subject to more scrutiny by you and your beneficiaries. You (and the successor trustee) must always remember that the successor trustee may be personally responsible if the terms of your trust are breached. In this way, you and your beneficiaries are protected.

REAL ESTATE

Real estate is unique in many respects. For one, every transaction relating to the property is formally recorded at an official registry. The names of the old owners, the new owners, the mortgagees, discharge of mortgages, attachments, and so on are all on record. And in many but not all states, when the real estate transferred to a trust, the trust itself is recorded as well. Once the trust is recorded, it may be that any changes or amendments to your trust may also be required to be recorded, and in some cases this could be inconvenient. For this reason, most attorneys have a simple form of trust especially designed to hold real estate.

Before you transfer any of your real estate to your trust, have a local attorney advise you as to any potential tax issues involved, as well as local laws regarding the holding of real estate in a trust, to be sure you are not creating any new problems. For instance, many states do not recognize a declaration of "homestead" that is made on a principal residence held in a trust. Typically, a homestead declaration that is properly made and recorded can protect the residence from attachment and sale by creditors of the homeowner. Although a few states (like Delaware, New Jersey, and Pennsylvania) offer no homestead protection, in others the protection can be quite substantial. In Massachusetts, for instance, it is a $500,000 (twice that if the homeowners are over age sixty-two), and in Texas, Kansas, Iowa, Oklahoma, and Florida it is unlimited. *Note*, however, that the Bankruptcy Abuse Prevention and Consumer Protection Act of 2005 imposes its own overriding limitations on homestead protection. Furthermore, if the property is mortgaged, be sure the transfer does not violate the terms of your mortgage. A bank holding a low-interest mortgage may like nothing better than to call the balance due on the mortgage because of some technical breach of the mortgage contract, even though the new owners are essentially the same as the old. Normally, the mortgage would not be called just because a declaration of homestead is recorded, especially since the homestead would *not* prohibit the bank from collecting on the mortgage note. Federal law prohibits a bank or other lender from calling a mortgage if the transfer of the property is to a living trust under which the borrower or spouse is the beneficiary. In any case, you should consult with your attorney.

BUSINESS INTERESTS

The trust to hold your business interests, whether they be in the form of a partnership, limited liability company, corporation, or sole proprietorship, may be the very same living trust that holds your bank accounts and securities, or it may be a special, separate trust recommended by your attorney. Here, particular attention should be given to selection of the person or organization (the successor trustee) who will have control of the business after you. It should be someone capable of handling that responsibility. If the person or organization you wish to name as successor trustee is different from the person you wish to run your business, this can easily be arranged either by a separate trust or by a special provision in your primary trust. Remember that under a trust you can provide that control of the business will be in one person's name, whereas benefits (payments of one type or another) may go to your family. If the business is jointly held, all of these choices are taken away from you. If the business is held in your own name, all of these choices are delayed by the probate process and the business is subjected to the other exposures of probate as well.

OTHER PROPERTY

Virtually every type of property may be held in a trust. Anything that is not mentioned above that you wish to put into your trust can be done so, merely by taking the necessary steps to transfer it legally to the trust. If there is a question or the manner of transfer eludes you, just ask yourself, "How was the item transferred to me in the first place?" It may have been by a bill of sale, deed, etc. In most cases, you can use the same approach, although it would not be a sale, since no payment is being made for the transfer to the trust. This is another area where your attorney can help you over the rough spots.

Items of tangible personal property usually have no formal title documentation, with the possible exception of automobiles and certain boats, which have "certificates of title." If you wish to hold tangible items of property in your trust, such as antiques, jewelry, furniture, etc., this can be done through a simple written statement, describing the items in detail and stating that you are holding them in your trust. You may also declare who is to receive the items on your death. Such a statement might say:

> I hereby declare that I have transferred the following items of property to the Bove Family Trust, dated August 19, 1988, and that I am holding the same, as Trustee, under the terms and conditions of that trust:
> [list and description of items]
> Upon my death, such items are to be divided equally between my two children. If either predeceases me, all to the survivor. If they both survive me and they cannot agree upon a division of these items within one month after my death, my trustee is directed to sell the remaining items and divide the proceeds equally between my two children.
> /S/ Alexander A. Bove, Jr.
> [Witness and/or notary is generally not necessary, but either or both won't hurt.]

Incidentally, life insurance policies are not usually transferred to a revocable trust, although they may be. Instead, it is customary to name the trust as *beneficiary* of the policies. By itself, this does not constitute a change of *ownership* of the policies. If actual ownership of the policies is to be transferred to a trust, it is usually an *irrevocable* trust, designed to save estate taxes on your death. (In this type of trust, you would *not* be the trustee, nor would you have any control over or rights to the trust assets. See more on this later in this chapter.)

If your plan calls for only one trust and all your property has been transferred to it, you should make a checklist of what is in your trust and keep the list up to date. New property should be acquired in the name of your trust rather than individually, if this is your plan, and you ought to review the whole arrangement with your attorney once each year.

Surprisingly, having a trust does not require any more record keeping than not having one. In other words, if you already have securities and bank accounts in your own name, you would, of course, keep your own records of these. If they are transferred to your trust, you'll keep the very same records, except that the title of those accounts will be in the name of the trust instead of your own name individually. Furthermore, unlike a will, a copy of the signed trust is adequate when you deal with brokers and banks, so the original can be safely left with your attorney or in your safe-deposit box.

Another advantage of a trust over a will is its "geographic" flexibility. When a family moves to a new state, they are often advised to make out a new will. If the same family happens to have a living trust, however, it would not normally be necessary to make out a new trust because the existing trust will be perfectly valid in the new state. And if this family does make out a new will, the new will can easily refer to the existing trust that was made out in the previous state.

DON'T LET THE IDEA OF A TRUST SCARE YOU

To many, the thought of a trust seems attractive, but then when they find that they must rearrange title to their assets, they get a little worried. Changing bank accounts, securities, business interests, and real estate can cause you to have second thoughts about the trust and question whether you're "doing the right thing." If this happens, remember that your trust is *revocable*—you can change it or cancel it, in whole or in part, anytime you wish at your absolute whim. Furthermore, *you* can be the trustee, so there is no loss of control.

Once you have separate trust accounts, you will find it much easier to deal with banks and transfer agents through your trust. Furthermore, you will become a little more accustomed to dealing with the trust yourself. In this respect, you will be buying and selling securities, opening accounts, etc., in the name of "John Smith, Trustee of the John Smith Trust, dated 12/3/04" instead of just "John Smith," or "John and Mildred Smith as joint tenants."

From these basics all trusts are built, and they can be molded into some pretty intricate and complicated structures, designed to meet a myriad of objectives of the settlor. What follows is a discussion of the numerous types of trusts created and used by attorneys for estate planning, family planning, charitable planning, etc., keeping in mind that a competent and expert attorney can combine many of these trusts. Note also that a number of objectives can be satisfied by a single trust (although you should keep in mind that putting everything into a single trust is not necessarily a desirable goal).

For instance, a marital deduction trust can readily be combined with a charitable trust or an asset protection trust, and a life insurance trust frequently doubles as a generation-skipping trust or a dynasty trust. Of course, these are all covered in detail in this chapter.

Trusts for the "Family"

For a married couple with children and a potentially taxable estate, the typical estate plan will include, in addition to wills, durable powers of attorney and health care proxies, and *two* living trusts, one established by each spouse. (See chapter 13 for more on estate taxes, but this generally means a combined estate in excess of $2 million for 2006, gradually increasing to $3.5 million for 2009.)

Each of these trusts would be revocable by the settlor spouse and, on his or her death, that trust will contain provisions that divide the original trust into two new irrevocable trusts: One, a marital deduction trust for the benefit of the surviving spouse, and the second, a bypass, or family trust for the benefit of the spouse and/or children (these trusts and their tax effects are described in more detail below). The effect of this split of trusts is basically to reduce estate taxes to zero on the first death *and* to help reduce estate taxes on the second death, while at the same time providing benefits for the surviving spouse and children.

THE MARITAL DEDUCTION TRUST

This is unquestionably one of the most important trusts in the estate plan of a married couple with a potentially taxable estate. If a trust is established for the surviving spouse and the requirements for qualifying for the marital deduction are accidentally missed, a veritable tax disaster (and probably a lawsuit for malpractice) will result. When the trust does qualify, *all* of the deceased spouse's assets that pass to the marital deduction trust will be free of estate tax, without limitation.

It is called a marital deduction trust because our federal estate tax laws allow a deduction against the taxable amount of an estate for those amounts that pass to a surviving spouse, without limitation. In other words, if John dies, leaving his entire $50 million estate to his surviving spouse (either outright or in a marital deduction trust), there will be *no* federal estate taxes. Technically, the calculation is:

Gross estate:	$50 million
Less deductions against estate tax:	(*$50 million*) marital deduction
Taxable estate:	- 0 -

If the deceased spouse leaves the assets outright to the surviving spouse, there is no question about the bequest qualifying for the marital deduction. If the bequest is left to a *trust,* however, the trust must meet certain requirements; otherwise, the deduction could be lost.

For a trust to qualify for the marital deduction, the surviving spouse must be the *only* beneficiary of the trust during her lifetime, and she must either be given the unrestricted power to dispose of the trust assets on her death, or all of the trust income must be distributed to her at least yearly during her lifetime, in which case the spouse who *creates* the trust can provide for disposition of the trust assets on the other spouse's death. This is called a "QTIP" trust, for qualified terminable interest property trust. The QTIP trust is frequently used in the case of second marriages where one or both spouses have children from a previous marriage and the settlor spouse wants to provide for the new spouse but also wants to be certain that his or her children will receive the trust assets on the surviving spouse's death.

For instance, John and Mary both have children from a previous marriage and each has an estate in excess of the tax-free amount. Each wants to provide for the other, but they also want to be sure that their respective estates will ultimately pass to their own children. They would establish, on death, reciprocal QTIP trusts. Each trust would provide that all of the trust income would be distributed at least annually (although typically, trust income is distributed quarterly or even monthly) to the surviving spouse. The trust could also provide that the trustee could make discretionary distributions of principal to that spouse. (Note that *no one* else may receive principal or income of the marital deduction trust during the life of the surviving spouse.) On the death of the surviving spouse, the remaining trust assets would pass to the children of the settlor spouse. (*Remember,* as with all trusts, this trust must be funded with the settlor spouse's assets in order for the plan to work. Jointly held assets or those where an individual beneficiary is named will not pass to the trust and the plan will be frustrated.)

The marital deduction trust is primarily tax-driven. In some if not most cases, a spouse is motivated to fund the marital deduction trust with a *smaller* amount than he or she otherwise would have in order to produce a lower overall estate tax in both estates.

For instance, in the case of John and Mary above, say that John has assets of $2.5 million and Mary has assets of $500,000, and say that at the time of John's death (2006) the tax-free amount is $2 million. If John leaves his entire estate of $2.5 million to Mary, there will be no estate tax on his death. However, Mary's estate will now total $3 million (John's $2.5 million plus her own $500,000), and (assuming the same $2 million exemption at her death) on Mary's death she will have a "taxable" estate of about $1 million, producing a tax of about $450,000! If instead John leaves $500,000 to a QTIP trust for Mary and the balance in a family trust for Mary (he could also include his children as beneficiaries), there will, as above, be no tax on his death, but the greater advantage will come on Mary's death. Assuming the values and exemption remain the same, Mary's estate will total $1 million ($500,000 from John's trust and $500,000 of her own) and there will be no estate tax on John's death and no estate tax on Mary's death, for a savings of $450,000, or *more* if their assets appreciate.

In the case of previous marriages, the marital trust, as suggested above, is often a QTIP trust, providing that on the spouse's death the remainder will pass to the first spouse's children. The other portion of the estate (typically, the "family" or "bypass" trust, as described below) may provide for the spouse, or the children, or both (or even the grandchildren in many cases). In any event, the spouse creating the trust has the option of deciding where the funds will go on the surviving spouse's death.

There may be cases—in fact, it is often the case—where neither spouse has been married before, where the settlor spouse wants the surviving spouse to have easy access to principal during her lifetime. There are a number of ways to accomplish this. One would be to give the trustee the power to make distributions of principal to the spouse. The trustee's discretion could be governed by a "standard," such as "comfort," "accustomed manner of living," or the usual, "health, maintenance, education, and support." (*Note* that "standards" should not be used arbitrarily and without expert advice, since there can be serious tax implications to using the wrong standards in a trust.) This option could be enhanced by naming the spouse beneficiary as the trustee. This is quite permissible from a legal and tax standpoint, but whether it is wise in a particular case will depend upon the particular family circumstances.

Another way to provide access to principal of the marital trust would be to give the spouse beneficiary the power to simply direct the trustee to make a principal distribution to her. This is called a "general power of appointment," and the power could be limited to a certain annual amount (e.g., $5,000 or 5 percent of the total, whichever is greater) or it could be unlimited (the entire balance). It would almost never be unlimited in a family trust or bypass trust, or any other trust that we did not want taxed in the spouse's estate.

As you can see, while a good deal of flexibility can be built into the marital deduction trust, there are some features that are inflexible if the marital deduction is desired. In addition to those explained above, the spouse's interest or benefits under the marital trust must be unconditional. That is, you *cannot* provide that benefits will cease if she remarries, or moves out of state, or fails to take care of the children or your elderly parent. Any such provision will cause the deduction to be *lost*, although you can condition benefits on the spouse's survival for a period not to exceed six months.

Trusts for a noncitizen spouse. As described above, the marital deduction can provide a deferral of estate taxes on an unlimited amount of money. Congress allowed this based on the fact that on the death of the surviving spouse the government would collect its estate tax on virtually all the deferred amount. A few years ago, however, it occurred to Congress that if a spouse had a strong connection to another country, she might be tempted to move back to that country after the death of her U.S. spouse, taking the money with her. In that event, the U.S. government would never get its tax.

So, around 1988, Congress enacted a law that materially changed the marital deduction where the deceased is survived by a spouse who is not a citizen of the United States. In fact, the new law *disallows* the marital deduction unless the assets passing to (or for the benefit of) the noncitizen spouse are placed in a "qualified domestic trust" (dubbed a QDOT). If the assets are not placed in a QDOT by the time the federal estate tax is to be paid for the deceased spouse's estate, then the entire amount will be subject to immediate tax.

To facilitate qualification for the deferral where the deceased spouse failed to create a QDOT for the noncitizen spouse, the law allows the noncitizen spouse to create her own QDOT after the death of the spouse. For instance, John dies and leaves his wife, Mary, who is *not* a U.S. citizen, an outright bequest of $900,000. If Mary does nothing, all of these assets will be subject to estate tax. If instead she creates a QDOT, no taxes will be due until she dies or, as described below, until the principal is distributed.

Mary can also eliminate the entire problem by *becoming* a U.S. citizen prior to the filing of the federal estate tax return (including extensions) in John's estate. In this case, the bequest would then qualify for the regular marital deduction and no QDOT would have to be created.

If a QDOT trust is required, the QDOT election must be made by the executor. The trust must be a trust for Mary's (the noncitizen spouse's) benefit, and it must provide that any distributions of *principal* (as opposed to income) will be subject to the trustee withholding the estate tax due on the distribution. (That is, the estate tax that would have resulted if the distributed principal from the QDOT was included and taxed in John's estate.) One of the QDOT trustees *must* be a U.S. citizen or a U.S. corporation. If the QDOT assets exceed $2 million, then one of the trustees must be a U.S. bank. If an individual trustee is used, then the individual U.S. trustee must post a bond or letter of credit to the IRS in the amount of 65 percent of the value of the trust assets to secure payment of the tax. If the trust assets are under $2 million, then no bond need be posted and a U.S. bank need not be a trustee, provided that no more than 35 percent of the trust assets consists of real estate located outside the United States. Also, if more than 35 percent of trust assets consists of non-U.S. real estate, then a bond *will* be required. If these requirements are not met, not only will the marital deduction be lost, but, if the assets are in a trust, the trustee of the trust will be *personally liable* for the tax. In short, the U.S. government wants to be sure it will get its money.

As noted, every distribution of principal from QDOT to the surviving spouse during her lifetime or at her death will be subject to payment of estate tax, and this tax is computed as if those amounts were included and taxed in the estate of the first spouse. In smaller estates, this can have a particularly negative result.

For instance, say that John has an estate of $3.3 million and he dies in 2006, when the tax-free amount is $2 million. The entire estate goes to Mary, a noncitizen. The first $2 million is "tax free" and the remaining $1.3 million is potentially taxable unless Mary puts it into a QDOT. If she does so, there will be no tax on John's death, but on Mary's subsequent death, the entire $1.3 million (or what is left of it) will be taxed not as part of Mary's estate but *as if* it was part of John's estate, and there will be a tax of over $500,000! (*Note* that distributions of principal from the QDOT trust during Mary's lifetime will also be subject to an "estate" tax as if included and taxed in John's estate.) On the other hand, if Mary was a citizen, or became one before John's estate tax return was filed, the tax on her death (assuming the values remained the same) as well as the tax on principal distributions from the trust would be *zero!*

Accordingly, with a couple where one spouse is not a U.S. citizen, some careful attention to planning can yield valuable results.

THE BYPASS TRUST

Like the marital trust, the so-called bypass trust is also tax-driven, since, if properly structured and administered, assets in such a trust can bypass (and therefore escape taxation in) the estate(s) of the beneficiaries. The bypass trust, also commonly called a "family" trust, a "credit shelter" trust, and an "exemption equivalent" trust, is designed to be funded, optimally, with the maximum allowable tax-free amount on the death of the creator (the settlor) of the trust. With this approach, there would be no estate tax on that amount on the settlor's death and no estate tax in the future upon termination of the trust. Potentially taxable estates that do not take advantage of the bypass trust in one form or another are literally throwing money away.

The bypassing of taxes in the estate of a trust beneficiary is based on the concept that the beneficiary did not create the trust, has no extensive control over it, or has limited control over it and cannot arbitrarily withdraw the principal. Under these circumstances the assets in the trust will escape taxation in the estate of a beneficiary on the beneficiary's death. Here's how it can work:

Donald creates a revocable trust for his own benefit during his lifetime. On his death, his trust provides that his wife, Daisy, may receive as much income and principal as the trustee decides to pay out for her benefit during her lifetime (*not* a marital deduction trust). As it happens, the trustee is a "friendly" trustee and is liberal in making distributions to Daisy. (There could also be situations where the trustee is instructed not to be liberal with distributions.) Even though Daisy can benefit from the trust, on her death none of the assets in that trust will be taxed in her estate. The same result will occur if one or more children were beneficiaries of this bypass trust. That is, they could receive benefits but the trust assets would not be taxed in their estate. However, if the assets pass to *their* children at death (Donald's grandchildren), *then* this would be a generation-skipping trust as well as a bypass trust, and there is a limit to the amount Donald can place in a generation-skipping trust (see page 259). There are additional benefits to a bypass trust, including protection of the trust assets from the creditors of a beneficiary and avoidance of probate of the trust assets in the beneficiary's estate. In short, there are numerous and significant advantages to using a bypass trust to provide for beneficiaries as opposed to just leaving them an outright distribution.

MINOR'S AND CHILDREN'S TRUSTS

There are two types of trusts most commonly used to provide for minors and children: "Minor's" trusts and so-called Crummey trusts. In both cases the trusts are generally used to effectuate gifts to benefit minors and/or young adults without giving them direct access to or control over the gifted funds.

Minor's trusts. The "minor's trust" is also referred as a "2503(c)" trust, which is a term suggesting a trust that conforms to the requirements of section 2503(c) of the Internal Revenue Code. This section states that if a trust meets certain requirements (noted below), then gifts to the trust will be treated as a gift to the child and will qualify for the annual gift tax exclusion,° even though the child will not receive the funds for a period of time. (As explained in greater detail in chapter 13, gifts that qualify for the annual exclusion are not subject to gift taxes and do not use up any of an individual's lifetime gift-tax credit.)

To qualify for this treatment, a separate trust instrument must be prepared and the trust must provide that:

- The minor (child) must be the only beneficiary of the trust, except that if the child dies before all assets are paid out and he has not directed otherwise in a will, the trust assets may be paid to or held for others (typically siblings);
- Any income that has accumulated, together with all of the remaining principal, must be distributed to the child or made available to him at age twenty-one; and
- On the death of the child before age twenty-one, he must have a right to dispose of the trust assets through his estate (although, as noted above, alternative beneficiaries may be named if the child fails to exercise this right).

As a general rule, it is *not* a good idea for a parent to be a trustee of this trust; otherwise, there is the possibility that the trust assets will be included in the parent's estate if the parent dies before the trust ends. Once established, the trust cannot be changed during its term, although the trustee can have great flexibility in distributing or retaining income and principal for the minor. The term *minor's trust* and the required termination at the child's

---

° As discussed in chapter 13, the tax code allows for gift-tax free annual gifts to an unlimited number of donees. For 2005 the limit per donee was $11,000 per year. Since 1982, the "annual exclusion" for tax-free gifts has been $10,000 per donee per calendar year. Beginning with 1999 gifts, however, the law directed that the $10,000 amount would be adjusted by the cost of living standard, but only by multiples to the nearest $1,000. This requirement caused the annual exclusion amount to be increased to $11,000 per donee per year beginning with gifts made in 2002.

age of twenty-one may appear inconsistent, since in virtually all states the age of majority is now eighteen. The age of twenty-one stems from earlier times when that was the age of majority, and no need to change it was ever recognized where this type of trust is concerned.

In fact, even twenty-one is not generally regarded as a sensible age to hand over large sums of money to a child. Therefore, many minor's trusts contain a provision stating that upon reaching age twenty-one, the child will be notified that he has a right to withdraw the entire balance of the trust. If the child does not exercise that right by notifying the trustee within thirty or sixty days of such notice (the "window"), then the funds will remain in the trust, *outside* the child's control, for an additional number of years (usually five to ten years). Assuming the child can be persuaded not to withdraw the funds during the window, the trust will then continue for the stated period. During this extended period the child will be taxed on all the trust income and capital gains, whether or not distributed to him, so the trust should contain a provision requiring the trustee to pay or distribute to the child an amount equal to the attributable taxes. Until the trust ends, the trustee will manage the trust assets for the benefit of the child, giving him what he reasonably needs but not necessarily what he requests. At the end of the period, all remaining assets are turned over to the child, who, at that time, will hopefully be wiser and more mature.

The tax implications of minor's trusts up to age twenty-one are fairly straightforward. Any income for the year that is held in the trust and not distributed to the child during the year is taxed to the trust. Income that is distributed to the child is taxed to the child (but be mindful of the "kiddie tax" if the child is under age fourteen; see chapter 13 for more on that). There will be no additional tax when the trust terminates and the assets (and accumulated income) are distributed to the child. If the child dies before the trust ends, the assets are included in the child's estate for estate tax purposes, although in most cases no tax will result.

The other trust for children. Although children (and grandchildren) can, of course, be named as beneficiaries of any type of trust other than a marital deduction trust, the "other" trust most commonly used for children (although its use is certainly not restricted to children) is called, in estate planning vernacular, the "Crummey trust."

The principle advantages of the Crummey trust over the minor's trust is that the Crummey trust can and often does have more than one beneficiary, and the Crummey trust does not have to end (or the funds made available) when a beneficiary reaches age twenty-one, or any age, for that matter.

And like the minor's trust, gifts to the Crummey trust can qualify for annual tax-free gifts. This qualification can be particularly important when you have a potentially taxable estate and several beneficiaries whom you want to benefit, without giving them the money (or other property to be gifted) outright. For instance, in 2005 a married couple with four children (and a generous heart) could transfer up to $88,000 per year (each spouse giving $11,000 to each child) of tax-free gifts to one Crummey trust for the benefit of their children.

In order to qualify for the annual tax-free gift, the gift must be subject to the "present enjoyment" of the donee (recipient). In other words, if the donee has to wait to receive the funds (as in the case of most trusts), a gift to the trust will not qualify as a tax-free gift and the donor will then have to apply a part of his "lifetime exemption" to the gift (more on this in chapter 13). The tax law provides a specific exception to this rule where a minor's trust is concerned [section 2503(c) trusts as described above], but gifts to most other trusts will not qualify, *unless* they are Crummey trusts or the equivalent.

A Crummey trust (named after a 1968 federal case on the gift-tax question, involving a taxpayer unfortunately named Crummey) is one that has a provision allowing each beneficiary the right or power (called a "Crummey power") to withdraw his or her share of the annual gifts to the trust, up to the annual tax-free gift limit. For instance, if Chester contributed $24,000 to a Crummey trust for the benefit of his three children, each child would have the right to withdraw $8,000.

As you may have quickly observed, it may not be a good idea to allow this withdrawal power to continue indefinitely or carry forward cumulatively from year to year. If we did this, what would be the sense of having the trust? The fact is that the typical arrangement is largely modeled after the original power that Crummey himself used.

The irrevocable trust established in 1962 by D. C. Crummey and his wife provided that each beneficiary would have the right to withdraw the lesser of the annual tax-free gift limit or his equal share of the annual gifts to the trust, *provided* he did so by December 31 of the year in which the gifts to the trust were made. If the beneficiary did not exercise his right to withdraw, he could not thereafter withdraw his share of that year's gifts, and such gifts would become a permanent part of the trust. Crummey, then, could *time* his gifts, making them, for instance, sometime in December, so his children only had a limited time in which to exercise their withdrawal rights. The IRS objected to this arrangement and that is how the Crummey case came to be. The court held that the right of withdrawal *did* give the beneficiaries the necessary present enjoyment (or at least the right to present enjoyment, even though some of the beneficiaries were so young that they could not, without a guardian, exercise their rights) and therefore Crummey's gifts to the trust qualified as tax-free gifts.

Further requirements evolved from the Crummey case giving practitioners a clear picture of how to draft Crummey powers to qualify for the tax-free gift:

- The beneficiaries *must be given notice* of their right to withdraw, indicating the amount they may withdraw and the manner in which to do it;
- The beneficiaries must be given a reasonable amount of time after receipt of the notice to act upon it (called a "window," and the window is usually thirty days); and
- The fact that a beneficiary may be an infant or very young child is not an issue. Typically, the notice of withdrawal right is sent to a parent on behalf of the child.

As taxpayers use Crummey powers more and more aggressively to remove assets from their taxable estates, the IRS is liking them less and less, and attacking aggressive cases more and more. In one case, at the time when the annual tax-free amount was $10,000 per donee, a taxpayer's Crummey trust gave sixteen beneficiaries the annual right to withdraw (allowing annual tax-free gifts of $160,000 to the trust), and provided that if they didn't withdraw only four of the sixteen would be able to receive distributions for their lives. The IRS took the trust to court. As it happened the IRS lost, but the IRS has publicly stated that it intends to actively pursue such aggressive uses of the Crummey power. Furthermore, there has been a least one proposal in Congress to pass legislation limiting the number of annual tax-free gifts a person may make.

It is not fatal if the trust does not have Crummey powers; in fact, many do not. However, without Crummey powers any gifts to the trust will have to be applied to the donor's lifetime exemption and, as explained in chapter 13, once that is used up, every gift (other than tax-free gifts) will then be subject to a gift tax.

The typical Crummey trust for children will be for a number of children and will terminate when a child reaches, say, age thirty or thirty-five or forty. In the meantime, the trust assets are managed by the trustee for the group of beneficiaries and funds are distributed as needed by each of them. Crummey trusts for the benefit of grandchildren must follow some special rules and are discussed later under the section on generation-skipping trusts.

The *tax rules* relating to Crummey trusts are somewhat complicated, but briefly, the beneficiaries are taxed on trust income based on their respective proportions of cumulative tax-free gifts left in the trust. This is because a failure to withdraw is treated, for tax purposes, as if the donee *did* make their withdrawal and then recontributed the same amount to the trust under which he is a beneficiary. Similarly, a portion of the assets of the Crummey trust will be in the estate of a beneficiary who dies. All of the results can be modified by varying the provisions of the trust and suffice it to say that such trusts should only be prepared by experts.

TRUSTS FOR UNMARRIED PARTNERS

When two people develop a long-term relationship that has virtually all the attributes of a "marriage" but without the legal contract of marriage, each of them should consider an estate plan that provides the other with benefits on a partner's death, without interference from the relatives of the deceased partner, and, if possible, with the benefit of any tax breaks that are available.

One basic tax break that is *not* available to unmarried partners is the marital deduction, since it is only available to individuals who are legally married. However, unmarried couples are able to make annual tax-free gifts to each other and to establish trusts for each other. In fact, unmarried couples can enjoy one tax-advantaged strategy that is not available to spouses or to children. This is called a grantor retained income trust (a "GRIT"). Until 1989 GRITs were used by individuals to transfer assets to a trust and retain the income for a period of years, after which the trust assets would belong to (usually) their children, at a highly reduced gift-tax value, thereby reducing the donor's estate. In 1990, however, the law changed to disallow GRITs for family members.

Since unmarried partners are not related to each other, the tax code does not prohibit one from creating a GRIT for the other. Briefly, a GRIT might work like this. During the term of the typical GRIT, the donor (creator) is only entitled to the income from the assets in the trust. Although the assets may be sold and the proceeds reinvested, the donor is never entitled to more than the income actually produced by the assets. For purposes of computing the value of the gift made by the donor to the residuary beneficiary, the tax regulations assume that a certain return was earned on the assets. In fact, the gift and estate tax advantages are increased if the assets grow more and earn less than the tax tables assume. If the donor dies during the term of the GRIT, all advantages are lost, and the full value of the trust is included in the donor's estate. This is not such a catastrophe as it may appear, however, as it merely leaves the donor in the same position as she was without the GRIT; the only loss would be the costs of implementing the GRIT.

For instance, Elizabeth, who has substantial assets, wishes to provide for her partner, Jan. Elizabeth establishes a fifteen-year GRIT and transfers $500,000 worth of securities to the GRIT. Under the terms of the GRIT, Elizabeth receives all the income from the securities for a fifteen-year period and, thereafter, the securities (or whatever they have become) belong to Jan (or they could continue to be held in trust for Jan's benefit).

Because the GRIT is irrevocable and Elizabeth has no right to recover the principal (as opposed to the *income* generated by the principal), Elizabeth is deemed to have made a gift to Jan, the person who will receive the principal at the end of the fifteen-year period. But since Jan has to wait fifteen years to receive the funds, the gift is certainly not one for "present enjoyment." Since it is not, the gift must be discounted to reflect the present value of what Jan will receive in fifteen years. In fact, depending on Elizabeth's age and the income rate assumed by the federal rate tables at the time of the gift, the gift could be, say, only about 28 percent of the $500,000 amount actually placed in the trust, or $141,500. That is, to make a gift of $500,000 to Jan fifteen years from now, Elizabeth may only have to apply $141,500 of her lifetime exemption.

Although the GRIT for unmarried couples is not quite as advantageous as the marital deduction, it can in some instances come close. Note, however, that the advantage offered by the GRIT may be affected by the age of the donor (the creator of the GRIT). If Elizabeth, in our example above, was age eighty, a fifteen-year GRIT would not be a good idea, since she may not outlive the term and no savings will be realized. And a five-year GRIT would offer considerably less tax advantage. This is because the closer we are (i.e., the less time) between the gift and the enjoyment of the gift, the lower the discount for gift-tax purposes and, correspondingly, the less the savings.

Another potential drawback of the GRIT is that although the appreciation on the gifted assets escapes estate tax, the donee (the beneficiary who receives the assets when the GRIT ends) may face a capital gain on a subsequent sale of the assets. This is because the donee/beneficiary's cost basis is the same as that of the donor. This is most easily explained by illustration. Elizabeth (age sixty) places $500,000 of stocks in a fifteen-year GRIT, and at the end of the GRIT the stocks will be given to Jan. Elizabeth paid $200,000 for the stocks many years ago. If Elizabeth dies twenty years later when the stocks are worth, say, $1 million, only $141,500 will be included in Elizabeth's estate. The difference of $858,500 will be estate tax free to Jan. However, Jan's *cost basis* in the stocks will be the same as Elizabeth's ($200,000), so that a sale by Jan at the market price of $1 million will produce an $800,000 capital gain. Note, however, that the capital gain rate of 20 percent is considerably less than the estate-tax rate, which begins at over 40 percent after applying the exclusion amount and increases to 50 percent depending on the size of the estate and the year of death.

Note also that the GRIT need not actually produce any specified amount of income. Furthermore, it may be funded with *any* type of property, not just securities. That is, the donor could fund it with rental real estate or a patent or a copyright interest, or even a residence, which generally produces no income at all, if a single-family dwelling. This is one instance where it pays to be "unrelated" as the tax laws make it prohibitive to do a GRIT for a close family member. (Where a family member is involved, a GRIT funded with a residence must meet certain strict requirements, as discussed below.)

In fact, with the exceptions of the marital deduction trust, the QDOT, and the children's trust, *every* type of trust discussed in this chapter can be used by and for unmarried partners. The selections and individual trust provisions would be those suited to the objectives of the individuals involved.

Another trust often used by unmarried partners is the Crummey trust (described in detail above). Although the amounts placed in the trust (generally, equal to the annual tax-free gift per beneficiary per year) are lower than in the GRIT, the gifts can accumulate over the years and there is no waiting period that must pass before the trust assets are out of the donor's estate. Furthermore, as described later in this chapter, "leverage" can be attained by using the trust funds to purchase life insurance on the donor. If properly structured, the trust can receive huge amounts of life insurance proceeds totally tax free for the benefit of the unmarried partner.

TRUSTS FOR THE DISABLED

When the family includes an individual who is disabled, a special trust or special trust provisions should be considered to protect the financial interests of that person. Of course, the term *disability* can have a wide range of meanings. Generally speaking, I am referring here to individuals who would not be able to care for themselves or whose interests would be better served by retaining control and management of the disabled person's inheritance or other assets in a trust.

In some cases, certain types of trusts are essential in order to preserve benefits the disabled person may be receiving. For example, in the case of a person who is eligible for Supplemental Security Income (SSI) benefits, the receipt of an inheritance or personal injury award would immediately disqualify that person from benefits, but if these funds are instead placed in a special trust for the individual's benefit, he would not be disqualified.

Even if a person is not receiving government benefits but is under a guardianship or conservatorship because of his disability, the outright receipt of an inheritance or gift will cause unnecessary complications and fees. Again, by placing the person's inheritance or other funds in a trust with appropriate provisions, the donor and the donee can avoid fees, publicity, and often even the need for court supervision. What types of trusts and provisions are appropriate?

While it is virtually impossible to suggest the exact provisions that should be placed in every trust for a disabled person, there are certain guidelines that, if followed by a competent practitioner, will help protect the funds and the beneficiary.

In the typical case of a family with a disabled child, a parent (or other relative) may want to provide for the disabled child on the parent's death. If the child is receiving or may in the future receive government benefits, an outright bequest to the child will, as noted above, disqualify the child from eligibility for benefits, which could be a very expensive loss. Although there are alternatives, such as leaving the disabled child's share to other children on the basis that they will use those funds for the child, such alternatives are risky and generally regarded as bad planning. Instead, the parent can consider placing the child's share in a "supplemental needs trust" or in a fully discretionary "special needs trust."

A supplemental needs trust is an irrevocable trust for the benefit of the disabled person (although in some cases it includes other beneficiaries in addition to the disabled person), and the operative provision states that the trustee may only make distributions to or for the disabled person to provide for the needs of that person *over and above* the person's basic needs for food, clothing, and shelter. The reason for this is the government regulation providing that if a person on certain disability benefits (SSI) has unrestricted access to assets in a trust to the extent that such assets may be used for the person's basic needs and support (i.e., food, clothing, and shelter), then those assets will be considered available to the person. Since the SSI program is a welfare program and eligibility is based on a lack of assets available to the individual to provide for his basic needs, then the individual could lose his eligibility if the trust assets are considered so available. In order to eliminate the possibility of this happening, the trustee of the supplemental needs trust is actually prohibited, by the special provision, from making distributions for the beneficiary's basic needs of food, clothing, and shelter.

Care must also be taken to ensure that the trust cannot be considered to be revocable by the beneficiary. Furthermore, many supplemental needs trusts have "self-destruct" provisions causing termination of the trust if the continued existence of the trust would cause the beneficiary to lose his benefits. While the self-destruct provision (discussed below) is useful, the trust should *not* provide that on such a termination the assets will be distributed to the disabled beneficiary.

The problem with the typical supplemental needs trust is that it is fairly rigid and shortsighted in its operation and restrictions. For instance, the typical supplemental needs trust will directly or indirectly prohibit the trustee from making distributions to the beneficiary that are or may be used for "food, clothing, or shelter" because such distributions could disqualify the beneficiary for SSI purposes or affect his benefits. In these cases, if the circumstances (or the government programs) change, we are stuck with the trust as it is (although the trust, if carefully drafted, could include certain special provisions such as a limited power to amend or a limited power of appointment held by a third party—both discussed elsewhere in this chapter). What the drafters of the supplemental needs trust clearly overlook (to the detriment of the beneficiary) is that unforeseen changes in the beneficiary's circumstances or even in the SSI program itself could warrant a more flexibly drafted trust. Furthermore, also apparently overlooked is the fact that a "prohibited" distribution from the trust for, let's say, rent, does not actually disqualify the beneficiary from public benefits, but rather it has the effect of merely reducing a monthly benefit, at the most, by one-third the benefit, under the one-third reduction rule.

With this in mind, many experts in this field use instead a fully discretionary trust that does not restrict the trustee to distributions for the beneficiary's supplemental needs. As explained earlier in this chapter, a trustee's powers and duties can range widely, dictated by the written terms of the trust. And distributions made from the trust to the beneficiaries can be mandatory (giving the trustee no choice) or discretionary. In addition, the trustee's discretion can be guided by additional provisions of the trust.

For instance, in the supplemental needs trust, the trustee has discretion to make distributions or not to make them, but *only* for the beneficiary's supplemental needs. In a fully discretionary special needs trust, the trustee has no such restrictions and may make distributions for any purpose whatsoever, at the trustee's discretion (usually accompanied by either or both of the words *sole* or *absolute* discretion). In addition, the fully discretionary trust usually contains (and *should* contain) a statement requesting the trustee, in exercising its discretion, to take into consideration whether the proposed distribution would have a negative effect on the beneficiary's eligibility for government benefits. Although technically this does not limit the trustee, it is a reminder of the settlor's intentions and assists the trustee in making a decision. It does *not* by itself affect the beneficiary's eligibility for benefits, so long as the beneficiary himself did not establish the trust. Thus, for example, it would be permissible for the trustee to make a distribution of, say, $1,000 for the beneficiary's rent, which would have the effect of causing the beneficiary's SSI payments, usually about $600, to be reduced for that month by $200 or so. Doesn't that make a lot more sense and offer a lot more flexibility than providing that the trustee simply cannot make such distributions?

A fully discretionary trust should contain as little language as possible relating to the extent of the trustee's discretion, as too many words in that context could be fatal to the protection otherwise offered by the trust. For instance, *fully* discretionary means there are no restrictions or guidelines governing the exercise of discretion. If a trust says, "The trustee may make such distributions to or for the beneficiary as the trustee in its absolute discretion deems appropriate for the beneficiary's *support, maintenance, and welfare*," it is *not* a fully discretionary trust. In fact, under the law of many if not most states, the beneficiary (and therefore the government, if the beneficiary is on a benefit program like SSI) can legally force the trustee to make distributions for the beneficiary's "support," etc. Accordingly, a well-drafted fully discretionary trust, if using the language above, would end that sentence at the word "appropriate."

The choice of whether parents (or other family members) should establish a supplemental needs trust or a fully discretionary trust for a disabled child depends in large part on family circumstances and almost as often on the family's legal adviser. A supplemental needs trust is frequently the choice only because the adviser is unclear on how the fully discretionary trust works. Many feel that the advantage of the supplemental needs trust is that its very language (of providing only for items *other than* food, clothing, or shelter) more or less guarantees that the existence of the trust will not affect the beneficiary's eligibility for the SSI program. In fact, federal regulations do not require that such provisions be included to ensure eligibility. The regulations *only* look to actual distributions made from the trust and the *use* or potential use of those distributions. In other words, if a trustee of a fully discretionary trust was aware of the SSI regulations (and he would have to be if there was a trust beneficiary on SSI), and was therefore careful not to make distributions that would affect the beneficiary's eligibility, there would be no difference between the two trusts—except for one important difference—the special needs trust restricts the trustee in distributions and could leave the family in a bad situation if circumstances and/or the regulations change. However, the discretionary trust leaves the trustee with full choice as to whether or not to make distributions and as to the amounts of any distributions that are made, and, in effect, the trustee can automatically adjust distributions to accommodate the changes.

Either the supplemental needs trust or the fully discretionary trust for a disabled individual can be established through the parent's will (a testamentary trust) or during the parent's lifetime (an inter vivos or "living" trust). Most knowledgeable practitioners agree that a living trust is the better choice. If a living trust is used, a parent may be the trustee, although if the parent has a potentially taxable estate and wants the proceeds of the special needs trust or discretionary trust to be out of his taxable estate, he may be better off having someone else serve as trustee, particularly if the trust is to hold life insurance on the parent's life (life insurance trusts are discussed starting on page 255).

In many cases the trust will provide benefits for other children as well as the disabled child, and this arrangement can actually give the trust much more flexibility. This question, however, must be carefully considered in each particular case, especially where the trust is established with the beneficiary's own funds (a self-settled trust). In any event, provisions must be made to dispose of any remaining trust assets on the death of the disabled person. If it is possible that the disabled person could have children, the parent may want to make provisions for them. Otherwise, typically the remainder will pass to the siblings of the disabled child.

Self-settled trusts. When a person establishes and funds a trust for himself, it is referred to as a "self-settled trust." (Note that a trust is still considered to be self-settled even though it may be established by a person's guardian or conservator, or at the order of a court, so long as it is funded with assets belonging to the beneficiary.) In some cases, however, a disabled beneficiary can establish a trust for his own benefit (with his own funds) and still qualify for government benefits. Briefly, if the person is on SSI and does not become institutionalized, he can establish a supplemental needs trust or a fully discretionary trust for his own benefit, being careful that no provision in the trust can be interpreted as giving the beneficiary the right to revoke the trust, and being equally careful not to include language that requires or requests the trustee to withhold distributions if they would affect the beneficiary's eligibility for benefits (this is called an "exculpatory" provision). This latter suggestion is because of case decisions and public policy rules relating to self-settled trusts.

There is another type of self-settled trust for a disabled person that in some regards falls under the fully discretionary category, but is regarded differently by practitioners because it is a "statutory" trust. That is, it is a trust for a disabled person that is specifically described under the federal law relating to the Medicaid program. This type of trust is called an "under 65 trust" and is discussed in greater detail on page 223. Briefly, it must be established for a disabled person under the age of sixty-five (although it can continue past that age), and on the beneficiary's death it must provide for repayment to the state for Medicaid benefits paid to the beneficiary. Any balance remaining in the trust may be paid to others, such as family members. During the beneficiary's lifetime, the trustee may have full discretion over payments to the beneficiary.

Self-destruct clause. Since the establishment and continuation of the special needs trust or discretionary trust (but *particularly* the special needs trust) is conditioned on the beneficiary's continued eligibility for benefits, the trust's purpose may be frustrated if its very existence causes the beneficiary to become ineligible. Accordingly, many such trusts contain a self-destruct provision that says something like, "If the existence of this trust causes Johnny to lose his benefits under the Social Security Income or other program, then this trust shall thereupon terminate, and the trustee shall distribute the remaining trust principal and undistributed income to Johnny's then surviving siblings in equal shares."

Self-destruct clauses are quite legal (although they could present a problem if the trust is self-settled), and are commonly used in special needs trusts.

Trusts for personal injury settlements. These trusts typically fall into the category of "trusts for the disabled," since the very nature of the personal injury settlement is to compensate a victim for injuries (a temporary or permanent disability) caused by another. Of course, not every personal injury settlement gives rise to the need for a trust. Smaller settlements and those where the victim has fully recovered by the time the settlement is received present a different situation. In those cases, while a trust may be advisable for general estate planning purposes, it need not be a special trust designed around the circumstances of the settlement.

Where the individual has not fully recovered, however, or may never fully recover, and in cases where the individual is receiving SSI or Medicaid benefits to provide for his care, the use of a trust may be essential to preserve those benefits as well as to preserve the settlement funds to provide for future care and enhancement of the individual's quality of life.

Although trusts can be created for personal injury settlements after a lump sum has been received, in cases where all or part of the settlement is structured, it is *extremely important* that a trust expert be consulted *before* the final settlement is negotiated. In most circumstances where a large recovery is involved, the settlement is often "structured"—that is, paid in specified periodic amounts over an extended period of time. Again, it is important that the trust expert be consulted in structuring the settlement, not only to preserve eligibility for any benefit programs but also to avoid the tax traps often present in such cases (the tax traps are discussed in chapter 13). Note the reference here to a "trust expert." No matter how outstanding the personal injury attorney, it is unlikely that he or she would have the expertise necessary to design, draft, and fund the trust to best suit the particular circumstances.

Where a trust is established to receive the proceeds of a personal injury settlement, it will generally be considered a self-settled trust, as discussed above. As pointed out, however, properly drafted self-settled trusts may nevertheless allow the beneficiary to continue to qualify for SSI or Medicaid.

Typically, the self-settled trust for personal injury settlements will be a supplemental needs trust or a discretionary trust, or one of the qualifying Medicaid trusts. There are also cases, however, where such a trust is not self-settled. It is not unusual, for instance, for a personal injury award to be apportioned between the victim and his spouse, or between the victim and his parents. In these cases, the spouse or more particularly the parent may want to use her share of the settlement proceeds to fund a trust for the benefit of the child. This type of trust would *not* be a self-settled trust and offers considerably more flexibility in providing for the disabled party, but at the same time it introduces some very complicated tax issues for the parent who establishes the trust. Accordingly, it should only be done by a trust expert.

Medicaid trusts. Medicaid is a needs-based (i.e., welfare) benefit program administered separately by each state, but funded in part by the federal government and in part by each state. A person qualifying for Medicaid is only allowed to have a minimal amount of assets, other than a home. Although each state may have certain differences in its particular Medicaid regulations, each must follow certain basic federal guidelines in order to be eligible for the federal subsidy. One of those guidelines is the waiting period imposed on a person who transfers assets and later applies for Medicaid benefits.

The basic rule (in every state) is that if a person makes a gift of assets and the gift is not connected with a trust, and if the person applies for Medicaid within thirty-six months of the date of the gift (the "look-back" period), then the amount of the gifted assets will be taken into consideration in determining whether the person will be entitled to Medicaid benefits. If the gift involves a *trust*, then the look-back period is generally sixty months.° However, subject to the notable exceptions for certain trusts as described below, if the trust to which the assets are transferred allows any benefits to be distributed to the person who established the trust, then the look-back period does not apply because federal law provides that the assets of a trust, to the extent they may be paid to the person establishing the trust, will be considered accessible to him for Medicaid eligibility purposes.

For instance, say that Chester creates and funds an irrevocable trust that provides that the trustee can pay to Chester any part or all of the trust income or principal as the trustee in its discretion deems appropriate. In this case, *all* of the trust assets are considered available to Chester, whether or not paid to him, and it will not matter whether he applies for Medicaid ten months or ten years after the trust is established. Keep in mind that even if the trust directs the trustee *not* to make any payment that would jeopardize or terminate Chester's eligibility for Medicaid, *all* of the trust assets would be considered available to Chester. Such a provision (called an "exculpatory clause") is useless to protect the assets of a self-settled trust.

In this type of trust where *no* discretion is given to the trustee, it does not matter who acts as trustee. It can be the settlor and/or the settlor's spouse, for example, or one or more children.

(This is but a cursory overview of only a few of the Medicaid rules, which are extensive, very complex, and frequently subject to exceptions. Readers who wish to do Medicaid planning should consult an expert in that field.)

° Note that states are continually trying to tighten these rules, so it is essential to check local law before making any transfers for this purpose.

Using these rules as a basis for planning, if we restrict the benefits we can receive from the trust and if we wait sixty months before applying for Medicaid (where relatively large transfers are made), then the restricted amount or portion can be protected. Here is how it can work in practice: Margo establishes an irrevocable trust to which she transfers $400,000 worth of investments. The terms of the trust allow the trustee to pay to Margo any dividends and interest from the investments, but *under no circumstances* is Margo to receive any of the trust principal. About fifty months after the trust is established Margo enters a nursing home. The *income* from her $400,000 trust is applied toward Margo's nursing home costs for the following ten months and Margo's family pays the balance of the costs. Just *after* the sixty-month period following the transfer to the trust, Margo applies for Medicaid benefits. Assuming she has no other assets (and assuming Margo does not reside in one of the nineteen states—so-called income-cap states—which deny Medicaid benefits to anyone receiving more than a certain amount of income,* even though the person may have no assets), Margo will then qualify for Medicaid. Although she will have to apply the trust income toward her care, the state will pay the balance of her care costs and the $400,000 of investments (plus whatever growth is realized) will be protected for her family.

It is common and advisable for the income-only Medicaid trust to contain estate planning provisions allowing for the trust to continue for the benefit of Margo's family after her death. It is also generally advisable, especially in view of the rapidly changing law in this area, to provide for a "safety valve" in this type of trust. This frequently takes the form of a provision that allows a trustee (*other than* the settlor or her spouse), or some other party outside the trust, to direct principal distributions out of the trust to the settlor's children or grandchildren, thus allowing the principal to be protected in the event of a later change in the law.

Special exceptions to the Medicaid trust rules. Under a 1993 change in federal law, three types of trusts were recognized as exceptions to the rules that would otherwise "count" the assets in a self-settled Medicaid trust and therefore disqualify the beneficiaries of such trusts. These three trusts are commonly called the "under-65 trust," the "pooled trust," and the "Miller trust."

---

* The nineteen income-cap states are: Alabama, Alaska, Arkansas, Colorado, Delaware, Florida, Georgia, Idaho, Iowa, Louisiana, Nevada, New Jersey, New Mexico, Oklahoma, South Carolina, South Dakota, Tennessee, Texas, and Wyoming.

The Miller trust, named after a court decision on a Medicaid issue, is a trust that is suitable to be used only in income-cap states. As noted above, the hard-to-understand rule in these states is that a person, even though certified to be in need of care and having zero assets, will not be able to qualify for Medicaid if her income exceeds the state-prescribed amount. For instance, say that Sally lives in Florida, an income-cap state. She has advanced Alzheimer's and needs institutionalization. She has no assets but receives a company pension of $1,510 per month. If the income cap in Florida is $1,500 per month, since Sally's income exceeds the cap, she *cannot* qualify for Medicaid!

The Miller trust law, however, provides that Sally's guardian can petition the Florida court to establish a Miller trust for Sally. The court would order that Sally's monthly pension be paid into the trust, and the trust would provide that the trustee may then pay to Sally (or to the nursing home) a monthly amount equal to $10 less than the income cap, thus allowing Sally to qualify for Medicaid. The law also requires, however, that any funds remaining in the trust on Sally's death (which wouldn't be much) be paid to the state to help reimburse it for the benefits paid to Sally without interest. Any type of income, including Social Security income, may be paid into a Miller trust, but *only income* may be used to fund this type of trust.

The pooled trust is a trust designed to hold the assets of more than one disabled individual (in separate accounts) and must be established by a nonprofit organization for this purpose. The same nonprofit organization must be the trustee of the trust. The individual's account within the pooled trust may be funded by the individual himself, by his guardian, parent, grandparent, or by a court. Although the individual's funds are assigned to a separate account, they may be invested in a "pool" with the funds of other disabled individuals. While the funds are in the pooled trust, the trustee may distribute such funds attributable to the individual's separate account and/or the income from those funds to the disabled individual on a discretionary basis. Since this is one of the "excepted" or safe harbor Medicaid trusts, the funds in the trust are not considered accessible to the individual, and therefore do not affect his eligibility for Medicaid. Like the Miller trust, there must be a pay-back provision on death, but the pooled trust payback is slightly different. On the individual's death the remaining funds in his separate trust account must either be applied to pay down the amount owed to the state for Medicaid benefits paid to or for the individual (without interest), *or* simply be added to the accounts of other individuals (who typically are totally unrelated to the individual). (Note that some states appear to be interpreting this provision rather harshly, attempting to limit the amount that may be retained by the pooled trust for other beneficiaries.) If there are adequate funds to reimburse the state in full and the state is, in fact, reimbursed, then any funds in excess of such reimbursement may be paid to those beneficiaries *outside* the trust as the individual designates in the trust (including his family).

The under-65 trust is by far the most useful and common of the three, since it allows for a greater possibility of preserving some of the individual's funds for his desired beneficiaries while still allowing the person to qualify for Medicaid. But like the other two trust exceptions, strict rules must be followed. The under-65 trust may be established by the individual's parent, grandparent, or legal guardian; or by a court. Unlike the pooled trust, it may *not* be established by the disabled individual himself. Furthermore, the trust must be established before the individual reaches age sixty-five, although, once established, it may continue beyond that age. The trust must be for the "sole benefit" of the individual. That is, *no one* but the individual may benefit from the trust until the state is reimbursed in full (without interest) on the individual's death. Thereafter, family members or other beneficiaries may receive benefits, if any trust assets remain.

There are two distinct advantages to the under-65 trust. One is that transfers to this trust are not treated as disqualifying transfers for Medicaid purposes, so an under-sixty-five disabled individual could have his assets transferred to this type of trust and immediately qualify for Medicaid. A second advantage is that the trust does not require an independent trustee (as does the pooled trust), so a family member may have control over the trust investments, which in turn could be arranged to benefit the individual and his family. For instance, say that the trustee used all or a substantial portion of the trust funds to invest in a family limited partnership as a limited partner. In the typical limited partnership agreement, no limited partner may force a liquidation or redemption (i.e., cashing in) of his share. Therefore, on the death of the disabled individual the trust's obligation to pay back the state could only be satisfied by an assignment of the limited partnership interest to the state. Such a transfer is likely to be prohibited by the partnership agreement except insofar as the partnership must allow the state to become an "assignee." As an assignee, the state could not force a liquidation of the partnership or demand distribution, although it would be entitled to its share of partnership distributions that the general partner decided to make. It is quite unlikely that the state would want to hold such an interest, and this could serve to give the remainder beneficiaries of the trust a great deal of leverage in negotiating a favorable settlement with the state.

In addition, the under-65 trust (as well as the pooled trust) allows the individual to take advantage of the "spread" between the amount the state pays for nursing home care (which must later be paid by the trust) and the private pay costs of care, which are generally 20 to 50 percent higher. Therefore, even if full reimbursement were made to the state, it would inevitably be less than if the individual paid on his own.

Asset Protection Trusts

It seems that we all want protection from creditors, whether we need it or not. Trusts are one form of legal vehicle that can be used to protect assets and there are a number of variations of these, both domestic and foreign. But there are also laws relating to asset transfers, including transfers to trusts a person makes for creditor protection purposes. In fact, a great and very complicated body of law has developed around the issue of whether an individual is or should be permitted to transfer his assets for the purpose of placing them beyond the reach of a creditor or potential creditor. Many such transfers may be attacked by the creditor as "fraudulent."

A fraudulent transfer (or "conveyance") is not fraudulent in the criminal sense of the law, but rather it refers to a transfer that is unfair to creditors and in violation of the concept of good-faith dealings with the rest of society. This is not at all to say that planning for creditor protection is automatically fraudulent. When properly done, it is quite legal and can positively protect assets. On the other hand, there should be (and there *are*) rules to prevent someone from, say, incurring a large debt and then intentionally transferring his assets away, thereby making him unable to pay the debt. These rules are called the fraudulent transfer (or fraudulent conveyance) rules and whether they have been violated is usually decided by a court (after the creditor wins a suit for his money or claim) based on the facts and circumstances of each individual case. Understandably, there are thousands of cases on the subject.

Furthermore, efforts made by creditors to rescind or reach transfers based on the fraudulent transfer rules are "actions within actions." That is, a creditor must take a *separate legal proceeding* during which the court conducts a separate hearing to determine whether a transfer was fraudulent. Such proceedings themselves can be drawn out and expensive.

In addition, there are time periods (called a "statute of limitations" or "period of limitations") within which a creditor must act; otherwise his right to attack the transfer is lost. Typically (although some states differ), the limitations period for attacking a fraudulent transfer in the United States is four years after the transfer. (Note that special rules and shorter periods apply in bankruptcy proceedings, but this situation is outside the scope of this discussion.)

As a general rule, if you make a transfer that falls into any of the following categories, it is likely that the transfer will be considered fraudulent:

a. *Transfer made with the actual intent to hinder, delay, or defraud a creditor.* Your "intent" is often difficult to prove, so the law contains a number of telltale actions that may be considered by the court, such as concealment of the transfer, transfer to close relatives or "insiders," transfer for less than full value, transfers that leave you "insolvent" (i.e., more debts than assets), transfers made right after you discover that you are being sued or about to be sued, or transfers made when you know that you have done something that has damaged someone and they are likely to sue you.

This last criterion often surprises people since the common misunderstanding seems to be, "If I haven't yet been served with the legal papers, I can still make some transfers." This is *not* the case.

b. *Incurrence of a debt beyond your ability to pay.* This, of course, presumes that before the incurrence of the debt you made a transfer for less than fair value and that had you kept the transferred asset you would have otherwise been able to pay the debt.

For example, say that you want to borrow $75,000 for an investment you think will make you rich, but you don't want to use your own money, so you arrange for a loan. Just prior to taking out the loan you transfer $100,000 to your spouse, leaving you with assets of about $150,000 and debts of about $140,000. You then borrow the $75,000 from the bank, which is glad to loan you the money because of your long and good financial standing with them. Unfortunately, the investment goes sour and now you can't pay the bank. Under those facts, the bank can recover what you owe from the $100,000 you transferred to your spouse, on the basis that it was a fraudulent transfer.

c. *Transfers that actually leave you insolvent.* This type of transfer may include those mentioned under "b" above, and both may be attacked by your present or *future* creditors—they include transfers made *while* you are insolvent as well as those that make you insolvent.

For instance, in the example in "b" above, say that you gave your spouse $150,000. This would have left you with more debts than expenses even before the bank loan, so the transfer would have rendered you insolvent. Under both rules, the bank would be able to go after the transferred funds.

d. *Transfers for less than fair value when you are engaging or about to engage in business (the "undercapitalization" rule).* Say that you intend to start a business that normally requires $50,000 in capital to operate. You have $50,000 (and that is all you have), but you don't want to risk it. You transfer $40,000 to your spouse and proceed with the business, putting in only $10,000. You run up $40,000 in business debts *or* you are faced with a $40,000 claim from a customer and decide to close the business. Under the thin capitalization rule, your creditors or customer could attack the gift to your spouse.

e. *Transfer to an insider (relative, employee) to pay a preexisting debt, where the insider had reasonable cause to believe you were insolvent.* You have run up quite a lot of debt, which includes $125,000 due to your brother-in-law for funds he advanced to you. You have about $380,000 in debt and $160,000 in assets and you are thinking of filing bankruptcy or at least just throwing yourself at the "mercy" of your creditors. However, you first pay your brother-in-law, who is aware of your problems and has growing concern over the $125,000 you owe him. (You are probably motivated to do this, believing that later on he may be willing to reloan you the funds, and besides, if you don't pay him, your sister will never speak to you again.) Unfortunately, you are not allowed to favor him as a creditor and, under these facts, your other creditors will be able to attack the funds paid to your brother-in-law.

As a result of the application of these rules over many years, we are left with the following potential outcomes where a *fraudulent transfer* is deemed by a court to have been made:

- Your creditors can reach assets or benefits that you can reach.
- Your creditors can receive what you have a right to receive.
- Your creditors can *reverse* an "unfair" (fraudulent) transfer.
- Your creditors can have your assets placed in the hands of a court-appointed receiver.
- Your creditor can attach, freeze, and/or force a sale of your assets.

And in certain cases,

- Your creditors can force you into bankruptcy.

(This is an extremely brief overview of the fraudulent transfer rules. Anyone concerned over the issue should consult an expert in the field.)

Of course, the other side of this coin is that if none of the above rules applies to you, or if the transfers were made some time ago, *outside* the period of limitations, then the assets will likely be protected and unreachable by your creditors. But that, of course, is only part of the answer. The examples above, for instance, illustrate transfers of assets to spouses, in-laws, etc.—who really wants to do that? What we really want is an arrangement where *we* can continue to enjoy our assets, at least to some extent, while still keeping them beyond the reach of our creditors. Is there a way to do this? Actually, there are a number of ways, and most involve the use of legal vehicles such as the corporation, the limited partnership, the limited liability company, the trust, or various and creative combinations of any or all of the above. In this case, however, we will focus on the *asset protection trust*.

WHAT IS AN ASSET PROTECTION TRUST?

Generally an asset protection trust is one where the settlor (the creator of the trust) can continue to enjoy benefits from assets she has transferred to the trust while placing those assets beyond the reach of her creditors. (Remember, this type of trust is called a self-settled trust.) In addition, the asset protection trust must at the same time be designed to take advantage of appropriate tax benefits. Whether the assets in such a trust can be reached by creditors depends on two essential factors:

1. Did the transfer of assets to the trust constitute a fraudulent conveyance? and
2. What rights does a creditor have against the trust assets under the law of the jurisdiction governing the trust?

As noted in the discussion above, if a transfer is deemed to be fraudulent, it won't matter what the law is regarding the trust, since the fraudulently transferred asset(s) can be reached as if the trust did not exist.

If the transfer is not fraudulent *or* if the period of limitations within which a creditor must attack the conveyance has expired, then we must look to the law of the jurisdiction of the trust (the governing law) to determine the creditor's rights.

WHAT LAW GOVERNS YOUR TRUST?

Somewhere, usually toward the end, in every well-drafted trust, you will see a statement something like, "This trust is established in [*the selected state or other jurisdiction*] and all matters relating to the trust be construed and administered according to the laws of that jurisdiction."

Is this all that is necessary to have the trust governed by the laws of a favorable jurisdiction? Does it matter that the person creating the trust does not live there? Would this mean that every time a question arises someone has to go to a court in the particular jurisdiction?

When we form a corporation or a partnership or a limited liability company, we have the freedom of choosing any state in the United States, or any country in the world, for that matter, simply by filing the necessary organizational documents in that state or country. It does not matter that we may never actually carry on a business or any other activity in that jurisdiction, only that we organized the entity there according to its laws. (How many times have we heard or seen the reference, "a Delaware Corporation," when it is apparent the company has no connection with Delaware?) Once we do that, all legal matters relating to the administration of the entity and the rights of its shareholders, partners, or members will be determined by the laws of the selected jurisdiction. Trusts are somewhat different.

While the jurisdiction of a trust may also be freely selected by the settlor, in order for his selection to be binding on the trust and the beneficiaries, the trust must have a *connection* (the law calls it a "nexus") with the chosen jurisdiction. For instance, say that Barry, a resident of Oklahoma, creates a trust for the benefit of his children, who reside in California, and funds it with real estate he owns, located in New York. He then names his brother, who lives in New Jersey, as the trustee. Barry decides that Delaware law would be best for his trust so he includes a statement in the trust that it shall be governed by the laws of Delaware. Is this valid? If not, what law would apply? The law of Oklahoma? New York? California? New Jersey?

First, since there is no connection whatever to the state of Delaware, the provision in Barry's trust attempting to make it a Delaware trust would be invalid. Next, in determining what law would apply, the court in this case would probably apply the law of New York because when a trust's principal assets are real estate, it is the law of the location of the real estate (the "law of the land") that will determine the jurisdiction (called the "situs") of the trust. If the trust had property in several states, the court would then have to consider all of the circumstances and, as a general rule, would apply the law of the jurisdiction that on balance has "the greatest interest" in the trust. In this case, it could be California because that is where all the beneficiaries are, but a definitive answer could not be given.

This is why a settlor wishing to have his trust governed in a jurisdiction other than his own must *provide* a connection. Perhaps the easiest way to do this is to select a trustee in the desired jurisdiction. The situs of the trustee is an adequate connection to establish the situs of the trust. Thus, had Barry simply selected a trustee in the state of Delaware, even (in some cases) to act as co-trustee with his brother, this would have been sufficient to bind the trust and establish the governing law. This would be the case even though at some future date the Delaware trustee resigned, although if he resigned immediately after appointment there would likely be a different result.

It is also interesting to note that the situs of a trust can be *changed* if the terms of the trust allow it. This can have far-reaching and complicated effects and should only be considered with expert advice.

THE SPENDTHRIFT TRUST RULES

The general rule of creditor protection in the United States where a self-settled trust is concerned is that your creditors can reach whatever benefits may be paid to you out of the trust. This is called the "spendthrift trust" rule and it works like this:

Denise creates and transfers assets to an irrevocable trust, which provides that the trustee may pay to Denise and/or her children any part or all of the trust income and/or principal, as the trustee deems appropriate in its sole discretion. In other words, Denise cannot order the trustee to make any payments from the trust; it is totally up to the trustee. This is a self-settled spendthrift trust and in all states except (as of this writing) Alaska, Delaware, Colorado, Nevada, Oklahoma, Rhode Island, Utah, and Missouri (as discussed later), and except for trusts qualifying in the aforementioned states, Denise's creditors can reach *all* of the assets in the trust. The fact that Denise's children are also beneficiaries has no bearing on that result. If the trust were revocable by Denise, the issue would be even clearer, since, as a general rule, her right to revoke the trust and take back all the assets could be reached by her creditors. Note that if Denise were *not* a beneficiary and the transfer was not fraudulent, her creditors could *not* reach the trust assets— although neither could she. It is this aspect of the spendthrift trust rule that actually makes it attractive to most families. That is, when a person creates a discretionary trust for the benefit of one or more *others*, creditors of those beneficiaries may not reach the trust assets. Many parents or other ancestors protect their beneficiaries' inheritances with this form of arrangement.

To illustrate, Steve, a widower with a substantial estate, made out a will leaving everything to his two sons equally. He knew one child was a little "loose" with money and the other had a shaky marriage, but he didn't know there was anything he could do. After Steve's death his concerns proved out; one child spent most of his money and lost the rest gambling, while the other was forced to give most of his share to his wife as a divorce settlement.

If, instead, Steve had established spendthrift trusts for the benefit of his two children (he could include their children as well), providing the usual safeguards prohibiting a beneficiary's creditors from reaching trust assets, then Steve's money would have been protected and remained intact to continue to provide benefits for his two sons for their lives, despite the debts or the divorce.

In the ordinary course of the typical estate planning practice, the situation often arises not just when planning for someone like Steve, but rather when planning for Steve's children. When individuals are getting estate planning or even financial advice, it is standard procedure to ask about potential or expected gifts of inheritances. If the circumstances warrant, the adviser will recommend that the parent(s) or other relative of the individual who has named them as a beneficiary consider instead establishing a spendthrift trust for that person. This would give the person benefits and reasonable access to the inheritance but would keep the inheritance beyond the reach of the beneficiary's creditors, and, if properly drafted, could escape taxes in his estate as well.

To illustrate, say that during a conference with her estate planner, Sally reports that a malpractice claim has recently been made against her and she is concerned that her insurance won't cover it. She also states that her eighty-four-year-old aunt, Sadie, recently made out a will naming Sally as the sole beneficiary. Aunt Sadie's estate is about $900,000, and Sally's estate is $1.6 million, which she intends to leave in trust for her children. If things are left as is and Aunt Sadie dies, Sally will receive the $900,000, which will then be immediately available to her creditors. In addition, Sally's estate will jump to $2.5 million, and on Sally's death (even if it occurred after 2006 when the tax-free amount is $2 million), the tax on that estate would be nearly a quarter million dollars.

If Sally's estate planner is worth her salt, she'll advise Sally to speak to Aunt Sadie about changing her will. She'll suggest (through Sally) that instead of an outright bequest to Sally, Sadie establish a spendthrift trust for

Sally's benefit, with liberal distribution arrangements for Sally (in fact, Sally could even be the trustee if the trust contains an ascertainable standard as explained earlier in this chapter). On Sally's death, what is left in the trust could go to Sally's children, protected from Sally's creditors and *completely free of estate taxes* in Sally's estate.

As mentioned above, there are exceptions to the rules—positive and negative. The negative exceptions to the spendthrift trust rules include the majority of states where a beneficiary's share of a spendthrift trust will be available to pay a creditor for "necessaries" furnished in good faith to the beneficiary and, in many cases, the beneficiary's child support obligations. In addition, in three states—Mississippi, Georgia, and Louisiana—spendthrift trust assets may be available to certain "tort" creditors of a beneficiary. (A tort is a wrong committed against another, such as assault and battery, stealing, or causing personal injuries by reckless driving or other negligent behavior.) These three states have carved out special exceptions to the spendthrift trust rules in certain of those cases, so if you are establishing a trust in one of those states, either consider establishing it elsewhere or consult an expert to be sure you understand the limitations that apply.

The positive exceptions to the spendthrift trust rules apply in Alaska, Delaware, Missouri, Nevada, Oklahoma, Rhode Island, South Dakota, and Utah, and, to a limited extent, Colorado (the list is growing annually). The types of trusts available in those states, together with other trusts that contain certain special protective provisions, are considered "domestic asset protection trusts."

DOMESTIC ASSET PROTECTION TRUSTS

These are self-settled trusts that are created, funded, and administered in certain states, and offer or purport to offer protection of trust assets from the creditors of the settlor. Because of this, they would, of course, be subject to the jurisdiction of U.S. courts and laws, including the spendthrift trust laws explained above. In the states mentioned above, and, to an extent, Colorado (let's call them, and others that will undoubtedly follow, the domestic asset protection trust [DAPT] states), the spendthrift trust rule as it applies to self-settled trusts has been abolished by statute if the trust complies with state law. Briefly, compliance with the law generally requires that:

- The trust must be irrevocable by the settlor (except in Oklahoma);
- The settlor must not be in default of child support payments;

- Distributions from the trust to the settlor must be fully discretionary (in Oklahoma the settlor may not be a beneficiary);
- Some of the trust assets must be deposited and administered in the protective state (in Oklahoma, all of the trust assets);
- At least one of the trustees must be a resident of the protective state or a bank or trust company with a principal place of business there; and
- Transfers to the trust were not fraudulent transfers.

Delaware has special exceptions to creditor protection even where all of the above requirements are met (e.g., alimony payments and certain personal injury claims), but aside from these special cases, the DAPT states apparently offer protection of assets without giving up use and enjoyment of those assets, in the ordinary course of events. Or do they? A number of experts in the field have raised the question of whether these trusts will stand up to a constitutional challenge, that is, whether a creditor who obtains a legal judgment in, say, New York, against the settlor/beneficiary of an Alaskan trust can require the state of Alaska to honor that judgment under the "full faith and credit" rule of the U.S. Constitution. Proponents of the Alaska-type trust argue that such a judgment need not be given full faith and credit because it was not a judgment against the *trust,* as the foreign court had no jurisdiction over the trust. Countering further, the opposing critical experts argue that even if the full faith and credit argument does not work, the federal bankruptcy rules would override the state law and allow a trustee in bankruptcy (of the settlor/beneficiary) to reach the trust assets. In both cases, the jury is still out.

PROTECTION THROUGH POWERS OF APPOINTMENT

Other options exist for domestic (as well as offshore) asset protection trusts but generally they are a "step down" from the best of all worlds offered by Delaware-type DAPT trusts (if they work). These alternatives involve an arrangement where someone other than the settlor is given the power to remove assets from the trust and place them elsewhere, such as in another trust. This power is called a "power of appointment." Power of appointment is the legal term meaning the power to redirect ownership of assets that are subject to the power. A power is a "general" power if the person who has the power (the powerholder) can redirect the ownership of the assets to *himself.* The power is a "limited" or "special" or "nongeneral" power if the power-holder cannot exercise the power to himself or for his own benefit. If the language creating the power permits it, the power can be exercised to place the assets in *another trust* (for the benefit of the individual objects of the power) rather than for the individuals directly.

To illustrate, Stewart creates a trust providing that the trustee can pay all the income to Stewart, but no principal. At the same time the trust allows Stewart's wife, Carolyn, the power to direct the trustee to pay trust principal to or for the benefit of any or all of Stewart's children. In this case, Carolyn has a special power of appointment in favor of Stewart's children (the objects of the power) and, at any time and for any reason, without restriction, she can exercise it by directing the trustee to pay such part or all of the trust principal (assets) to the children as she chooses, or to a new trust for their benefit. *Note* that the exercise of such a power is *not* a new transfer. It is regarded as merely a completion of the initial transfer (by Stewart) that became subject to the power

The beauty of this arrangement is that the exercise of the power is not a fraudulent conveyance by Stewart, since his transfer was made earlier when he funded the trust. And it was not made by Carolyn since the trust assets did not belong to her. Furthermore, there is considerable law supporting the fact that a court could not order Carolyn to exercise or not to exercise her power. Accordingly, if the trust income being received by Stewart were in jeopardy of attack by Stewart's creditors, Carolyn could exercise her power and remove the principal of the trust, which in turn would remove the income.

The obvious problem with this picture is that Stewart now has neither income nor principal. Is there a way that we could leave "open" the possibility that at some future date Stewart could regain use of the income or the principal?

Supposing that Carolyn's power over the trust principal extended to anyone *except* Carolyn or her own benefit? If this were the case, when trouble struck, Carolyn could exercise her power in a *revocable* manner (this is permissible, allowing her the opportunity of reexercising it again later) into a trust for the benefit of her children. Then later, when the coast is clear, Carolyn revokes the first exercise and makes a second exercise of the power into a new trust for the benefit of Stewart.

PROTECTION THROUGH THE POWER TO AMEND

Akin to the power of appointment is the power to *amend* a trust. Most people (including attorneys) instinctively regard this as a power held by the *settlor*. In fact, it is quite possible to give someone *other than the settlor* the power to amend the settlor's trust. Under the law, a power to amend is a power of appointment so that if this power is utilized, it must be drafted very carefully to result in the correct power being granted, presumably a special power.

The power to amend a trust would work in much the same way as a power of appointment, but with the added advantage that the trust assets need not be removed from the trust; the trust would merely be amended by the powerholder to achieve the desired effect. For instance, the desired effect may simply be to remove the settlor as a beneficiary.

THE PROTECTOR

Though this may sound like the title of a new TV series, it is in fact a commonly used trust provision by attorneys specializing in asset protection planning. The role of protector is viewed by some as having originated in overseas trusts and family foundations. It typically involved a trusted family friend who would be given veto power over trust distributions that were to be made to beneficiaries, but in many cases the protector might have even broader powers, including the power to add or remove beneficiaries. The protector would *not* be a trustee, but he may be given the power to remove and replace trustees. As can be seen, it is or can be a very powerful position "outside" the trust.

As noted, protectors are more often used in offshore trusts and, in such cases, it is important to provide that the protector may *not* be a U.S. person or entity who would ordinarily be subject to the jurisdiction, so as to avoid U.S. court jurisdiction over the protector. More and more they are being used in domestic trusts as trust attorneys become more familiar with their use, although up until the past few years it was virtually unheard of in U.S. trusts. Now there are a number of states (e.g., Delaware, Utah, South Dakota) that actually have laws specifically providing for the appointment of a protector. As a general rule, the protector should *not* be a beneficiary of the trust.

Note that there are a myriad of legal and tax intricacies and potentially complicated consequences of maneuvers involving powers of appointment, powers to amend, and the use of trust protectors. These suggestions are only hypothetical to illustrate the potential uses of these provisions for domestic creditor protection purposes. Where domestic creditor protection measures are not sufficient, the more serious planners will turn to the offshore trust—the "Great Wall" of asset protection.

Offshore Asset Protection Trusts

Some say the concept of asset protection using foreign jurisdictions, ironically, actually began in the United States. During World War II many German (and other countries') citizens attempting to escape Nazi dominance and control moved their assets to the United States. As part of their move to confiscate assets the German courts ruled that those assets "illegally" moved "offshore" should be returned to Germany and the Third Reich, and German judgments were issued accordingly. German representatives then attempted to collect on these judgments against funds held in the United States. The U.S. courts, however, held that in the absence of "comity" (where international jurisdictions may recognize certain of each other's judgments out of fairness and respect), these "foreign" judgments were neither recognized nor enforceable in this country, and there was certainly no treaty between the two countries providing for reciprocal recognition of judgments—hence those assets were unreachable by the individuals' German "creditors," even though the creditors had a legal judgment against them. This is the fundamental concept of how the offshore asset protection trust works, only reversing the direction of the assets and the location of the creditors.

In the typical asset protection trust, a U.S. person will establish a living trust in an offshore jurisdiction that has no reciprocal judgment recognition agreement with the United States and usually no tax treaty (although, as noted later, the offshore trust is *not* usually established to avoid taxes— almost all offshore asset protection trusts are tax neutral). The assets that are to be protected will actually be transferred to this trust and held offshore. There is little benefit to leaving assets onshore as it simply leaves them vulnerable to the order of a U.S. court.

Once the assets are settled offshore in the trust, creditors must jump considerable hurdles at considerable expense to get at them. And by "creditors" we do not mean only your typical bad debt or personal injury claimant. Many offshore trusts have been established to avoid claims of forced heirship (see chapter 7) by spouses and children, and even to protect funds in the event of a divorce. In one case, a very wealthy businessman named Hess placed millions in a Gibraltar trust. His wife later sued for divorce, and she also sued in Gibraltar claiming the transfer to the trust was fraudulent and should therefore be available to her as a creditor, only to have the legal door slammed in her face. The assets in Hess's Gibraltar trust were unreachable to her.

Due to the average person's concern about moving money a few thousand (or more) miles away and placing it in the hands of some bank or trust company they never heard of, some onshore advisers recommend an arrangement whereby the funds and investments remain onshore in the individual's control until "the suit hits the fan." In addition to keeping the funds close by, this arrangement may temporarily postpone the extensive reporting requirements associated with foreign trusts, as discussed below. This result is typically accomplished by establishing a family limited partnership and transferring the targeted assets to that partnership. The individual (and her spouse, if appropriate) will act as the general partner (but holding only a 1 percent or 2 percent partnership share), and therefore they control all investments and distributions. The limited partner, holding a 98 or 99 percent share, is a domestic trust that later *becomes* a foreign (*offshore*) trust. Everything stays this way until trouble strikes, at which time all investments are liquidated (note that there may be a capital gains tax to pay on liquidation) and the partnership is dissolved, with ultimate distribution of assets to the "partners." The liquidation of assets is necessary to facilitate an immediate transfer (e.g., by wire or cashier's check) to the offshore trustee. On dissolution, a partnership pays its partnership debts (here there would likely be none) and then pays out the funds to the partners according to their shares. One of the partners is the trust. Simultaneous with the partnership liquidation, the domestic trustee resigns and the foreign co-trustee takes over. Certain trust provisions are triggered, and the trust becomes an offshore trust. Since the offshore trust is a 98 or 99 percent partner, virtually all of the partnership funds would be immediately moved offshore, out of harm's way.

At some point, however, the assets must be moved outside the United States, and there must be an offshore trustee who is not subject to the jurisdiction of U.S. courts. And while the onshore partnership arrangement may offer a degree of comfort, it also involves the likelihood of paying a gains tax when the assets are liquidated, which is *not* the case if the assets have been placed in the offshore trust at the outset. Furthermore, while assets are held in the United States, or even where they may be offshore but held in U.S. companies, there is always the risk that a creditor can convince a court to reach or perhaps freeze those assets, preventing movement or protection offshore, as they are technically within the U.S. court's reach. For this reason, the really serious asset protection plan may involve offshore trusts holding non–U.S. investments.

Although the typical offshore trust is irrevocable, this is not a deterrent to its establishment, since its provisions are extremely flexible. Such a trust is typically designed to provide exclusively for the individual and, if desired, for her family as well. Also, there are often provisions for amendment by the trustee or by a protector if deemed to be in the best interests of the beneficiaries, and for the appointment of a protector. As explained above, a protector is not a trustee, but simply an individual or entity outside the trust who can have the power to veto distributions, add or remove beneficiaries, and hold other powers designed to insure flexibility. Since the settlor herself does not have these powers, a court could not order her to exercise them. Offshore trusts also will usually include a "flee" clause, which allows the trustee to actually move the legal location (the "situs") of the trust to another offshore jurisdiction if the trust is in jeopardy in its present jurisdiction.

In its actual operation, the offshore trust works just like any other trust. The trustee invests the assets and makes distributions to the beneficiaries as provided by the terms of the trust. Thus, so long as advisable, the settlor could receive income and principal payments as needed. If trouble strikes, distributions to the settlor would cease, and they could be made to his spouse or even for other purposes, such as payment of the settlor's mortgage or other bills. Once the claim was settled, distributions to the settlor could be resumed. There will also be provisions for continued management of assets and distributions after the settlor's death. In fact, the trust will contain all the usual estate tax marital deduction and bypass trust (even generation-skipping trust) provisions as discussed earlier, just as if it were an onshore trust. Furthermore, the individual's will will be coordinated with the trust, as is customarily done.

OFFSHORE TRUST TAX ISSUES

Although the offshore trust will typically contain provisions designed to minimize estate taxes, it is designed to be "tax neutral" for *income* tax purposes. This means there are neither income tax advantages nor disadvantages in establishing it (with the possible exception of the gain on liquidation if it is funded with a U.S. partnership—but note that any gain is because of the need to liquidate the U.S. partnership and *not* because of the existence of the offshore trust). The tax neutrality is primarily due to the fact that the trust is intentionally designed to be a "grantor" trust for U.S. income tax purposes. As discussed in more detail in chapter 13, a grantor trust is one where, because of certain provisions contained in the trust, all trust income, losses, deductions, gains, etc., are *passed through* to the settlor. That is, the trust pays no income taxes; all taxes on trust income or gains are paid by the settlor, whether she receives them or not. On the settlor's death, the assets in the trust are treated like any other asset in her estate. Nevertheless, it is extremely important to note that although the establishment of a foreign asset protection trust does *not* normally bring about any extra taxes, it *does* bring about the requirement to file additional tax information forms each year. Failure to file the necessary annual foreign trust tax information forms with the IRS can result in a penalty of 35 percent of the amount transferred to the trust. (Taxes and the required tax forms are discussed in the next chapter.)

CREDITOR'S ATTACK ON A FOREIGN TRUST

Because the trust and the trust assets are located in a jurisdiction that does not recognize U.S. court judgments, a creditor would actually have to initiate *new* legal proceedings in the offshore jurisdiction. This means that he would have to hire an attorney in the foreign jurisdiction and pay legal fees up front—attorneys in asset protection jurisdictions do not work on a contingent fee basis. In addition, in most instances the creditor would have to produce evidence and witnesses to prove his whole case, as he would (or already has, at great expense) in the United States. Furthermore, many of these jurisdictions require that the creditor post a bond, usually a *cash* bond, before he is allowed to bring suit, to cover court costs and fees in the event he is not successful.

In short, it is a formidable and expensive proceeding, chosen by only the most determined creditors and usually only in chasing large judgments. Unofficial but very reliable reports show that better than 95 percent of such attacks are either unsuccessful or settle for 5 to 10 cents on the dollar. This is not to indicate, however, that all offshore trusts are creditor proof, *nor* that you should or can create one in the face of a lawsuit.

In this sense, there is, perhaps, both good news and bad news with respect to offshore asset protection trusts. The good news is that the above observations illustrating the tremendous difficulty and expense that face a creditor seeking to attack such a trust are absolutely true and proven so. The bad news is that one way their virtual imperviousness to a creditor's attack has been proven is through a blatant abuse of their protective features by con men and other individuals of dubious character. The cases resulting from these abuses have, of course, been the ones that have made the headlines and the ones that in some respects have given a "bad image" to such trusts. This is quite unfair for those perfectly legitimate individuals who establish such trusts with nothing to run from and nothing to hide. Nevertheless, as badly motivated as they were, here are a couple of examples of actual cases dealing with offshore trusts.

In one case, a New York business owner who we'll call "Porky" needed additional funds to carry on his business. His company borrowed $1 million from a major New York bank and Porky personally guaranteed the loan. Shortly thereafter, through a combination of a downturn in business and his own substantial withdrawals from the company, Porky and the company defaulted on the loan. When the bank came to collect on his personal guarantee, Porky filed for bankruptcy. After lying to the bankruptcy trustee as well as to the court, Porky finally admitted that he had transferred substantial (perhaps $1 million or more) to an offshore trust he had established in the Channel Islands. This was done while he knew of the company's circumstances and while his personal guarantee was in effect (in short, he had clearly made a series of fraudulent transfers). The net result, after proceedings in a New York bankruptcy court, was that the court refused to acknowledge the validity of the offshore trust and so considered the funds "available" to Porky, but the result of all this was not that any money was legally recovered from the offshore trust; rather it was merely that Porky's debt was not discharged by the bankruptcy proceedings. What did the bank, his major creditor, do? According to reliable sources, they simply settled for 20 to 30 cents on the dollar, obviously deciding that to pursue Porky's money in the offshore trust was simply not worth it.

In another notorious and abusive case, a couple we'll call Bonnie and Clyde owned a chain of bookstores. Like Porky, Bonnie and Clyde needed money to carry on their business and so took out and personally guaranteed a $20 million(!) loan from a major bank. Undoubtedly, the bank extended the loan not only on account of the business but also on account of the fact that, unlike Porky, Bonnie and Clyde had substantial personal assets outside the company. As the story must go, the business went sour and the bank called the note. Bonnie and Clyde stalled and the bank brought legal action. Unbelievably, in the midst of and after legal proceedings against them, which resulted in an order for payment, Bonnie and Clyde established a trust in the Cook Islands and funded it with about $18 million of their assets. This time, the bank took forceful action against Bonnie and Clyde and their trust, even to the extent of suing in the Cook Islands as well as in the United States. All this took time (and lots of money), of course, and in the meantime, Bonnie and Clyde filed for bankruptcy. After numerous and expensive legal skirmishes that gained little ground, and with no certainty of success, the trustee in bankruptcy, in response to an offer on behalf of Bonnie and

Clyde to settle the dispute for about half the $20-odd-million-dollar debt, recommended to the court that the offer be accepted, which it was. Unlike the movie, Bonnie and Clyde got away with the (balance of the) money.

In both of the above cases, the debtors clearly made fraudulent transfers and it seems unfair that their legitimate creditors could not collect what was due them. As noted earlier, this may be the dark side of such planning, but it does demonstrate the strength of the concept in general. What is not so apparent or prominently reported are the thousands of legitimate professionals and business people who in good faith and with no present claims against them establish offshore asset protection trusts and can then "sleep at night," knowing that a substantial part of their wealth is protected for themselves and their family. There is nothing unusual or unfair about this.

As for fraudulent transfers, remember that the fraudulent transfer rules apply all over the world, as it is a valid public policy principle, and *if a transfer to an offshore trust is deemed fraudulent, the trust may be successfully attacked.* However, these rules are regarded quite differently in most offshore asset protection jurisdictions. First, there are much shorter periods of limitations within which a creditor must bring an action *in* the foreign jurisdiction and *within* the allowable period from the date the claim arose to void the transfer. Typically, the offshore period of limitations is two years (e.g., the Cook Islands and the Bahamas), and in some jurisdictions the protection is *immediate,* so long as the transfer to the trust did not render you insolvent (e.g., Gibraltar). Note that in virtually all offshore jurisdictions the protection is immediate as to any claims that arose *after* the trust was settled (and funded). Second, the burden of proof as to whether the transfer was fraudulent is much higher. In the Cook Islands, for instance, the creditor must prove, *in* the Cook Islands, *beyond a reasonable doubt,* that the transfer was fraudulent *as to that creditor.* A formidable and expensive burden; no wonder most creditors settle.

While in Porky's case the bank decided it would not be worth it to go to the foreign jurisdiction to attempt to prove the transfer fraudulent, in the case of Bonnie and Clyde, where many millions were involved, it clearly would have been worth it—*if* the bank could win. Once the bank got there, hired lawyers, and began the battle, however, the picture dimmed more than a bit. They definitely had a good case, at least on its face, but how do you prove a fraudulent transfer? Generally by showing evidence of the intent of the debtor/transferor. In this instance, the best way to show intent would be the communications and correspondence between Bonnie and Clyde and the law firm that helped them create the offshore trust, and that's exactly what the bank's lawyers targeted. But this was clearly privileged attorney/client information—or was it? In fact, there is a "fraud" exception to the attorney/client privilege and the court ultimately held that it applied here—but not to every document. All documents would therefore have to be examined, with opportunities for exceptions, objections by the parties' attorneys, and so on. With the prospect of months if not years of litigation on this matter alone, with no certainty or even a likelihood of success, it is not surprising that the trustee in bankruptcy recommended settlement.

It is also important to explain that the question of insolvency in this context often requires the person (the settlor) to take into consideration not only her actual debts, but also those debts and claims that may be *pending* or *expected* (e.g., where you know you have caused damages giving rise to a claim, but the claim has not yet been formally filed). In this regard, most competent attorneys who practice in this area will have their clients make a complete disclosure and sign an affidavit of solvency before agreeing to prepare and implement an asset protection plan. Some attorneys even do a credit check and outstanding case review before proceeding with the plan. In addition, virtually all responsible offshore trustees will require a written statement by the attorney and another by the client, disclosing assets and liabilities as well as known or anticipated claims, and showing that the individual will not be rendered insolvent by the transfer to the offshore trust.

SETUP AND ANNUAL COSTS OF AN OFFSHORE TRUST

Due to the complexity of an offshore asset protection plan, the degree of expertise required, and the many details involved, the experienced asset protection attorney will generally charge fees ranging from $12,000 to $25,000 (sometimes even more) for the average plan and documents. The offshore trustee fees are generally competitive with local professional trustees, and their charges usually run from $3,000 to $4,000 per year, but, as in this country, they may be higher depending on the amount of assets under management. Note that due to the amount of your assets typically being protected, the broad scope of the knowledge and expertise involved, and the intricate trust provisions often required, this is *not* an area where you would shop around for the cheapest price.

Another item of costs that recently became noteworthy are the costs associated with preparing the numerous forms and reports now required by the IRS when a foreign (offshore) trust is used. As a result of the IRS belief that individuals with funded offshore asset protection trusts were not reporting the income earned in such trusts, they convinced Congress to pass laws requiring extensive reports and forms when a foreign trust is used, providing a severe penalty (35 percent of the assets in the trust!) for failure to comply. *Note that all this reporting doesn't mean any additional taxes.* It merely means that the IRS wants to be kept fully informed of the existence and funding of your foreign trust. Of course, you needn't personally worry about this since these forms and reports are normally prepared by your accountant or tax attorney. The fees for this work, however, can range from $1,000 to $2,500 annually in the average situation.

All in all, the costs associated with the offshore trust plan are generally three or four times the costs of a local plan without asset protection features. But this should not be a deterrent if asset protection is the objective. What is it worth to protect your nest egg of $750,000 or $1 million or more? How much are you paying for malpractice or other liability insurance? Or do you have none? Once a lawsuit is filed against you, you would quickly wish you had such a plan when you saw all your assets placed in jeopardy and possibly frozen by a court for a few years, waiting for a judgment.

Tax-Oriented Trusts

A number of trusts have been designed for the primary purpose of taking advantage of certain tax laws, and they fall into two general categories: those that benefit only the family, and those that benefit the family and one or more qualified charities. These trusts are all subject to detailed requirements in formation and operation in order to realize the tax benefits.

Charitable/family trusts include the *charitable remainder trust* and the *charitable lead trust.*

THE CHARITABLE REMAINDER TRUST (CRT)

This is an irrevocable trust to which a person (the settlor) can transfer assets and retain either a fixed dollar amount of annual income (called a charitable remainder *annuity* trust), or a fixed percentage of the trust assets valued each year (called a charitable remainder *unitrust*). The tax code provides for minimums in either case for the trust to qualify. In the case of the annuity trust, the payment must be at least 5 percent of the initial value of the trust assets, and no assets may be added after that. With the unitrust, the payments must be no less than 5 percent of the value of the trust assets from year to year. Assets may be added to a unitrust trust at any time, but not to an annuity trust. It is also necessary that the projected remainder (based on the retained interest and the applicable IRS tables) be no less than 10 percent of the original contribution to the trust.

The income from either trust can be paid to the settlor for a fixed term of years up to a maximum of twenty years, or for the person's lifetime. At the end of the period (if a term is chosen) or on the settlor's death, the balance remaining in the trust (the "remainder") must pass to a qualified charity. In either case there can be secondary (or more) beneficiaries after the settlor, but a secondary beneficiary other than the settlor's spouse produces adverse tax consequences and also can materially reduce the amount of the charitable gift.

Because the trust is irrevocable and the payments fixed or determinable, and because the remainder must go to a qualified charity, the settlor is entitled to an income tax *deduction* (up to allowable limits) at the time the trust is funded. The amount of the deduction is calculated according to IRS tables (a complicated exercise that is usually and happily computed by the charity named in the trust), and it reflects the present value of the remainder that is to pass to the charity at the end of the trust. Although getting an income tax deduction today for a gift that will continue to be used by you (in the form of income) and may not be paid to the charity for many years ought to be enough of a bonus, there is an even greater bonus that accompanies this type of trust. The tax code provides that the trust itself is not taxable. The only tax that is paid is that which becomes due as a result of distributions from the trust to the individual beneficiary (typically the settlor or his spouse). This means that if a settlor transferred assets to a CRT and the CRT sold those assets at a huge capital gain, there would be no tax to pay on that gain unless at some point the gain was distributed to the settlor. This can result in an indefinite deferral of a virtually unlimited amount of tax. Here's how it could work.

Katherine, a single person age sixty, has 6,000 shares of stock in IBM, her principal asset, which she acquired many years ago at a cost of about $40,000. At $80 per share, the stock is now worth $480,000. The problem is that IBM pays a dividend of less than 1 percent, or about $3,500 per year on the 6,000 shares. Although Katherine could sell the stock and invest in a higher-paying investment, she is reluctant to do so because of a capital gain of $440,000 (which could result in a tax of over $60,000).

Katherine is a perfect candidate for a CRT. She could create a charitable remainder unitrust paying her, say, 8 percent annually for her lifetime. On her death, the remainder would pass to her favorite charity. As soon as the trust is executed, Katherine can transfer the IBM stock to the trust. The trustee of the trust can *immediately* sell the stock and, assuming the same value, reinvest the full proceeds of $480,000. No tax will be paid on the gain by the trust.

The particular investment returns that the trustee realizes is important for long-term purposes, since Katherine will be receiving 8 percent of the value of the trust, valued *each year,* so if the value increases, Katherine's income will increase as well (and, of course, the converse would be true). In any event, for the first year, the trust will pay Katherine $38,400, and, assuming the value of assets remain constant, she will receive $38,400 per year for the rest of her life. Compared with the $3,500 she was receiving on the same amount, this is quite an improvement.

The tax that Katherine will pay on the $38,400 will depend on the trustee's investments and the source of the income derived by the trust. If the trustee received $40,000 of dividends and paid out $38,400 to Katherine, her income is deemed to be dividend income and taxed accordingly. Note that the trustee *must* pay Katherine 8 percent of the value of the trust assets, regardless of whether they actually earn 8 percent. If Katherine is paid out more than the trust earns, she is considered to be receiving back part of the principal (or the capital gain).

For instance, if the annual payment is to be $38,400, but the trust assets only earned $28,400 for the year, then the balance of $10,000 is deemed to come from the principal, and this is when the capital gain on the stock would be drawn out. Thus, Katherine would have $28,400 of dividend income and $10,000 of capital gain to report. Often this is actually an advantage, since capital gain is generally taxed lower than ordinary income.

Another important tax benefit is that Katherine would be entitled to an income tax deduction of about $125,000 in the year she funds the trust, for the present value of her gift to charity.

CHARITABLE REMAINDER TRUST RETIREMENT FUND

And if that isn't attractive enough, it can get even better. A certain type of CRT can be designed to accumulate tax-deferred appreciation until such time as you decide to retire and take an income for life (or for a term of years). Where a unitrust is involved, the tax code allows the trust to provide that if the trust has no income for the year or less than the required percentage payment, then only the actual amount earned need be paid out. For instance, if the required payment was 6 percent of the assets but they only earned 2 percent, then only the 2 percent would be paid. This is called a net income CRUT (the "U" is for unitrust).

The code also allows such a trust to keep a running tab of the shortfall and to *make up* the shortfall in future years when the trust income increases. This is called a "net income with makeup" CRUT, or NIMCRUT. Even though the NIMCRUT can be structured to generate large distributions to the beneficiary/settlor in later years, the settlor's income tax deduction when the trust is created is calculated in the same manner as if the trust were a straight CRUT. Here is how a NIMCRUT might work.

Conrad has a large parcel of undeveloped land that he purchased long ago for a song. It is now worth about $500,000 and rising steadily because of the area. His plan has been to hold the land until he needs the money and then invest what's left after taxes to produce income for himself and his wife. Conrad creates a 6 percent NIMCRUT, which is to pay him 6 percent of the trust's value as income each year for his life, then the same amount for his wife's life, and then the remainder to three charities selected by them. If in any year the trust earns less than 6 percent, the shortfall may be made up in future years in which the trust earns more than 6 percent, to the extent of the excess income (over 6 percent) for that year.

The land is contributed to the trust and, based on Conrad's and his wife's ages and the 6 percent return, the $500,000 value of the land contributed to the trust results in a current income tax deduction to Conrad of about $120,000. The land produces no income, so no distributions are made, and the makeup account begins to build up. Furthermore, as the land appreciates in value each year, the 6 percent buildup also increases from $30,000 the first year to $72,000 in year ten when the land is worth $1.2 million. In that year the trustee of Conrad's trust sells the land for $1.2 million (net proceeds), and neither the trust nor Conrad will pay any tax on the gain in the year of sale (and may never pay a tax on it). The trustee invests the sale proceeds for a return of 8 percent, or $96,000 for the year.

Since the required payout is 6 percent, the trustee must first pay out $72,000 for the year (6 percent of $1.2 million). The income balance of $24,000 ($96,000 less $72,000) may then be applied toward the balance in the makeup account, which now stands at about $500,000. If the trust continues to earn 8 percent and the value of the principal remains constant, Conrad (and then his wife) will receive the full $96,000 each year until the makeup account is paid down, or about twenty years. If the return or the value of the principal changes, the payments will go up or down accordingly.

Each payment received by Conrad is first treated and taxed as ordinary income to the extent that the trust has any ordinary income that has not been distributed. If that is exhausted, then the payments begin to reflect capital gains that have not previously been distributed. In the typical NIMCRUT of this sort, the payments are made up largely of dividend or interest with only a small part, if any, being capital gain.

As noted, on Conrad's death, his wife will then be entitled to the 6 percent annual payout (or $72,000) if the value of the trust assets remains at $1.2 million. In addition, as stated earlier, she is entitled to recover any unpaid makeup amounts that accrued during Conrad's lifetime. The value of the unpaid makeup amounts and the wife's 6 percent income interest for her life is included in Conrad's estate for tax purposes, but there will be no tax on it because it qualifies for the estate tax marital deduction as a QTIP trust (see the discussion earlier in this chapter).

CHARITABLE LEAD TRUST (CLT)

A charitable *lead* trust (CLT) is, in a certain sense, the opposite of a charitable remainder trust (CRT). Whereas a CRT pays income to an individual for a period of time and then pays the remainder to one or more charities, the lead trust pays *income* to one or more charities for a period of time, then pays the remainder to one or more individuals. Like the CRT, the CLT must be irrevocable and can be a "unitrust" (a "CLUT") with fixed percentage of income for its term or an "annuity" trust (a "CLAT") with fixed annual payment for its term. Whether a CLUT or a CLAT, the lead trust, unlike the CRT, which can have a makeup provision if there is inadequate income in some years, *must* make its prescribed payments every year. And unlike the CRT, the CLT is not tax exempt and cannot defer tax on a gain. In fact, the income tax advantages of the CLT are usually negligible. It is more often used for its estate tax advantages, which are gained by virtue of the *discount* the settlor receives on the remainder that passes to his beneficiaries. The discount is applied to the gift because the donee will not receive the gift for several years. Here is how it works.

If a person makes a gift of $100 today, the gift is clearly $100. If, instead, the person says, "I'm setting aside $100, which will be paid to you in ten years," then *today* the gift is not worth $100 to the donee. Taking it a step further, if the person says, "I'm setting aside $100; 7 percent of this will be paid each year to my church, and at the end of ten years, you'll get what's left," now we have still a different picture. If the account earns more than

7 percent, we'll have more than $100 left. But if it earns less, or substantially less, we may have nothing left. So, what is the value of the gift today?

The IRS has tables and procedures that enable us to arrive at a present value of the future gift based on the prescribed payout compared with the estimated rate of return established by the IRS over the period. In using these tables for planning purposes against what we believe will be the realistic rate of return, we can get a considerable tax advantage with the charitable lead trust.

To illustrate: Jack placed $200,000 into a charitable lead annuity trust providing that his alma mater will receive 8 percent or $16,000 per year income from the trust for fifteen years. At the end of the fifteen-year period, the balance remaining in the trust will pass to Jack's two children. At the time Jack creates the trust the IRS tables assume just over a 6 percent return (regardless of what is actually earned). Based on this return, the term of the trust, and the prescribed payment, the IRS will treat this as a gift of about $44,000 to Jack's children. If, in fact, the invested funds produced a return of 12 percent, the remainder value passing to the children at the end of the fifteen-year term will be nearly $500,000! In other words, in this example Jack's children would receive $500,000 totally tax-free and free of taxes in Jack's estate, and Jack would report a gift of only $44,000. Note that Jack would pay the income tax on the annual income of the CLT, reduced by the 8 percent passing to charity (unless he elected to deduct the present value of the charitable payments in full at the outset, in which case he would pay a tax on all of the CLT income for the term).

In effect, this is an added benefit to his children since they will receive the accumulated income on which Jack has already paid the income tax. Even though the children may receive substantially more than the calculated amount of the gift according to IRS tables, the table amount is the controlling factor. This is the principal advantage of the CLT.

The charitable lead unitrust can also be used as a generation-skipping device (to avoid estate taxes in a child's estate), but the lead *annuity* trust should not be used for this purpose. If the estate is large enough and the projected actual annual return sufficient, the CLUT can be very effectively used on a person's death to pass on huge amount of funds, gift and estate tax free to grandchildren. For instance, say that Jackie had a $30 million estate and no spouse. On her death she leaves $20 million in a CLUT with a rate of return for the charity and a term of years calculated at the time of her death so as to produce a remainder at or near zero, with the remainder at the end of the twenty-year period passing to her grandchildren (or great-grandchildren). This means that the $20 million would *not* be taxed in Jackie's estate, since there is *no* projected remainder to pass to her beneficiaries. If, however, the return on the $20 million was more than the applicable IRS rate on her death, the grandchildren could receive *millions* in tax-free dollars. In fact, this is almost exactly what Jacqueline Kennedy Onassis did in her estate.

TAX-ORIENTED FAMILY TRUSTS

These trusts are all motivated almost exclusively by tax laws that the trusts use to the family's advantage by saving gift taxes, estate taxes, income taxes, or any combination of these. Although tax planners are constantly coming up with new ideas, new trusts, or new versions of old trusts, the basic group of trusts in this category and discussed in this section include retained interest trusts, personal residence trusts, "defective" trusts, life insurance trusts, and dynasty or generation-skipping trusts.

GRANTOR RETAINED INTEREST TRUSTS (GRITS)

This category generally includes trusts where the settlor (grantor) retains an interest in the trust for himself—typically, some amount of income or the right to use the trust property. In this section, it will be more appropriate to call the settlor the *grantor,* since this type of trust is commonly referred to as a "grantor retained income trust" or GRIT. In a GRIT, the grantor usually transfers income-producing assets and receives the *income* from those assets for a term of years selected by the grantor. At the end of the selected term, the remaining assets pass to the named beneficiary (the "remainder-man"). The advantage is similar to that described in the charitable lead trust discussed above—a discount on the value of the gift of the remainder. If the grantor outlives the term of the GRIT, the trust assets will be excluded from his estate, regardless of their value. The bad news (for some) is that no savings and adverse tax consequences will result if the beneficiaries of the GRIT are members of the grantor's close family. The good news is that this does not include nieces or nephews, nor does it include unmarried partners. In this regard, a more detailed discussion of the GRIT appears in the section on trusts for unmarried partners earlier in this chapter.

The sister to the GRIT, but with a much wider application, is the GRAT (grantor retained annuity trust). This differs from the GRIT in that the grantor must receive a *fixed annual payment* for the term of the GRAT. Like the GRIT, the term of the GRAT may be selected by the grantor; there is no minimum or maximum. The trick is, as it is with all of the retained income trusts, to select a term that the grantor will outlive, since if he dies before the end of the term, most, if not all, of the hoped-for tax savings will be lost, as explained below.

The most effective use of the GRAT will occur when the property transferred to the GRAT generates a higher income than the income assumed under the tax code (the so-called section 7520 rate), similar to the concept described above for the charitable lead trust. In this case, however, it is the *grantor* who will be receiving the income.

For instance, say that Sal, age sixty-six, transfers shares of his closely held company to a twelve-year GRAT. The shares are appraised at $600,000 (after taking an appropriate discount for the minority interest and the fact that the shares are not readily saleable), and the GRAT must pay him $76,000 per year for the twelve-year period. The company is classified as an "S" Corporation, which means that its profits are passed through to its shareholders. At the end of the twelve-year term, the shares (or what remains) will pass to Sal's three adult children. Based on the applicable IRS rate, after taking into account the payments that must be made to Sal over the term of the trust (and assuming that the IRS agrees with the appraised value of the shares), Sal is considered to be making a gift of only about $100,000 when he creates and funds the trust. This is the case regardless of what is actually left at the end of the term.

As it happens, the shares that Sal has transferred to the trust are actually generating income of $126,000 per year, which is more than the required payments. In this case, the excess income remains in the trust, but because the trust is a "grantor" trust, the entire amount of the trust's taxable income, not just the amount he receives, is nevertheless taxed to Sal. In this event, Sal has the option, when he creates the trust, of requiring the trustee to distribute to Sal, in *addition* to the specified annuity payments, an amount equal to his tax liability on the undistributed income that remains in the trust. For instance, if after the required payments there was excess income of $50,000 and Sal's tax on that amount was $16,000, then the trustee could distribute an additional $16,000 to Sal to pay the tax; the remaining $34,000 would remain in the trust, to be invested with the trust assets, until the end of the term, when it would all be distributed to the children, tax-free.

Note that all required payments to Sal, the grantor, *must* be made each year. If for some reason there was not enough cash to make the payment, then shares of stock, at their then appraised value, could be distributed in satisfaction of the payment. Some commentators have suggested that the trustee of the GRAT could give the grantor a promissory note for the payment, but in the opinion of most experts, this is asking for trouble, and the IRS is likely to disqualify the entire GRAT.

Taxes. If by the end of the twelve-year term, the stock has appreciated in value to $2 million and there are additional accumulated cash and investments of $500,000, Sal's children will receive the entire amount of $2.5 million totally tax free, even though Sal's original gift was only about $100,000. The other side of this coin is that, as described in more detail in the next chapter, the children's *cost basis* in the shares will be the same as Sal's original cost basis. Thus, a later sale of the shares is likely to produce a capital gain. On balance, however, the tax savings to the family will be huge so long as Sal outlives the term. If Sal dies before the end of the twelve-year term, most or all of the tax savings will be lost, since the IRS position is that the trust assets would be fully includable in Sal's estate for estate tax purposes. There is a good argument that something less than the full value of the assets will be included, but this issue has not yet been decided by the courts.

It should be noted that the grantor's grandchildren should *not* be the remainder beneficiaries of a GRAT at the end of the term. This is because the rules relating to the generation-skipping tax (the "GST," discussed in chapter 13) as they relate to this type of trust would require the grantor to apply his GST exemption at the *termination* of the trust, when the value presumably would be at its highest.

Trustee. During the twelve-year term of the trust, Sal, if he wishes, can be the trustee with no adverse tax consequences. After the term, however, he should not remain as trustee, unless his only function is to terminate the trust and distribute the assets to his children. In some cases, especially where the children are minors or there is some other reason to keep the assets in trust, the trust will continue after the term and in such event the grantor should *not* be the trustee. To do so could cause the trust assets to be included in the grantor's estate on his death after the term, when otherwise it would not be. A disastrous result.

Grantor retained unitrust (GRUT). A third type of retained interest trust will be mentioned only briefly here for the record, since it is generally of little use for estate planning. It is the grantor retained unitrust (GRUT). We can recall from the discussion of the charitable remainder unitrust above that a unitrust is one where the grantor (in this case) retains the right to receive a fixed percentage of the trust assets each year. For instance, Gigi places $100,000 in a six-year GRUT, retaining the right to receive a 6 percent unitrust interest per year. The first year she would receive $6,000. Each year thereafter for the term Gigi would receive 6 percent of whatever the value was for that year. The main planning purpose of a retained interest trust is to "freeze" the value of the asset at the time the trust is created and to have increases in income and appreciation of the asset accrue for the beneficiaries. Since the GRUT would increase the income paid to the grantor as the asset appreciates, it is generally agreed that the GRAT is the far better estate planning vehicle.

THE QUALIFIED PERSONAL RESIDENCE TRUST (QPRT)

Like the other three retained interest trusts, the personal residence trust must be irrevocable, the term of the trust may be selected by the grantor, and the trick is to select a term that will end before the grantor's death. If you do this and meet the requirements discussed below, it could result in substantial estate tax savings on your principal residence.

The benefit of the qualified personal residence trust (QPRT) is the ability to transfer a personal residence to chosen beneficiaries at a discount, often a very substantial discount, from its actual value. In the typical case, Mom and Dad own their home jointly. If they wish to establish a QPRT, it is generally advisable for one spouse to transfer his or her share of the home to the other, and that spouse will, a short while later, transfer the entire home to a QPRT. It is possible for the spouses to make a joint transfer to the same QPRT, but the drafting issues that must be properly addressed so as not to run afoul of the tax laws are too complicated to warrant it. If they must do it together, it is easier if each transfers his/her half to a separate QPRT. For obvious reasons, then one QPRT by one spouse is the usual choice. And the choice of spouse is important as well. If possible, it should be the one who's younger or healthier (or both), so as to increase the chances that the spouse creating the QPRT will outlive the term.

As mentioned above, the choice of term is purely subjective, but one place to begin is the life expectancy tables used by the IRS. The reason these are significant is that the discount you will get at the outset will be larger as you get closer to your life expectancy and beyond. This, in turn, is because most QPRTs are (and should be) drafted to cause a termination of the trust and a "reversion" of the property to the grantor's estate if he dies before the end of the term. As the term gets closer to or exceeds the grantor's life expectancy, the chances of his outliving the term decrease, hence the less the chance the beneficiaries have of ever getting the property, hence the smaller the gift.

For instance, if a healthy eighty-year-old establishes a ten-year QPRT (more than his life expectancy) and the property comes back into his estate if he dies before the term, he will be entitled to an 83 percent discount on the gift! In other words, if his residence has a market value of $300,000 at the time of the transfer to the QPRT, his gift, for gift tax purposes, will be only $51,000.

The QPRT may only be funded with one *personal residence* (and in some cases a nominal amount of funds to pay three months' expenses). A person may not have more than two QPRTs, and one of them must be for her *principal* residence. Therefore, a vacation home can be transferred to a QPRT, provided the grantor uses it at least fourteen days each year. A married couple could actually have *three* QPRTs: one for the principal residence, one for the husband's vacation home, and one for the wife's vacation home. If they had separate principal residences or wanted to split their joint residence into two QPRTs, then the couple could have four QPRTs. In practice, there are seldom more than two.

The residence must continue to be used as the grantor's personal residence throughout the term of the QPRT. There is a special exception if the grantor is institutionalized (i.e., hospitalized or in a nursing home), but otherwise, ceasing to use it as a residence causes the QPRT to become disqualified. Nevertheless, if the residence is destroyed or damaged an exception applies, and if the residence is sold, the proceeds should be used to purchase another residence within two years. If the proceeds are not used for another residence, there is a complicated rule that requires the QPRT to convert to a GRAT, and that the GRAT begin making payments to the grantor based on the original value of the residence when it was placed in the QPRT, for the remainder of the QPRT term.

A condo could be used in a QPRT, as could shares in a cooperative. Problems or questions arise where the residence consists of something more than a house, such as a house, several barns, cottages, and one hundred acres of land. Can all this be placed in one QPRT if it is my "personal residence"? The rule is not entirely clear and is constantly being examined by the IRS, but the approach seems to be that appurtenant buildings used by the grantor for residential purposes and land that is reasonably appropriate for the particular residence's size and location would be approved.

Putting a mortgaged residence in a QPRT is generally a bad idea since the part of each payment that constitutes principal will be an additional gift to the remainder beneficiaries.

For a while, advisers were recommending that the grantor who established a QPRT *purchase* the residence back from the QPRT just prior to the end of the term. This would have produced an almost too good to be true result, which the IRS quickly squashed by issuing tax regulations that require a QPRT to state in its terms that the grantor (and the grantor's spouse) is prohibited from purchasing the residence from the QPRT.

At the end of the term, the residence belongs to the beneficiaries, or to the trust if the trust is to continue. The grantor and his spouse no longer own the home and no longer have the legal right to live there. Not to worry. The QPRT can contain a provision that requires the trustee to lease the residence to you (at fair market rent, of course) for reasonable periods of time, with extensions, etc. In other words occupancy by the grantor and spouse can be protected for as long as they like. After the term, the residence can be sold (if not leased by the grantor), but the grantor, since he is not a beneficiary of the trust, would get no benefit from the sale.

Taxes. During the term, the QPRT is structured as a grantor trust and so all income and gains are taxed to the grantor. (See a discussion of "grantor" trusts in the next chapter.) If the principal residence is sold from the QPRT during the term, the gain will be eligible for the $250,000 capital gain exclusion (or $500,000 if married, even though only one spouse is the grantor). But remember the rules stated above where the trust ceases to be a QPRT.

After the term, the grantor is no longer the owner for tax purposes, so all income is taxed to the trust, or to the beneficiaries if distributed, depending on the terms of the trust. If the residence is sold, the trust or the beneficiaries will have a capital gain since their cost basis is equal to that of the grantor. This is, perhaps, somewhat of a downside to the QPRT, but it must be compared with the considerable estate tax savings likely to result if the grantor outlives the term of the trust.

Here is an illustration of the potential tax costs of a QPRT. Ray transfers his home to a ten-year QPRT. The home is worth $300,000 and the IRS tables indicate that Ray has made a gift to his children (the remaindermen) in the amount of $51,000. Ray's cost basis in the home is $40,000. Ten years pass and now the home belongs to the children. Ray begins to rent the home from the children at a fair rental of $1,800 per month. The rent payments are income to the children, less expenses, taxes, etc., and depreciation based on $40,000 minus the cost of the land. In year fourteen Ray dies, and the value of the home is $700,000. Only the $51,000 gift is included in Ray's estate; the balance (in value) of $649,000 is free of estate taxes, for a savings of as much as $325,000. The children then sell the home for $700,000 after expenses. They will have a capital gain of about $660,000 (that is, $700,000 sale proceeds less their cost basis of $40,000—actually the $40,000 will be further reduced by the depreciation deductions taken during the rental period). The capital gains tax will be about $132,000 (20 percent of $660,000).

In this illustration the net savings to the children was $325,000 less $132,000 or $193,000, a substantial amount. However, there may be other factors to consider that would materially change the picture. For instance, if Ray did not have a large estate to begin with, the estate taxes may in fact be *less* than the capital gains taxes, and it would be better to *keep* the residence. Thus, before a QPRT is employed, your adviser should make a careful comparison of the projected results with it and without it.

PERSONAL RESIDENCE TRUST (PRT)

This is a seldom used alternative to the QPRT and basically must follow all of the same rules discussed above except for one major difference: with the personal residence trust (PRT), the home may *not* be sold during the term. Since this "locks in" the grantor, the PRT is not used very often.

THE "DEFECTIVE" TRUST

One might wonder why anyone would want a defective trust, and what do we mean by "defective" anyway? In a number of tax-planning schemes, the grantor of a trust may enter into a sale or other transaction with the trust. Where the grantor is not a beneficiary and has no control over the trust, it is often the case that the grantor and the trust will be treated not only as two separate *legal* entities but as separate *tax* entities as well. Under our complicated tax laws, however, it is also possible for a grantor and a trust to be treated as the *same* entity for *income* tax purposes but different entities for *estate* tax purposes. This will be the result if the trust is "defective," and sometimes it is a desirable result.

For instance, say that Fred creates a trust for his children and over the years the trust accumulates $400,000 of liquid assets. Fred happens to have a piece of real estate worth $350,000 that he would like his children to have. Fred's cost basis in the real estate is $50,000. Fred can sell the real estate to his children's trust for $350,000 cash, but of course, he will then have a $300,000 gain since he and the trust are separate taxpayers for income tax purposes.

If, instead, Fred's trust were a "defective" trust (sometimes called an "intentionally defective grantor trust"), it would be classified as a "grantor" trust for income tax purposes, and Fred and the trust would be considered the same taxpayer (see "Grantor Trusts" in chapter 13). Since a taxpayer cannot sell property to himself, the sale of real estate from Fred to his defective trust, although still *legally* a sale, is ignored for tax purposes and therefore produces *no capital gain.*

The trade-off (with taxes, there has to be one) is that the trust will not get a new cost basis in the real estate. It's basis will be $50,000, the same as Fred's basis. There is still another benefit, however. All of the post-sale appreciation on the real estate will escape taxes in Fred's estate, because Fred and the trust are separate entities for *estate tax* purposes.

With only a slight modification, the sale-to-a-defective-trust idea can be even more attractive for family planning. In the above example, say that the children's trust only had $50,000 instead of $400,000, and Fred's real estate is rental property, producing a good income. Instead of a cash sale, the defective trust can buy the real estate for a promissory note, bearing interest. Remember, the sales price is a fair one, usually backed by an independent appraisal. The promissory note, however, need only bear interest at the minimum rate prescribed by the tax code. And since the income tax laws ignore the tax effect of the sale, the interest payments to Fred are not taxable to him. But don't get too excited about this, as the rental payments *are* taxable to Fred, just as if he never made the transfer, since the trust is treated as a grantor trust. As with the earlier illustration of the GRAT, Fred is taxed on all the income of the defective trust, even though the only payments he is entitled to receive are the *interest* payments.

The advantage, again, is that on Fred's death, only the value of the *note* is included in his estate; after the sale, all of the appreciation on the real estate escapes tax.

To make a trust defective for income tax purposes, the drafter of the trust merely needs to include one or more specific provisions that result in the trust being treated as a grantor trust. Some of the typical provisions include:

- Permitting someone who has no interest in the trust to add a beneficiary (other than the grantor);
- Giving the grantor's spouse certain powers over the trust; and
- Giving the grantor the power to exchange assets in the trust for other assets of equal value.

Remember, these are brief illustrations; the actual drafting and sale arrangements are complicated and should be undertaken only by expert tax attorneys.

THE IRREVOCABLE LIFE INSURANCE TRUST (ILIT)

Sometimes referred to (especially by this author) as "the last meaningful estate tax loophole," the irrevocable life insurance trust (ILIT) provides an accessible means of producing estate tax free dollars that is without equal in terms of the potential savings measured against what the grantor has to give up in return.

Before we talk about the incredible benefits of ILITs, however, it is important to understand the basics of how life insurance proceeds may be subject to estate tax. Estate taxation of life insurance proceeds centers around ownership of the policy and payment of the proceeds. If the proceeds of a policy are paid to the insured person's "estate," then they will be fully subject to tax on the insured person's death. The term *estate* in this context includes the executor of the estate, creditors of the estate, or any other beneficiary arrangement that requires the proceeds to be used to pay a debt, claim, expense, or liability of the insured person's estate. For instance, it is not unusual for an insurance policy to be taken out on a person, either by the person's creditor or by the person himself at the request of the creditor, to cover payment of the person's debt should he die before the debt is paid off. If that happens and the policy proceeds are used to pay the debt, they will be subject to estate tax in the person's estate, *regardless* of who owns the policy.

This does not mean that proceeds of a life insurance policy cannot ever be used to pay the deceased person's estate taxes, as they often are. It does mean that if there is an *obligation* to use the proceeds for that purpose, they will be subject to a tax. However, if a beneficiary other than the "estate" receives the proceeds and decides to loan them to the estate for taxes, or if the beneficiary of the insurance policy has inherited other assets and doesn't want to sell them, certainly she can instead decide to use the insurance proceeds to pay the taxes.

The other cause of estate taxation of life insurance is *ownership* of the policy. Many (if not most) people confuse owner with beneficiary. The beneficiary of a policy is *not* necessarily the owner. The owner is the one who has the right to borrow against the policy, the right to name or change the beneficiary, the right to cancel or surrender the policy, exchange the policy, etc. The tax code and regulations make it clear that if the insured person holds any of these "incidents" of ownership, the *full* policy proceeds will be included in his estate. And this can be the case even if the incidents of ownership are held by an entity that the insured *controls*, such as a corporation or a trust.

Note, however, that this does not automatically mean the proceeds will actually produce a tax. There could be other factors that would reduce or eliminate the taxes. For instance, if a person owns a policy on her own life under which her spouse is named as beneficiary, the proceeds are fully included in her estate on death, but there will be no tax on the proceeds because the receipt of funds by the spouse qualifies for the estate tax marital deduction. The problem in that event is the inclusion of those funds in the estate of the surviving spouse, to the extent of those funds remaining at death. This is where the ILIT can save the day . . . and the taxes.

The ILIT should be irrevocable because we don't want anyone treated as the owner of the trust, as will be seen later. The purpose of this is to offer the opportunity of escaping taxes not just in one estate, but in several estates. The ILIT is typically a trust for the benefit of the spouse and/or children and is a very common part of the estate plans of families whose estates exceed the "tax-free" amount (e.g., $1.5 million for 2005, $2 million for 2006; see chapter 13).

If the individual already has a life insurance policy, ownership of the policy can be *assigned* (transferred) to the ILIT. This is done by signing an "irrevocable assignment form" available from the insurance company or from the agent. Proper completion of the form will indicate that the ILIT will be the new owner *and* the beneficiary. It would be a serious mistake to name a beneficiary other than the ILIT. When an existing policy is transferred to an ILIT (or to anyone, for that matter), the tax code provides that if the insured/transferor dies within three years of the date the policy is transferred, then the proceeds of the policy will be included in his estate for tax purposes. Note that this does not mean the beneficiary will not receive the money; it merely means that the deceased insured's estate tax return will report the proceeds as part of the estate in computing the tax.

For this reason, where the insured has a spouse, the ILIT will usually contain a "fail-safe" clause, providing that if the insured/transferor dies within three years of the transfer of any policy to the ILIT, then the proceeds of such policies will be held separately under the ILIT and administered for the surviving spouse in a way that will qualify for the estate tax marital deduction. This arrangement will render those proceeds tax-free if the insured dies within three years and is survived by his spouse. The trade-off is that whatever is left of these proceeds will then be included in the estate of the surviving spouse. If the insured dies after the crucial three-year period, the fail-safe clause would not apply and the entire trust could provide for the family.

The three-year concern is completely avoided if the policy is purchased at the outset by the trustee of the ILIT. This way there is *no* policy transfer, so no three-year period to worry about. (It is not unusual for an ILIT to contain both new policies and transferred polices.)

SECOND-TO-DIE OR SURVIVORSHIP OR JOINT LIFE INSURANCE

Because the estate tax marital deduction can and usually does produce a zero estate tax on the first spouse's death but results in a large estate tax on the surviving spouse's death, a need (and a huge market) arose for a product that would accommodate this problem. Without hesitation, the insurance industry offered a special type of policy that would insure any two people and pay off on the second death (i.e., on the death of the survivor of the two insureds). What's more, the second-to-die policy usually would be much cheaper than a single life policy, since, effectively, the risk is spread out. As a result, many ILITs hold one or more of these "second-to-die" or "joint-life" insurance policies. In some cases the provisions of the trust would not change, but in others, a second ILIT should be created to hold these policies. Unfortunately, no general rule can be stated except to get the best expert advice.

"CRUMMEY" POWERS IN THE INSURANCE TRUST

Once the policies are in the trust, the premiums have to be paid. Ideally, they should be paid by the trustee of the trust, who typically receives the money from the settlor of the trust (usually the insured person). In order for the transfers to the trust to be free of gift taxes, the trust must be structured so that transfers to the trust are considered to be gifts to the beneficiaries of the trust; this is accomplished by giving the beneficiaries the power to *withdraw* the transferred amounts. This power of withdrawal (called a "Crummey" power after the name of a case that decided the issue) is usually limited to the tax-free gift amount of $10,000 per beneficiary per year. In addition, the beneficiaries are given only a short time to withdraw (a "window"), typically thirty days, after they receive written notice by the trustee that a contribution has been made to the trust. They then will have thirty days after receipt of the letter to withdraw their share of $X. It is very important for tax purposes that these notices are sent and records are kept accordingly.

Hopefully (and typically), the beneficiaries will not withdraw and at the expiration of the window the trustee can use the funds to pay the premium of the life insurance policy. If a beneficiary did withdraw his share, it is likely that the settlor would reconsider continuation of his contributions and, without these, the policy would lapse. He might also reconsider the share of that beneficiary in the rest of his estate; in the usual case, wise beneficiaries will not exercise their right of withdrawal.

OPERATION OF THE ILIT

The ILIT generally does not accumulate or hold many assets other than the life insurance policies during the life of the insured, so the only trust administration consists of receiving the contributions, sending out withdrawal notices, and paying the policy premiums when due. When the insured dies, however, the picture changes considerably. At that time the trustee will collect, perhaps, hundreds of thousands, and in not a few cases, millions of dollars, and the ILIT shifts into gear.

As noted above, an ILIT may be designed to continue for many lives or it may be designed to end shortly after the death of the insured. The first objective for estate tax purposes is that the proceeds be excluded from the estate of the insured, and that is accomplished as stated earlier in this section. Thereafter, the specific provisions of how the proceeds will be administered and how long the trust will last are up to the settlor and her advisers. Often, the ILIT will provide benefits for the surviving spouse and the children, at the discretion of the trustee, for the life of the surviving spouse. On the death of the surviving spouse, the remaining assets could be divided among the children equally, either outright or when they reach certain ages. If there are grandchildren, the trust could continue to provide benefits to the children for their lives, then to the grandchildren for their lives, and then the assets would be paid out to great-grandchildren some years later, all *without estate taxes* in any preceding estate. This is a generation-skipping trust and involves some very careful drafting and planning.

As a good general rule, the trustee of the ILIT should be an "independent" trustee, that is, someone (or some institution such as a bank or trust company) who is not a beneficiary of the trust and not subordinate to or controlled by the settlor. This allows the trust to have considerably greater flexibility in its operation. It is permissible for family members or beneficiaries, and in some cases even the settlor, to have the power to remove and replace trustees, but this is a delicate area and should be approved by expert advisers.

GENERATION-SKIPPING TRANSFERS (GST) AND DYNASTY TRUSTS

The basic concept of estate taxation centers around ownership of assets at death and the retention of control and enjoyment over assets that the deceased person has transferred before death. In other words, if I transferred assets to a trust that provided for you for your lifetime and then for your children for their lifetimes, and then perhaps for your grandchildren, and after that, to your great-grandchildren, no one of you would ever have owned those assets, nor would any of you have transferred any of the assets. Therefore, there would be no estate tax on those assets on your death, or on your children's death, or grandchildren's deaths, or when your great-grandchildren received them. Depending upon how much you originally placed in the trust, the savings could easily run into the *millions* of dollars. Can this be done?

The answer is yes, and it is called generation skipping. Although there are certain limitations placed on generation-skipping transfers (GST) because of its extensive use (or abuse, in the eyes of Congress and the IRS) by the mega-rich from the 1930s to the 1970s, opportunities still remain to save huge amounts of taxes under present law. Before we begin the discussion, however, it is appropriate to warn you that the GST rules and regulations are among the most complex and intricate areas of the tax code. (A simple—if that's possible—explanation of the GST tax is offered in chapter 13.) Lengthy legal texts have been written on the subject, and it is impossible to review the details and numerous considerations in a discussion of this type. Therefore, what follows is a brief overview of its workings to give you an idea of how you might use GST planning.

As explained at the outset of this section, the basic concept of GST planning is to provide a trust for the benefit of younger-generation individuals (let's assume they are lineal descendants, specifically, children, grandchildren, great-grandchildren, etc., although they need not be), in such a way that those individuals can enjoy all the benefits of the trust assets without owning them for tax purposes. In other words, the trust assets will not be taxed in the estates of the successive generations so long as these assets remain in trust.

To illustrate, in her will, Christine leaves $1.5 million to an irrevocable GST trust for the benefit of her two children and three grandchildren. Such a trust would normally provide that the trustee, in its discretion, can distribute any amounts of income and/or principal for the benefit of any or all of the five beneficiaries. The distributions need not be equal. The trustee could arrange to make regular payments of income to children, could pay tuition for the grandchildren, could pay for vacations, insurance, painting the house, car or mortgage payments, or anything else the trustee decides is appropriate. On the other hand, there could be periods where the trustee makes no distributions.

Let's say the funds are invested wisely. Over the years they grow to $4 million, and then the two children die of "old age." There would be no estate taxes and no probate on the children's deaths, and the trust could continue, on the same basis, for the lives of the grandchildren. Over the years the grandchildren have married and have children (Christine's great-grandchildren) and as the great-grandchildren are born, they automatically become beneficiaries of this GST trust. A number of years (usually twenty-one) after the death of the last surviving grandchild, the trust will end and the remaining balance will be distributed to the great-grandchildren, presumably in equal shares. There will be no estate tax or probate on the trust assets on the death of the grandchildren nor on the distribution to the great-grandchildren. In all, the trust will have run about one hundred years with no estate taxes after the first tax on Christine's death, and no probate, ever. (There could be probate and/or tax on the estates of the great-grandchildren if they failed to plan, but even this could be avoided, using what is called a GST supertrust.)

The reason Christine chose to fund her GST trust with $1.5 million is because that happens to be the GST tax exemption each person is allowed in 2005 under the federal tax code. If she had funded it with more than $1.5 million, the trust would have been forever "tainted" in part with perpetual exposure to the high GST tax, unless she had a spouse who agreed to use a part or all of his GST exemption. Furthermore, it should be noted that the GST exemption is an exemption from the GST tax and *not* from the gift or estate tax.

Like the gift tax and estate tax allowances, the GST exemption amount is scheduled for changes over the next several years. For 2005 it is $1.5 million, for 2006 through 2008 it increases to $2 million, for 2009 it is $3.5 million, and in 2010 it is repealed (no GST tax). But then, unless the law changes, it is reinstated in 2011, and the exemption drops back to the 2003 level of $1.06 million, with a GST tax rate of 55 percent.

It is also important to understand that, as explained in the next chapter, the generation-skipping transfer tax is a special tax *separate* from the gift and estate tax, and it is imposed when certain transfers are made to persons who are two or more generations younger than the person who makes the transfer (e.g., a person who makes a gift to grandchildren or great-grandchildren). And unlike estate and gift taxes, the GST tax is not graduated. It is imposed at a flat rate (the *highest* estate tax rate) and can be almost confiscatory. For example, say that Christine has a second trust with $1 million in it and on her death, instead of passing to her children, it passes to her three grandchildren. Since she has already used her GST tax exemption, and depending on the year of her death, the GST tax on the $1 million will be as high as $550,000 or as "low" as $450,000(!), and this would be *in addition* to any estate tax on the $1 million! In other words, almost the *entire* $1 million would be paid in taxes.

The $1.5 million GST exemption may be used just about any way the transferor wishes—such as by outright gift or in a GST trust. (But if she makes a lifetime gift in excess of $1 million, she will have to pay a gift tax on the excess. Furthermore, whether or not a gift tax is due, a gift tax return should be filed to record the allocation of her GST exemption for the transfer.) As illustrated above, a GST trust is clearly the most sensible way to use it since it can continue for more than two generations. Gifts that qualify as "tax-free" gifts under the tax code (i.e., the annual exclusion gifts and qualifying gifts for medical expenses and tuition) are additionally exempt (beyond the GST exemption), so grandparents in high estate tax brackets employ these exemptions often.

THE GST SUPERTRUST

Huge leverage can be realized on the GST exemption through the use of life insurance. For instance, Ruth creates a GST trust and contributes $1 million cash to it. The trustee of the trust uses the $1 million to purchase $10 million of insurance on Ruth's life. Since the trust was funded with an amount that did not exceed Ruth's GST tax exemption, the full $10 million *and whatever it grows to in the future* can be forever exempt from GST taxes *and* from estate taxes. When the numbers move into this neighborhood, the question arises as to whether such a huge amount even ought to be handed over to beneficiaries. As suggested by the illustration in Christine's case, the extended GST trust often lasts about one hundred years. If funds are wisely invested and not lavishly distributed, the balance could easily grow into $100 million or $500 million or more! This is often referred to as a "dynasty" trust, sort of a GST supertrust.

The term of one hundred years is a carryover from the English common law and based on the concept that while it is all right to keep property in trust, somebody must own the property sometime. Otherwise, carrying it to the extreme, so much property would end up in trust where it would never be sold or passed along for other generations to sell that it would hinder the normal growth and development of communities. It was thought, then, that a rule ought to be made that prohibits perpetual trusts except where charities are involved, and that a long-enough trust period for anyone's purposes should be measured by the duration of the life of an individual (any individual) called "a life in being," plus an additional twenty-one years. Under favorable circumstances this would add up to about one hundred years. Therefore, every trust (except those where the funds go to or are held for charity) must terminate by then, or a court will order it terminated. This is called "the rule against perpetuities."

But times change, at least in some places. Although every state in this country had adopted some version of the rule against perpetuities, a few states decided, for reasons unnecessary to explore, that it would *not* be harmful to the particular state's communities to allow a private (noncharitable) trust to last more than one hundred years; in fact, they could last *forever,* however long that is. Thus a number of states have abolished the rule against perpetuities for trusts created and governed under the laws of that state. See, for instance, the law of Alaska, Delaware (except for real estate), Idaho, South Dakota, and Wisconsin.

In other words, in the illustration above, Ruth could establish her trust in, say, South Dakota, by naming a South Dakota trustee and having the trust administered there. Getting off to a healthy $10 million tax-free start on Ruth's death, the trust could provide estate-tax free distributions and accumulations forever. This can produce a pretty impressive result. How impressive? If after annual distributions and administration fees, the trust netted only a 5 percent after-tax return, it would grow to about *$20 billion* in 160 years! This kind of money would certainly provide handsomely for Ruth's children, grandchildren, great-grandchildren, great-great-grandchildren, great-great-great . . . wait a second! Ruth has two children and two grandchildren. What if that's the end of the line? What if the trust does grow to $20 billion in 160 years and there are only one or two beneficiaries? Or none? What if South Dakota sinks?

One of the most difficult and abstract aspects of truly long-term trusts is deciding on provisions for beneficiaries and situations so remote as to be almost impossible to imagine. For this reason experienced drafters build in a great deal of flexibility to allow for totally unforeseeable circumstances, including changes in the law. It is not uncommon in a long-term trust to see provisions that allow changing the location and governing law of the trust, amending the trust, even terminating the trust if its purposes can't be met. Nevertheless, even with all the expert advice, it is at best a complicated, thought-provoking, and often expensive exercise with few if any "right" answers.

S CORPORATION TRUSTS

An "S corporation" is a corporation that qualifies for and has made (along with its shareholders) the special federal tax election under subchapter S of the tax code to bypass the tax at the corporate level and be taxed only at the shareholder level. In effect, a qualifying S corporation (S corp.) pays no tax on its income. Instead, the shareholders pay the tax on the corporate taxable income in proportion to the percentage of shares they own in the corporation, similar to partners of a partnership. (A number of states allow a corporation to elect this treatment for state income tax purposes.) That is, a 15 percent shareholder will pay a tax on 15 percent of the corporate taxable income, whether or not it is distributed to her.

There are a number of requirements that must be met before a corporation can qualify as an S corp., and the one pertinent to this discussion is that only certain types of trusts may be shareholders of an S corp. If the trusts do not meet the strict requirements, the S corp. could *lose* its qualification (which sometimes inadvertently happens) and the results can be extremely costly in additional taxes, as well as an inability to reinstate the election for a number of years.

Only four types of trust will qualify as S corp. shareholders: a grantor trust, a qualified subchapter S trust (QSST), an electing small business trust (ESBT), and a voting trust.

The *grantor trust* qualification is relatively easy, since any trust that qualifies as a grantor trust will be eligible to hold S corp. stock. It does not matter what the terms of the trust may be and no election needs to be made so long as the trust is a grantor trust and the grantor is a U.S. citizen or resident. If you recall, a grantor trust is one where the grantor (settlor) is treated as the owner of the trust for federal income tax purposes, and so there is no tax at the trust level: all income and losses are passed through to the grantor. (This is discussed again in detail in the next chapter.) For S corp. purposes, then, every revocable trust can hold S corp. stock, as can grantor retained income trusts (GRITs), grantor regained annuity trusts and unitrusts (GRATs and GRUTs), and defective grantor trusts.

The QSST exception is quite different from the grantor trust exception in that the terms of the trust itself must meet certain requirements, and the beneficiary of the trust must join in making the S corp. election for tax purposes. To qualify, a QSST can only have one current income beneficiary, except that spouses can be co-beneficiaries of the income of a QSST if they are both U.S. citizens or U.S. residents and they file a joint federal income tax return. Except where spouses are concerned, the QSST may only have *one* current income beneficiary, and in any event *all* of the trust income *must* be distributed to the current income beneficiary. Furthermore, during that beneficiary's lifetime, if any *principal* distributions are made from the QSST, they may *only* be made to the income beneficiary. No other beneficiary may receive principal during the income beneficiary's lifetime. On the income beneficiary's death, however, the trust may provide that the principal will pass to other beneficiaries. If the trust continues after the beneficiary's death and continues to hold S Corp. stock, it must qualify again as either a QSST, a grantor trust, or an ESBT (described below); otherwise the S corp. could lose its election.

The QSST may also be drafted to last for a period of years rather than for the lifetime of the income beneficiary, but in this case the principal must pass to the income beneficiary at the end of the term. It cannot pass to another unless the income beneficiary dies before the end of the term.

Trusts that may not have originally been intended specifically as QSSTs may nevertheless qualify as QSSTs and therefore may hold S corp. stock provided they meet the income distribution requirements. For instance, a minor's trust [a 2503(c) trust] will qualify, as will a QTIP trust because the terms of both of these trusts meet all the requirement of a QSST, except for the mandatory distribution of income. If, in fact, all of the trust's income is distributed, the minor's trust or QTIP trust will then meet the requirements.

One of the planning drawbacks to the QSST is the inability to provide for several beneficiaries in a single trust giving the trustee the power to distribute or not distribute the income among those beneficiaries at its discretion. A trust that overcomes this drawback, but not without a cost, is the electing small business trust ESBT.

The ESBT is the only trust that may hold S corp. stock, have more than one beneficiary, and allow the trustee discretion over distributions, without causing a loss of the S corp. election. Since it is regarded as a "tax break" by Congress and the IRS, the ESBT must meet special, strict requirements.

First, all beneficiaries must be qualified S corp. shareholders—that is, where individual beneficiaries are concerned, each must be a U.S. citizen or resident. Next, the trustee of the trust must elect to have the trust treated as an ESBT. Next, the portion of the trust attributable to S corp. stock is treated as a *separate trust* for income tax purposes, and taxed separately at the *highest* income tax rate. This separate tax treatment for some trust income and not other, with the required separate accounts and computations, can make an ESBT an accountant's nightmare (or dream, depending on how you look at it). And the issue of paying the highest tax on all S corp. income in the ESBT will be an additional cost, but in cases where the income and distributions are large to begin with (i.e., already in the 39.6 percent tax bracket), it won't matter. The bottom line seems to be that if large amounts of income can regularly be paid on S corp. stock, and if the settlor wants one trust to benefit a number of beneficiaries with discretion to treat them unequally, and if other estate planning considerations favor the use of the ESBT, then it could be the best way to hold the S corp. stock—but there are a lot of "ifs" here.

Special Purpose Trusts

As has, I hope, become apparent throughout the chapter, the trust is probably the most flexible document in the estate planner's book. As further indication of just how flexible, this section discusses three special purpose trusts (the actual number is limited only by the estate planner's imagination) designed and drafted to accommodate special situations or objectives, as well as a fourth, perhaps the ultimate special purpose trust, itself simply called a "purpose" trust. Keep in mind that the first three special purpose trusts, as with all trusts, will have one or more trustees, with a mechanism for trustee replacement; one or more beneficiaries, with provisions covering all possible changes, such as death, disability, etc.; a "corpus," or assets transferred to the trustee; and provisions covering the management and disposition of those assets in all circumstances, up to the termination of the trust. The fourth type, the purpose trust, need not have any beneficiaries.

THE NOMINEE TRUST

This is a "special purpose" trust that covers an almost infinite number of special purposes. That is, the nominee trust is often created solely to suit a particular situation requiring the use of a simple but private trust, although it does have two common functions—to avoid probate with privacy and facilitate transfers of the trust property. The nominee trust is a unique type of trust that, in fact, is not always a trust. Also occasionally referred to as an Illinois land trust, a "blind" trust, and an agency trust, the nominee trust is often regarded as a relationship where the trustee merely acts as the *agent* of the beneficiaries. As an "agency" trust, the arrangement has, in some courts, been held to be a hybrid between a trust and an agency. An agency relationship occurs when you authorize someone to do something for you, giving specific instructions, and when the job is done the agency ends. This is not usually the case with the nominee trust, even though some nominee trusts are purposely drafted so that the trustee can *only* act as the agent of the beneficiaries, as specifically instructed by them. I raise this agency issue only because no discussion of nominee trusts would be accurate without it. Despite this, however, they are generally treated as *trusts* and from here on we'll talk of the nominee trust as a *trust*.

The need for the nominee trust originated in those states that require a trust to be recorded in the state's registry of deeds if the trust is to hold real estate in that state. Because the typical estate planning trust contains so much personal information that grantors would not want as public record, a trust was created that had virtually no personal information but would satisfy the state's conveyancing and title concerns. Effectively, the only provisions needed for recording such trusts would include adequate trustee powers to deal with the property, an orderly succession of trustees, a provision protecting third parties who deal with the trustees, and little else. What's missing? The beneficiaries.

The truly unique feature of the nominee trust is that the identity and shares of the beneficiaries are set forth in a document *separate* from the rest of the trust, allowing the rest of the trust to be recorded (or a copy of the trust to be given to banks, stockbrokers, etc.) without disclosing the identity or shares of the beneficiaries or any other personal information. This separate document, legally a part of the trust, is typically called a "schedule of beneficial interests" (SBI), and it is a perfectly legal arrangement that does not affect the validity of the trust. Instead, it allows a copy of the trust (but *without* the SBI) to be readily recorded or given to parties dealing with the trustee who want to see a copy for their "protection," or, as in the case of banks or stockbrokers, who want to have a copy of the trust for their records.

Typically, the grantor (owner) of the assets will be the trustee of the nominee trust, succeeded by his spouse and/or children, or other close individuals. In small estates, the grantor and his spouse can be the beneficiaries, possibly followed by the children (all as stated on the SBI), and the primary function of the nominee trust—to avoid probate—will be carried out simply and quickly. In larger estates, however, the SBI would probably show the grantor's more elaborate estate planning trust as the beneficiary of the nominee trust, thus completing the picture and allowing all assets to be easily placed in trust without disclosing any personal information. Since the nominee trust is normally a revocable, grantor trust, it is ignored for tax purposes and does not complicate the overall plan.

As noted above, the nominee trust also greatly facilitates ownership and gifts of real estate, simply by changing the SBI instead of having to execute and record a deed for a fractional share of the property every time a gift is made. In cases where real estate is transferred piecemeal to a number of donees over a period of time, it not only avoids recording fees but avoids the need for twenty or thirty or more deeds. If this approach is used for such gifts, however, be absolutely *certain* that the grantor does not have the unilateral power, or even the power by majority interest, to amend the nominee trust or control the distributions to beneficiaries; otherwise, the IRS will claim that the full value of the property should be included in the grantor's estate, regardless of who is named on the SBI.

It is also an excellent way to hold real estate that is located in a state other than that of your domicile. This is briefly described in chapter 11, under "Out-of-State Real Estate." In such situations, unless the real estate is held under a survivorship interest or in a trust, it will be necessary to have double probate on your death (once in your own state and again in the state where the real estate is located). A nominee trust can easily be used to hold the out-of-state property and avoid probate in both estates.

Don't be surprised if your attorney is not familiar with nominee trusts. Although they are valid and may be used in every state that recognizes trusts, they are not necessarily used in every state, particularly in those states, such as New Hampshire and California, that do not require a trust holding real estate to be recorded. Furthermore, in those states that truly have simplified probate, they are also less necessary. In any event, they are available as another way to avoid probate and ensure privacy, even in those states.

THE VOTING TRUST

The special purpose served with a voting trust is to transfer the right to vote shares of stock without losing control of the stock itself or any other rights associated with it, such as appreciation, dividends, or other distributions. The voting trust is most often used with closely held companies where it is deemed advisable to allow one or more specific individuals to vote the stock. It is the trustee of the voting trust who is entitled to vote the stock held in the trust, and thus the individuals who are to have the vote will be appointed as the trustees of the voting trust. A voting trust can be revocable or irrevocable; typically they are irrevocable for a period of years, or for the life of the key person, or until the company is sold, or any other arrangement that suits the objectives and is within the law. Although many states have a special limitation period on voting trusts, typically ten years (e.g., New York), some allow the trust to last as long as any other noncharitable trusts (i.e., about one hundred years, as discussed in the previous section).

A voting trust normally pays no taxes and files no tax returns, as it holds only the right to vote and, if it receives any dividends, it does so merely as an agent of the shareholder. Funds or other trust assets are not managed as they would be with another type of trust. In practice, it is not uncommon for a closely held company to pay dividends directly to the shareholders even though the stock is held by a voting trust.

Shareholders wishing to establish a voting trust will actually transfer their shares to the trustees of the trust. The corporation is notified of the transfer, receives a copy of the trust, and actually issues a new stock certificate in the name of the trustees of the voting trust for the total number of shares transferred to the trust. The trustees in turn will issue to each shareholder a "voting trust certificate" for the number of shares they transferred to the trust. When the voting trust terminates, the shares of stock are transferred back to the shareholders.

Voting trusts are often used when a parent transfers voting stock to a child or where a parent (or other relative) wants to leave shares of stock to one or more children through her estate on the condition that the shares subsequently be transferred to a voting trust with preselected trustees, to ensure the continuation of proper management and control of the company. As noted above, however, some states limit the term of such trusts to ten years, with one ten-year extension. If a more permanent arrangement is required, the stock could be transferred to a standard trust (i.e., not a voting trust) that can last for up to one hundred years in most states, or the company could simply issue two classes of stock—voting and nonvoting.

Remember, the existence of the voting trust has nothing to do with the dispassion of the shares on your death. Accordingly, they should be dealt with separately, as any other asset. In this regard, there is no reason why the voting trust certificate could not be held by your living trust, so the shares will avoid probate and be distributed according to your estate plan.

STOCK OR BUSINESS PURCHASE TRUST

The special purpose of a stock or business purchase trust is to arrange for the purchase of a business interest or shares of a corporation on the death (and sometimes the disability) of a business owner or shareholder (the "owner"). It is primarily used where the owners are actively participating in a business or professional practice. In many such cases, it is wise to arrange for an automatic buyout on death or disability through a trust for a number of reasons:

- To produce an immediate source of cash to provide for the owner and for his family without having to wait for an estate representative to be appointed or a dispute to be settled;
- To produce funds to help pay any estate tax that may be due;
- To arrange for an orderly sale at a fair value rather than a forced sale at a bargain price;
- To allow a buyout at a previously agreed-upon price without interference from the deceased or disabled owner's beneficiaries; or
- To avoid having the surviving owner be forced to work with a new partner whom he or she may not want or who may not act in the best interest of the business.

In the typical business purchase trust the owners will transfer their interests in a form of escrow to the trustee of the trust. The escrow arrangement is one where the trustee has absolutely no obligations until such time as an owner were to die or become disabled (to the point where he could not perform his functions in the business). In the event of a disability, the agreement usually requires the owner to be disabled for a period of twelve months before the buyout would take place. In the usual case, the buyout is funded by life and disability *buyout* (not disability income) policies on the owners, and the policies are made payable to the trustee. This way, when the event happens, the trustee receives the funds, buys out the particular interest, and transfers the funds to the owner's beneficiary (if the owner is deceased) or to the owner or his representative (if the owner is disabled). Since the trustee already has the necessary transfer documents and the binding agreement to sell, he does not have to wait until the deceased's estate is probated, or to get approval from the deceased's beneficiaries. This is not to say that it would be impossible to take legal proceedings to question the buyout, since legal proceedings can be initiated in just about any situation. However, there would be a binding agreement signed by the deceased or disabled person, and the burden of proof that it was somehow not binding or should be overturned would be on the challenger, at his or her expense.

If the agreement is not funded with life or disability insurance, then the payments must be made by the business or by the purchasing owner. In this event care must be taken to work out a realistic arrangement for payment that does not bankrupt the business.

The price or formula for the buyout should be included in the trust agreement. It is usually best to have a formula that is simply applied to the facts and financial status existing at the time of the buyout. As a fail-safe provision, many agreements simply call for an independent appraisal to set the price.

As with all trusts, this one also requires the assistance of an attorney with considerable experience in drafting and implementing this particular type of trust, as well as the complicated tax implications of the different methods of funding the buyout.

PURPOSE TRUST

Briefly, a purpose trust is a trust established for a *purpose* rather than for specified or named beneficiaries. This concept is totally contradictory to one of the most basic principles of trust law, which is that a trust *must* have beneficiaries; otherwise there would be no one to enforce the trust and, therefore, no trust. In at least one respect, however, this concept is not new. After all, a charitable trust is typically established for a purpose and typically has no identifiable beneficiaries, but it has never raised the eyebrows of a trust lawyer or a judge. For instance, a trust established to maintain a public park or to fund medical research is nothing unusual, and if properly drafted is seldom questioned since such trusts are regarded as charitable and may be enforced by the attorney general for the benefit of the public. The "new" concept referred to here is the noncharitable purpose trust. An example of a noncharitable purpose trust would include one where a settlor established a trust to maintain his collection of antique automobiles, or perhaps one for the purpose of constructing a home for the maintenance and care of his pets and all their offspring. Such trusts would, under trust law, still be regarded as purpose trusts even though there may be individuals who happen to benefit from the trust carrying out its purpose, or beneficiaries who may take the trust's remainder when the purpose of the trust is satisfied or the trust terminates for some other reason.

For instance, in the illustration above, a valid purpose trust could be established for the maintenance of the settlor's collection of automobiles and, if the settlor's child or children were using the automobiles, they would indirectly benefit from the trust, although under trust law they would not be considered beneficiaries and would have no standing to enforce the trust. Similarly, the trust could provide that if and when the automobiles were unusable or disposed of, or simply after a set period of time, the trust would terminate and the settlor's children would receive any assets (e.g., the automobiles) remaining in the trust. The fact that the children are designated remaindermen after the purpose is carried out does not change the character of the trust or by itself give it validity as a trust. Note, however, that in those states that do not recognize purpose trusts, a trust with these provisions would be totally disregarded as void, and one of two things would happen. Either the bequest would pass directly to the children without regard to the instructions to maintain the automobiles, or the entire bequest would fail and pass by intestacy (absence of a will) through the settlor's estate. Cases have held both ways.

The offshore jurisdictions that have recognized purpose trusts have done so through formal legislation. They include, among others, the Isle of Man, Jersey, British Virgin Islands, Bermuda, Cayman Islands, Cook Islands, and Nevis. There are also some states that have adopted purpose trust law, but in a far more limited way than the offshore jurisdictions. The thrust in the United States to adopt purpose trust legislation appears to be largely related to and motivated by the public's desire to be able to establish valid trusts for their pets, although other "honorary" trusts (such as trusts to maintain gravesites or masses) are usually allowed on the same basis.

Generally, the states that allow purpose trusts limit the term of such a trust to twenty-one years. Interestingly, the wording of the law does not invalidate the trust after the twenty-one-year period; it merely declares the trust to be unenforceable. Presumably, then, a court could, upon petition, declare the trust invalid, inasmuch as its terms are unenforceable. When that happens, unless otherwise provided in the trust, the corpus would revert to the settlor or her estate. It would be unusual, if not a lack of foresight, if a drafter did not provide for disposition of the trust property after the purpose was carried out or in the event it could not be carried out.

A few states allow some form of purpose trust through case law (e.g., Pennsylvania), but whether through case law or a uniform act or code, the application and use of purpose trusts in the United States is extremely narrow and the term unnecessarily limited. For instance, if an individual wished to provide for the long-term maintenance of a private building without mingling that asset with other assets in a "person" trust (one that provided for individual beneficiaries, where dispositive disputes could arise and restraint on sale of the property could be overridden), why should he be limited to twenty-one years?

Accordingly, if a person in the United States wished to establish a purpose trust for a longer term than permitted in the applicable state, it would be a simple matter to settle one in any of the several offshore jurisdictions recognizing such purpose trusts, and then administer it in the United States.

Whether the purpose trust is created offshore or onshore, it must meet certain requirements, as with other trusts, or it will fail, despite the potentially broad scope of such a trust. The first requirement is that the trust be subject to enforcement. Most of the offshore statutes as well as the Uniform Trust Code require the trust to name an enforcer to enforce the terms of the trust (sort of a private attorney general) and provide for court appointment of one if the trust fails to do so.

Next, the purpose or object of the trust must be certain, reasonable, and possible. The case of the late famous author, George Bernard Shaw, is a good illustration of a purpose trust that seems to fail on all three counts. In his will, Shaw directed that the residue of his estate be held in several trusts for, among other unusual purposes, the study of the advantages of developing a phonetic alphabet and the determination of the number of living persons who speak and write English based on the twenty-six-letter alphabet, "at any and every moment in the world." The forty-seven-clause, lengthy, and complicated will, written in part by Shaw himself at age ninety-four, who is described by the court as having been "a kind of itching powder to the British public," generated the obvious question of whether the trusts were valid and enforceable. In its holding that they were not, on the basis that they were not for a charitable purpose (since the United Kingdom did not and still does not recognize noncharitable purpose trusts), the opinion also indicated that at least some of the purposes were virtually impossible to carry out.

Even if the purpose is possible to carry out, the court will not enforce it if it is wasteful, useless, or otherwise against public policy. An interesting illustration of this principle is the case of Anne Maria Burdett, whose will devised her home and contents to trustees, directing that on the day of her funeral the trustees arrange to have the doors and windows of her home bricked and boarded up "and nailed with good long nails," and basically kept "in state" for twenty years after her death; thereafter it would pass to named beneficiaries (remaindermen). Her will was contested by the remaindermen, but in the meanwhile the house was, in fact, bricked and boarded up as directed. Not surprisingly, extensive litigation ensued; ten years later the remaindermen's appeal was successful, and the court ordered the trust property unboarded, unbricked, and sold, and the trust was to be terminated on the basis that it was wasteful, useless, and did not constitute a disposition of the property.

Of course there are numerous other terms to consider, such as selection of trustee and enforcer, successors to both, registration requirements, etc., and, of course, the purpose and duration of the trust.

As to which jurisdiction to select, there are, of course, numerous factors to consider, both domestic and offshore, including the purpose and term of the trust, the most logical place for administration, the laws of the jurisdictions under consideration (i.e., the flexibility of the applicable statute), and, perhaps, your travel preferences.

While the illustrative cases discussed earlier may be interesting, if not entertaining narratives of would-be purpose trusts, what are the practical uses of such trusts that gave rise to their growing recognition and developing legislation? The answer is that modern-day purpose trusts can be used for personal or philanthropic purposes that do not otherwise qualify as charitable, for instance, to hold and provide for control of a family business (indefinitely, in jurisdictions not bound by the rule against perpetuities); for maintenance and preservation of family or business property without interference by beneficiaries; to provide complete privacy and creditor protection where, for instance, the purpose of the purpose trust is to maintain a noncharitable foundation for the benefit of the settlor and members of the settlor's family; and quite commonly, to hold ownership of companies that lease assets to other companies for off-balance-sheet transactions.

And remember, even though the trust may be established in an offshore jurisdiction, if the settlor is a U.S. person we still have the U.S. tax laws to think about (see chapter 13). Since this is the case, perhaps we would want to consider importing the offshore trust to the United States. That is, so long as the local offshore jurisdictional requirements of the purpose trust are met, it may generally be administered anywhere in the world, including the United States. Therefore, it should be possible to establish a purpose trust in an offshore jurisdiction, then, after a short time, move it to the United States while retaining the governing law of the original jurisdiction. If certain other requirements are met, this could eliminate the need to file the aforementioned reports with the IRS. And as U.S. planners become more and more familiar with purpose trusts, no doubt more and more purposes will be found.

13

Probate, Trusts, and Taxes

There is only one difference between the tax collector and the taxidermist—the taxidermist leaves the hide.

—M. Chaplin, former director of the IRS

Anyone who has been through a tax audit might well feel that way. And anyone who has suffered through the deadly, double-barreled combination of a will contest *and* a tax audit usually comes to the painful realization that man is the only animal that can be skinned more than once.

What never ceases to amaze me, however, is that despite their loathing to pay taxes and equal loathing to pay legal fees, most people bring *both* a contest and an audit upon themselves and their families by failing to take a few necessary and fairly easy steps to avoid them. In chapter 12, for instance, I point out a way to avoid probate in not just one estate but two or more, without the risks attendant to joint ownership, the expensive alternative that is used by most families. And in this chapter, I go further in pointing out how to save thousands in estate taxes by using one or more trusts. Will you take advantage of these ideas, or will yours be just another family that gets skinned more than once?

Probate vs. Taxes

One of the most common and persistent misconceptions is that avoiding probate means avoiding taxes. *This is simply not so.* It is quite possible to have an estate that totally avoids probate but that is fully subject to estate taxes. The legal principles and rules on which probate and taxes are based are totally different and each serves a totally different function.

Remember, probate is the legal process in each state by which property that was in the deceased person's name can pass to his heirs or beneficiaries after debts and expenses of the estate are paid. By itself, the probate process does not generate any revenue to either the state or the federal government in the form of taxes.

Taxes, on the other hand, *estate* taxes, that is, are based on ownership, control, and enjoyment of property, *regardless* of whether or not the particular item of property was or was not probated. Jointly held property is a perfect example of this, as discussed in more detail below. For instance, say that after Mom's death, Dad places his home and all the rest of his estate in joint names with Daughter. On Dad's death, his entire estate will past to Daughter as surviving joint owner without probate, but, at the same time, Dad's *entire estate* will be subject to estate taxes. Understanding this difference between the *legal* consequences of ownership (where it goes and who gets it) and the *tax* consequences (what is subject to tax) is essential to developing the best plan for your family.

A WORD ABOUT OUR TAX SYSTEM

Justice Oliver Wendell Holmes said, "Taxes are what we pay for a civilized society." Well, we must be awfully civilized, since there is not much we do without paying a tax, sometimes a huge tax. The money we earn is taxed, and the money we earn on the money we earn is taxed; if we give money away we can be taxed; and what we have left when we die is subject to tax. We are not, however, any different from most other "civilized" countries, and you may be surprised to learn that when compared with other major countries, our taxes are actually lower than most.

Like most "civilized" tax systems, ours imposes taxes in three major areas: on income earned by the taxpayer; on gifts made by a taxpayer to another person; and on transfers made on account of a taxpayer's death. The last two are referred to as wealth transfer taxes and generally complement each other. For instance, if there was an estate tax but no gift tax, a person could give away all of her assets during life and pay no tax on the transfer of that wealth to another generation. All of our tax laws are very carefully drafted to allow for a minimum of "loopholes" (note that a minimum is better than none), and this includes careful attention and consideration to the numerous situations where trusts are involved. As explained in more detail below, there are cases where trusts are ignored for tax purposes and other cases where the trust is taxed on its own. What follows is a brief explanation of how all this works, first with respect to income taxes, then gift taxes, and, finally, estate taxes.

Trusts and Income Taxes

Let's start with a *common misconception.* It is commonly thought that every trust must pay its own tax on income earned by the assets held in the trust. For some reason, this conclusion is even firmer if that trust is irrevocable. This is a dangerous, misleading, and often *costly* misunderstanding of the tax laws. Whether a trust will be treated as a separate taxpayer *depends upon the terms of the trust,* and for our purposes, this can be boiled down to one simple rule.

If the trust is a "grantor trust" (explained below), it will be *ignored* for income tax purposes and will pay *no* income tax. All of the trust income will be taxed to the person who is treated as the grantor of the trust, whether it is paid out or held in the trust. If the trust is *not* a grantor trust, then, as described later, the *trust* will be taxed on income that is not paid out to its beneficiaries. The question then becomes, What makes a trust a "grantor trust"?

Grantor trusts. Because trusts can be so flexible and may be tailor-made to fit almost any situation, and because careful custom-tailoring can often save income taxes, Congress decided many years ago to set down a number of rules that will determine whether a trust will be treated as a grantor trust. (These rules are contained in sections 671–679 of the Internal Revenue Code.) If by application of any one or more of these rules a trust is treated as a grantor trust, then all trust income, losses, and any other tax result, characteristic, or penalty will be attributed to the *grantor.* (It is important to note that it is also possible for a trust to be *partly* a grantor trust and *partly* a separate taxable entity, depending on the circumstances of funding and on the terms of the trust. Furthermore, depending on the same two issues, a trust can have more than one grantor. Don't blame me for the complexity.)

The grantor is the taxpayer (usually an individual, although not necessarily; it could also be an entity, such as a corporation) who directly or indirectly transferred the money, property, or other assets to the trust, or who is treated as the "owner" of the trust, due to the application of the grantor trust rules in the tax code.

More often than not, a grantor trust is intentionally made that way, but occasionally a slipup occurs and a trust that is intended to be separate taxable entity (such as a minor's trust, as discussed in chapter 12) ends up as a grantor trust and is taxed to the person who funded it. The most typical example of a grantor trust is a *revocable* trust, designed primarily to avoid probate, or a revocable estate planning trust. The settlor's right to revoke such a trust causes the trust to be treated as a grantor trust.

Briefly, if a trust contains *any* of the following provisions, it will be treated as a grantor trust, *regardless of whether it is revocable or irrevocable,* and *regardless of whether the income is paid out to the grantor:*

A provision—

- allowing the grantor or her spouse to revoke or change the terms of the trust;
- allowing the trustee to pay out or accumulate the trust income for the grantor or her spouse;
- allowing the grantor or her spouse to withdraw trust funds;
- allowing the grantor or anyone else to direct the trustee to pay trust funds to someone other than a beneficiary;
- allowing the trust assets to be returned to the grantor or her spouse within a certain period;
- allowing the grantor or her spouse to buy from or sell to the trust or to borrow money under less than fair market value terms; or
- allowing the trustee or anyone else to add beneficiaries to the trust.

In addition, a trust will be a grantor trust if a *U.S. citizen or resident* transfers assets to a foreign (offshore) trust that has a U.S. beneficiary (in which case the U.S. transferor is treated as the grantor *regardless* of the terms of the trust). *Note also* that all "U.S. persons" are subject to U.S. income tax on their *worldwide* income. A U.S. person includes not only U.S. citizens (wherever in the world they may reside) but also U.S. residents, even though noncitizens. Thus, a European citizen who lives and works in the United States and who meets the residency test (a complicated formula, but generally more than six months per year) will similarly be subject to U.S. income tax on his worldwide income, even though he may also be taxed in his home country.

Note that the foregoing is an abbreviated review of the grantor trust rules. Although the discussion reflects the basic situations where the grantor will be taxed on trust income, the rules can be extended to other situations, and they can be extremely complicated and tricky in their application.

Nevertheless, this overview will give you a good idea of when you may or may not be taxed on trust income, even though it is not distributed to you.

To illustrate, say that Kay transfers $100,000 to an irrevocable trust. The terms of the trust give the trustee the discretion to make (or not to make) distributions of trust income and principal to Kay and her daughters, Ella and Emma, in any shares the trustee deems appropriate. In 2005 the trustee received $6,000 of interest income on the trust funds and paid out $2,000 to Ella and $2,000 to Emma. Nothing was paid out to Kay. The remaining $2,000 was kept in the trust and invested.

Under the grantor trust rules, Kay is treated as the tax "owner" of all of the assets *and* income of the trust, and, therefore, Kay is taxed on the entire $6,000 of interest income received by the trust, even though she did not receive (nor could she demand) a penny. Clearly, then, having a grantor trust should be an intentional result rather than a mistake.

It is important to note that there are certain instances where a trust can be a grantor trust as to the trust *income* but not as to the trust *principal*. The primary difference in this case is that capital gains (which are generally treated as attributable to the trust principal) realized by the trust would not be taxed to the grantor, but to the trust. Any competent tax attorney drafting a trust will know whether this arrangement is desirable and how to achieve it.

Retained interest trusts. Tax issues with these types of trusts are only briefly discussed here because they are covered in chapter 12 and are very commonly used in tax planning. Generally, all of the retained interest trusts (GRITs, GRATs, GRUTs, and QPRTs) are *grantor* trusts because in every such trust the trustee is directed to pay the income or a specified amount (or equivalent value of property) to the grantor. Furthermore, if there is even a *possibility* that the trustee may have to use some of the trust principal to meet the required payment under the GRAT, GRUT, or QPRT (and this is typically the case), then the trust will be a grantor trust as to both income and principal. Accordingly, the grantor is taxed on all of the trust income in the typical retained interest trust whether or not it is distributed to her. As pointed out and illustrated in the discussion of such trusts in chapter 12, however, this arrangement could actually prove to be a tax benefit to the grantor by resulting in a tax-free gift of the remaining undistributed income to the other beneficiaries.

Other trusts. This includes any trust that is not treated as a grantor trust (i.e., a nongrantor trust). Interestingly, a trust could be drafted so that in some years it is a grantor trust, and in others it is not. For purposes of this discussion we will assume the trust starts as and remains a nongrantor trust.

Simple and complex trusts. Nongrantor trusts are separate taxable entities and are characterized (for income tax purposes) as "complex" or "simple." A simple trust is one that is required by its terms to distribute all of its income each year and may not make any charitable distributions presently or in the future. Any trust that is not a simple trust is a complex trust, but typically a complex trust is one that allows for discretionary distributions of income and/or principal.

The basic rule of trust taxation for nongrantor trusts is that the trust is taxed on the amount of income it receives and does not distribute to its beneficiaries for the tax year. Distributions of trust income made from the trust to its beneficiaries in a given tax year are *deductible* by the trust to the extent of its taxable income for the year, and taxed as income to the beneficiaries, again to the extent of the trust's taxable income for the year. To illustrate, say that the Doright Trust (a complex trust) receives bank interest income of $5,000 on trust funds and distributes $3,500 to its beneficiary, Bill Doright. The Doright Trust will report $5,000 interest income received, show a $3,500 deduction for distribution to beneficiary Bill, and pay a tax on the $1,500 of income it did not distribute ($5,000 income less the $3,500 distributions). Bill Doright will report the $3,500 trust distribution on his income tax return for the year.

If the Doright Trust distributed *more* than its income for the year, say $6,000, then $5,000 would be taxable income to Bill Doright, and $1,000 would be a tax-free distribution of principal. This is a very simple illustration, and the application of these rules can get quite complicated. An example would be where the trust has different types of income for the year, such as dividends, interest, capital gains, and tax-exempt income, and where there are several beneficiaries, each receiving different amounts. (As a general rule, capital gains are taxed to the trust.) It might also be noted that the tax law allows a trustee of a nongrantor trust to distribute income received by the trust in a given year up to sixty-five days after the end of that year (called "the sixty-five-day rule") and have the distribution treated as if it was made within the previous calendar year. There are also circumstances where a trust may accumulate and pay a tax on income for years, and then pay out the accumulated income to the beneficiaries. And then there are special rules when multiple trusts have been established for the same beneficiary. These situations are beyond the scope of this discussion, but your tax adviser should be able to guide you through such situations.

Special rules for structured settlement payments. In many personal injury settlements the injured party will be advised to receive the settlement over a period of years instead of in a lump sum. This is called a "structured settlement." For instance, say that Lew, the injured party, may be offered the choice of a lump-sum payment of $1.3 million, or $75,000 per year for the rest of his life, with a guarantee of payments over forty years. (In other words, if Lew died in nine years, his family or other named beneficiaries could receive the payments for the thirty-one-year balance of the guaranteed term.)

One of the reasons this option may be chosen (although it should *not* be the only reason) is that the tax code provides that payments received on account of personal injuries or sickness are *free* of income taxes, whether received in a lump sum or over a period of time. This is so even though a part of the structured settlement payments are actually interest on the lump sum.

Accordingly, if the structured settlement payments are made to a trust established by the injured party, the payments will still be tax free. If, however, after the payments are received by the trust, they are invested and earn income, then, of course, the income earned on such investments will be currently taxable (typically under the grantor trust rules), as described above.

The *trap* that accompanies structured settlements is not related to income taxes but *estate* taxes, as discussed in greater detail below.

TAX TO TRUST BENEFICIARIES

Income distributions. From the discussion above, it should be clear that trust beneficiaries are only taxed on income and in some cases capital gains that are distributed to them by the trust, *except* for trusts of which the beneficiary is treated as the *grantor,* and *except* for trusts under which the beneficiary has the *right* to receive all the income. In the latter two cases, the beneficiary is taxed on all the income whether or not it is distributed to him.

From the beneficiaries' perspective, however, the issue of beneficiaries' taxes is made quite simple because in cases other than grantor trusts, the trustee will give each beneficiary of the trust an IRS form "K-1" each year. A copy of the K-1 form must be filed with the trust's income tax return, and it tells the IRS and the beneficiary exactly how much income or loss and/or capital gains or loss that each beneficiary should report on his or her personal income tax return.

Termination distributions. When the trust ends, or when a final distribution is made of a particular beneficiary's share, there is generally no income tax on this distribution except to the extent that it might include the beneficiary's share of the current year's income and capital gains. The portion of the distribution that consists of principal is generally not subject to income taxes. In fact, there could even be a *loss* carried through to the beneficiary, since the termination and final tax year of a trust is the occasion that allows capital losses to be passed through to beneficiaries. However, if the beneficiary receives assets other than cash on a termination distribution, she may have a gain when she later sells these assets, depending on the "cost basis" of the assets. Cost basis means the "tax" cost of the asset for determining a capital gain or loss on sale. In general, on the distribution of an asset from a trust that is not an income distribution, the beneficiary's basis will be the same as the basis held by the trust. The trustee would give the beneficiary this information.

So, for example, if the trust has a cost basis of $2,500 in 100 shares of XYZ stock worth $10,000, and distributes the 100 shares to Ben as his share of the trust, Ben will have a cost basis of $2,500 in the shares. If he later sells them for $10,000, he will have a $7,500 capital gain.

On the other hand, if the trustee is required by the trust to give Ben a $10,000 bequest, and, in satisfaction of this, the trustee gives Ben the 100 shares of XYZ stock worth $10,000, then the *trust* will have a capital gain of $7,500, since it is satisfying a $10,000 obligation with an asset that cost only $2,500. Ben, in this case, would then have a basis of $10,000 in the stock, and if he sold it at that price he would have no gain or loss.

TRUST REPORTING REQUIREMENTS AND TAX RATES

Nongrantor trusts. Trusts other than grantor trusts (and other than charitable trusts) must file an income tax return on IRS form 1041 for each year that the trust has *any* taxable income, or gross income (which may or may not be taxable) of more than $600 for the year. Such trusts must use a calendar year. In addition to the 1041 form, the trustee must file copies of the K-1 forms the trustee sent to each trust beneficiary, as described above. If any beneficiary of the trust is a nonresident alien, then the trustee must file a 1041 form even if it has no income. The trust income tax return is due on April 15 following the calendar year of the trust, and, like individuals, trusts are entitled to an automatic three-month extension for filing the return by filing IRS form 8736.

Trusts must pay estimated taxes under rules similar to those for individuals. A trust need not pay estimated taxes on amounts distributed to beneficiaries, since these amounts are not taxable to the trust. Generally, the trustee would estimate the amount of income he expects to have left *after* distributions and deductible expenses, and pay an estimated tax on that amount. Since estimated taxes are paid quarterly, the trustee can calculate the amount on an ongoing basis. If the trustee pays too much in estimated tax, he can treat the excess as having been paid by the beneficiary. This way, the beneficiary would not have to pay as much additional estimated tax on the distribution. However, the amount the trustee credits to the beneficiary as an estimated tax payment is itself treated as an additional distribution from the trust.

Grantor trusts. If the grantor or his spouse is the trustee or one of the trustees of the grantor trust, then *no income tax return need be filed for the trust. Note* that this is the case regardless of whether the trust is revocable or irrevocable. The grantor simply reports all the trust income on his own federal income tax return (IRS form 1040). (Most states with income taxes follow the same rule, but be sure to check your state's rules.) Furthermore, grantor trusts in this category *do not* have a separate federal tax identification number. The grantor simply uses his own Social Security number for all trust accounts, as discussed in chapter 12.

If neither the grantor nor his spouse is a trustee of the grantor trust, then a separate trust tax identification number should be obtained and a 1041 form (trust income tax return) should be filed, but *no taxes* will be paid. The 1041 form will contain only the grantor's name, address, and Social Security number, indicating on the form that the trust is a grantor trust by checking the appropriate box. The trustee will attach a statement to the 1041 showing the income received by the trust and stating that it is reported on the grantor's individual income tax return (as it will be).

Foreign trusts. As pointed out in chapter 12, foreign trusts established by U.S. citizens and residents (typically for asset protection purposes) are now required to file a myriad of forms and statement with the IRS each year. Without discussing each form and statement in detail, this will give you an idea of the extent of the reporting involved: you *must* file: IRS form 56, form TDF 90-22.1, form 1041, forms 3520 and 3520-A, a "background information" statement for the foreign trust, a balance sheet and income statement for the foreign trust, a foreign trust "owner statement," and a foreign grantor trust beneficiary statement. Obviously, a knowledgeable tax attorney or tax accountant familiar with those requirements must be employed. Note, however, that if there is a good reason for you to establish a foreign trust (e.g., for asset protection purposes), the filing requirements should not discourage the plan. Advisers who regularly do this type of work usually do it for a reasonable fee.

Trust income tax rates. At one time (prior to 1994), the income tax rates of trusts were similar to those of an unmarried individual and offered an opportunity to save taxes by "shifting" income to a trust. For instance, a taxpayer in the 50 percent income tax bracket could create a trust for his children and place some of his investments in the trust, which would pay a tax as low as 11 percent on the same income. In some cases, he could later get the investments back from the trust. That was then.

In fact, it was this very arrangement that ultimately led Congress to enact the "kiddie tax," described below, and the grantor trust rules, described above, to prevent the shifting of income without giving up something in return. Nevertheless, the difference in tax rates continued to offer potential for tax savings until 1994, when Congress dramatically revised the tax rate tables for trusts, substantially curtailing any meaningful tax savings solely through the difference in rates. Thus, while there is still the possibility of shifting income to the lower bracket of a trust, it will only be of value for the first $7,000 or $8,000 of trust income retained by the trust because, as the trust income exceeds that amount, the rate quickly jumps to 35 percent, which is the highest rate for individuals and married couples. The following table should illustrate the dramatic difference in rates:

Taxpayer	*2005 taxable income*	*Tax rate*
Individual	Over $250,000.00	35 percent
Married couple	$250,000.00	35 percent
Trust	$7,500.00	35 percent

In view of the above, whenever possible, good tax planning will attempt to keep trust taxable income in the lower brackets (say, up to $3,500) and distribute the rest to beneficiaries who are also in lower brackets, so that the overall rate on the total trust income (both retained and distributed) is kept as low as possible. As noted with the next section, however, the trustee must also be mindful of the *age* of the beneficiary.

THE KIDDIE TAX

In its never-ending effort to attack tax savings plans developed by taxpayers and their advisers, Congress in 1986 adapted the kiddie tax. Simply stated, the kiddie tax law provides that if a child under the age of fourteen receives unearned income (e.g., dividends, interest, royalties), then that income, over a certain annual allowance, will be taxed at the *parent's highest tax rate*. For 2004 the allowance was $1,500. The first $750 is tax-free, and the next $750 is taxed at the child's own rate of 10 percent.

To illustrate, say that Fauntleroy, age nine, is the beneficiary of a trust, and in 2004 the trustee distributed $3,300 to him. Fauntleroy's parents earn a lot and are in the 35 percent tax bracket. Because he is under age fourteen, Fauntleroy will pay a tax of 35 percent of $1,800 ($3,300 less his allowance of $1,500) or $630, plus a tax of 10 percent on the "second" $750, for a total tax of $705.

If Fauntleroy's parents file their tax returns separately, the rate applicable to his kiddie tax will be the higher of the two parents' rates. If they are separated, the rate will be that of the custodial parent.

Accordingly, trustees of minor's trusts and other trusts where the beneficiaries may be under age fourteen at year-end must always keep in mind the tax consequences of the distributions. Ideally, it should be kept under the annual allowance. Alternatively, the trustee can invest in low-yielding investments or capital gain–oriented investments, or even tax-deferred (EE) government savings bonds. Zero coupon taxable bonds are no help since a portion of the interest must be reported each year. Once the child reaches the age of fourteen, however, all income received by or taxable to the child will be taxed at her own individual tax rate.

Trusts and Gift Taxes

Overview of the gift tax rules. Federal (and a few states' laws) impose a *gift tax* on the transfer of property by gift from one individual to another for less than its fair value. There are exemptions and exclusions from the tax that change from time to time and that allow for gifts that are not taxed (commonly referred to as "tax-free" gifts). For instance, for 2005 a person (the "donor") could give up to $11,000 annually to each of any number of donees (the persons receiving the gifts) without paying a gift tax. This is called the "annual exclusion" gift. (You may be aware that for many years, the annual tax-free gift was $10,000 per donee. In 2002, due to an inflationary adjustment required under the tax law relating to annual gifts, that amount was increased to $11,000.) In addition, a person can give *any amount* for medical care (which includes medical insurance premiums) and for tuition payments on account of a donee. However, to qualify for the gift tax exclusion, gifts for medical care and tuition *must* be paid *directly* to the educational institution or provider of medical care. If they are paid to the individual, they will be treated as part of and limited to the annual exclusion.

Since each donor is allowed an annual tax-free gift for each donee, then husband and wife, as *two* donors, can give up to twice the allowable amount to any number of donees they wish during each calendar year. Accordingly, if Mom and Dad have four children and five grandchildren, they could give away $198,000 each year ($22,000 x 9), free of gift taxes—if they had the money.

And because of a special rule that allows one spouse to permit the other to use his annual tax-free allowance, the gift *need not come equally from both spouses.* For instance, if Mom has all the money and wants to make a $22,000 gift to Son, she can do so by having Dad consent to her use of his $11,000 allowance (note that in this case none of the gift actually comes from Dad). Dad does this by signing Mom's gift-tax return (IRS form 709, due April 15 of the year following the gift, as explained below), indicating his consent to the use of his annual exclusion allowance. If the couple is not married, they cannot split gifts like this. In that case, each would have to make his or her own gifts from his or her own funds.

The annual exclusion must be a "present interest" in order to be tax free. This concept can be complicated and elusive, but it basically means that the donee must be able to enjoy the gift when it is given to him rather than wait for years to get it. For instance, if Dad says to Son, "I have given your uncle $11,000 to hold for you until you get married," then unless Son is to be (and gets) married within the calendar year, the gift is not one of a present interest, and it will not qualify for the annual exclusion.

Gift-tax credits. Gifts that are within the annual exclusion may be repeated year after year without limitation. Gifts that exceed the exclusion or that do not qualify for the exclusion will be subject to the gift tax. Before a gift tax is actually paid, however, every individual is allowed a *credit* toward the gift tax. And once a gift exceeds the tax-free exclusion, it generates a tax against which the donor's credit *must* be applied; the donor does not have a choice. When the total gifts for the year exceed the allowable annual exclusions, it must be reported on a gift tax return, IRS form 709, which must be filed each year by the same due date as the donor's income tax return. Once the cumulative total of taxable gifts generates a tax that exceeds the donor's tax credit, then every taxable gift thereafter will generate an out-of-pocket gift tax. (See illustrations below.)

The allowable "tax free" amount one may give away is commonly expressed in terms of the amount of dollars in gifts (or estate value) that may be transferred rather than in terms of the actual credit itself. For instance, using the IRS gift tables, in 2005, a gift tax credit of $345,800 converts to a gift of $1 million. In addition, the allowance and the tax rate are under a schedule of annual changes that run to 2011. Furthermore, the estate tax but not the gift tax is scheduled to be repealed in 2010 (for one year), then reinstated. Most knowledgeable commentators believe the following schedule will be changed before 2010:

Gift Taxes

Year	Tax-free gift*	Top rate of tax on excess
2001	$675,000	55% or 60%
2002	$1,000,000	50%
2003	$1,000,000	49%
2004	$1,000,000	48%
2005	$1,000,000	47%
2006	$1,000,000	46%
2007	$1,000,000	45%
2008	$1,000,000	45%
2009	$1,000,000	45%
2010	$1,000,000	35%
2011	$1,000,000	55%

*The amount equal to the "applicable exclusion amount" under sections 2505 and 2010(c) of the Internal Revenue Code. They are not annual allowances, so that once used up, all future gifts in excess of the annual exclusion, marital deduction gifts, and charitable gifts would be fully taxable.

To illustrate the relation between the annual exclusion and the tax-free allowance (the applicable exclusion amount), say that in 2005, Mom (a widow) makes a $56,000 gift to Daughter and a $26,000 gift to Son. Mom would file a gift tax return on April 15, 2006, showing the two gifts, but *each* would be reduced by the annual exclusion of $11,000, so the gift tax return would show taxable gifts of $45,000 to Daughter and $15,000 to Son. There would be no out-of-pocket tax to pay on the total technically taxable gifts of $60,000 ($45,000 and $15,000), since this is far less than Mom's credit equivalent of $1 million for 2005. Then in 2006, Mom makes additional gifts of $311,000 to Daughter and $256,000 to Son. After reducing each of these gifts by the annual exclusion, Mom's total gifts for 2006 are $545,000

($300,000 + $245,000). To see whether Mom now owes a gift tax, we must *add* to this total the previous year's taxable gifts of $60,000, for a grand total of $605,000 ($60,000 for 2005 and $545,000 for 2006). Since the allowable cumulative tax-free total is $1 million, Mom will not have to pay a gift tax.

To illustrate further, if Mom's total cumulative taxable gifts through the year 2006 were $605,000, in 2007 she could make additional gifts of $395,000 over the annual exclusion without paying a gift tax, since the tax-free cumulative total is $1 million. Say that in 2007, she made an additional taxable gift of $445,000 (for a cumulative total of $605,000 plus $445,000, or $1.05 million), she would then *pay a gift tax* of about $28,000 on the $50,000 excess over the "tax-free" amount. That is, Mom's cumulative taxable gifts through 2007 are $1.05 million. If in the same year, she made another $30,000 of taxable gifts, her cumulative total would be $1.08 million. A gift tax is then computed on this *total,* and she would receive a credit for the previous amounts of gift tax paid or credited. The difference will be the gift tax on the $30,000 *at the bracket applicable to the new total.*

Therefore, although the gift-tax rates appear to begin at 18 percent, because of the tax credit and the cumulative nature of the tax as described above, the *effective* beginning gift-tax rate is *45 percent,* and unless the law is changed it climbs to a high of 55 percent on cumulative taxable gifts after 2010. Remember, tax-free gifts qualifying for the annual exclusion, tax-free gifts between spouses, and tax-free gifts to qualifying charities will never have a bearing on the cumulative total.

In order for the gift tax to apply or even for a tax-free gift to be made, the gift must be *complete,* that is, the donor, in the words of the gift tax regulations, "must have parted with dominion and control" of the gifted property. An outright transfer to a donee with no strings attached is the clearest example, since the donee becomes the absolute owner of the property. Where gifts to trusts are involved, however, many tricky questions can arise. Certainly there is no question that a transfer to the donor's *revocable* trust is not a completed gift because the donor can simply revoke or amend the trust and take the gift back. Gifts to irrevocable trusts are not quite as conclusive, as explained in more detail below.

The gift may be one of money, jewelry, stocks, bonds, real estate, a life insurance policy, even a copyright interest in a book. It can be anything that is capable of ownership and transfer. The amount of the gift for gift-tax purposes is the *fair value* of the property *on the date of the gift.* It does not matter that the donor paid much less than it is now worth. The only significance of the donor's purchase price is that it will generally determine the donee's cost basis if the gifted property is later sold. For instance, say that you paid $1,000 for a painting that is now worth $10,000, and you make a gift of it to your daughter, who sells it for $10,000. You have made a $10,000 gift *and* your daughter has a $9,000 capital gain. *Note* that you cannot get around this by "selling" her the painting for $1. A "sale" for $1 is only a true sale if that's all the property is worth.

Gifts between spouses enjoy special treatment. There is no limit to the amount each spouse can give to the other without a gift tax. So if Barry gives his wife, Jane, a $5 million diamond for their anniversary, there is no gift tax and no use of his applicable exclusion amount. Gifts to a spouse through the use of a *trust*, however, may not offer the same result unless the trust meets certain requirements. If the spouse has a full withdrawal power, it will be gift tax free, or if the trust qualifies as a QTIP trust, as explained in chapter 12, it will be gift tax free.

Note that the above discussion on gift taxes is intentionally brief and little more than an overview of the basics. It is offered to give you a general understanding of such taxes to help you follow the concepts and tax savings ideas discussed in chapters 12 and 13.

Gifts on creating a trust. As explained above, the gift tax rules apply when one person makes a gift to another. If a person makes a gift to a trust, who is the donee? Is it the trustee? Probably not, since we know that the trustee does not receive trust assets for his own benefit. Then it must be the beneficiaries. But if that is the case, what about the fact that the beneficiaries may not get to use or receive the gift for years, depending on the terms of the trust, or that some beneficiaries may never receive it at all? It is this fact that prevents a gift to a trust from qualifying for the annual exclusion *unless* the trust contains certain specific provisions.

The trust provisions required to obtain the necessary gift-tax exclusion are somewhat simple in concept, but the tax and legal ramifications can be extensive and most are beyond the scope of this discussion. Briefly, for a trust beneficiary to be considered a donee with a present interest in the gift, she merely needs to be given the right to withdraw the gift from the trust. This right, or power of withdrawal, by the beneficiary has been ruled (first by the courts and then by the IRS) to be the same as making the gift directly to the beneficiary, thereby qualifying the gift to the trust for the annual exclusion. This is the case even though the beneficiary does not actually withdraw the gift. The right to withdraw is commonly called a "Crummey power" (see chapter 12).

Trusts that contain Crummey powers are often referred to as "Crummey trusts," meaning that gifts to the trust will or should qualify for the annual exclusion because of the existence of the withdrawal powers. It is a safe bet that there is not a single tax attorney, tax accountant, or financial planner in the country who is not familiar with Crummey and his legacy. Little did Mr. Crummey know that his name would go down in tax history and generate a household phrase to be used by tax advisers for decades to come (although some of us might have preferred his name was "Nifty," or "Smart," or even "Worthy," as opposed to "Crummey").

The Crummey power is usually part of an irrevocable trust (remember, if the trust is revocable by the donor, no gift takes place) and typically provides that once the donor makes a gift to the trust, the trustee will notify the beneficiary of the gift and of the amount the beneficiary may withdraw. The beneficiary will have, say, thirty days after receiving the notice to advise the trustee if she wants to exercise the withdrawal right. If she does not notify the trustee that she wishes to withdraw the funds (some trusts require that she decline in writing), then the power to withdraw expires, and the funds that she could have withdrawn will remain in the trust and be managed according to its terms.

It is not unusual for there to be several beneficiaries of a Crummey trust and the amount of the donor's gifts may be increased accordingly. For instance, if Jerry establishes a Crummey trust for his four children and the annual exclusion at the time is $11,000 per donee, he and his wife could contribute up to $88,000 each year to the trust, gift tax free ($11,000 per donor x 4 children [donees] x 2 donors). Crummey powers are very often used in irrevocable life insurance trusts (as explained in the discussion in chapter 12) to allow the donor/insured to pay the premiums on insurance policies on his life through gifts to the trust, without gift or estate tax consequences.

When you think about it, this right of withdrawal or Crummey power is a pretty neat thing. If the beneficiaries holding the power never exercise it, quite a lot of money could pile up in the trust, gift-tax free. And if we are pretty sure the power won't be exercised, we could name as many beneficiaries as possible to have the power, and then provide that once their power lapsed, other beneficiaries (the ones we really want) could receive distributions.

To illustrate, say that Leo has four married children, who have a total of six grandchildren, five of whom are also married. Leo creates a Crummey trust providing that all of his children and grandchildren and all of their spouses will have Crummey withdrawal powers for thirty days after any contributions to the trust. After the thirty-day period any amounts not withdrawn will remain in the trust for the benefit of Leo's four children, rather than for all of the "donees." Leo contributes $209,000 to the trust (four children, four spouses, six grandchildren, five spouses = 19 x $11,000 = $209,000). Leo claims nineteen annual exclusions. Will this fly?

The IRS has repeatedly attacked this type of situation and has vigorously taken the position that unless the beneficiary with the withdrawal power holds an interest in the trust other than the bare Crummey power, the IRS will *disallow* the exclusion. In this case, only the four children were "real" beneficiaries. If the grandchildren stood to become beneficiaries after the children, the arrangement would probably be accepted, but as for the spouses, it would likely be a lost cause, since they have nothing more than the withdrawal power. It is also worthy of note that both the IRS and Congress are pushing for limitations on the number of annual exclusions a person can use each year. Expect to see more on this in the future.

Not every trust will have Crummey powers. There are situations where the donor will not want the beneficiaries to have withdrawal powers, or where, for tax purposes, it is advisable not to have them. A typical case would be a generation-skipping trust (see a discussion of the GST trust in chapter 12). If one GST trust is to be established for a number of beneficiaries (say, children, grandchildren, and great-grandchildren), it is usually far more practical and desirable for long-term tax planning to forego the use of the annual exclusion and simply apply the donor's (and spouse's, if appropriate) gift-tax credit to the transfers to the GST trust.

Gifts on terminating the trust. This is an easy one. If the trust is irrevocable and a completed gift was made on its creation, then there will be no further gift when the trust is terminated and the trust assets are distributed to the beneficiaries. As with anything that is as complex and far-reaching as the field of trusts, however, there could be exceptions, but this is the general rule. On the other hand, if the trust was revocable to begin with, then no completed gift was made at that time, and if the assets are distributed on termination to someone other than the original donor, there will be a gift of the fair market value of the trust assets on termination, from the donor to the recipient/donee of the assets.

Trusts and Estate Taxes—Overview of the Estate Tax System

Provisions of the Internal Revenue Code go to great length to include in your estate the value of any and all property with which you are even remotely connected, and even some property with which you feel you have severed all connections. This is not to say that nothing escapes taxes, but rather to orient you to the theory of the tax laws so as to increase your general understanding and reduce the surprises that result from misunderstanding.

One of the more common misconceptions, for instance, is that every estate will pay an estate tax. In fact, it is just the opposite. Most estates pay *no* federal estate tax. This is primarily because the portion of the estate that passes to the deceased's surviving spouse is tax free (this is called the marital deduction), and most people are married! And even where there is no surviving spouse, a certain portion of the estate is still not taxed. In 2005, for instance, the tax-free amount for estates is $1.5 million, and that number gradually increases until it reaches $3.5 million in 2009, as shown in the table below. (I have included numbers dating back to 2001 since tax laws, and especially estate tax laws, are still political punching bags; it seems unlikely, however, that the tax-free amount will sink back to 2001 levels.)

Estate Taxes

Year	Tax-free estate*	Top rate of tax on excess
2001	$675,000	55% or 60%
2002	$1 million	50%
2003	$1 million	49%
2004	$1.5 million	48%
2005	$1.5 million	47%
2006	$2 million	46%
2007	$2 million	45%
2008	$2 million	45%
2009	$3.5 million	45%
2010	Repealed	0
2011	$1,000,000	55%

*Note that this amount not only will include the value of all assets otherwise includible in the deceased's estate but it will *also* include the amount of all lifetime gifts made by the deceased during his lifetime, adjusted by annual exclusions and marital deduction and charitable gifts.

Remember that allowable deductions from the taxable estate will generally apply *before* the tax-free allowances are applied, so in some cases, the allowance may never get to be used, which, as illustrated in the discussion on the bypass trust, can be a big loss for the family. Surprisingly, married couples often get "bailed out" of a lack of planning by the application of the marital deduction, but even in those cases, the lack of planning can ulti-mately cost a small fortune in taxes. For example, if Frank has a $5 million estate and leaves it all to his wife, Lorraine, there will be no federal estate tax, since the amount passing to his wife is not taxed, without limitation. On Lorraine's subsequent death, however, since there is no surviving spouse, the full amount of the estate (less debts and expenses) would be subject to tax, and then the allowable exemption would be applied. Thus, Lorraine's estate tax in 2006 would be based on $5 million less debts and expenses and the tax-free allowance. Say that debts and expenses were $100,000, the estate tax in her estate would then be about $1.4 million! If she remarried and left enough to her new spouse, the tax could be zero. It's almost worth getting married!

The other significant aspect of our estate tax system (an aspect that often is not clearly understood) is that all lifetime taxable gifts are *added back* to the donor's estate at his death. This does *not* mean that the donees of the gifts have to give them back; rather it means that the cumulative dollar amount of the donor's lifetime taxable gifts are shown on the donor's estate tax return to arrive at a "gross estate" figure that reflects *all* the includible property attributable to the donor on his death, which requires the addition of all of his lifetime taxable gifts. The term *taxable gifts* is the key because tax-free or exempt gifts are not added back. This is the primary reason that people with larger estates try to make as many annual exclusion tax-free gifts as they can before death, as these are not added back. So, if larger gifts are added back, why make them at all? Because all *appreciation* on the value of the gift after it is made escapes estate tax.

To illustrate, say that Jane, a widow, has an estate of $2 million that includes a parcel of choice real estate worth about $600,000. She decides to make a gift of the real estate to her three children. She does so in 2005 and on April 15, 2006, she files a gift-tax return (which should include a formal appraisal of the property with the return) showing the gift of $600,000, less her annual exclusion (x 3 children) of $33,000, for a taxable gift of $567,000. Since this is below her allowable exemption of $1 million, Jane will pay no gift tax.

Three years after the gift, Jane dies, with the remainder of her estate intact at $1.4 million ($2 million less the $600,000 gift). At the time of Jane's death, however, the parcel of real estate she gave to her children had appre-ciated to a value of $1.8 million. Jane's estate tax return will show the $1.4 million she retained *plus* the $567,000 lifetime taxable gift to her children, for a gross estate of $1.967 million. Her estate will be entitled to the tax-free equivalent of $2 million (for the year 2008) and so no estate tax will be due. The $1.2 million *appreciation* on the parcel of real estate gifted to the children ($1.8 million value less the gift value of $600,000) completely *escapes tax* in Jane's estate and is tax free to the children.

Note that if Jane had kept the property to her death, her estate would have totaled $3.2 million and a tax of over $500,000 would have been due! The other side of the gift-tax coin is that with the gift, the children would take Jane's low cost-basis in the property for the purpose of calculating the children's capital gain or loss (see discussion on this under gift taxes) and any depreciation deductions. But even if Jane's basis was near *zero* (unlikely), the children's tax on the gain would be less than *half* the estate tax.

Trusts and the generation-skipping transfer tax. As if our tax laws are not complicated enough, we now have to contend with a special tax *separate* from the gift tax, the income tax, and the estate tax, called the generation-skipping transfer (GST) tax. I will offer what I feel is a simple explanation (as simple as I can make it) of the GST tax for purposes of helping readers understand the potential, serious GST tax traps, and the basic reasons for some of the GST tax planning strategies discussed here and in chapter 12. But please heed this warning: the GST tax is one of the most complicated areas of the tax code and you should *never* attempt GST tax planning without expert advice.

The GST tax is a tax imposed on transfers that are to benefit individuals who are two or more generations younger than the person making the transfer. Such individuals are called "skip-persons." Where family members are concerned (including nieces and nephews), the identification of skip-persons is pretty straightforward—it would include grandchildren (and more remote descendants) of the transferor, and grandnieces and grandnephews (and their descendants) of the transferor, regardless of the number of years in age difference between the transferor and the skip-person. Where non-family members are concerned, however, the rule calls for a thirty-seven-and-a-half-year age spread between the transferor and the younger beneficiarywho would then be a skip-person.

To illustrate, say that Herbert, age seventy-six, makes a gift to his grand-nephew, Harvey, age forty. Even though their age difference is not thirty-seven and a half years, there would be a GST tax because the "family" rule will apply. On the other hand, if Herbert made the gift to his live-in companion, Anna, age forty, there would be *no* GST tax, since Anna is not thirty-seven and a half or more years younger than Herbert. And if Herbert wanted to make a large gift to Anna, he could marry her and pay no GST tax because spouses are always considered to be in the same generation regardless of their age difference.

The GST tax is one that should be avoided at almost all costs since it is applied *in addition* to any other tax that is due, and there is only one rate, equal to the *highest* estate tax rate. (However, everyone is entitled to a one-time GST tax exemption in the amount of $1.03 million, as of 2005.) Thus, say that Rockyfella leaves $1 million of his gazillion-dollar estate to his grandchildren. Assuming his GST tax exemption (discussed below) does not apply and that the highest estate tax rate at the time is 45 percent, there will be a GST tax of $450,000 on the transfer, and *another* $450,000 of estate tax—a total of $900,000 in taxes on the $1 million. (And believe it or not, when the GST tax is applied to certain lifetime transfers [gifts], the tax can be *more* than the amount given away!)

The GST tax applies to both lifetime and death-time transfers to skip-persons, although there is some slight relief. The first is that lifetime gifts to skip-persons that qualify for the annual gift-tax exclusion (see explanation of this in chapter 12) are exempt from the GST tax. For example, Grandpa can give $11,000 annually to as many of his grandchildren as he wishes with no exposure to the GST tax. In addition, as noted above, everyone is entitled to a GST tax exemption in the amount of $1.03 million (as of 2005). This exemption may be used during life or at death or a combination thereof, but can only be used once. When the transfers are made to a trust that includes skip-persons, the laws get exponentially more complicated, so it is extremely important that a knowledgeable adviser is consulted.

What is included in your estate? The next most common concern is the concept of what is included in your estate when computing the tax. *Note* that when we say something is "included" in your estate, we do not mean that the item is somehow taken back or handed over to your executor. What we mean is that the *value* of the item for estate tax purposes (usually the fair value at the date of death) is shown on the estate tax return for purposes of computing the estate tax. If the inclusion of these items produces a tax that the executor or trustee cannot pay, there is a legal mechanism by which the IRS can collect against the items themselves in proportion to the tax generated by each.

As to the general rule of includibility, you can assume for starters that the value of any property over which you have *control,* or property that you have given away but retained the right to *use and enjoy,* or property that you simply *own,* will be included in your estate for tax purposes. To expand on this just a bit, let's look at some specific items and forms of ownership and see how they are taxed in an estate.

1. *Jointly owned property.* If you were a joint owner of any assets with someone other than your spouse, then the *full* value of the jointly held assets will be included in your taxable estate, *unless* (and to the extent) the other joint owner can *prove* to the IRS's satisfaction that he or she contributed to the property. Contributions by the surviving joint owner that can be traced back to gifts from the deceased are *not* considered contributions.

If you and your spouse were the only two joint owners, then only one-half of the joint property will be included in your estate. While it's true that this one-half will not be subject to federal estate tax because of the marital deduction, remember that the full value of that property will then be included in the estate of the surviving spouse on her later death, often costing extra in estate taxes.

2. *Life insurance.* If you were the *owner* of a policy on your life, or if you had any "incidents of ownership" (the right to change the beneficiary, cash in the policy, borrow against it, or cancel it), either individually or as trustee of a trust, or if the policy proceeds were payable to your estate or executor, or required to be used to pay debts, expenses, or taxes, then the *full proceeds* of the policy will be includable in your taxable estate—*even though* the proceeds avoid probate. Most people confuse ownership of a policy with designation of beneficiary. *The beneficiary is not necessarily the owner,* and, except as just noted, has little to do with the policy's includibility in the estate, as explained in chapter 12.

3. *Property in trusts.* As a general rule, your gross estate will include the *full* value of any assets in a trust created by you that is revocable by you, or controllable by you (such as where you could change beneficiaries), or where you retained the right to receive income or principal for your life, or for a period that did not end before your death. In fact, the includibility rules on trusts in the estate of the person who created the trusts can be divided into two categories: trusts in which the creator has retained some interest or benefit (retained interest trusts), and trusts in which you have retained some control (retained control trusts).

Similarly, when we apply the retained interest concept to asset protection trusts, special needs trusts (for Medicaid or other benefit programs), and personal injury settlement trusts established to receive a personal injury settlement, the result is that the full value of the trust assets is generally included in the deceased beneficiary's estate.

In the typical case, all of the foregoing trusts but one will have either funds or property to use as a resource from which to pay any estate tax that may be due, if there are no other funds available to pay the tax. The trustee of the trust will be obliged to do so. The one trust where this may not be the case—resulting in a potentially serious problem—is the personal injury settlement trust funded with structured settlement payments (structured settlement trusts).

Structured settlement trusts tax trap. As noted in the income tax discussion above, personal injury settlements are often "structured," meaning that the injured party (the "plaintiff") will accept periodic payments extended over a number of years instead of in a lump sum. The choice is often motivated by the fact that such payments are usually income tax free. In most cases, as a matter of good estate planning (if not made otherwise necessary for Medicaid planning), such structured settlements are caused to be put into a trust.

Although structured settlements enjoy a special income tax break, however, there is no corresponding estate-tax relief. Our federal estate tax laws are very clear in their treatment of unpaid settlement proceeds to which the plaintiff is entitled: They are *fully taxable* to the extent of their present value on the death of the plaintiff. This is the trap.

To illustrate, say that Henry, a minor, is awarded a settlement payable over his life but no less than forty years. The settlement has a present value of $6 million. In year five, Henry dies and at that time the settlement has a remaining present value of $5.6 million.

Assuming no other asset in Henry's estate, and assuming that the contract did not provide for accelerated payment or commutation on Henry's death (something to ask for), the unpaid balance of the structured settlement is *fully includible in* Henry's estate and, depending on the year of death, will generate a federal estate tax of about $1.6 million.

Since the insurance company is under no obligation to advance payments (unless negotiated in the contract as suggested above), how will these estate taxes be paid? Will the IRS agree to take a portion of each payment received by the beneficiaries?

If the estate tax liability is not paid by nine months after the date of death, interest begins to run on the unpaid amount.

Fortunately, the tax code allows for an extension of time of up to ten years to pay the tax. But even if the full ten years' extension is allowed, interest on the unpaid balance of the tax must also be paid, at a rate undoubtedly higher than the rate paid under the settlement. In most cases, therefore, the tax and interest will consume the settlement payments for years, and the named beneficiaries will get nothing until the estate taxes (and interest) are paid in full. In smaller estates, or in estates where there is a surviving spouse and the trust is designed to take advantage of the marital deduction, the problem can be lessened or even eliminated.

Although each case is different and special circumstances may allow a solution to the problem to be found (such as the purchase of life insurance on the plaintiff), there is no easy remedy, and in some cases, as with Henry, there is no remedy at all, *unless* the plaintiff or his attorney can get the settlement company to agree that if the plaintiff dies within the term, they will accelerate an amount of the payments sufficient to pay the estate tax on the settlement.

Retained interest trusts. The tax code and numerous cases on the issue have been very clear about the following rule: If you transfer assets to a trust and under the terms of the trust you are entitled to receive the income for your life or for a period that does not end before your death, then all of the trust assets will be includible in your estate at death. This will be so even though the trust is irrevocable and you have no right whatever to the principal nor any rights to control the trust.

When we apply this concept to the retained interest trusts of GRITs, GRATs, GRUTs, and QPRTs discussed in chapter 12, it should be clear that if the grantor of any of those trusts should die before the end of the term, the full value of the trust assets will be included in the grantor's estate (with the possible exception of the GRAT, where something less may be included in certain circumstances).

Retained control trusts. This issue is much more involved, but the basic string leading to includibility is where the grantor keeps too much control over a trust. What is too much control is easy to describe in extreme cases, such as where the grantor reserves the right to add or remove beneficiaries or change shares, or to change the terms of the trust, or where the grantor names himself as trustee with unlimited discretion. In these cases, the *entire* trust assets are includible in the grantor's estate even though the grantor retained no benefits from the trust. The question is much more difficult in more subtle cases, such as where the grantor reserves the seemingly harmless right to remove and replace trustees of a discretionary trust. As a general rule, retaining control of a nature that would, even indirectly, give the grantor the ability to control trust distributions is dangerous. One way to deal with this is to give such control to one or more individuals who are close to the grantor and whose judgment would likely be consistent with the grantor's judgment in similar circumstances. Most tax attorneys prefer this route rather than to walk close to the line and risk estate inclusion by attempting to give the grantor control that is just short of what would cause estate includibility. But frequently, grantor and third-party control can be combined to arrive at a satisfactory result.

For instance, as a general rule it is always wise to have a mechanism in a trust to change trustees. As suggested above, however, giving the grantor the power to remove and replace trustees is considered somewhat aggressive. Instead, a third party who understands the grantor's wishes in creating the trust may have the power to remove the trustee, and the grantor may have the power to fill any vacancy in the trusteeship or vice versa. Note that this arrangement would *not* extend to the making of any changes to the trust's dispositive provisions (i.e., who gets what and when).

In short, a considerable degree of control of power to change the trust or even the beneficiaries can be given to others, but in general cannot be retained by the grantor without risking includibility of the entire trust assets in the grantor's estate.

4. Retirement plan proceeds. Fully includible in your estate (*and* they will also be subject to *income* tax when withdrawn by the beneficiaries).

5. Gifts within three years of your death. Not includible, except in two cases. One is where ownership of a life insurance policy on your life was transferred by you within three years of your death, in which case the *entire* policy proceeds will be included in your estate for estate tax purposes. If you manage to live for more than three years after the transfer, the policy proceeds will escape tax, assuming there is no other reason they may be included. (Note that this rule has nothing to do with the adding back of lifetime taxable gifts, as there is no three-year limit on that.)

The second case where a three-year rule applies is where you have made a transfer of property, retained an interest in the property transferred (such as a life estate or an income or other interest in a trust), and gave away or released that interest within three years of your death. On your death within the three-year period, the full value of the subject property will be added back to your estate.

6. Property held under a tenancy in common. Generally, only your proportionate share of the property is included in your estate.

7. Property in which you hold a life estate. A life estate is the right to occupy or use or receive the income from property during a person's (the life tenant's) lifetime. It automatically expires on the life tenant's death, and no further action is required for the owners (the "remaindermen") to own the property. If you transferred the underlying property and retained a life estate, then the full value of the property will be included in your estate, *even though* you made a completed gift of the remainder (the full value of the property minus the calculated value of your life estate) on the original transfer. If *someone else* transferred the property and *gave you* a life estate in it, then *none* of the value of the property would be included in your estate, since you never had ownership of the property. (See also the comment in part 5 above.)

8. *Assets held in your own name.* Fully includible in your estate and fully subject to probate as well.

Taxable value. The value at which all of the above assets will be subject to tax in your estate is the fair market value on the date of your death. There is also an election available to value the assets six months after the date of death and, in some cases, this can prove advantageous (such as a big drop in the stock market within that time period). In addition, there are special use valuation elections for real estate used in a farm or other business, and a special tax break given to closely held businesses. These elections and tax reductions, however, only apply if certain specific conditions are met. Perhaps the biggest estate tax break is that given to surviving spouses in the form of the unlimited marital deduction (discussed in more detail in chapter 12), rendering estate transfers to the surviving spouse completely free of estate taxes.

14

Dealing with Lawyers

To employ an attorney I ne'er was inclined;
They are pests to society, the sharks of mankind;
To avoid that base tribe my own will I now draw;
May I ever escape coming under their paw.

—from the will of William Ruffell

I believe it can be said safely that as a class we lawyers do not enjoy the highest regard of the public. And unfortunately, this disregard goes way back. Lawyers are unaffectionately referred to in a biblical passage by Luke, which begins, "Woe unto you also, ye lawyers!," and who hasn't heard, at least ten times, Shakespeare's unfortunately famous line from *Henry VI*, "The first thing we do, let's kill all the lawyers"? (Although, in fact, Shakespeare's rebel, Jack Code, calls for the death not only of lawyers but of all scholars and gentlemen.)

But what *is* the first thing we do when we have a will problem, an estate problem, or a trust problem? We call our lawyers and ask for their help. Many people are fortunate enough to have an excellent and trusting relationship with their lawyers, while others use them only when and if they have absolutely no other choice. Many are fortunate enough to find a good, competent lawyer who does a thorough and efficient job for a (believe it or not) fair fee, while others have the misfortune to hire an incompetent. Worse yet, the problem often is that neither the client nor the lawyer realizes he is incompetent until it's too late.

Perhaps the first rule to learn, if you want to find a good lawyer, is not to prejudge him or her. *Don't* assume all lawyers are alike or of equal competence or incompetence and, above all, don't start off the relationship with an attitude of mistrust. Just as a tip, I can tell you that I don't trust clients who don't trust me. If a client comes in with a major chip on his shoulder, assuming that I'm going to cheat him or give him minimum representation with maximum fee, then I ask him to find another attorney.

To make a lawyer-client relationship work best for both, there must be, at least until it is otherwise indicated, a relationship of *mutual* trust and confidence. But this does not mean that you will never have a disagreement or that your lawyer will never make a mistake or that you are stuck with each other forever. As I will explain, as objectively as I can (since I have been a client as well as a lawyer), when it comes to dealing with lawyers, there is a time to speak and a time to listen, a time to pay and a time to be paid, a time to hire and a time to fire.

Hiring an Estate-Planning Lawyer

Just about everyone thinks that just about every lawyer can draft a will. Basically, this is true. But as I have explained, *a will is not an estate plan*. Therefore, to develop the best estate plan for your family, you need a lawyer who is competent at estate planning, not just at drafting wills. And remember also that you should not be the person to decide that all you need is a simple will. In most cases, I have found that clients are led to this decision more by a desire to spend less on legal fees than by an informed judgment.

Finding an estate-planning lawyer is somewhat less difficult than finding an estate-settlement lawyer, because estate planning is more of an acknowledged specialty among lawyers. There are numerous estate-planning organizations and most of them have lawyer-referral services, which are a bit more reliable than the general lawyer-referral services offered by most bar associations. Before you resort to the bar association, a good way to begin is to investigate whether your city has an "estate-planning council." These organizations are made up of professionals who specialize in estate planning, and most have their own lawyer-referral services. Call the one closest to you and get the names of two or three lawyers in your area you can interview. In addition, or as an alternative if you cannot locate the estate-planning council, you can contact the trust department at one or two local banks and ask them to give you the names of local lawyers they would recommend to prepare your estate plan. Compare the two or three lists you get from these various sources to see if there are any names that are common to all of them. If so, it is likely that those lawyers do a good deal of estate planning. In any event, set up interviews with two or three of these lawyers and tell them ahead of time that you are *interviewing* lawyers to do your estate plan.

Be respectful of the free time they may give you and prepare your questions beforehand. Your questions should include: (1) What's your feeling about avoiding probate? (2) What are your general recommendations on choosing an executor? (3) Do you recommend that I act as trustee of my own living trust? (4) Can you advise me on how to transfer assets to my living trust? (5) What will your fees be?

The answers you receive to these questions should give you a rough idea of how comfortable and knowledgeable the lawyer is in the field of estate planning. If he gets defensive about avoiding probate, for instance, he may be one of those lawyers whose attitude about probate is, "What's all the fuss about?" (meaning, "You'll be dead. What should you care about the delays and extra costs?"). And if he suggests that he should be the executor of your estate, or that you can't be trustee of your own revocable trust, politely cut the meeting short and go on to your next interview.

After you have made your selection, be frank and open with the lawyer: Tell him your concerns and make your objectives clear. Don't be afraid to ask questions throughout the relationship, but be prepared to pay for the time he spends answering them. Finally, if you intend to get a second opinion on your plan, tell him so, and don't be upset if the second opinion turns up some suggested changes. So long as they are not major, you should stick with your initial selection. If the changes are major, the lawyer himself should then have some explaining (or perhaps refunding) to do.

Hiring an Estate-Settlement Lawyer

When someone in your family or someone close to you dies and you are responsible for settling the estate, one of the first things you do is seek the advice of an estate lawyer, if for no other reason than to find out just what you are supposed to do. Do you pay all the deceased's bills? File his tax return? Collect on his life insurance? How do you locate all of his property? Can you withdraw the funds from his joint bank account? How do you sell his car? Can you do all this on your own without a lawyer?

DO YOU NEED A LAWYER AT ALL?
Even in the smallest estates, there are often questions that arise, that require at least the consultation of an experienced lawyer to prevent your doing the

wrong thing, which could lead to trouble and more legal fees later. Quite often, however, particularly in small- to medium-sized (in relation to the tax laws) nonprobate estates, it is not necessary to hire a lawyer to settle the estate. You may only need a few hours of consultation to guide you through the necessary steps. And in some cases, particularly where there are no disputes or other problems, you may not need a lawyer at all.

For instance, Mom and Pop have sold their home and live in a retirement community. Their only assets consist of two joint bank accounts totaling $65,000. On Pop's death, assuming he died of natural causes, there is nothing for Mom to do to settle his estate. It is not necessary to probate his will, there will be no estate or inheritance tax, no lawsuits, and Mom has free access to the bank accounts without the need for legal action.

Even where there is a probate estate, if the size of the probate estate is small (the allowable amount varies from state to state, ranging from $5,000 to $100,000) and the family situation is simple (a spouse and/or children), then, as discussed in chapter 7, most states have simplified probate procedures. In such cases, these procedures allow for the settlement of the estate with the mere filing of one or two forms, which the clerk of the court will usually help you complete.

For larger estates, however, where more formal probate is required by law, or where the estate distribution may be more complicated, or where a contest takes place, you would be foolish to attempt to handle the matter without an experienced estate attorney. In which case, how do you determine if you need one, and where do you find one?

In general, if you find yourself with the responsibility of planning or settling an estate, it is a good idea to consult with an estate attorney to have him advise you on just what your responsibilities are and whether he feels you can handle them on your own. It may sound silly to suggest going to an attorney to ask if you need an attorney, but, aside from books like this, there is nowhere else to go, except to the probate court itself. *If* you can get the clerk of the court to listen to and evaluate your case, he *may* advise you on it, but I have found that, except in the simplest of cases, the clerks usually play it safe and direct you to an attorney

I suggest you pick the best estate attorney you can find, rather than someone who looks like he needs work and will do the job cheaply, and be prepared to pay for the time and advice he gives you. Be frank about why you are there. Don't give him the impression you don't trust him, but rather that you wish to do as much as you can on your own, and you recognize the value of competent professional assistance. If you *think* you have a small and simple estate, but the attorney still tells you it's complicated and will require a lot of work, get a second opinion. Better to pay for two or even three consultations than to hire someone whose advice you question from the very beginning. If it turns out that you *do* need an attorney, which in many cases you can figure out for yourself without the need for a consultation, then get the best you can afford.

WHERE TO FIND AN ESTATE-SETTLEMENT LAWYER

They may be everywhere, but they are tough to find. It's not at all difficult to find one who would be quite pleased to help you settle the estate, but will he do it well? Many people suggest asking friends and neighbors if they know of a good estate lawyer you can use, and this is one route you may take, although not a very reliable one, in my opinion, unless your friend or neighbor is in a position to be able to compare the particular attorney's work with others.

The next best resource, though, again, in my opinion, not solidly reliable, is that of the local bar association. Bar associations have lawyer-referral services, providing names of attorneys in specified areas of the law to anyone who asks. For instance, you can call the local bar association's lawyer-referral service and ask for the names of one or two lawyers or law firms that handle the settlement of estates, and they will supply you with referrals.

The problem is that aside from having the attorneys complete a brief questionnaire, the bar associations do nothing to ascertain whether or not the attorneys to whom they refer you are true specialists or even of above-average competence in the particular area of law. In fact, if an attorney decides that he wants to receive referrals in a particular area of the law—settling estates, for example—he simply registers with the local bar association lawyer-referral service and represents that he has extensive experience in that area. He is then placed on their list of "estate-settlement lawyers," and, depending on where he is on the list, his name is given to callers who ask to be referred to estate lawyers. A lawyer would not normally seek referrals in an area with which he was not familiar or experienced, particularly in light of the dramatically increased tendency to sue lawyers for malpractice, and, therefore, a referral from the bar association ought to lead you to a lawyer who has some experience in the requested field. However, under the typical bar association referral system, there is no assurance that the lawyer referred to you is outstanding or even particularly competent in the applicable area.

Larger, more successful law firms almost always have specialists in every area, including estate settlement. Boston has its Ropes and Gray; New York has its White & Case; Chicago, its Baker & McKenzie; and San Francisco, its Pillsbury, Madison. Each of these firms has hundreds of lawyers, specialists in every known field, and no job is too big or too small, *provided* you have the money. In firms like these, if the size of the estate matches the size of the law firm, you'll probably get competent advice and service—but you'll pay for it. So where does that leave all of the in-between estates and estates where a giant law firm is not desirable for some reason?

Perhaps the best source of referrals to good lawyers is lawyers themselves. They know who is at the top of their profession, who wins the most will contests, who is consulted by their brethren on complicated trust *and estate* tax matters, who is called in as an expert witness to interpret trust law or a will question, and who *they* use to handle their *own* estates. I know of no outside resource that can match this. So rather than going to an unknown estate lawyer (unless of course you know of one already), find a lawyer that you or a friend or neighbor has used in the past or are familiar with now, and ask him who is the best estate lawyer in the area. This referral is far more likely to bring you to an acknowledged specialist than any of the other sources.

Once you have the names of at least two estate lawyers, you should consider interviewing them before reaching a decision. Unfortunately, this interview is more to get an overall impression of the attorney and his firm than it is to see if he gives you the right answers to your questions. Short of having another lawyer do the interviewing, there is little way to telling whether he knows how to settle estates, except for his own assurances to you that he can do it.

There have been occasions where lawyers have before the fact hired (or attempted to hire) *themselves* as attorneys for the estate. Every so often you will see a provision in a will that says something like, "I direct my executor to engage the law firm of Tadpole and Snodgrass to act as attorneys for my estate." Aside from the question of ethics in attempting to preclude the executor from hiring the lawyer of his choice, such a provision is *not* binding on the executor and he is under *no* obligation to employ the lawyer as "directed" by the testator. For the drafting lawyer to add this type of instruction is considered to be unprofessional and in poor taste, and in some cases can lead to trouble.

In one estate, for instance, the testator's will instructed his executor to "select Ralph Moody as the attorney for the executor of the will and as attorney for the estate." (Ralph also drafted the will.) When the testator died, his executrix followed his instructions and engaged Ralph to handle the estate.

Shortly thereafter, however, she became quite dissatisfied with his services. She asked him to withdraw from the case and offered to pay for his services to date, hiring another lawyer to continue. Ralph *refused* to withdraw and sued the estate for breach of contract, claiming that it was obliged to continue using his services as lawyer for the estate. The executrix was then forced to petition the court to order Ralph's removal and instruct him not to interfere with estate settlement.

The court quickly approved the discharging of Ralph, stating:

> Because of the special relation of attorney and client, the law permits the termination of that relationship in a manner not recognized with respect to other contracts. The client has the absolute right to discharge the attorney and terminate the relation at any time with or without cause, no matter how arbitrary his action may seem. The provision in the will directing the executor to hire the lawyer is not binding. It is merely advisory, even though the language used frequently sounds mandatory. The executor is not bound to accept an attorney whom he does not select.

Note that this type of provision is quite different from one selecting the lawyers as *executor* of your estate. As discussed earlier, this is quite acceptable, assuming it is *your* decision, and in such cases it is likely that the lawyer, as executor, will hire himself or his law firm as lawyer for the estate, which is not a problem so long as they do a good job. If, however, you have named someone else as executor, and your lawyer adds a provision in your will requiring that he or his firm should be the lawyers for your estate, I would ask him to remove the provision, at *his firm's* expense.

Lawyers' Fees—Planning Estates

The easiest estates to settle are those that are well planned during the *lifetime* of the deceased. To most people, an "estate plan" means having a will. In fact, if your estate is properly planned, the will is only a tiny part of your estate plan, and if you haven't already learned from reading this book, passing your estate through your will is the most vulnerable, time-consuming, and expensive way to pass your estate. Therefore, money spent on a good estate plan to simplify estate settlement, save taxes, and avoid probate is money well spent—as long as you don't overspend in proportion to the value of your estate.

The story is told of the woman who walked into the lawyer's office, telling him that she wanted him to plan her estate. He said he would be glad to, but he required a $5,000 retainer. She made out the check, handed it to him, then he said, "Thank you. Now, tell me about your estate," to which she replied, "You just took it!"

It's one thing to declare how valuable a good estate plan may be, but it's another to pay for it. If the cost is disproportionate to the value or size of the estate, then the client has been done a disservice.

Fees for estate planning are as varied and as volatile as the winds and there are no "standard" guidelines. For many years, lawyers would draft wills as "loss leaders," charging token amounts such as $50 or $75 for the will, in the hopes of attracting other business or in the hopes of being able to handle the estate of the person when he died. And if the lawyer was allowed to handle the estate, the loss leader usually paid off, since a $75 will was in most cases hardly adequate to deal with the complexities in settling an estate. Then along came the living trust and the realization that with competent and expert advice a family could avoid probate and save thousands in estate taxes as well. This is what we call "estate planning."

Because every estate and family situation is different, it is difficult to standardize estate-planning fees. In embarrassing contrast to the $75 will, I have seen lawyers charge as much as $5,000 for a will and $10,000 for a trust. And some attorneys, without justification, charge a percentage of the estate to prepare the estate plan. A trust, by itself, should not cost $10,000 or a will $5,000, except in complicated circumstances that involve an extraordinary amount of time and expertise. As to charging a percentage of the estate, I cannot see how this bears any relation to the work done, except that in some cases, larger, more complicated estates do involve more time and expertise. In such cases, I believe it would be fair to agree to a fee based on the time the lawyers must spend on the plan, together with a premium if some particular expertise is effectively employed, but *not* a fee based on the size of the estate.

There have been cases where instead of charging an immediate fee, a lawyer will accept a share of the estate. This arrangement raises ethical questions, to say the least, and it is likely that the attorney would *not* be entitled to a share of the estate, although he would be entitled to be paid fairly for the services he performed. There are also situations where the testator thinks so highly of the lawyer that in addition to the fee for preparing the plan, he wants to give him a share of the estate. Here, the lawyer may be entitled to the grantor's bequest, depending upon the circumstances, but even in the most honest of cases, a bequest to the lawyer who prepares the will raises strong suspicions of fraud or undue influence, in addition to the serious ethical questions involved. As a general rule, lawyers agree and ethical rules *require* that in such cases the will should be prepared by another lawyer, with the possible exception of cases where the lawyer receiving the bequest may be closely related to the testator, such as a child, sibling, niece, nephew, etc. Otherwise, it is not at all unusual for the court to void the bequest to the lawyer who drafted the will, while leaving the remaining provisions intact.

This statement may confuse you if you have seen or heard of a situation where the lawyer who drafted the will received a bequest without incident. This is quite possible. Remember that unless it was informed, the court normally would have no way of knowing that one of the beneficiaries was also the lawyer who prepared the will. Therefore, if no one objects, the lawyer will receive the bequest. And also remember that *only* ones who can object, as pointed out in chapter 10, are those people who would stand to benefit if their objections are successful. Note, that in these cases, even though a person does not have standing to object to the will, if she feels that fraud or undue influence has been committed, she can nevertheless report the matter to the local agency governing the professional behavior of lawyers.

Before you engage an attorney to do your plan, get at least an estimate, if not a fixed fee, for the work to be done. A fair way to approach the problem (which I have used with great success) is to have an initial conference to review your family and financial situation and to determine your objectives in setting up an estate plan. After this review, a letter of recommendations is prepared and sent to you, describing the work to be done and an estimate of the fees the lawyer will charge to complete it. The conference and letter are paid for separately, so that if for some reason you wish to stop at that point or have the work done elsewhere, you are free to do so, and you still have the benefit of the conference and recommendations. The letter of recommendations is also quite useful if you wish to show it to another lawyer to get a second opinion.

You should be aware that in order to get through this first step of analysis of your existing situation and recommendations of a plan, you must disclose to the lawyer *all* of the details of your family and financial situation. Occasionally, I find that some clients are reluctant to tell me everything they have for fear that I might charge them more. Estate-planning attorneys generally do *not* base their fees on the size of your estate. The estate plan for a $500,000 estate may well cost the same amount as the estate plan for a $2 million estate, depending on the family circumstances and objectives. And speaking of objectives, these are the *most* important things to communicate to your estate lawyer, since this will determine the basic structure of your plan. What good would it be if your lawyer creates a trust for you but the provisions of your trust do not accomplish your wishes?

Lawyers' Fees—Settling Estates

Lawyers love estates. Especially probate estates. And most especially, large probate estates. The bigger the probate estate, the bigger the fee—it stands to reason. There is much more work for the lawyer to do and much more responsibility than for nonprobate estates. But is this the lawyer's fault? We have a tendency to criticize lawyers for charging so much to settle an estate, but, in fact, the more costly estates, from the standpoint of legal fees, are the result of a poor estate plan or no plan, and are generally not the fault of the lawyers.

Regardless of where the fault lies, however, what is a fair fee to settle an estate? As with executors' fees, the underlying rule a probate court applies when deciding on contested legal fees is, "What is reasonable under the circumstances, taking into consideration the nature, extent, and complexity of the services performed?" Although a fee of 1 percent of an estate may be unreasonable in one case, a 10 percent fee may be quite reasonable in another. And a number of states have preestablished fees that an attorney may charge in settling a probate estate, with rates similar in fashion to those of executors' fees, for instance, 5 percent of the first $5,000, 4 percent of the next $20,000, 3 percent of the next $75,000, etc. Most states, however, simply adhere to the test of reasonableness and look at each case on its own. Since attorneys' fees must be approved by the probate court before payment, a beneficiary or executor who thinks the attorney is charging too much can object to the payment of the fee, and the court will review it.

When the court reviews a contested attorney's fee, it will look carefully at the size and nature of the estate, then examine the attorney's report of what was done and how much time it took, and it will also consider whether the amount of time the lawyer claims to have spent on the case was reasonable under the circumstances. In one case, a lawyer, in defending his fee, claimed to have spent "a great deal of time and considerable difficulty" in selling some stock represented by forty-eight certificates in fourteen different corporations. The court's inquiry revealed, however, that the securities were sold through a stockbroker and the lawyer's time primarily consisted of making copies of the certificates and talking to the broker. The court cut the lawyer's requested fee by two-thirds.

In another case, however, a lawyer spent nearly one thousand hours of his time over a nine-year period on estate matters. He produced a detailed time log, itemizing all of his activities on behalf of the estate, and this was corroborated by other evidence. The court allowed him the full fee of $85,000.

In many cases, the lawyer will, in the course of representing the estate, perform services that are outside the normal course of estate representation and this will often warrant an additional fee. For instance, if the estate is sued by a creditor, or if there is a will contest, this will require considerable extra legal time. Other examples would include the sale of estate property or the running of a business. A classic example of additional fees for business-related matters is illustrated in the Saperstein estate.

Abe Saperstein was the founder and owner of the world-famous Harlem Globetrotters basketball team. Saperstein owned the team as a sole proprietorship, and on his death the executor had the obligation of managing the team. Since the objective was ultimately to sell the team, one of the first things done to facilitate a sale was to form a corporation to hold ownership of the team. Because of the nature of the estate and the complexity of the laws regarding sports teams, incorporating involved extensive legal work. In addition, Saperstein never bothered to have any of the key players sign contracts; this posed a serious impediment to a sale. The executor and the attorneys then negotiated with the "star players"—Meadowlark Lemon, Fred Neal, Robert Hall, and Hubert Ausbie—and were successful in getting them to sign favorable contracts. The lawyers and executors continued to improve the operation of the team to a point where it began to show a profit, and it was ultimately sold to the Potter Palmer Group for $3.71 million. The lawyers received a fee of $123,000 for the incorporation and other business work, and they asked for an additional fee of $140,000 for estate services. Saperstein's beneficiaries objected.

At the trial, the beneficiaries pointed out that it was the *executor* and not the lawyers who did most of the work and that the lawyers submitted no time records to substantiate any work that they did do. The court noted, however, that it was established that the lawyer had material involvement in the weekly operations of the Globetrotter team business, that they negotiated the contracts with the key players, that they were instrumental in developing the profitability and ultimately the sale of the team at a price almost double that of the value on the date of Saperstein's death. "This was," the court said, "an unusual and unique estate, requiring extraordinary and broad-ranging legal and nonlegal services." The fee was considered reasonable under all the circumstances, and allowed.

In discussing the matter of fees with your estate lawyer, you should be sure that you *both* understand just what the fee arrangement will be and, at least in general terms, what it will include. As explained earlier, the fee would normally cover all matters routinely settling the estate, including the filing of necessary forms to probate the will, assisting in the preparation and filing of inventory and accounts, assistance in collection of estate assets, and other routine matters. What is usually *not* included is negotiation and sale of estate assets (unless the transaction is nominal), handling of will contests or objections to accounts by beneficiaries, and handling of suits brought by creditors. Some lawyers, especially tax lawyers, will also handle the preparation and filing of the estate tax returns as part of their representation.

Depending on the state in which the estate is being administered, you may be required to pay a fixed fee according to the state's schedule of allowable fees, or you may agree on a percentage of the estate, or you may simply arrange to pay an hourly fee for routine matters and a negotiated fee for extraordinary work (which I feel is best). If you do agree upon an hourly fee, ask the lawyer to send you a monthly statement showing the time spent to date, so you can keep abreast of your costs.

Remember, these fee arrangements are on behalf of the estate. If you are on the "other side," acting *against* the estate, there are no state-regulated fees and it is up to you and your lawyer to reach an agreement. In a will contest, for instance, your lawyer may ask for a nonreturnable retainer against a percentage (one-third to one-half) of the recovery he wins for you. On the other hand, if you are simply objecting to an accounting, the fee will normally be on an hourly basis.

Whether you are for or against the estate, however, and whatever fee arrangement you agree upon, ask your lawyer to explain it in a letter to you. I guarantee that this will come in handy for both of you because, when it comes to money, we all have a tendency to be "forgetful."

Firing an Estate Lawyer

At some point between the petition for probate of the will and the allowance of the final account of the executor or administrator, you may decide that you are unhappy with your lawyer and you want to fire him. But is it that easy? Can the lawyer obstruct the settlement of the estate if he refuses to be fired? And what if he won't return the estate files and papers to you?

Before you even think about firing the lawyer you hired to handle the estate, you should first be sure of your reasons for firing him. If it is simply a lack of communication, of which many lawyers are guilty, this by itself is not a good reason, since, despite it, he may be doing a superb job in settling the estate. If there has been no communication, put the pressure on him to bring you up to date immediately. If he neglects your calls and letters, show up at his office and demand to see someone regarding the status of the estate. If this doesn't work, maybe it's more than a lack of communication and you should consider changing lawyers.

If you are receiving regular reports and communication is not a problem, but you are nevertheless dissatisfied with your lawyer's performance, once again you should try to identify the problems. I find that if clients are not made aware of the amount of time it takes to settle an estate, they think that any delays are the lawyer's fault, no matter how efficient the lawyer may be. If it is something other than the delays that bothers you, before you do fire your lawyer, get a second opinion on his performance. Consult with another estate lawyer, describing the situation as best you can; you might even give the second lawyer the authorization to call or write to your lawyer for additional information to help him evaluate the situation. I have seen a number of situations where just a call or a letter from another lawyer investigating the matter will snap the first lawyer into action.

If it turns out that your first lawyer is simply incompetent and is not handling the estate properly, one of two things can happen on inquiry from your "new" lawyer (after you have told the first he has been fired). One, he may recognize the fact that he can't handle the estate and gladly turn over the files, provided you pay him for work he has done to date. If you feel this is fair, you can pay; otherwise you can fight it, but he still has to turn over the files—he cannot keep them as hostage for payment.

The second possibility is that your original lawyer will ignore the fact that you are firing him and simply continue to do work on the estate, asserting that he has some sort of "right" to continue. This is improper. Remember that as a client, you have the *absolute right* to discharge your attorney at any time with or without cause, no matter how arbitrary your decision may seem. The only stipulation the court makes is that you may be required to pay a fair fee for the work done to the date of the discharge.

If the lawyer ignores your instructions or refuses to return the estate files and records to you, then you may have to resort to filing a complaint with the disciplinary committee of the local bar board. Before you do this, though, you should understand that it will necessitate some time and involvement on your part. Bar associations are quite responsive to a client's complaint, but they don't automatically prejudge the lawyer to be wrong or the client to be right. Usually they'll ask each party (the client and the lawyer) to detail his or her side of the story, and then they will reach a decision. The process could require you to take the time to respond to subsequent inquiries by the board and in some cases you may be required to attend a hearing, although a hearing would be unlikely in the simple case of a refusal to return files. In short, you should use a complaint only as a last resort; bringing a formal complaint to the bar board, however, will usually motivate all but the most cantankerous lawyers to cooperate, since the board has the power to recommend suspension or even disbarment for professional misbehavior.

Before you make the move to fire your lawyer, be sure you have a new lawyer ready to take over the handling of the estate. The procedure for finding the new lawyer will presumably be no different from that for finding the first, and don't be discouraged if you find that you have to change lawyers partway through the settlement of the estate. It is not unusual to use more than one attorney in estate settlements. This is because despite the initial screening or interviewing process, it is sometimes difficult to tell whether the attorney you initially choose will be able to do the job. It may only later become apparent that he is not adequately familiar with handling estates or that he simply does not have the time to work on your case. In either event, as soon as you realize that you would be better off changing lawyers, you should start looking for another. The longer you wait, the longer it will take to settle the estate, and the greater the exposure to interest and penalties for late payment of taxes or other expenses. Remember, you are not obliged to keep a lawyer, only to pay him the fair value for the services rendered.

Often the problem, or at least a part of the problem, is not the lawyer but the estate itself. That is, a poorly planned estate can make a reasonably good lawyer, who may have had no trouble with a well-planned estate, look bad. And if the lawyer is of marginal competence to begin with, a poorly planned estate will simply make matters worse. But, regardless of the competence of the lawyer, when estate complications arise, legal fees go up, it takes more time to settle the estate, and clients often get mad at the lawyer because of it. The good news is that much of this can be avoided by having a well-planned estate.

Estate settlement can be made extremely smooth and legal fees kept to a minimum by having your own estate plan in good order, keeping in mind that although you should always have a will, a will is *not* by itself an estate plan. In most instances, your estate plan will include a will, a durable power of attorney, and at least one living trust, with the important understanding that ownership of your assets must be coordinated with these documents or your plan will fail.

When all of this is done, you can feel as Ishmael did in the novel *Moby-Dick*, when he said after signing his will,

> I felt all the easier: a stone was rolled away from my heart. Besides, all the days I should now live would be as good as the days the Lazarus lived. . . . I survived myself.

Appendix I

Sample Will and
Codicil Forms

(Sample) Last Will and Testament of

_____

I, _____, now of (CITY), (COUNTY), (STATE), do make and declare this to be my Last Will and Testament, hereby revoking all Wills and Codicils I have made before this.

ARTICLE I: *Appointment of Executor.* I nominate and appoint my husband, _____, Executor of this Will. In the event that my said husband declines or is unable to serve or ceases to serve as Executor, then I nominate and appoint _____ as Executor. I request that no Executor or successor in such capacity, or any other fiduciary hereunder, shall be required to furnish any sureties on his or her official bond in said capacity, and that any of the same be appointed and serve in a temporary capacity upon application.

ARTICLE II: *Appointment of Guardians.* In the event that any child of mine has not attained the age of majority at the time of my death, I nominate and appoint my husband, _____, as guardian of the property of such minor child or children. In the event that my said husband for any reason is unable to serve or ceases to serve as such guardian before all of my children attain the age of majority, then I nominate and appoint _____ as guardian of the person and property of any child of mine during his or her minority. I direct that any guardian hereunder be permitted and authorized to qualify and act as such in any jurisdiction without furnishing any bond or other security.

ARTICLE III: *Specific Bequests.*

   (A) I give the sum of _____ thousand dollars ($_____,000) to my brother, _____, if he survives me;

   (B) I give to my son, _____, my collection of woodworking tools and equipment, if he survives me;

   (C) I give to my daughter, _____, my oil painting of Alexander the Great, by Guido Reni, if she survives me;

   (D) I give the sum of _____ ($_____) to the pastor of St. Sebastion's Church, Maintown, for the purchase of a ceiling fan to cool the parishioners on hot days;

   (E) I give to my daughter, _____, if she survives me, the parcel of real estate I own located at 400 Beacon Street, Boston, Massachusetts.

ARTICLE IV: *Bequest of Tangible Personal Property.* I give and bequeath all my tangible personal property, not otherwise disposed of hereunder, together with any unexpired insurance thereon, to my husband, _____, if he survives me. In the event my said husband does not survive me, then I give and bequeath the property referred to in this ARTICLE IV to my children who survive me, in substantially equal shares, to be divided as they shall agree, or if they fail to agree within six (6) months after the date of my death, as my Executor shall determine.

ARTICLE V. *Bequest of Residuary Estate.* All of the remainder of my estate, I give and bequeath to my husband, _____, if he survives me. In the event my said husband does not survive me, then I give and bequeath the property referred to in this ARTICLE V to my children who survive, me, in equal shares, provided that if any of my children should predecease me leaving issue who survive me, one such equal share shall pass to such issue by right of representation.

ARTICLE VI: *Survival and Simultaneous Death.* For all purposes of this Will, a person shall not be considered to survive me or another if he or she shall die within sixty (60) days after my death or the death of such other. If my husband and I shall die under circumstances where it is impossible to determine which of us predeceased the other, then I shall be deemed to have survived my husband. [*Note:* The "deemed" surviving spouse shall generally be the one with the smaller estate. Also, both Wills should be consistent, so that in this case, the husband's Will will declare that his wife will be deemed to have survived him.]

ARTICLE VII: *Taxes.* I direct that all estate, inheritance, and other death taxes of any nature payable by reason of my death whether with respect to property passing under this Will or property not passing under this Will (except for any such taxes arising solely as a result of any power of appointment I may have at my death), shall be paid out of my residuary estate without apportionment.

ARTICLE VIII: Powers of Executor—General. My Executor shall have full power and authority without the necessity of order of court to sell, at either public or private sale, or to exchange, lease, pledge, or mortgage, in such manner and on such terms as my Executor deems advisable, any or all property, real or personal, belonging to my estate and to execute all deeds, assignments, mortgages, leases, or other instruments necessary or proper for those purposes; to adjust, compromise, or otherwise settle claims of any nature in favor of or against my estate on such terms as my Executor deems advisable; to make distributions wholly or partly in kind by allotting or transferring specific securities or other real or personal property or undivided interests therein at then-current values; to retain any securities or other property owned by me at the time of my death, although the same may not, without this instruction, be considered a proper investment for Executors; and generally to perform any acts and to execute any instruments with respect to such property as if my Executor were the absolute owner thereof, but no power under this Will shall be exercised or exercisable if it would defeat qualification for any marital or charitable deduction otherwise available to my estate for estate tax purposes. Notwithstanding any other provisions of this Will, my Executor shall, to the extent possible, not use any property otherwise excludable from my estate for estate tax purposes for payment of any obligations of my estate, including any obligations for taxes.

ARTICLE IX: Powers of Executor—Taxes. I hereby vest my Executor with full power to do everything he deems desirable in connection with any tax matter involving to any extent myself, my family, or my estate. My Executor shall have full power and discretion to make, or to determine not to make, any and all elections available to me or to my estate with respect to income, gift, estate, or generation-skipping taxes, and my Executor's determination shall be final and binding on all parties. No compensation adjustments of any sort shall be required as a result of any election made or not made by my Executor pursuant to this authority.

ARTICLE X: Exculpatory Provisions. My Executor shall not be liable for any act done or omitted to be done in good faith nor for any loss to or diminution of my estate unless caused by his own willful malfeasance or default; nor shall any Executor or Administrator hereunder be liable for the act or omission of any other Executor or Administrator hereunder. No interest shall be payable on any legacy or bequest hereunder, regardless of statute or court rule, and regardless of when such legacy or bequest is paid, so long as my Executor shall act in good faith in making any such payment or distribution.

ARTICLE XI: Unascertained Beneficiaries. If any occasion shall arise during the administration of my estate or in connection with any matter or procedure affecting my estate calling for the appointment of a person to represent the interests of persons unborn or unascertained or the interests of any other person, I direct that such appointment shall be dispensed with, if permitted under law.

IN WITNESS WHEREOF, I, _____, do hereby declare that I sign and execute this instrument as my Last Will, that I sign it in the presence of each of the said witnesses, and as my free and voluntary act, this _____ day of _____, 20____.

_____
(Name)

We, the undersigned witnesses,° each do hereby declare in the presence of the aforesaid Testator (Testatrix) that the Testator (Testatrix) signed and executed this instrument as his/her Last Will in the presence of each of us, that he/she signed it willingly, that each of us hereby signs this Will as witness in his/her presence and in the presence of each other, and that to the best of our knowledge, the Testator (Testatrix) is of sound mind, and under no constraint or undue influence.

_____ residing at _____
Witness   _____

_____ residing at _____
Witness   _____

_____ residing at _____
Witness   _____

STATE OF _____

_____, ss.
(County)

Subscribed, sworn to, and acknowledged before me by the said Testator (Testatrix) and witnessed this _____ day of _____, 20_____.

_____
NOTARY PUBLIC
My Commission Expires: _____

_____

Note: In some cases, it may be wise to add a non-contest provision. See page 323.

°Most states require only two witnesses.

(Sample) Codicil

Codicil to the Will of _____

I, _____, of (CITY), (COUNTY), (STATE), having
made my Last Will dated _____, 20_____, hereby make this Codicil to my said Will:
1. I hereby revoke the appointment of my husband as Executor in Article I, and
   in his place I name my son, _____, to serve as Executor;
2. Article III, part (A), containing a specific bequest to my brother, is deleted
   and the following part (A) is substituted in its place:
   "(A) I give the sum of _____ thousand dollars ($_____,000) to
   my sister, _____, if she survives me." and
3. The specific bequest of _____dollars in part (D) of Article III is
   increased to the sum of _____dollars ($_____).
   In all other respects I ratify and confirm my said Will, this _____ day
   of _____, 20_____.

   Signed, _____
   (Name)

We, the undersigned witnesses,* each do hereby declare in the presence of
the aforesaid Testator (Testatrix) that the Testator (Testatrix) signed and executed this instrument as his/her Codicil to a Will dated _____
in the presence of each of us, that he/she signed it willingly, that each of us
hereby signs this Codicil as witness in his/her presence and in the presence of
each other, and that to the best of our knowledge, the Testator (Testatrix) is of
sound mind, and under no constraint or undue influence.

_____ residing at _____
Witness   _____
_____ residing at _____
Witness   _____
_____ residing at _____
Witness   _____

STATE OF _____
_____, ss.
(County)
   Subscribed, sworn to, and acknowledged before me by the said Testator
(Testatrix) and witnesses this _____ day of _____, 20_____.

_____
NOTARY PUBLIC
My Commission Expires: _____

_____
*Most states require only two witnesses.

Appendix II

Special Will Provisions

INTENTIONAL OMISSION OF ISSUE

"I have intentionally, and not through accident or mistake, made no provisions in this Will for my son (daughter), _____, and for any other of my issue hereafter born or adopted."

AVOIDANCE OF GUARDIAN AD LITEM (FOR UNBORN OR UNASCERTAINED BENEFICIARIES)

"If any occasion shall arise during the administration of my estate or in connection with any matter, thing, or procedure affecting my estate, calling for the appointment of a person to represent the interests of persons unborn or unascertained, or the interests of any other person, I direct that such appointment shall be dispensed with, if permitted under law."

DECLARATION OF INTENT (FOR JOINTLY OWNED ASSETS)

"It is my purpose and intent that any savings, checking, or other accounts established by me or in any savings, banking, or other financial institutions, and any securities, including certificates of deposit or similar 'money market' investments, on which I have designated my husband or any of my children* as a joint tenant, shall, upon my death, become the sole and absolute property of each respective surviving joint tenant. It is my intent that such funds and securities are not to be considered a part of my probate estate, nor are such funds or securities to be considered as being disposed of by this Will."

---

* If there is someone other than a spouse or a child whom you have named as a joint owner with you, and you wish him or her to receive the jointly held funds, he or she should be identified here.

NONCONTESTABILITY OF BEQUESTS

"All gifts, bequests, legacies, and devises contained in this Will are given upon the express condition that the respective beneficiaries shall not directly or indirectly contest or oppose, or appear against the allowance and probate of this Will, or take action in any court to have it set aside or annulled in whole or in part. If any such action is taken or participated in by a beneficiary hereunder, whether or not such contest or action is based on probable cause, then I revoke and declare void the gift, bequest, legacy, devise, share, or interest given to such beneficiary, and such share or interest shall instead go to the beneficiaries under the residuary clause of this Will, but excluding said contesting beneficiary and his heirs.

"If all the beneficiaries hereunder participate in any such action against this Will, then my residuary estate shall pass to the Fleming Home for Chickens, in Hull, Massachusetts."

BEQUEST OF TANGIBLE PERSONAL PROPERTY

"Except as otherwise disposed of by this Will, I give all of my tangible personal property to my children who survive me, in shares of substantially equal value, to be divided by rotation, after drawing lots. Items that are normally parts of sets shall, wherever possible, be kept together. Any disputes with respect to any of such tangible property under this ARTICLE that are not resolved within six (6) months after the date of my death, shall be finally resolved by my independent Executor. When used in this Will, the term 'independent Executor' shall mean any duly appointed executor or administrator with the Will Annexed other than my issue or their spouses.

"If no such executor is then serving, a majority of my surviving children shall appoint an independent Executor, solely for the purpose of resolving the disputes relating to my tangible property. If they cannot agree on a choice within nine (9) months after my death, then an independent Executor shall be appointed by the court, upon application of one of my children, for the aforesaid purpose. If, in the opinion of my independent Executor, such disputes cannot be speedily and satisfactorily resolved, he may sell the remaining tangible personal property hereunder at fair market value and divide the net proceeds equally among my surviving children, taking into account the value of any items of such property they may have previously received hereunder."

EXECUTOR'S AUTHORITY TO CONTINUE BUSINESS

"My Executor shall have full power and authority, without the necessity of order of court, to determine all questions relating to the operation, conduct, management, liquidation, sale, incorporation, capitalization, personnel, and all other matters in connection with the carrying on of, or the winding up of, the business known as _____, currently carried on in (CITY), (STATE). All receipts and disbursements in connection with any carrying on of or winding up of said business shall be handled as a separate account in the name of said business, and in such manner as my Executor deems appropriate."

(POUROVER PROVISION) BEQUEST OF RESIDUARY ESTATE

"All the remainder of my estate, I give, devise, and bequeath to the Trustee under a Declaration of Trust dated _____, by and between (NAME) as Settlor and (NAME) as Trustee (referred to as 'THE [NAME] TRUST'), to be added to the principal of the Trust estate created thereunder, and to be held, administered, and distributed in all respects as an integral part thereof, pursuant to the terms of said Trust as the same has been or hereafter at any time or from time to time may be amended. If the aforesaid Trust shall be declared invalid for any reason, I give, devise, and bequeath the said remainder of my estate to the aforesaid Trustee, IN TRUST, nevertheless, to be held and administered as a Testamentary Trust, in the manner, and to the persons and upon the same terms and conditions as are set forth in the said Trust."

APPENDIX III

Sample Durable Power
of Attorney Form

CAUTION: *These provisions are offered only for illustration of the concepts discussed in this book. They should not be arbitrarily used in any documents without consulting a knowledgeable attorney nor without a careful examination of their compliance with local law and with the intention and purpose of the applicable document.*

(Sample) Durable Power of Attorney
of

_____

    Know all people by these presents that I, _____, of [CITY], [COUNTY], [STATE], do hereby revoke all Powers of Attorney executed by me before this date, and I now hereby make, constitute, and appoint _____ _____ , of [CITY], [COUNTY], [STATE], as my true and lawful Attorney-in-Fact for me and in my name, place, and stead to act under the following provisions and to have the following powers:

1. ***General Powers and Scope.*** To exercise or perform any act, power, duty, right, or obligation whatsoever that I now have or may hereafter acquire relating to any person, matter, transaction, or property, real or personal, tangible or intangible, present, contingent or expectant, now possessed or hereafter acquired by me, including without limitation, the specifically enumerated powers granted below. As an expression of my intent hereunder, my Attorney-in-Fact shall have full power and authority to do everything necessary in exercising any of the powers herein granted as fully as I might or could do if personally present.

2. ***Powers of Collection, Payment, and Enforcement.*** To demand, sue for, collect, compromise, recover, and receive all debts, moneys, property interests, claims, and demands whatsoever, which are now due or which may hereafter become due to me, including the right to institute any legal or equitable proceedings therefor; and to execute and deliver on my behalf and in my name, any and all endorsements, elections, releases, receipts, or discharges for the same.

3. ***Banking Powers.*** To make, execute, deliver, and endorse notes, drafts, checks, certificates of deposit, and orders for the payment of money or other property from or to me or to my order; to make deposits or withdrawals on any accounts in banks or other financial institutions on my behalf; to borrow money and execute promissory notes in my name, and as security therefor, to pledge, mortgage or hypothecate any property, real or personal; to execute personal guaranties of the debts of another person or entity.

4. ***Power with Respect to Entities or Forms of Ownership and Related Transfers.*** To create, amend, or terminate one or more trusts, partnerships, corporations, limited liability companies, co-tenancies, or any other form of ownership or entity for the purpose of dealing with any property or property interest of any nature that I may have or hereafter acquire, under such terms and with such provisions as my attorney deems in my best interests and those of my family; to transfer any or all property, tangible, intangible, personal, or real, in which I may have any interest, into any form of entity or ownership, including, without limitation, co-tenancies, trusts, whether revocable or irrevocable, and whether created by me or by my Attorney-in-Fact on my behalf, and whether or not such entity or entities were created before or after the execution of this Durable Power of Attorney. In this regard, the fact that my Attorney-in-Fact may be a remainderman, partner, shareholder, member, co-tenant, or beneficiary of any such entity in connection with any such transfer hereunder shall not affect the validity thereof, nor, by itself, constitute a breach of my Attorney-in-Fact's fiduciary duty hereunder.

5. ***Power to Acquire, Manage, Lease, and Sell.*** To make, execute, and deliver deeds, mortgages, liens, releases, conveyances, leases, subleases, purchase and sale agreements, contracts of indemnity and insurance, and contracts of every nature in relation to both real and personal property, on such terms and conditions as my attorney shall deem proper; to manage or to become involved in the management of any such real or personal property.

To receive and give receipt for all rents and income to which I am or may become entitled, and to pay therefrom all necessary expenses for the maintenance, upkeep, care, improvement, and protection of my property; to pay the net income therefrom from time to time to me or in such manner as I shall direct, or in the absence of such payment to me or such direction, to invest the same in my Attorney-in-Fact's best judgment.

To carry on, manage, or become involved in the management of any business in which I may have an interest and to carry out any act of management that may be appropriate to such involvement; to enter into and/or carry out the provisions of an agreement for the sale or transfer of any business interest or the stock therein, upon such terms and conditions, including the making of such representations, warranties, and indemnities, as my Attorney-in-Fact shall deem consistent with my intentions and any negotiations begun by me or on my behalf.

6. **Powers as to Investments.** To purchase, pledge, hypothecate, sell (including short sales and sales that may result in a loss), transfer, or otherwise deal in any way with all forms of investments, including without limitation, securities, options, rights, warrants, general and limited partnership interests, trust units, and all forms of securities issued by the United States Government (or any other government, domestic or foreign), or any division, branch, or agency thereof; to act as my proxy with power of substitution; to vote all stocks or other securities in my name relative to any individual or corporate action; to deposit any stocks or other securities in connection with any plans of protective or reorganizational committees; to purchase, accept, exercise, or sell rights to subscribe for securities; to endorse securities or any agreements relating thereto; to create, utilize, terminate, and otherwise deal with accounts (including margin accounts).

7. **Powers with Respect to Mail.** To enter any mailbox that I shall have hired, whether at a United States Post Office or elsewhere, and to surrender possession of any mailbox and terminate the lease thereof; to sign for any certified or registered mail directed to me, whether it is via United States mail, foreign mail, or private delivery service, and to execute any order required to forward mail to any location selected by my Attorney-in-Fact.

8. **Powers over Safe-Deposit Boxes.** To have access to all my safe-deposit boxes, whether in my name alone or held jointly with others, and to surrender possession of any safe-deposit box and terminate the lease thereof [including, without limitation, the box situated at _____
_____ BANK, _____ branch, CITY, COUNTY, STATE].

9. **Powers with Respect to Insurance Contracts.** To have full authority to deal with any policies of insurance on my life, or policies on the life or lives of others, but excluding any such policies on the life of my Attorney-in-Fact, in which I may have any interest, including, but not limited to, the right to irrevocably assign, surrender, borrow against, convert, or change the beneficiaries thereof, or to take any other action with respect

to such policies as my Attorney-in-Fact shall deem proper and consistent with my intentions or objectives; to receive payments under any disability, income, or other contract and to deal in every other respect with such disability, income, or other contracts.

10. **Use of Funds for My Care.** To incur, pay, and satisfy any expenses and obligations for my comfort, benefit, and care, as are necessary and desirable in my Attorney-in-Fact's sole discretion.

11. **Powers as to Taxes.** To prepare, execute, and file any tax returns or statements on my behalf and to pay or compromise any or all taxes or apply for and collect any refunds due; to make any tax elections on my behalf or which I am entitled to make; to appear and represent me at any level before the U.S. Tax Court, any state court, any federal district or appellate court, the U.S. Treasury Department, the Internal Revenue Service, the [STATE] Department of Revenue, or any other taxing authority, in connection with any matter involving taxes in which I am a party; to execute any claims for refund, protests, applications for abatement, and consents to any waivers of determination and assessment of taxes, and to agree to a later determination and assessment of taxes than is provided by any statute of limitations; to receive, endorse, and collect any checks in settlement of any refund of taxes; to request, receive, and examine copies of any tax returns, reports, and other information from the U.S. Treasury Department or any other taxing authority.

12. **Power to Make Gifts and to Disclaim.** To make gifts of my property either outright or in trust to or for the health, education, maintenance, or support of such persons as, in the opinion of my Attorney-in-Fact, would be the donees I might choose, including my Attorney-in-Fact, having in mind the resources, both public and private, available for my care after the making of such gifts, and having in mind the objective of preserving the largest amount of my property for my family as a whole. My Attorney-in-Fact shall also have the power to obtain appraisals in connection with the making of any such gifts. My Attorney-in-Fact shall also have the power to disclaim any bequests or other interests to which I may become entitled from any source whatsoever, and to execute any documents necessary to effect such disclaimer(s), even if my Attorney-in-Fact may personally benefit from such disclaimer.

13. **Power to Employ Agents.** To employ, compensate, and discharge such agents on such terms as my Attorney-in-Fact deems appropriate to carry out any acts authorized or contemplated hereunder.

14. **Powers with Respect to Retirement Plans, Education Plans, and Annuities.** To establish, contribute to, and deal with in any way any form of so-called retirement plan for my benefit as a participant or under which I may be named as a beneficiary, including without limitation, any interest I may have in any annuities, Individual Retirement

Accounts, Keogh plans, and any other form of pension or employee benefit plan; to establish, contribute to, and deal with in any manner any so-called education savings plan, including without limitation, Section 529 plans; to change beneficiaries of my account or on my behalf in any such plan, designating such beneficiaries as my Attorney-in-Fact determines to be consistent with my wishes; to waive any spousal rights I may have to benefits from any plan under which my spouse is a participant; to borrow against or withdraw from my plan accounts on such terms as my Attorney-in-Fact deems appropriate; to select any form of payment option or to modify options I may have selected; to accept any benefits or lump-sum payments on my behalf and to "roll over" any such benefits on my behalf.

15. ***Powers with Respect to Medical Information.*** To have access to and obtain any information or medical records governed by the Health Insurance Portability and Accountability Act of 1996 and any applicable federal or state regulations.

16. ***Third-Party Reliance or Refusal.*** Any party dealing with my Attorney-in-Fact hereunder may rely absolutely on the authority granted herein and need not look to the application of any proceeds nor the authority of my Attorney-in-Fact as to any action taken hereunder. In this regard, no person who may in good faith act in reliance upon the representations of my Attorney-in-Fact or the authority granted hereunder shall incur any liability to me or my estate as a result of such act.

    If a third party refuses to deal with my Attorney-in-Fact or acknowledge this power, my Attorney-in-Fact is authorized and encouraged to take legal action to carry out the desired transaction and to recover any costs or damages resulting from said third party's failure to recognize and honor this power.

17. ***Successor Attorneys-in-Fact.*** If _____ [Andrew Agent] for any reason ceases or is unable to serve under this Durable Power of Attorney, then I grant the same aforesaid powers in every respect to _____ [Bertha Agent II], of [CITY, STATE]. A written statement by _____ [Bertha Agent II] as to the cessation or inability of _____ [Andrew Agent] to serve shall be conclusive evidence of such fact, and any third party may rely upon the same in dealing with [him/her]under this Durable Power of Attorney. If neither _____ [Bertha Agent II] nor _____ [Andrew Agent] for any reason is able to serve under this power, then I grant the same aforesaid powers in every respect to _____ [Celeste Agent III], of [CITY, STATE]. A written statement by _____ [Celeste Agent III] as to the cessation or inability of _____ [Andrew Agent] and _____ [Bertha Agent II] to serve

shall be conclusive evidence of such fact, and any third party may rely upon the same in dealing with under this Durable Power of Attorney. If _____ [Celeste Agent III], _____ [Andrew Agent], and _____ [Bertha Agent II] are all unable to serve, then a substitute Attorney-in-Fact may be appointed by the last of them to serve in a written, acknowledged statement attached hereto.

18. ***Guardianship.*** If a petition is filed in any court for the appointment of a guardian or a conservator to care for me or my estate, then I nominate _____ [Donald Guardian] as such appointee. If [he/she] is not able to serve, then I nominate _____ [Ellen Guardian II] in [his/her] stead. If neither _____ [Ellen Guardian II] nor _____ [Donald Guardian] is able to serve, then I nominate _____ [Frank Guardian III] in their stead. Nothing in this part shall be construed as a direction that such a petition be filed or such appointment be made, and it is my express wish that such action be taken only when and if absolutely necessary.

19. ***Reliance on Copies of This Power.*** A photostatic copy or facsimile or electronic transfer of this Durable Power of Attorney, as executed, may be treated as an original power by any third party dealing with my Attorney-in-Fact.

20. ***Disability or Incompetence.*** This Durable Power of Attorney in _____ [Andrew Agent] or in _____ [Bertha Agent II] or in _____ [Celeste Agent III] or in [his/her] successor, as the case may be, shall not be affected by my subsequent disability or incapacity.

21. ***Ratification of Attorneys-in-Fact Acts.*** I hereby ratify and confirm whatever my Attorney-in-Fact shall lawfully do under these presents.

IN WITNESS WHEREOF, I have hereunto set my hand and seal this _____ _____day of _____, 20____.

_____
[Name/Signature]

County of_____   STATE OF _____

On this ___ day of _____, 20__ before me personally appeared the above named _____, who is either personally known to me or proved to me through satisfactory evidence of identification, which was a current driver's license, to be the person whose name is signed on the preceding document, and who acknowledged to me that he/she signed it as his/her free act and deed.

_____
Notary Public
My Commission Expires: _____

Signature of Attorney-in-Fact:

_____   ._____
[Andrew Agent]   Witness

_____

Important Note: In some states (e.g., Florida) it is either required or recommended that the Durable Power of Attorney be witnessed by two independent witnesses (in addition to the notarization) if the power may be used to deal with real estate located in the subject state.

APPENDIX IV

Executor's Checklist

NOTE: *With the exception of the deadline for filing the estate tax returns, the time periods indicated on the following checklist in which the items should be begun or completed are offered* only *as general guides, and meeting these time periods is normally possible only under the best of circumstances. Often, the key family members are too distraught over the loss of a loved one to act promptly, or the required information is not immediately available. Nevertheless, it is always a good idea to engage the estate attorney as promptly as possible after a person's death because, in many instances, the attorney can proceed to take some or all of the steps outlined below, thereby taking the pressure off the family members.*

I. WITHIN THE FIRST WEEK AFTER DECEDENT'S DEATH
   A. Arrange a conference with decedent's immediate family and gather all available information as to decedent's assets, debts, location of personal financial and business financial data, and estate-plan documents.
   B. Meet with decedent's attorney, or the attorney you select to handle the estate, and:
      1. Bring an inventory of all assets that you are able to locate, in which decedent held sole ownership or held a joint interest.
      2. Bring an inventory of all decedent's debts outstanding at the time of death.
      3. Bring all decedent's legal documents that you can find: wills, trusts, contracts, buy-sell agreements, partnership agreements, employment contracts, leases, corporate record books.

4. Bring all decedent's personal income tax returns for the three years preceding death, and business tax returns for the five years preceding death.

5. Ask your attorney to outline briefly for you the steps to be taken during the administration/settlement of the estate.

6. Ask your attorney to explain his fees in representing the estate. Have him confirm the arrangement in a letter.

C. Compile and review decedent's most recent (past six months to one year) personal and financial statements.

D. If decedent owned a bank safe-deposit box, arrange to have it opened and then inventory all the contents.

E. After inventory of safe-deposit box is completed, remove those documents from the safe-deposit box that require immediate action to be taken (stocks, bonds, other paper representation of passive investments, leases, notes, etc.).

F. If decedent left a surviving spouse, arrange with the spouse to prepare a monthly budget of her expenses.

G. If decedent left surviving dependents, determine all sources of income that can be applied for their immediate benefit.

H. After consulting with estate's attorney, determine whether you will need to open probate proceedings in the probate court (this is a matter of the amount of probate assets and the statutory monetary threshold for filing probate proceedings in the particular state the decedent was domiciled in at the time of his death).

If probate is necessary, complete and have signed the required court papers in order to commence probate proceedings.

I. If there are no members of decedent's family living in decedent's home at time of death, or if decedent did not leave a surviving spouse, then immediately arrange to seal decedent's home. (After the home has been sealed, do not enter it alone until a complete inventory and appraisal of the contents has been completed.)

J. Contact or meet with decedent's accountant. The accountant will be able to provide you with critical information about decedent's financial arrangements, business investments, and tax filings.

K. Contact or meet with decedent's broker. The broker will be able to provide you with critical information about decedent's portfolio, passive investments, etc.

1. It is often necessary to take immediate action with regard to certain types of passive investments that are risky and need to be watched closely, such as puts, calls, or commodity contracts. Often executors

will need to sell such assets, and reinvest in more stable investments in order to ensure the preservation of the estate's assets.

    2. Cancel open orders on brokerage accounts.

    3. Check all investments to see whether any have short deadlines for exercising any rights: stock options, warrants, purchase rights, and pension plans.

L. Determine whether the decedent had casualty policies and assets that need to be insured.

    1. Re-evaluate the coverage, and if it is not adequate to protect the value of the estate assets, increase the coverage. Also determine whether you want to change insurance companies.

    2. Determine who the new owner of the policy should be (it will be the surviving joint owner of the asset, the trustee of the trust in which the asset is now held, or the administrator/executor of the estate) and arrange to have new endorsements on the policies.

    3. Review the homeowner's policy and arrange, if not already the case, to have the policy insure the contents of the home for the replacement value, not the fair market value.

M. If decedent owned a car at time of death, change the automobile registration and insurance coverage over to the new owner's name. (Depending on the state's statutes, this might be done outside the probate court. Furthermore, some states allow the surviving spouse to continue to operate the car under the same policy for the duration of the policy period.)

N. Discuss with family members and estate's attorney all possible issues and areas in which the estate might be subject to liability. Take all necessary steps to reduce or eliminate the estate's exposure to such liability.

O. If decedent owned an interest in a closely held business, go to the business's headquarters and review all physical assets on-site (you might want to arrange for an immediate inventory in order to prevent any losses of such assets). Also, make the necessary arrangements to see that the business is continued, or terminated, if appropriate, in an orderly fashion.

P. Inspect all real estate parcels decedent owned at time of his death.

Q. File (or arrange for funeral home to file) on behalf of widow for Social Security death benefits, survivor's benefits, and Veteran's Administration death benefits.

R. Secure several certified copies of death certificate, which you will need for court filings, insurance policies, etc.

II. WITHIN TWO WEEKS AFTER DEATH

A. Complete the following probate administrative proceedings:

1. File petition for letters testamentary (i.e., probate of will).
2. If necessary, arrange for witnesses to will to testify as to proper execution of the will.
3. Publish creditors' notices in accordance with the court rules or state statutes.
4. If appropriate, obtain heirs' assents or file proper notices of the filing of the will to all heirs. Heirs and beneficiaries should be sent a copy of the will.

B. Apply for widow's allowances and dependents' allowances or awards, where necessary and appropriate.
C. Apply for a federal tax identification number for the estate.
D. Arrange with the surviving spouse to recover all decedent's mail, or in the alternative, arrange to have all mail delivered to your address or held for your pickup.
E. Apply to recover from or have benefits issued to appropriate beneficiaries of all decedent's life insurance policies, and at that time notify every insurance company to forward the Form 712 to yourself, or to the estate's attorney. (*Note:* A Form 712 [or the equivalent] must be filed with the estate's estate tax returns for *each* policy on the life of the decedent.)
F. If decedent's death resulted from accident, determine whether the estate should file any claims pursuant to accidental death, life insurance policies, disability claims, health insurance policies, or job-related claims.
G. Review decedent's credit card agreements to:

1. Determine whether there is any available life insurance coverage on any of the cards' loans or balances.
2. Cancel all credit cards, or change title to the name of the surviving spouse, where appropriate.

H. If decedent owned an interest in a closely held business that was subject to a buy-sell agreement, commence such proceedings (to sell his share of the business) in accordance with the terms of the agreement.
I. Open an estate account (consider whether to open only a checking account, or a combined checking/savings or money market account).
J. Arrange with health insurance carriers to continue coverage of surviving spouse and dependents, where possible.

III. WITHIN ONE MONTH AFTER DEATH

    A. Arrange for appraisals on all real estate and personal property and businesses.

        1. Enter into a written agreement with the appraiser; the agreement should contain the deadline when the appraisal will be due, a date on which you will forward the appraiser a written remainder, and a provision allowing you to hire another appraiser if the appraisal is not delivered as promised, and that you will not be obligated to reimburse the appraiser for his services unless and until the appraisal report is completed and delivered.

        2. When hiring an appraiser for real estate and closely held businesses, hire someone who has a well-developed reputation for making such appraisals and is known by the state's revenue department, or has at least handled substantial estate appraisals and knows how to conduct himself before a tax audit.

        3. Appraisals must be obtained on all real estate, closely held businesses, personal property items of value (refer to your state's statutes on the threshold for requiring an appraisal on an item of tangible personal property; some states set the limit at $3,000), rare coins, antiques, jewelry, paintings, or other collections, oil and gas interests, interests in partnerships, real estate ventures.

        4. Obtain values of all passive investments such as stocks, bonds, etc. This can usually be obtained through a broker. Review with the estate's attorney the figure the IRS and state taxing authorities want to receive. (Often it is the mean fair-market-value selling price on the day of decedent's death, but there are some intricacies involved in this analysis. Your broker can usually supply you with this information at no charge.)

    B. Determine whether the estate is a party to any lawsuits, whether already existing or pending, and if so, determine whether the estate is plaintiff or defendant. Review the proceedings with the attorney handling the lawsuit.

    C. Begin to estimate available cash sources to the estate and amounts of estate taxes and administration expenses.

    D. Arrange for or collect decedent's ongoing accounts receivable such as rents, royalties, and loan payments.

    E. Review with estate's attorney and heirs whether any postmortem (after death) estate planning is advisable (this usually consists of making disclaimers to achieve estate tax savings in the estates of the heirs, in particular, decedent's surviving spouse). Disclaimers have very strict time requirements and often complicated filing requirements, so review this early on, as it often takes some time for the heirs to reach a decision on such matters.

F. Obtain copies of all gift tax returns that decedent filed during his life. Usually, estate's attorney will want copies of these as well.

G. Determine what the state requires to be done in order for you to obtain inheritance or death tax releases on the estate assets. This varies, and in some states can be done only at the time you file the state estate or inheritance tax return.

H. If anyone owned a life insurance policy on decedent's life that you intend to claim is excludable from the estate, arrange with the insurance company to receive the original policy once the proceeds are paid to the beneficiary. You will need to submit the policy (or the insurance company form 712) with the federal estate tax return in order to establish that no tax is due from the estate on that policy. (*Note* the distinction between owner and beneficiary. If the deceased *owned* the policy, the proceeds will be counted in his estate for estate tax purposes.)

IV. WITHIN THREE MONTHS AFTER DEATH

A. Review and assess with the estate's attorney whether any of decedent's closely held corporate stock can be redeemed and the proceeds used to pay federal estate taxes and administration expenses.

B. Pay the decedent's funeral bills and the expenses of decedent's last illness, if any. Make an effort to determine and locate the decedent's creditors and notify them of his death.

C. Determine whether it is advisable to make an early withdrawal of any CDs held by decedent. (This can be done without a penalty pursuant to federal treasury regulations.)

D. File state and federal *income* tax returns, if necessary, for the last taxable year of decedent's life.

E. Where decedent did not make specific bequests of his personal property, proceed to distribute the personal property items in accordance with the decedent's will.

F. Make an inventory of all gifts decedent made within three years of death. This information will be necessary for filing the federal estate tax return. Most states will require the same information for either the three years or the two years preceding death, depending on the state's tax regulations.

G. Confer with estate's attorney or tax adviser to determine whether the estate's accumulated income should be accumulated or distributed.

H. Confer with estate's attorney or accountant to determine whether the estate should elect a fiscal or annual tax year.

I. If decedent owned real estate in other states at the time of his death, arrange for ancillary probate proceedings in those jurisdictions.

V. SIX TO NINE MONTHS AFTER DEATH (OR MORE, DEPENDING ON TAX OR LEGAL DELAYS)

    A. This is the time period in which you will be working with the estate's attorney and possibly an accountant in preparing the estate's federal and state estate tax returns. (The return is due nine months after death—there are many guidelines and booklets available on this, from the IRS, that review and explain how these returns must be completed.)

    B. Thoroughly document the backup material for each schedule of the estate return; this will assist you in the event the estate is audited.

    C. If there are more than adequate funds in the estate to cover any increased taxes or expenses on account of audits or other foreseeable costs, make distribution of the specific bequests in the will, after obtaining signed releases from the beneficiaries of those bequests.

    D. Upon the completion of the estate administration, and after payment and filing of estate and fiduciary tax returns, and upon completion of any tax audit, prepare and file the final account with the court (if a probate estate), sending a copy of each beneficiary together with a release for the beneficiary to sign. After signed releases are received, have your final account allowed by the court and, at the same time, make distribution of the balance of the estate to the beneficiaries. If a trust is a beneficiary, that share should be given to the trustee of the trust.

    E. Record tax releases on real estate, where necessary.

    F. Ask the estate's attorney to review the surviving spouse's estate plan to determine whether any immediate changes need to be made to that plan, such as a new will, a living trust, a durable power of attorney, or a gift-giving plan.

Glossary

Abatement. The forced reduction of shares or bequests when the testator's estate has insufficient assets to pay all debts, expenses, and bequests in full.

Accounting. The financial statement submitted to the court and to the beneficiaries by the executor (or trustee, in the case of a trust), showing all probate (or trust) assets in the estate (or trust) and all transactions affecting or arising from those assets, from the time the executor or administrator (or trustee) was appointed. Accountings are usually filed on an annual basis.

Ademption. When an item of property that was mentioned in the will is subsequently sold or otherwise disposed of before death, thereby preventing the beneficiary from inheriting the item.

Administration. The management of the estate of a deceased person.

Administration expenses. All the expenses connected with settling an estate, including executor's or administrator's fees, attorney's and accountant's fees, court fees, and the expenses related to estate property.

Administrator. A person named by a court to handle the settlement of the estate of a person who dies without a will, or for a deceased who had a will but no named executor.

Administrator—C.T.A. (cum testamento annexo). When there is a will but no executor named in the will or the ones named decline or are unavailable, then an administrator is appointed "with the will annexed."

Administrator—De bonis non. An administrator appointed to succeed a previous administrator and settle the remainder of the estate.

Advancement. An amount given to an heir by the deceased during his lifetime intended as an "advance" against the heir's share under the will.

Ancillary administration. Additional probate proceedings that must be carried out when the deceased owned property in a state or states other than that where he had his principal residence.

Applicable exclusion amount. Formerly referred to as the unified credit, it is the tax credit allowed under the federal tax code that is applied to gift or estate taxes that may be due.

Asset protection trust. A trust, domestic or offshore, that is designed to protect the assets of the settlor while at the same time allowing the settlor to be a beneficiary.

Attestation clause. A statement at the end of the will saying that the witnesses saw the testator sign, in their presence, and that they then signed in his presence and in each other's presence.

Attorney-in-fact. Under a power of attorney (durable or otherwise), the person named to act as legal agent for the person who gives the power of attorney.

Beneficiary. A person who is entitled to receive benefits (usually money or other property) from a trust or an estate.

Bequest. A gift of money or other property under a will or trust.

Charitable lead trust (CLT). An irrevocable trust where the income of the trust is paid to a charity for a specified term of years, and the remainder passes to beneficiaries (usually family) specified by the grantor. Virtually the opposite of a charitable remainder trust.

Charitable remainder trust (CRT). An irrevocable trust where the grantor retains an income for life and the remainder passes to a qualified charity. The CRT is tax exempt, and it may sell the grantor's appreciated assets and pay no capital gains tax. In addition, the grantor is usually entitled to a present income tax deduction for the future gift to charity.

Codicil. An amendment to a previous will, but executed with the same formalities as a will.

Common disaster. Where two or more people, including the testator and a beneficiary, die in the same accident and it is impossible to tell who died first.

Common property. Property that is held by two or more parties under one of the forms of co-ownership, i.e., joint tenancy, tenancy in common, tenancy by the entirety, or community property.

Community property. In the states of Arizona, California, Idaho, Louisiana, Nevada, New Mexico, Texas, Washington, and, to a certain extent, Wisconsin, property that is acquired by husband and wife during their marriage. (In most of these states gifts and inheritances are excluded.) Spouses each have a one-half interest in their community property and therefore only one-half of such property can be disposed of by will.

Convenience account. An account—usually a bank account—that has been opened in joint names but only for the convenience of one of the joint owners and not with the intent that the noncontributing owner receive the balance in the account. As a result, the account could be part of a deceased owner's probate estate.

Corporate trustee. An organization such as a bank or a trust company that receives, holds, and manages money and other property for a fee from members of the public under a trust agreement.

Co-tenancy. When two or more parties own the same property at the same time and the property remains undivided.

Co-tenant. One of the owners under a co-tenancy.

Co-trustee. Another person, often a family member, who serves with the trustee in helping to make decisions concerning the trust.

Crummey power. A provision, typically in a trust, where a beneficiary is given the power, which usually lasts thirty to sixty days, to withdraw his share of a contribution made to the trust by the settlor or some other party. The purpose of the power is to cause the contribution to the trust to qualify as a tax-free gift to the beneficiary or beneficiaries.

Crummey trust. A trust that contains Crummey powers, although otherwise it could be any type of trust.

Devise. A gift of real estate under a will.

Disclaimer. When a beneficiary or heir under a will, an estate, or a trust does not wish to accept the bequest, he may disclaim it without tax consequences, if he does so within a certain time, usually nine months, after he becomes entitled to the bequest.

Discretionary trust. A trust that allows the trustee to decide "in its discretion" how much to distribute to the beneficiaries from time to time.

Domicile. The place where a person permanently resides, even though he may not spend all or even a majority of his time there.

Donee. A person who receives a gift.

Donor. A person who makes a gift; sometimes one who creates a trust (see **Settlor**).

Durable power of attorney. (See also **Power of attorney.**) If a power of attorney is a "durable" power, it must be in writing, and, unlike a power that is not a durable power, the right to act under a durable power continues even through the person giving the power has become legally incompetent. A power of attorney, whether durable or not, expires on the giver's death.

Dynasty trust. An irrevocable trust intended to last (and grow) for several generations after the settlor (in some states, forever), bypassing estate taxes in each successive generation. (See **Generation-skipping trust** and **Rule against perpetuities.**)

Escheat. If a person has no will and no heirs, his property returns (escheats) to the state, after payment of debts and expenses.

Executor. A person (or organization) named in a will to handle the settlement of the estate according to the will.

Family trust. In common usage, a trust agreement that provides for a certain portion of the estate or trust to be set aside in a separate trust to operate for the benefit of the family (spouse or children or both).

Fiduciary. Anyone responsible for the custody or management of property belonging to others, such as an executor, administrator, trustee, guardian, or conservator.

Fiduciary duty. The high degree of trust, responsibility, and objectiveness required of anyone acting as a fiduciary.

Fraudulent conveyance or transfer. A transfer that is deemed to have been made with the intent (express or implied) to defeat or prejudice the claim of a known or future creditor, and may therefore cause the transferred property to be considered available to satisfy the claim of the creditor.

Funding. The transfer of property to a trust.

Generation-skipping trust. A trust that is designed to provide benefits for two or more successive generations after that of the grantor without being exposed to estate tax from generation to generation, and as well to avoid the generation-skipping tax (GST) imposed when a person attempts to provide for someone two or more generations younger than himself. The younger generations may but need not be lineal descendants of the settlor/grantor. There is a $1 million per grantor GST exemption. (See **Dynasty trust** and **Rule against perpetuities.**)

Gift. The transfer of any type of property from one individual to another without consideration (payment).

Gift tax. The federal (and sometimes state) tax levied on the act of making a taxable gift, usually charged to the donor.

Gift tax exclusion. The amount of a gift that is not subject to a gift tax, usually measured or allowed on an annual basis.

Grantor. A person who creates a trust—also called donor, settlor.

Grantor retained annuity trust (GRAT). An irrevocable trust for a specified term of years, during which the grantor will receive a specified annual sum (an annuity) and after which the remaining trust assets belong to the remainder beneficiaries, outside the grantor's estate.

Grantor retained interest trust (GRIT). Similar to the GRAT, except that the annual payments to the grantor may be tied to the actual income of the trust. Close family members may not be remainder beneficiaries of a GRIT.

Grantor trust. A trust that, for income tax purposes, is treated as owned by the grantor and that results in all income of the trust being taxed to him.

Guardian ad litem. A representative (usually an attorney) appointed by the court to represent the interest of a minor or incompetent person.

Heir. The person or persons who will inherit according to the laws of a state when a person dies without a will.

Holographic will. A will that is completely handwritten by the testator and signed and dated by him, with or without witnesses. An unwitnessed holographic will is valid in only a few states.

Incompetent. A person who has been legally declared by a court to be unable to handle his own affairs.

Intangible personal property. Property other than real estate and other than property that can be "touched." Examples of intangible property: stocks, bonds, bank accounts, copyrights, patents, etc., as they all merely represent the right to receive something of value.

In-terrorem clause. A statement in a will or trust providing that any beneficiary who contests the document or in any way interferes with its operation will forfeit his share. Binding in most states.

Inter vivos trust. A trust created while the creator of it is alive—a "living" trust.

Intestate. When a person dies without a will, he dies intestate.

Inventory. A list of all the estate assets that come in the hands of the executor or administrator of the estate. The inventory must be filed with the court within a prescribed period after the fiduciary is appointed.

Irrevocable life insurance trust (ILIT). A trust that holds (as owner and beneficiary) one or more life insurance policies on the settlor's life and is typically designed to produce estate-tax-free benefits, which would include the proceeds of the life insurance, to the settlor's family or others.

Irrevocable trust. A trust that cannot be changed or revoked by the person who created it

Issue. Lineal descendants of a person, i.e., children, grandchildren, great-grandchildren, etc.

Joint ownership. When two or more people own the same property at the same time, generally in equal shares, with the understanding that on the death of any one, the survivor(s) will own the whole.

Joint property. Any property in joint ownership form (not just real estate).

Joint tenancy. Same as **Joint ownership.**

Joint tenant. One of the joint owners in a joint ownership or a joint tenancy.

Joint will. One will that is declared to be the will of two persons, usually husband and wife, signed by both and witnessed as a regular will. Joint wills are generally a bad idea.

Kiddie tax. The income tax imposed on the unearned income (dividends, interest) in excess of an annual exemption, on a child under age fourteen. The tax on the excess income is imposed at the parent's highest tax rate.

Lapsed gift. A gift or bequest that is not paid to the named beneficiary because he or she is deceased and the will did not provide for the bequest to be paid to another.

Letters of administration. The official document given by the court authorizing the executor or administrator to act. Also known as letters testamentary.

Life estate. The right to the use of property during one's lifetime only, after which the property belongs to the "remaindermen" outright.

Life tenant. A person who has a life estate.

Living trust. A trust created during the lifetime of the person who created it.

Living will. Not a will at all but a legal declaration (signed and witnessed like a will) that in the event of a catastrophic illness, the person does not (or does) wish to be kept alive by artificial means or heroic measures.

Marital deduction. A deduction for estate and gift tax purposes for the amount of property that passes to a spouse from the other spouse.

Marital deduction trust. A trust established to receive an amount on behalf of the surviving spouse that qualifies for the marital deduction.

Miller trust. A "safe harbor" trust under the Medicaid rules, allowing a trust to be funded with the *income* of a Medicaid beneficiary in an "income-cap" state, so that the beneficiary may qualify for Medicaid.

Nominee trust. A special purpose trust, originally designed to hold real estate and thus sometimes called a "realty trust," where the identity of the beneficiaries is contained in a document *separate* from the rest of the trust.

Noncontest clause. See **In-terrorem clause.**

Noncupative will. An oral will, allowed only in extreme cases (and not in all states) such as where the testator faces imminent death.

Nonprobate property. Property owned or partially owned by the deceased but which does not pass through his probate estate, such as jointly held property or property in a living trust.

Offshore trust. A trust that is settled and governed by the laws of a jurisdiction other than the United States. In the vernacular, generally one that is literally offshore, such as Gibraltar, the Cook Islands, the Bahamas, etc., and generally used for asset protection purposes. (See **Asset protection trusts.**)

Partition. The right of a co-tenant and in some cases a life-tenant to have the commonly held property divided by court order. Where real estate is concerned, this usually means a court-ordered sale of the property and division of the net proceeds.

Per capita. When a distribution or share is given equally to each person in a group, as opposed to **per stirpes.**

Personal property. Any property other than real estate.

Personal residence trust (PRT). An irrevocable trust to which a grantor may transfer a personal residence (one per trust, maximum two trusts) and retain the right to live there for a specified term of years, after which, if the grantor survives the term, the residence escapes tax in the grantor's estate.

Per stirpes. When a distribution or share is given by right of a person's ancestor. For instance, if the testator leaves his estate to his two sons "or their issue, per stirpes," and both sons are deceased, son A leaving one child, son B leaving four children, then A's child will take one-half the estate and B's children will share the other half.

Pooled trust. A "safe harbor" trust under the Medicaid rules allowing a trust established by a charitable organization to receive and pool funding from individuals eligible to receive Medicaid. Assets contributed to such a trust are ignored for Medicaid eligibility purposes if on the individual's death any trust distributions from the individual's account are used first to reimburse the state for benefits paid to or for the individual.

Pourover provision. A provision in a will that usually gives the bulk of the estate to a living trust created by the testator before or at the time the will is signed.

Power of appointment. The power to dispose of property held under someone else's will or trust, although a person could transfer property and *retain* a power of appointment for himself.

Power of attorney. A document (or verbal instruction) giving someone the right, which can be broad or very limited, to legally act for the person giving the power, typically with respect to administrative and financial matters. If a power of attorney is a "durable" power, it must be in writing, and unlike a power that is not a durable power, the right to act under a durable power continues even through the person giving the power has become legally incompetent. A power of attorney, whether durable or not, expires on the giver's death.

Pretermitted heir. A child or other lineal descendant who has been improperly omitted from the will.

Probate. The procedure in each state required to settle legally the estate of a deceased person and transfer his "probate property."

Probate property. Property that may be transferred only through the probate procedure and would therefore include property or proceeds payable to the estate of the deceased, as well as property titled in the deceased's name alone or as a tenant in common.

Protector. A person or entity other than a trustee who is given certain powers over the trust, such as the power to veto trust distributions, change trustees, etc.

Purpose trust. A trust that is established for a purpose (e.g., furtherance of a business, maintenance of a building, care of a pet) rather than for specified beneficiaries. Not recognized in every state, but recognized in most offshore jurisdictions.

Qualified domestic trust (QDOT). A trust that is used if the surviving spouse is not a U.S. citizen. If a QDOT is not used in such a case the marital deduction is lost.

Qualified personal residence trust (QPRT). The same as a PRT except that in a QPRT the residence may be sold without losing the tax benefits of the trust.

Qualified terminable interest (QTIP) trust. A trust leaving mandatory income to a spouse and optionally principal at the discretion of a trustee, where the spouse has no control over the disposition of the remaining trust principal at her death. The QTIP trust can qualify for the estate tax marital deduction.

Realty trust. See **Nominee trust.**

Release. The document that the executor, administrator, or trustee will ask the beneficiaries to sign before receiving their bequest, releasing the estate or trust from further liability.

Remainderman. The person(s) designated to receive what is left when a trust or estate terminates.

Residuary estate. Whatever remains of the estate after payment of debts, expenses, taxes, and specific bequests. In a "pourover" will, the residuary estate is left to a living trust.

Retained interest. Typically in a trust, whether revocable or irrevocable, where the settlor has retained some part or interest, such as an income stream, in the property transferred to the trust.

Revocable trust. A trust that may at any time be altered, amended, or revoked by the creator.

Right of severance. The right of a co-tenant to separate or divide commonly held property under a joint tenancy or a tenancy in common.

Right of survivorship. The right of a joint tenant (but not a tenant in common) to take the whole of the jointly held property if he survives the other joint tenant(s).

Rule against perpetuities. A rule of trust law providing that a family-type (i.e., noncharitable) trust must terminate at a certain future time. In general, it works out to ninety to one hundred years after the transfer becomes irrevocable. Many states have abolished or revised the rule and allow such trusts to continue without limitation or decades past the hundred-year rule.

Self-settled trust. A trust where the person creating the trust (the settlor) is also the beneficiary or one of the beneficiaries of that trust.

Settlor. A person who creates a trust.

Severance. The act of dividing commonly held property (see **Partition**).

Special needs trust—SNT. A trust naming a disabled person as beneficiary, established by another person, providing the trustee with complete discretion to make (or not to make) distributions to or for the beneficiary, having in mind both the beneficiary's special needs and benefits that may be available to the beneficiary outside the trust.

Spendthrift provision. The provision in a trust agreement that allows the donor to place the share of the beneficiary out of reach of the beneficiary's creditors. The funds of this particular beneficiary (other than the donor), while in the trust, cannot be attached or recovered by someone suing the beneficiary. (See also **Asset protection trust.**)

Spray provision. A provision in a trust giving the trustee the discretion to make unequal distributions among the beneficiaries. Also known as sprinkle provision.

Stepped-up cost basis. An increased (usually) tax cost in property that takes effect when that property is received as the result of a person's death and included in the person's estate for estate tax purposes.

Street-name securities. Stocks or bonds of a customer that are held in the name of the brokerage house for ease of transfer.

Structured settlement trust. A trust that is funded with payments to be received over a period of time as the result of a settlement in a personal-injury lawsuit.

Successor executor. A person named in a will to replace the first-named executor if for any reason he is not able to serve.

Successor trustee. A person appointed to replace the original trustee when the original trustee ceases to serve for any reason.

Supplemental needs trust. A special trust established for a person who is receiving or who may be receiving benefits under a welfare benefit program where the trust provides benefits that are over and above (supplemental to) the person's basic needs for food, clothing, and shelter. The assets in a properly drafted supplemental needs trust will not affect the person's eligibility for government benefits. This type of trust may or may not be the same as a special needs trust, depending on the respective terms.

Tangible personal property. Property other than real estate that has inherent value and can be touched, such as jewelry, furniture, clothing, automobiles, boats, machinery, etc.

Tenancy by the entirety. A special form of joint tenancy in which only husband and wife can be co-tenants and neither (alone) can cause a division of the property.

Tenancy in common. When two or more parties own the same property at the same time, but not necessarily in equal shares, and there is no right of survivorship, so that a deceased co-tenant's share passes through his estate. Any co-tenant can cause a division of the property (see **Partition**).

Testamentary. By or under a will.

Testamentary trust. A trust created under the terms of a will, and therefore only effective through the probate process. A testamentary trust also requires the filing of annual accountings to the probate court, whereas a living trust only requires accountings to the beneficiaries.

Testate. Dying with a will.

Testator. The person who makes a will.

Transferee. One who receives transferred property.

Transferor. One who transfers property.

Trust. A relationship in which one person (the trustee) is the holder of the legal title to property (the trust property) to keep or use for the benefit of another person (the beneficiary), although in some cases a person can be a trustee and also a beneficiary of the same trust.

Trustee. An individual or professional organization that holds the legal title to property and manages it for the benefit of another person or persons. It is also possible for a person to be trustee of a trust in which she is also a beneficiary.

Under 65 trust. A "safe harbor" trust under the Medicaid laws, allowing a discretionary trust to be established for a person who is under the age of sixty-five and allowing the assets in such a trust to be ignored for Medicaid eligibility purposes, if the trust provides for reimbursement to the state on the death of the beneficiary.

Undivided interest. A share of property that has not been physically set aside or divided, such as a joint interest in a home or a tenancy in common in stocks.

Undue influence. Persuading a person to change his will in a way he would not have done on his own.

Unified credit. A tax credit, allowed by the federal government, which may be applied toward either gift or estate taxes that may be due.

Index

About the Author

ALEXANDER A. BOVE JR. is a prominent attorney and nationally known lecturer with nearly thirty years of expertise in trusts and estate law. He is also admitted to practice in England and Wales. A former legal and financial columnist for *The Boston Globe,* he is a retired adjunct professor of law at Boston University Law School. He lives in Boston.